Development Problems and Prospects in Pacific Islands States

DEVELOPMENT PROBLEMS AND PROSPECTS IN PACIFIC ISLANDS STATES

B. C. PRASAD
AND
D. C. ROY
EDITORS

Nova Science Publishers, Inc.
New York

For permission to use material from this book please contact us:
Telephone 631-231-7269; Fax 631-231-8175
Web Site: http://www.novapublishers.com

LIBRARY OF CONGRESS CATALOGING-IN-PUBLICATION DATA

Development problems and prospects in Pacific Islands states : readings in world development / Biman Prasad and K.C. Roy.

p. cm.

Includes bibliographical references and index.

ISBN 978-1-60021-793-7 (hardcover)

1. Islands of the Pacific--Economic conditions--21st century. 2. Pacific Area--Economic conditions--21st century. 3. Islands of the Pacific--Social conditions--21st century. 4. Pacific Area--Social conditions--21st century. 5. Islands of the Pacific--Environmental conditions--History--21st century. 6. Pacific Area--Environmental conditions--History--21st century. I. Prasad, Biman C. II. Roy, K. C. (Kartik Chandra), 1941-

HC681.D48 2007

338.995--dc22

2007021136

Published by Nova Science Publishers, Inc. ✢ New York

CONTENTS

PREFACE

Pacific Island countries are undergoing fundamental political and economic changes due to the process of globalization. Many of them are struggling to come to grips with the global economic challenges of participating in a world of freer trade. Their smallness, distance from the major markets and vulnerability to natural disasters presents special challenges. Globalisation, however, also provides a window of opportunity for some of them to improve their economic growth performance through increasing exports, investment and technological advancement and labour mobility.

This book deals with a number of important issues relevant for improving the economic growth performances of the Pacific Island countries. Good governance, developing appropriate and quality institutions to promote investment and exports are major challenges for most of them. In addition, the volume also provides case studies discussing the role of foreign aid, remittances and labour mobility, role of the agricultural sector, role of the informal sector, management of public finances, and the state of the public sector reform.

The editors wish to thank the University of Queensland, Brisbane, Australia and the University of the South Pacific, Suva, Fiji for providing them with the facilities to complete this manuscript.

The editors also wish to thank Ms. Maya Columbus of Nova Science, New York, for agreeing to publish this volume and to all others who have been involved in the completion of this manuscript in one way or another.

Biman C. Prasad
School of Economics
The University of the South Pacific
Suva, Fiji Islands

Kartick C. Roy
School of Economics
University of Queensland
Brisbane, Australia

In: Development Problems and Prospects in Pacific Islands ISBN: 978-1-60021-793-7
Editors: B. C. Prasad, D. C. Roy, pp. 1-7

Chapter 1

GROWTH AND DEVELOPMENT IN THE PACIFIC ISLANDS: AN OVERVIEW OF ISSUES

Biman C. Prasad and Kartick Roy

1. INTRODUCTION

Pacific Island countries (PICs) are a very diverse group with varied culture, traditions and language. In addition, the diversity in the size of their economies presents special challenges for their development. Niue with a population of 1,700 is the smallest and Papua New Guinea with a population of about 5 million is the biggest and with the largest amount of natural resources. Almost all the PICs have in the last decade faced serious economic problems characterized by low levels of economic growth (see table 1.1). Unemployment, poverty and other social problems have been increasing in all these countries. The economic performance of the PICs has generally been weak despite high investment ratios recorded (ADB, 2000). The weak performance is attributed to both lower external demand due to global economic slowdown, and domestic structural problems relating to the small size of the economies, remoteness from the main markets, narrow resources base, political instability, civil unrest, market rigidities, depletion of already limited resources and dominance of the public sector (PIFS, 2002). Over the last six years up to 2004, the PICs have experienced variable but generally low growth rates. From a weighted average growth rate in GDP of 6 per cent in 1999, the GDP growth rate fell to -1 per cent in 2000 and -0.8 per cent in 2001. With a recorded GDP growth rate of 1 per cent in 2002, performance improved in 2003 and 2004 with average growth rates in GDP of 2.6 per cent and 2.7 per cent respectively. In the context of a predicted weaker international economic environment, it is expected that economic growth in the Pacific Region will decline to 2.3 per cent in 2005 (ADB, 2005).

Table 1.1. Growth Rate of GDP (% per year)

PICs	*1996*	*1997*	*1998*	*1999*	*2000*	*2001*	*2002*	*2003*	*2004*	*2005**
Average	5.6	-3.4	-1.0	6.6	-1.0	-.08	0.9	2.6	2.7	2.3

Source: ADB Outlook, 2005 Update.
* provisional/estimates.

The challenges facing small island developing states (SIDS) in the Pacific and other regions have been articulated in a number of specific international forums (See for example UN, 2002). The first global conference on the sustainable development of SIDS was held in Barbados in 1994, followed by a call at the World Summit of Sustainable development in Johannesburg in September 2002 for a special conference for a programme of action. The Barbados +10 was held in Mauritius in January 2005. As pointed out by the UN in its Millennium Project (UN, 2005) implementation of the Barbados programme is vital for achieving the millennium development goals (MDG) goals. The Barbados programme was the first intergovernmental policy initiative to integrate the SIDS into the world economy. However, after a decade this has not been implemented due to the lack of external resources and commitments from the developed countries.

Two major global processes bring out the challenges more clearly and urgently for the PICs. The first includes the multilateral trade negotiations under the World Trade Organisation (WTO) and the second is the targets set by the United Nations under the MDG. These challenges therefore have to be considered within the framework of these two processes. It is important for policy makers and politicians to understand these processes more extensively if PICs are to develop policy prescriptions for sustainable development.

2. Problems and Prospects for Growth and Development in the PICs

Across the Asian Pacific region, the least developed and Pacific island countries remain marginalized, unable to participate fully in the region's dynamism. South Asia, where GDP growth rates have risen dramatically in the last two years, must sustain that growth and translate it into a better quality of life for the poor. Central Asian economies are making good progress, but integration into the wider global economy remains a daunting challenge. In East and South-East Asia, pockets of poverty continue to exist.

Pacific Island countries face many difficult problems as also do many other small economies around the world. For the Pacific Island these include physical disadvantages, remoteness, smallness and dispersion. These characteristics of PICs raise significantly the cost of doing business. As pointed out by Winters and Martin (2004) most small economies have cost of doing business disadvantages which put them in significant difficulties for achieving high levels of economic growth.

The ability of PICs to raise the performance of the services sector remains viable. Tourism development provides a particular opportunity for many them, as the potential for manufacturing in many smaller PICs is very small and limited. While the tropical island nature of the PICs provides better opportunities for tourism, significant investment in the development of infrastructure is needed in many of them to reap the full potential of the tourism industry.

Agriculture remains an important source of income and employment in the majority of the PICs, though investment in this sector needs to be raised significantly. For the bigger Melanesian countries such as Papua New Guinea, Vanuatu, Solomon Islands and Fiji, agriculture remains vital for their economic progress. Unfortunately, as pointed out by Reddy and Duncan (2006), the productivity in agriculture has been declining in the PICs. For the PICs to raise the level of agricultural production, the issue of productivity has to be addressed. Important constraints such as the management of land and the communal nature of property rights provides special challenges for the development of agriculture in the PICs.

Almost all PICs suffer from the lack of appropriate human resources and physical infrastructure. In addition many of the PICs suffer from monopolistic control of the delivery of public utilities. The lack of competition in this area has raised the price of these utilities and is one of the major costs of doing business. This affects the level of investment in these countries. The level and quality of human resources is affected by the quality of primary and secondary education. While many PICs have high enrolment rates in both primary and secondary levels, countries such as Papua New Guinea, Solomon Islands and Vanuatu lag behind. The lack of formal sector employment opportunities for youth in these countries also reduces the demand for primary and secondary education.

The tourism industry makes a significant contribution to many Pacific island economies. Tourism numbers have been increasing steadily in many of the countries, led by Fiji. The prospect for the tourism industry lies in the attractiveness of the PICs including their tropical climate and undisturbed beaches. It also includes a combination of factors, including the growing demand for safe destinations, increased marketing and increased air capacity and the entry of low-cost carriers. However, this is an industry that is also most vulnerable to political instability and natural disasters, and the threat of terrorism always remains a distant fear. Several of the PICs and most notably Solomon Islands, Fiji and Tonga, have been affected by political instabilities. Fiji has suffered 4 coups in the last twenty years and this has affected its potential to achieve its target of a billion tourists a year.

In addition to the tourism industry, remittances from Pacific Island migrants continue to be an attractive prospect for raising the level of living standards of PICs people. A recent World Bank (2006) report on the Pacific argues strongly for labour mobility and calls for policies to enhance this. It argues that PICs prospects for growth over the years have been elusive and it is increasingly difficult for the 40 per cent of the population who are youths to find employment in their own countries.

3. MDG Targets for the Pacific Islands

According to the Millennium Project report the following areas will need to be carefully considered if Small Island Developing States (SIDS) such the Pacific Islands are to achieve any of the goals by 2015. These are as follows: (1) Science and Technology. Developing appropriate information and communications technology can help PICs to overcome isolation, and barriers to scale, and to support the development of service based industries like tourism and financial services. PICs will have to use these reforms to move away from primary based industries to more manufacturing and service-based industries. Many of the PICs, however, have monopolistic structures in their communication industry and this keeps costs high and therefore affects the development of other industries. (2) Urban and Rural investment strategies for the Development of Infrastructure. Many of the PICs face serious problems with the infrastructure, such as poor roads, poor airport, sea port facilities and lack of clean water and sanitation. Improvements in these are crucial for attracting investment in key growth industries such as tourism and financial services. PICs would need support for the development of infrastructure- aid for infrastructure must precede aid for trade if trade is to be enhanced; (3) Climate Change and Environmental Management. Extreme climatic conditions and natural disasters impose a significant economic and social costs to PICs and often inhibits development. Appropriate infrastructure for disaster management and risk strategies would be required to mitigate against damages. In this area PICs would need support from developed countries. Many of the PICs have fragile environment and are affected by damage to ecosystems, depletion of fish stocks and coral reefs. They need to put in strategies for proper environmental management. (4) Regional and Public goods; these are important in delivering basic services to the poor. Regional cooperation and integration would and should provide opportunities for these countries to overcome some of the difficulties that may be created by smallness.

4. Global and Regional Challenges

Apart from the problem areas noted above there are specific regional concerns, many of which overlap and are concerns in many of the PICs. The Millennium report, for example, identifies the issue of health services and education for the Caribbean region. In terms of health the report points out that HIV prevalence in the Caribbean is second only to Sub-Saharan Africa. The maternal mortality rate remains high, for example reaching 680 deaths per 100,000 births in Haiti. In terms of education, job training and skills development will be a major challenge in view of the erosion of preferences for bananas and textiles in the world markets.

Many of the Pacific Islands countries face similar challenges but national averages in some of these countries mask the disparities between urban and rural areas, and small and big islands within each the countries. The case of Solomon Islands is a good example of the government's inability to provide basic health and education facilities for its people. Investment in education and health is vital for many of the Pacific Island countries if they are to achieve some of the MDG goals.

The second global economic process, which poses difficult challenges but also opportunities for PICs, is the multilateral trade negotiations under the WTO. It is well recognized that international trade can be a powerful driver of economic growth and poverty reduction. It is, however, not a panacea for all economic ills of a country, in particular, if countries fail to adopt complementary policies such as investments in infrastructure, human capital, macroeconomic stability and institutional reforms. The current negotiations under the WTO involve trade in agricultural products, trade in services, non-agricultural market access, rules, trade facilitation, intellectual property (TRIPS Agreement), trade and environment, special and differential treatment and dispute settlement procedures. While all these are important for PICs, the main focus at the Hong Kong Ministerial meeting was on Agriculture, NAMA and Special and Differential treatment and trade in services.

The Monterrey Consensus outlined two areas on which MDG-based international trade policy should focus. The first is that market access and terms of trade should be improved for the poor countries and improving their supply side competitiveness for low-income countries exports through increased investment in the infrastructure such as roads, electricity, ports and trade facilitation.

The first issue that poses serious challenges in the negotiations is the preferential market access and erosion of preferences for PICs. It is well known that PICs are beneficiaries of many varieties of trade preferences, and generally deriving from their relationships with their former colonial powers. Many of the preferences available to PICs are through special programmes such as the Caribbean Basin Initiative, Cariban of Canada or SPARTECA of Australia and New Zealand, and the European Union grants special preferences to many PICs by virtue of Cotonou Partnership Agreement between African, Caribbean and Pacific (ACP) countries and members of the European Union. Some PICs are, however, beneficiaries of preferential agreements under the least developed countries (LDCs) categories. At the first WTO Ministerial Conference in 1996 members agreed on the importance of granting trade preferences to LDCs. This was followed through successive ministerial conferences and the 6^{Th} Ministerial Conference in Hong Kong agreed to grant duty free access to LDC exports. Some of the PICs will be beneficiaries of this agreement.

Other preferential access is provided by the US and Japan and some PICs benefit from this as well. In 2000, for example, the US approved the Africa Growth Opportunity Act through which the Generalised System of Preferences (GSP) of the US was expanded to include the range of products including clothing and textiles. Japan also reviewed its GSP in 2000 to provide duty free access to the Japanese market for industrial products from LDCs. The Japanese GSP was further reviewed and extended for another decade until 31 March 2014 and LDCs Kiribati and Tuvalu were added to the list of beneficiaries. In 2003 Japan further improved its GSP and the number of agriculture and fisheries products under duty free and quota free treatment was increased from 300 to 500 items for LDCs.

In March 2001 the EU adopted the "Everything But Arms" (EBA) initiative to provide duty and quota free access to all products but arms and special trade regimes for bananas and sugar until preferences are phased out.[1] Small and Vulnerable economies as a group at the recent Hong Kong Ministerial meeting asked that banana, rice and sugar be brought under the 'sensitive' product category.

The new ACP-EU Cotonou agreement, which superseded the Lome IV Convention provides for an 8-year roll over of the preferences previously granted under the Lome IV, with minor improvements until 2008.

Canada also provides preferences under its GSP programme as well. In January 2003, Canada granted duty free and quota-free access to LDCs, except for dairy, eggs and poultry. Clothing and textile was added in 2003.[2] Australia and New Zealand provide important markets for Pacific SIDS and give duty and quota- free access to LDCs of the Pacific (Kiribati, Samoa, Solomon Islands, Tuvalu and Vanuatu). The South Pacific Regional Trade

---

[1] For Banana the phasing out period is 2002-2006 and for sugar and rice 2006-2009.

[2] For details of Canada's GSP and rules of origin see UNCTAD (2003) " Trade Preferences for LDCs: An early assessment and possible improvements".

and Economic Cooperation Agreement (SPARTECA) is a non-reciprocal agreement providing duty free and unrestricted concessionary access to their markets.

Despite all the preferential treatment granted by the developed countries, the effectiveness of the GSP remains questionable. Studies show that only a handful of countries really benefit from trade preferences.[3] Judging from the experiences of countries such as Fiji, and some of the Caribbean and Indian Ocean countries, it is clear that trade preferences have not been able to encourage investment and generate export diversification; rather, they have to some extent created preference-dependent export and preferential depended efficiencies. This is especially the case for ACP countries under the four Lome Convention and now under the Cotonou Agreement.

What is important now, however, for PICs is how to counter the continuing erosion of trade preferences and policies to integrate their economies into the international economy and reap the benefits of global trading regimes.

Since the creation of the WTO, which is a major force for trade liberalisation, high rates of trade preferences have diminished and further negotiations will eventually mean more erosion and in some case no preferences at all. For example, many countries are now taking disputes to the WTO and these disputes when settled are likely to erode preferences. Some of the disputes are (1) Banana Dispute (2) Sugar Dispute- Brazil and Australia/Thailand and the EU over subsidies in the EU sugar regime (3) The Thailand-Philippines/EU, over margins for preference for canned tuna from Fiji, Mauritius, Papua New Guinea, Fiji and Seychelles; and (4) the current negotiations over the fisheries subsidies under the WTO, could undermine the revenue potential of small island economies, many of them dependent on access fees for their revenue.

The Pacific Plan adopted in 2004 is a result of the review of the state of regionalism by the Pacific Island Leaders in view of new global and regional economic challenges. This plan has been adopted also in recognition of the fact that PIC economic performance has been on the slide for the last 5 years. In addition, poor governance, corruption, political and social instability has put further pressures to re-look at regional cooperation. The plan further puts emphasis on strengthening regional cooperation and promoting sustainable development in the region. The long-term the challenge for PICs is to create capacity to reap the benefits and opportunities that may be available through increasing global economic integration. Many PICs will continue to face significant economic problems in future as they make adjustment to the various pressures of global trading regimes and changing global economic environment. To meet these challenges PICs would have to put more emphasis on raising productivity and improving the governance structures, which remain poor in comparision to economies that have done well. These challenges have also been highlighted in the Pacific 2020 plan, developed by the Australian Government (AusAID, 2006).

In addition, Pacific Island countries have been characterized by increasing political instability, bad governance and corruption. In particular, recent political instability in Tonga, Solomon Islands and Fiji has exposed a fear that the whole region may be politically unstable. This already has serious impacts on tourism, foreign investment and economic growth. PIC policy makers and political leaders have serious choices to make in terms of polices that ought to be pursued to bring economic prosperity to their countries. This will not be an easy

---

[3] See for example Inama (2003).

choice in the current economic and political climate and it may take considerable time for many of them to recover from serious economic decline.

References

Asian Development Bank (ADB). (2000) *Development Banking in the Pacific- Experience and Alternatives*, ADB, Manila

Asian Development Bank (ADB). (2005) *Outlook 2005, Publication Highlights*, Oxford University Press

AusAID (2006) *Pacific 2020: Challenges and Opportunities for Growth, Australian Department of Foreign Affairs and Trade:* AusAid: Canberra.

Inama, S. (2003) "Trade Preferences and the World Trade Organization Negotiations on Market Access." *Journal of World Trade,* 37(5): 959–76.

Pacific Islands Forum Secretariat (PIFS). (2002) *Economic Outlook*, Suva (*http://www .forumsec.org.fj)*

Reddy, M and R. Duncan (2006) "Productivity of Pacific Islands Agriculture: Issues and Challenges", *ICFAI Journal of Agricultural Economics*, 3(2):16-31.

UN (2002) "Review of Progress in the Implementation of the Programme of Action for the Sustainable Development of Small Island Developing States", *Report of the Secretary General.* E/CN.17/2004/1. Economic and Social Council, New York.

UNCTAD (2003) "Trade Preferences For Ldcs: An Early Assessment Of Benefits And Possible Improvements." Unctad/ITCD/TSB/2003/8. Geneva.

Winters, A. and Martin, J. (2004) *When Comparative Advantage Is Not Enough:* Business Costs in Small Remote Economies: Centre for Economic Policy Research, London and Centre for Economic Performance, London School of Economics, Department of Economics, University of Sussex, Brighton.

World Bank (2006) *Expanding Job Opportunities for Pacific Islanders Through Labour Mobility at Home and Away,* World Bank: Sydney.

In: Development Problems and Prospects in Pacific Islands ISBN: 978-1-60021-793-7
Editors: B. C. Prasad, D. C. Roy, pp. 9-21

Chapter 2

GLOBALIZATION AND THE ECONOMIC FUTURE OF SMALL ISOLATED NATIONS, PARTICULARLY IN THE PACIFIC*

Clem Tisdell

1. INTRODUCTION

Economic globalization has proceeded at a fast pace in recent times as demonstrated by several measures (Tisdell, 2005a; Tisdell and Sen, 2004). For example, the per centage of gross global output traded rose from around 12 per cent in 1960 to 24 per cent in 2002 (Tisdell, 2005a, p.6). The level of foreign direct investment has also risen substantially in magnitude and as a proportion of global output in recent decades, as have short-term money movements. The per centage of the world's population engaging in international travel has shown a strong upward trend (Tisdell, 2005b) and there has been an explosion in the extent of international electronic communication, partly as a result of technological advances.

On the other hand, growth in international labour movements appears to have been less rapid even though substantial international movements of labour do occur. These involve both short-term movements ('guest' workers) and permanent migration. Furthermore, the ageing of populations in many developing countries and perceived skill shortages in these countries are catalysts for relaxation of requirements for labour migration to more developed countries. Despite this, the international market for labour appears to involve more restrictions than other global markets.

Economic globalization involves the international extension of markets. In popular parlance, it covers the concepts of borderless economies and the global village. Its economic consequences for nations are liable to differ. Some nations may make little economic gain from the process of globalization, or even lose, whereas others may reap substantial economic

---

* A revised version of a paper presented at the 5th IIDS International Conference on Governance and Development to be held at The University of the South Pacific, Suva, Fiji Islands, 1-4 December 2005.

benefit from it. Furthermore, the ways in which nations may gain or lose from globalization can differ significantly.

Small isolated economies, such as many Pacific islands economies, have limited scope for benefiting from the process of economic globalization because of their geographical isolation from large markets. This combined with their small home markets denies such countries economies of scale and of agglomeration. Their natural barriers to international trade are substantial and are likely to remain even when man-made barriers to global trade are reduced considerably. Tuvalu, for example, virtually has no exports of goods because of its natural situation and Kiribati has few exports (Tisdell, 2000).

On the other hand, some of the larger Pacific island counties, such as Fiji, obtain a significant share of their foreign exchange receipt from their exports. In 2000, for example, Fiji's exports amounted to about 45 per cent of its GDP, and that of Papua New Guinea in 2002 was equal to about 27 per cent of its GDP. These economies, therefore, appear to be more dependent on the global trading economy than small atoll economies. There are, of course, other ways of achieving international dependence, for example, via international labour movements and remittances. The scope for this type of dependence also differs widely amongst Pacific island countries (PICs) (Connell and Brown, 2005). The nature and degree of economic interdependence of PICs with the global economy varies greatly. With this in mind, let us discuss generally the prospects for international trade in goods and services for these countries, the scope for changed international capital movements and labour movements, given the ongoing process of economic globalization.

2. International Trade in Goods and Services and PICs

While for some PICs, such as PNG and Fiji, international trade is their main link to the global economy for others, such as Tuvalu and Kiribati, international trade is of no or of little importance. In the case of Samoa, international trade is of moderate importance. Thus there are large differences in the degree to which PICs are linked to the global economy via international trade in goods and services. This position is unlikely to change as man-made barriers to international trade are reduced because of the considerable variations in the size of the economies of PICs, in their availability and diversity of resources, and in their physical costs of accessing international markets. For these reasons, one would expect the international trade possibilities of Kiribati and Tuvalu, for example, to remain quite limited compared to Fiji and PNG as economic globalization proceeds. That is not to say that these atoll economies have had no economic benefits from international contact. They have been able to obtain some benefits from the global economy, for instance, from royalties charged for tuna fishing rights in their waters, and from being able to supply seamen for international shipping lines.

Not only does the dependence of PICs on international trade in commodities differ greatly but within PICs, various social groups and communities have widely varying degrees of dependence on such trade. There appears, however, to have been no systematic study of the degree of this variation by social groups. However, one might expect urban populations to be more dependent on markets and international trade and foreign exchange for their livelihoods than rural populations. In Fiji, market and international trade dependence of Fijian Indians is most likely greater on average than for Melanesian Fijians given that Fijian Indians have only very limited land rights (Prasad and Tisdell, 2006). Fijians in remote areas probably engage in much less trade than those in more central places.[1]

It should, however, be noted that the proportion of a household's income or output entering trade is just one consideration in examining the importance of trade for the welfare of the household. A household, for example, that earns 5% of its income in cash might be economically more vulnerable to say a 20% decline in cash income than one that earns all of its income in cash. The former may be forced to forego market necessities whereas the latter household may only have to give up market luxuries. Assessment of the degree of economic dependence of households in PICs on market exchange is quite complex.

While many PICs may seem to have dualistic economies, probably most are not well represented by such a binary dichotomous relationship. The dependence of their population on markets, on cash, or on external economic factors probably forms a continuous relationship. A possible hypothetical relationship of this kind is shown in Figure 2.1 by the relative frequency curve ABCD. This curve indicates that no households in this hypothetical economy are without any cash income but that for a large number, cash accounts form a low proportion of their income. The hypothetical relationship in Figure 1 displays a bimodal distribution of 'dependence' of households on cash income, even though earning of all income in cash has the greatest relative frequency. Nevertheless, most individuals in this hypothetical country depend to some extent on non-cash income.

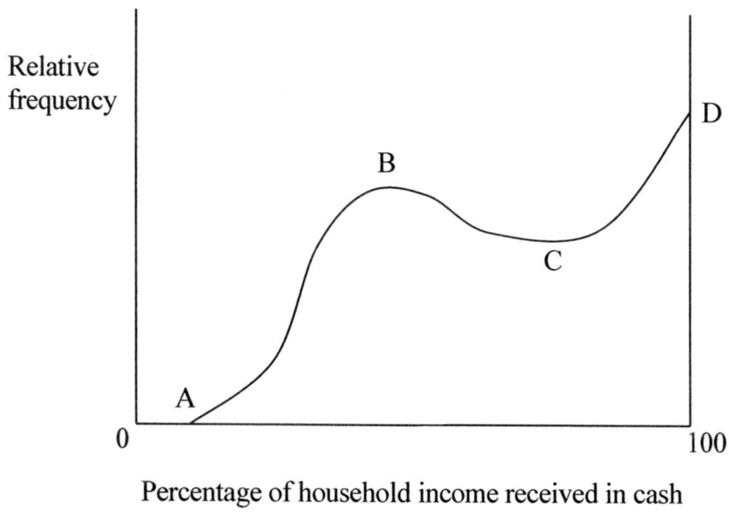

Figure 2.1. Relative frequency with which households in a hypothetical economy obtain different per centages of their income in cash.

[1] Even in the case of Fiji, subsistence income is very important for the livelihoods of many. According to the National Income Accounts prepared by the Fiji Islands' Bureau of Statistics, subsistence production in agriculture, forestry and fisheries accounted for about 42 per cent of the value of production of this sector in 2002. It accounted for a level of production valued at FJ$229 million and significantly exceeded the value of sugarcane production. The estimated value of subsistence agricultural production in 2002 was approximately equal to that of sugarcane production, but exceeded it in 2001. The economic significance of subsistence production in PICs appears often to be neglected in policy formulation.

Relative frequency curves of the 'dependence' of households on cash, market exchange, exports, foreign transactions and so on for PICs have not been estimated but would be revealing. In higher income countries, such as Australia, almost the entire population is dependent completely on cash for its income. The exceptions in Australia would include some Australian Aborigines and Torres Straits Islanders and alternative lifestyle groups.

Economic globalization and market extension have different consequences for households depending upon how dependent they are on markets and the cash economy for their income. Also, in the Pacific one has to give particular attention to the nature of economic obligations within the family. Amongst indigenous people, the family is often a very extended family so that earners of cash in such a family have wide obligations to share cash. Thus the loss of a government job by one family member can adversely affect the welfare of many family members. Economic restructuring of the public service, such as occurred in Solomon Islands, can therefore, result in widespread economic hardship where staff numbers in the public service are reduced.

Despite the fact that PICs differ greatly in their degree of dependence on trade in goods and services to generate income, all have significant links with the global economy. None are autarkic. International links of importance to countries such as Kiribati and Tuvalu are remittances from their sailors employed on foreign vessels, royalties obtained from foreign countries granted rights to catch tuna in their EEZs, and economic returns from mostly foreign investment of the government's capital reserve funds. In the case of W. Samoa, remittances from Samoans living and working abroad are a major source of foreign income and an important link to the world economy.

With growing economic globalization, it may be very difficult for many PICs to benefit from export-led growth. Fiji, in particular, may experience considerable economic difficulty given its export dependence on sugar production and garment manufacture. Markets for the output of both of these face increasing international market fluidity. PNG, and many PICs, are highly dependent on extractive industries for foreign exchange earnings. There is a risk that the rents from such industries will be unequally distributed and will not be used to bring about lasting economic development in the countries concerned. The rents of PICs may be used for consumption or even for investment abroad.

It is worthwhile, therefore, considering the likely impact of increasing freedom of capital movements on PICs and also the potentially greater freedom of international movement of labour. Freedom in international movement of capital is now well established as a plank of economic globalization policies. Easier movement of labour internationally is a subject of increasing debate.

3. International Capital Movements and PICs

In recent times, higher income countries have reduced their aid to developing countries, including PICs. There have been suggestions that with appropriate governance and the freeing of capital markets, private investment might compensate for this loss. However, in many resource-poor remote economies, this is probably a false hope. Greater freedom of resource movement globally may drain away their resources and reduce their long-term economic growth. Globally they can become declining regions of the world, a decline accelerated by greater freedom of international resource movements. It is normal for some regions of the world to decline and for their population levels to fall as economic development proceeds and as market extension occurs. In addition, there is often a net capital outflow from declining regions. Whether such changes are socially desirable or not is often a matter of contention.

Consider some simple theoretical possibilities as far as capital movement is concerned. Suppose that the only 2.2 represent its available supply of investment funds which is supposed for simplicity to be inelastic. Line ABC in this figure represents the marginal efficiency of capital in this economy and line DBE indicates the global return on investment. If domestic savings cannot be invested abroad, the total return on savings will be equal to the area of quadrilateral 0GCA. However, if investment can be undertaken freely abroad, savings invested at home will fall from x_1 to x_0 while the remainder of savings will be invested abroad. As a result, savers/investors increase their income by an amount equal to the area of the triangle BCE. The overall returns on investible funds increase but there is less capital formation in the domestic economy.

Reduced capital formation in the domestic economy can be expected to result in less employment in the private market sector of the domestic economy. While those who are able to save substantial sums (mostly the better off) will gain from free international flows of funds, those who depend for their livelihood on the sale of their labour in this hypothetical economy can be expected to lose. They can expect lower wages and reduced employment as a result of a decline in the domestic demand for labour.

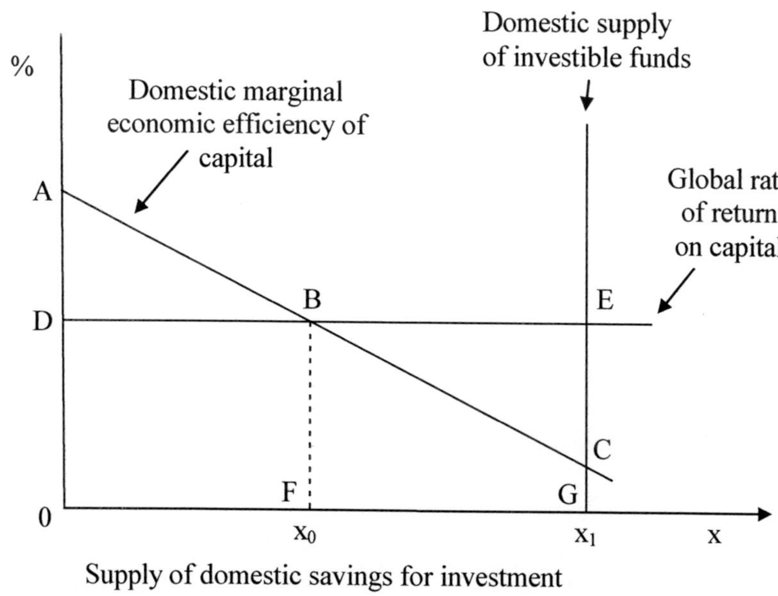

Figure 2.2. Illustration of how the free flows of funds for capital formation can result in an outflow of investible funds from a disadvantaged economy.

This is illustrated in Figure 2.3. There the line SS represents the supply of labour and the line D_1D_1 represents the demand for labour when all domestic savings are invested at home. The equilibrium in the labour market is then E_1. Suppose, however, that as a result of deregulation, a high proportion of local savings is invested abroad. As a result, the demand curve for labour in the domestic economy might fall from D_1D_1 to D_2D_2. The equilibrium in the domestic labour market then alters from E_1 to E_2. Consequently, the level of domestic employment of labour declines and the wage rate is reduced. The net results possibly will be an increase in the inequality of income in this hypothetical disadvantaged economy with income shifting in favour of the wealthier members of the community. Wage earners will be disadvantaged.

However, the above ignores the possibility that, as a result of deregulation of capital markets, there could be greater inflows of capital to disadvantaged economies, such as those of many PICs. Foreigners may be able to undertake investment opportunities that locals lack the skills, market connections and technology to undertake successfully. However, in many cases, the inflow of such investment is likely to be considerably less than the outflow of local savings. This is because the limited resources and the market disadvantages of many PICs provide little scope for profitable foreign investment. Furthermore, in some larger PICs, such as PNG, where foreign investment is considerable, it is often in extractive industries, such as mineral production. Economic leakages from foreign direct investment in such industries tends to be high, and extractive industries usually have limited sustainability.

In addition, there are, frequently, socio-political impediments to foreign and local investment in many PICs. These include lack of availability of secure private property rights in land (Prasad and Tisdell, 2006), the political instability of some nations, corruption, and problems in achieving effective governance. These are the outcomes of cultural traditions and historical experience. They are difficult to change quickly. Furthermore, there can be considerable social conflict about the desirability of altering institutions associated with cultural traditions. It is unrealistic to imagine that a quick 'social fix' is possible, even assuming that it is desirable.

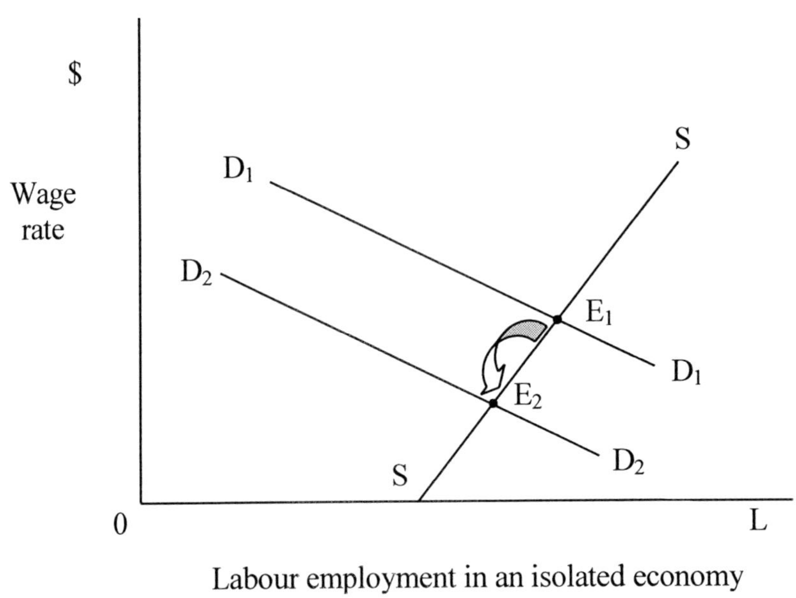

Figure 2.3. Outflows of capital from a disadvantaged hypothetical economy can reduce domestic wages and employment.

Thus, the prospect for economic growth being fostered in most PICs by the process of economic globalization involving free international capital markets seems to be dim. In fact, several PICs, such as Fiji, could experience negative economic impacts from economic globalization. Therefore, international labour movements need to be considered as a means to provide economic help to individuals living in such countries.

4. International Labour Movements and PICs

According to neoclassical economic theory, free movements of labour, including international movements, will result in economic gain if labour movements are currently restricted. Labour will tend to migrate from low income regions to higher income regions. In a frictionless, competitive economic world, labour movements will continue until the value of the marginal product of labour is equal in all regions and incomes are equal for those with equal skills and ability. Such free movements would bring about a potential Paretian improvement in economic welfare or a Kaldor-Hicks economic gain according to neoclassical economic theory.

Therefore, according to this point of view, migration from PICs to richer Pacific Rim countries, such as Australia and New Zealand, can increase incomes in the Pacific Region as a whole. It may also reduce the amount of foreign aid needed to maintain income levels in PICs, as discussed by Tisdell (1990) in Chapter 10, "Foreign Assistance to Resource-poor Developing Countries: Aid versus International Migration".

In practice, however, the economic impacts of such migration are likely to be complex. For example, its economic impact will vary depending on the relationship between the value of production in a country and the size of its population (Tisdell, 1990, Ch.10). Neoclassical economic models have normally been based on the assumption of diminishing marginal productivity. If this applies, out migration should raise per capita incomes in PICs. However, it could result in some countries or currently inhabited islands becoming completely depopulated because their maximum per capita income is less than that obtainable elsewhere in the world. For these areas, migration would result in a mathematical corner-point solution. The optimal economic solution could be to depopulate some islands completely in the Pacific and maybe even some small Pacific countries. Whether or not that would be desirable from other viewpoints could be contentious.

But we cannot be sure that a neoclassical production model of a Ricardian-type (see Tisdell, 2005c, Ch.1) applies. It may be that as the population of a country expands, it first experiences increasing returns to production then decreasing returns with further increases in population. If this Marshallian type situation prevails, then emigration from PICs may reduce the per capita incomes of remaining residents, not increase them as in the Ricardian case (Tisdell, 1990, Ch.10). Thus, Marshallian non-convexity in the production function will further stimulate out migration. It might, however, be offset (at least to some extent) by remittances to PICs by migrants.

It seems likely that non-convexities in national production do occur and that the Ricardian-type production function does not apply, or only applies in a few cases. Free migration from PICs could reduce per capita incomes in some of these, such as possibly Fiji. That could, however, be compensated for to some extent by remittances for emigrants.

The matter is further complicated by the presence of shared goods and services, the availability of which is heavily dependent on concentrations of populations. These include external economic benefits and disbenefits of being located in an area where population is concentrated, such as urban area or a 'centre' country. As a country or an area becomes depopulated, external economic benefits per capita may eventually fall, and further stimulate migration to central places (Tisdell, 1990, Ch.9). Thus the centre grows as a result of these externalities and the periphery further declines. Consequently, it is clear that the economic impacts of migration are more complicated than indicated by the Ricardian-type neoclassical production model. Non-convexities in the production function and the presence of economic externalities dependent on concentrations of population may prevent the occurrence of a Paretian optimal outcome when free migration is allowed (Tisdell et al., 2004). Yet easier international migration could be better from an economic (and arguably a social) point of view than one where international migration is highly restricted. Even if easier international migration does not give ideal results, it could be more desirable than maintaining the status quo.

5. Political Pressures for Easier Immigration to Higher Income Countries

Debate about whether residents of PICs should have easier labour access, including migration possibilities, to Pacific Rim countries, such as Australia, intensified in 2005. At the Pacific Islands Forum in 2005 held in Port Moresby, Pacific island leaders pressed for easier labour access of their residents to Australia. Such a development is seen by many as a logical follow up to a free trade area in the South Pacific, and would be analogous to the evolution of free markets in the European Union. In the case of the EU, greater freedom of trade within the EU was followed by greater freedom of labour movements.

An aspect of this debate has been the claim that Pacific islanders should be granted easier access to Australia for employment as seasonal workers (Maclellan and Mares, 2005). It is argued that this will create greater economic opportunities for unskilled or low skilled Pacific islanders, many of whom are under employed or unemployed. It may also provide a cheaper source of labour for seasonal employment on Australian farms, particularly in horticulture. Australian horticulturalists face considerable competition from imports as a result of reduced barriers to international trade. Several other higher income countries are employing cheap migrant labour in labour-intensive operations in horticulture; for example, Mexicans in the USA and North Africans in Spain.

In addition, it can be observed that many countries make considerable use of low-cost foreign 'guest' workers on short-term contracts, many of whom are low skilled. While this is a well known fact in relation to oil-rich nations, such as Brunei in the Asia-Pacific region, it is also true of other countries, such as Singapore, Malaysia, Thailand (see, for example, Kaur, 2004) and even Hong Kong. In the case of Singapore, Malaysia and Thailand, some of their industries are kept internationally more competitive as a result of the use of guest workers on lower pay than demanded by their nationals. Considerations of international competitiveness may, therefore, also entice nations such as Australia to adopt similar policies as economic globalization proceeds. As Australian labour markets become increasingly deregulated, the scope for labour contracts involving lower wages will increase particularly if a large supply of foreign guest workers from low income countries becomes available.

The above indicates that economic globalization can increase pressures in more developed countries in favour of the import of low-cost relatively low-skilled labour. However, various economic interest groups (mostly employers) in higher income countries have also argued that in order to maintain their international competitiveness in a globalising world, it is important for them to be allowed to import skilled labour. Currently, it is much easier for skilled persons to migrate to Australia than the unskilled or those with few skills. Australia's current policies add to the 'brain-drain' in PICs.[2] To some extent, PICs counteract this by employing skilled Africans but this in turn adds to the brain drain from Africa.

Thus, it seems that growing international competition arising from the processes of economic globalization is causing different employer groups with differing labour requirements to support easier short-term and long-term immigration of both skilled and unskilled persons. This is seen as a way to cope with international competitive pressures arising from globalization.

Given the limited income and employment opportunities in small isolated economies, including PICs, their leaders are generally supportive of more liberal international labour movements, particularly if their emigrants are likely to return significant amounts of remittances to their home countries. At the same time, they are aware of the extra burden that they may face as a result of loss of skilled persons, such as medical practitioners and nurses.

Another reason why many higher income countries have become more receptive to the immigration of non-elderly persons, is that they are faced by an ageing population and a dwindling workforce relative to their total population. The burden of supporting the elderly in higher income countries may be eased by immigration of non-elderly persons. This strategy is, for example, being followed by Spain (Rojas, 2005). Australia, like Japan and many European countries, is one of the higher income countries that is experiencing an ageing population. This does not, however, appear to be a major problem for the USA possibly because of its large influx of Latin Americans.

On the other hand, the possibility should not be overlooked that poorly planned immigration programmes can be the source of social problems, highlighted, for example, by the rioting in France in November 2005 in poor suburbs dominated by immigrants from North Africa.

Immigrants may be especially vulnerable in a deregulated labour market. There is a danger that they will be subject to prejudice and discrimination in the workplace. Because of their weak bargaining position, long-term conditions of work may suffer. This could become an issue in Australia with the increasing deregulation of industrial relations. Ghettoes of socially disadvantaged could evolve, as appears to have happened in France and in the USA. Australia has become a more unequal society as globalization has proceeded. Bob Gregory (2004) has found that there is increasing geographical stratification of income groups in Australia; the poor are increasingly located in proximity to each other and so also are the rich.

However, the number of Pacific islanders in relation to Australia's population is not large and not all will want or be allowed to migrate. Some Pacific islanders already have excellent opportunities to migrate such as Samoans and Cook Islanders but residents of resource-poor Kiribati and Tuvalu do not. This raises the question of whether residents of some PICs should be given a priority in sending migrants to Australia. If so, how should the selection be made?

---

[2] For some discussion of issues involving the brain-drain in small island economies, see McKee and Tisdell (1990, Ch.8).

Should preference be given to migrants from resource-poor atoll countries, or to countries, such as Fiji, which are likely to be quite vulnerable to the loss of international market protection as globalization proceeds?

In its Pacific policy discussion paper, the Australia Labor Party (ALP) indicates its support for a limited number of short-term employment visas, specifically for Pacific islanders to enable them to gain greater access to the Australian labour market (Sercombe, 2005). Their stays would be limited to 12 months or less. For seasonal workers, stays could be of as little as 3 months duration. The numbers being considered are modest; initially starting at 5,000 in year 1 and rising to 10,000 in year 5. The ACTU has indicated qualified support for the scheme.

Pacific leaders at the Pacific Islands Forum held in PNG in October 2005 requested the Australian and New Zealand prime ministers allow greater access to Australia and New Zealand for seasonal work by their residents. However, this was rejected by both. Miss Clark (the New Zealand Prime Minister) was reported as saying that "New Zealand is concerned about the erosion of working standards and the rise in the number of illegal visa overstayers" as well as the fact that "some small Pacific states had virtually become unviable because their working populations had moved to New Zealand" (Shanahan, 2005).

6. Further Discussion and Concluding Comments

It is often claimed by proponents of laissez-faire economic systems that market deregulation and freer international trade will stimulate private investment. Furthermore, it is sometimes suggested that government investment tends to 'crowd out' private investment, and that, therefore, a reduction in public investment may further stimulate private investment. However, none of these effects have happened in Fiji in recent times. Private investment as a per centage of Fiji's GDP has fallen since 1980 although the Fijian economy has become more open and less regulated, and at the same time investment by the public sector has also declined sharply (see Prasad and Tisdell, 2006, Table 4.7).

In Table 2.1, the openness of the Fijian economy as indicated by its exports as a per centage of its GDP for the period 1980-2000 can be compared with its level of private investment as a per centage of its GDP. It is apparent that with the growing openness of the Fijian economy,[3] its private investment as a per centage of its GDP has fallen considerably.

Figure 4 shows the scatter of observations for private investment as a per centage of its GDP in comparison to Fiji's exports as a per centage of its GDP for the period 1980-2000. It can be seen that a negative relationship exists between the degree of openness of Fiji's economy and its level of private investment as a per centage of its GDP. For each 10% increase in openness of Fiji's economy, its level of private investments as a per centage of its GDP tended to decline by about 3.2%.

[3] There is some indication from Fiji Islands' Bureau of Statistics that exports as a per centage of Fiji's GDP have started to decline. This may be because remittances have started to rise strongly as a source of its foreign exchange earnings.

Table 2.1. Openness of the Fijian economy (Exports as a Per centage of its GDP) in the 1980s and the 1990s and private investment as a per centage of its GDP in the same period

Year	Exports as a Per centage of GDP	Private Investment as a Per centage of GDP
1980	18.45	14.9
1981	15.66	13.7
1982	17.12	11.1
1983	15.77	10.9
1984	16.88	11.4
1985	17.09	13.6
1986	17.24	11.0
1987	23.47	10.9
1988	25.38	7.5
1989	27.72	6.4
1990	30.01	5.5
1991	27.38	5.2
1992	25.72	3.6
1993	26.38	4.7
1994	28.79	4.1
1995	36.19	4.1
1996	42.84	4.2
1997	35.42	3.7
1998	41.22	4.7
1999	44.31	4.7
2000	45.54	3.1

Source: Asian Development Bank, 2002 and Fiji Islands Bureau of Statistics, various years.

These results are consistent with the theoretical hypothesis put forward above that global market deregulation could lead to net capital outflows from some PICs or more generally reduce the level of private investment. There may, however, be other factors, such as political stability, that have contributed to Fiji's experience apart from the greater openness of its economy and reduced investment by the public sector.

The results indicate that it is by no means clear that growing economic globalization involving freer international markets will stimulate economic development in all Pacific countries. Certainly some might be expected to experience net capital outflows or declines in investment, and if international labour movements become easier, declining populations. One would expect, in a 'borderless economic world', some nations to experience economic and demographic decline whereas others will prosper as economic globalization proceeds. Just as some regions in large countries decline as they become more strongly integrated with the national market, so also several PICs can expect to experience economic and demographic decline as they become more fully integrated with the global economy and their mobile resources (such as capital and labour) move offshore to obtain higher economic returns. In the neoclassical economic world, such movements are an important step towards the achievement of global economic efficiency, even though it is recognised that they may result in the economic decline of some regions.[4]

An additional point not discussed above, but considered by Tisdell and Fairbairn (1984), is that those PICs which increase their export dependence in a globalising world are likely, as a result of the law of comparative advantage, to become even more specialised in production than previously. They become even less diversified in production than before. They are then particularly vulnerable to changes in the international economy. They are likely to find economic adjustment more difficult than in the case of large economies and they can face long-term economic sustainability problems of the type discussed by Tisdell and Fairbairn (1984).[5]

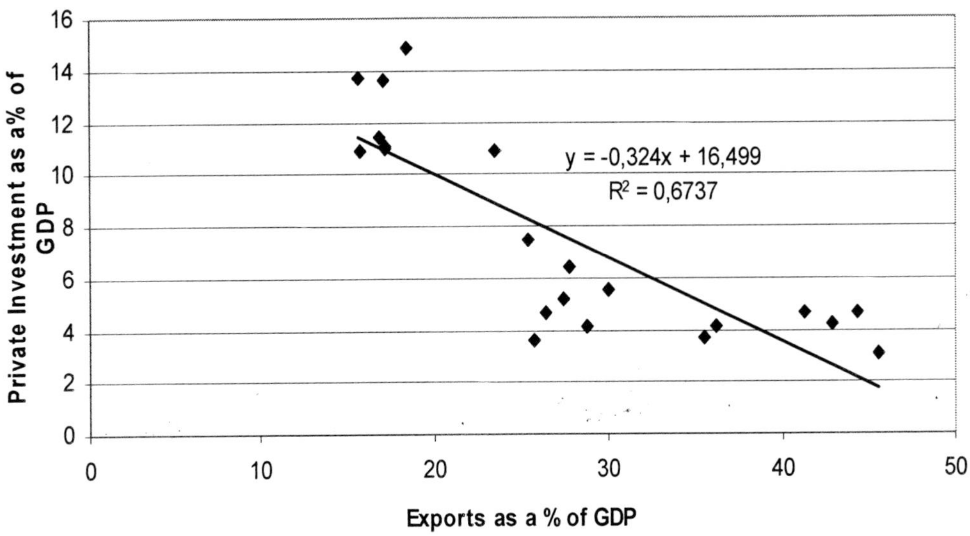

Figure 2.4. Openness of the Fijian Economy versus Private Investment 1980-2000.

References

Connell, J. and Brown, R. (2005) *Remittances in the Pacific – An Overview*. Asian Development Bank, Manila.

Gregory, R.G. (2004) Growing locational disadvantage in Australian cities. Pp.128-157 in P. Compton (ed.) *Australian Macroeconomic Policy Debates: Contributions from the Shann Memorial Lectures 1991-2000*, University of Western Australia Press, Crawley, WA.

Kaur, A. (2004) Economic globalization and the 'new' labour migration in Southeast Asia. Pp.244-266 in C. Tisdell and R.K. Sen (eds) *Economic Globalization: Social Conflicts, Labour and Environmental Issues*. Edward Elgar, Cheltenham, UK and Northampton, Mass.

[4] Other economic models, such as centre-periphery models, also recognize that freer international markets may result in the economic decline of some regions. However, their proponents usually reject the neoclassical claim that global market liberalisation will promote global economic efficiency.

[5] I would like to thank Dr Glyn Edwards for research assistance and Genevieve Larsen for her help in the preparation of this article.

Maclellan, N. and Mares, P. (2005) Labour mobility in the Pacific: creating seasonal work programs in Australia. A paper presented at a conference on "Globalization, Governance and the Pacific Islands", State, Society and Governance in Melanesia Project, Australian National University, Canberra, 25-27 October 2005.

McKee, D.L. and Tisdell, C. (1990) *Development Issues in Small Island Economies.* Praeger, New York.

Prasad, B. and Tisdell, C. (2006) *Institutions, Economic Performance and Sustainable Development: A Case Study of the Fiji Islands.* Nova Science, New York.

Rojas, J.A. (2005) Immigration to ease the ageing problem in developed countries: the Spanish case. Pp.182-196 in C.A. Tisdell (ed) *Globalization and World Economic Policies.* Serials Publications, New Delhi.

Sercombe, Bob (2005) *Towards a Pacific Community.* Shadow Minister for Overseas Aid and Pacific Island Affairs, Parliament House, Canberra.

Shanahan, D. (2005) Howard, Clark shut out seasonal workers. *The Australian*, 25 October 2005. http://www.theaustralian.news.com.au/printpage/0,59242,17038068,00.html [Accessed 02/11/05].

Tisdell, C. (1990) *Natural Resources, Growth, and Development.* Praeger, New York.

Tisdell, C. (2000) Implementation of the Programme of Action in Least Developed Countries in the Pacific. Pp.150-255 in *Review of Implementation of the Programme of Action for the Least Developed Countries in the 1990s: Subregional Studies.* ESCAP Least Developed Countries Series, No.5, United Nations, New York.

Tisdell, C. (2005a) An overview of globalization and economic policy response. Pp.1-16 in C.

Tisdell (ed) *Globalization and World Economic Policies.* Serials Publications, New Delhi.

Tisdell, C. (2005b) Tourism development and globalization: experiences and policies of China and Australia. Pp.421-436 in C. Tisdell (ed) *Globalization and World Economic Policies.* Serials Publications, New Delhi.

Tisdell, C. (2005c) *Economics of Environmental Conservation: Second Edition.* Edward Elgar, Cheltenham, UK and Northampton, Mass.

Tisdell, C.A. and Fairbairn, T.I. (1984) Subsistence economies and unsustainable development and trade: some simple theory. *Journal of Development Studies* 20, 227-241.

Tisdell, C. and Sen, R.K. (2004) An overview of economic globalization: its momentum and its consequences examined. Pp.3-23 in C. Tisdell and R.K. Sen (eds) *Economic Globalization: Social Conflicts, Labour and Environmental Issues.* Edward Elgar, Cheltenham, UK and Northampton, Mass.

Tisdell, C., Svizzero, S. and Lasselle, L. (2004) Unequal gains of nations from globalization. Pp.71-86 in C. Tisdell and R.K. Sen (eds) *Economic Globalization: Social Conflicts, Labour and Environmental Issues.* Edward Elgar, Cheltenham, UK and Northampton, Mass.

In: Development Problems and Prospects in Pacific Islands ISBN: 978-1-60021-793-7
Editors: B. C. Prasad, D. C. Roy, pp. 23-30

Chapter 3

THE PACIFIC PLAN AND LABOUR MOBILITY

Robbie Robertson*

1. INTRODUCTION

The Pacific Plan is a regional strategy to establish an enabling framework to assist Forum Island Countries (FICs)[1] deal with a changing global environment, whose interface with the FICs is already set with the 1993 Melanesian Spearhead Group Trade Agreement (MSGTA), the 2001 Pacific Island Countries Trade Agreement (PICTA), the European Union Regional Economic Partnership Agreement (REPA) due in 2007, and Pacific Closer Economic Relations (PACER) to follow after 2007[2].

The plans link with national development lies in its use of regionalism to offset many of the anticipated problems trade liberalization poses for FICs. Labour mobility is raised in this context, with the recognition that it possesses a development capacity, a capacity in fact that goes far beyond the oft-mentioned use of unskilled labour.

---

* The author wishes to acknowledge the assistance of the Pacific Islands Forum and the Asian Development Bank in the development of this paper. Much of it builds on the background papers of the Pacific Plan, in particular ADB-CS (2005).

[1] The Pacific Islands Forum (PIF) is comprised of 14 FICs: Cook Is, Fiji, FSM, Kiribati, Marshall Is, Nauru, Niue, Palau, PNG, Samoa, Solomon Is, Tonga, Tuvalu, and Vanuatu and 2 Forum Developed Countries (FDCs): Australia and New Zealand. French Polynesia, New Caledonia, and Timor Leste have special observer status. Tokelau (population 1,500) may join when it gains self governing status in 2006. The Forum began in 1971 and is serviced by the Pacific Islands Forum Secretariat (PIFS), headquartered in Suva, Fiji. A Pacific Plan was first called for by an Eminent Persons Group in 2004 and the PIFS's draft plan was endorsed by the PIF in October 2005.

[2] The MSGTA is a free trade agreement between Fiji, Papua New Guinea, Solomon Is, and Vanuatu which commits members to phased tariff reductions except on excluded items. PICTA is a similar agreement applicable to all the FICs. As of late 2005 Cook Is, Tonga, Samoa, Fiji, Nauru, PNG and Vanuatu had signalled their intention to implement PICTA during 2006 at the latest, phasing in tariff reductions over 10 years. PACER is related to free trade in goods between the FICs and FDCs. Negotiations for this (either collectively or individually) are scheduled to start by 2011 or when Fiji, PNG and Samoa conclude their REPA. The Pacific REPA is one of six regional development agreements between the European Union and the Africa Caribbean Pacific (ACP) signatories to the former Lomé preferential trade agreements and its 2000 Cotonou successor. Its free trade component is theoretically dependent on the prior implementation of PICTA or the extension of MSGTA to include Samoa.

In this regard the Pacific Plan defies definition as a Forum Developed Country (FDC: Australia and New Zealand) tool[3]. If anything it is a challenge to FDCs to engage as equal partners. However, its message to FICs and FDCs alike is that connectivity makes the difference.

The Pacific Plan regards regionalism in three ways. The first and perhaps most common form concerns regional cooperation. Regional cooperation occurs at many civil society levels, for example in sports, religion and arts. Politically it involves dialogues and agreements between governments, such as Pacific Island Forum (PIF) ministerial meetings, declarations and treaties. The second involves the regional provision of public services, that is, the pooling together of national services at the regional level. Tertiary education provided to 12 FICs through their jointly owned University of the South Pacific, and the common management of tuna resources by the Forum Fisheries Agency are two successful examples. The third form - regional integration- is the most recent and controversial, and involves the lowering of barriers such as quarantine measures, import taxes and passport requirements for the exchange of goods, services and people between countries. It is regional integration that the Pacific Plan most seeks to facilitate.

2. Why Deeper Regional Integration is the Central Focus of the Pacific Plan

The FIC region faces challenges, not least because of its special nature. What most distinguishes it from many regions is its lack of connectedness, in part due to the fact that its countries are scattered across the world's largest ocean. Remoteness from each other and from major trading nations, high transportation costs, and scattered populations, all serve to raise the cost of services and business. As a formal region it is also distinguished by its membership: 14 developing countries, 2 developed countries, with 1 country having observer status and 2 territories associate membership.

In global population terms the region is very small with only 9 million people (34 million including FDCs), of whom 88% (excluding the FDCs) are in Melanesia. Melanesia comprises Papua New Guinea (PNG), Solomon Islands, Vanuatu, New Caledonia and Fiji. Together they possess 98% of the land mass of FICs. Five countries (in ascending order: Niue, Tuvalu, Nauru, the Cook Islands and Palau) have populations under 20,000; 4 (the Marshall Islands, Kiribati, Tonga and the Federated States of Micronesia (FSM)) between 50,000 and 110,000, 4 (Samoa, Vanuatu, the Solomon Islands, and Fiji) between 170,000 and 1 million, and 1 (PNG) has nearly 6 million.

This diversity is repeated in many other forms. In part due to its lack of historical connectedness, the region possesses over 1000 different languages. As noted already, land area varies widely from 462,840 sq km in PNG to 21 sq km Nauru. So too social indicators: population growth rates range from 3.6% in the Marshalls to -3.4% in the Cooks; life expectancy from 73 years in Samoa to 54 years in PNG; adult literacy from 99% in Tonga to 56% in PNG; per capita GDP from USD5,708 in Palau to $421 in Kiribati; poverty from 38%

---

[3] This allegation has been made constantly throughout 2005. See for example Powell (1985), Jayaraman (1985a) and Casimira (2005).

in Kiribati to 0% in Niue; child mortality/1000 live births from 88 in PNG to 12 in FSM; and household access to improved water from 100% in Niue to 30% in the Solomons. Not surprisingly economic data exhibit the same diversity: ODA as a proportion of GNP ranges from 48% in the Marshalls to 1.8% in Fiji; goods & services exports as a proportion of GDP from 69% in Fiji to 7.9% in the Marshalls; and remittances as a proportion of GDP from 55% in Tonga to 0.8% in Palau (UNDP, 2004).

Of course FICs also share features that are common to many regions, most notably those concerning poor communications infrastructure, poverty, and the lack of political will and critical mass to drive change. These sometimes translate into considerable national threats, for example to health from communicable diseases. AIDS could reduce PNG's workforce 40% by 2020. Currently 2% of its adult population has HIV-AIDS, a proportion increasing 30% pa. Lifestyle illnesses also pose a serious threat to the well being of FIC peoples. In Fiji 15% of the population has diabetes, and over 13% of infants and 15% of children are considered obese (ADB-CS, 2005: 27; The Australian, 2005; Prasad, 2006).

There are also threats to livelihoods from unsustainable resource management. During the 1990s 97% of all forests in the Solomons were licensed for harvesting (ADB-CS, 2005: 31). Cross-border crime also poses threats to national security; a problem particularly for PNG, Bougainville, and the Solomons.

Poor governance combined with a lack of internal security carries particular threats to the region's political voice. In some states rapid population, urban growth and high proportions of young people (on average 50% of the region's population is under 25 years) increase the risk of political manipulation, especially when most states have failed to build a national consensus. The consequences can be catastrophic. PNG's per capital income has declined 10% since 1975. In the Solomons civil strife between 1997 and 2000 reduced GDP per capita by 40%, and in Fiji three coups cost the country US$4.3b or $5,456 per capita pa 1987-2000 (ADB-CS, 2005: 13-14).

The region's environments are also threatened by climate change, especially atolls many of which are less than 5 metres above sea level, and from pollution. Low economic growth, globalizing markets, and the loss of preferential market access also threaten the viability of many island communities. In part this is due to the failure of postcolonial strategies, such as import substitution, which has left many governments dependent on tariffs for income at a time when new trade practices demand difficult changes in sources for revenue collection.

All these threats contribute to a decline in social well being. Five countries are classified by the United Nations as Less Developed Countries (LDCs): Kiribati, Samoa, Tuvalu, Vanuatu, and the Solomons). Even in Fiji and PNG, poverty levels exceed 25% of populations. Ironically, resource poor states often do better. UN Human Development Indices rate Palau at 0.77, the Cook Islands 0.78, Samoa 0.72, and Niue 0.74 compared with 0.65 for Tuvalu, 0.59 for Kiribati, 0.59 for Vanuatu, 0.54 for PNG and 0.41 for the Solomon Islands (UNDP, 2006). The difference as we shall see lies in connectivity.

We could also add to this list of threats, a fear of regional imbalance and dominance by one or more of the FICs or FDCs. Such fears are common in all regions. But the issue should not be dominance but how regionalism can transform dominance to the benefit of all parties. This too is a goal of the Pacific Plan.

However, as with other regions –the Economic Community of West African States (ECOWAS), the Caribbean Community (CARICOM), and the South American Mercado Comŭn del Sur (Mercosur)- the key difficulty will be maintaining political support for regionalism from national leaders and citizens alike (Brewster, 2003; Aryeeteey, 2001; Malamud, 2001). Indeed the legitimacy of the Plan depends to a large extent on its appeal to the citizenry. Much of the nature of the Plan is shaped by an awareness of that need.

3. Labour Mobility and the Premises on which the Pacific Plan is Based

The Pacific Plan is an island response to the perceived consequences of globalization, trade liberalization, and civil strife facing Pacific states. It is also a response to the uneven record of 10 years of Regional Reform. In 2004 an Eminent Persons Group (EPG) recommended a Pacific Plan of action to strengthen the existing Forum and to promote greater engagement with Pacific territories and civil society groups (EPG, 2004). The EPG was aware that if trade issues dominated the agenda, regionalism could suffer. Liberalization alone could not reduce disparities between nations or create opportunities for convergence. It could not compensate for the lack of diversification in domestic economies and meet the costs of change.

The Pacific Plan is a response to that recognition and contains three premises. First: to be successful the Plan must address the fundamental challenges facing the region. Hence its 24 initiatives for the greater provision of regional services to overcome capacity constraints, improve governance, and promote the fundamentals for increased economic growth (for example, quarantine and customs services). These initiatives are designed to be implemented quickly and to deliver immediate benefits of a magnitude capable of sustaining the momentum for regionalism ($14 billion over 10 years)(ADB—CS, 2005: 154), something lacking in many other examples of regionalism. The Forum meeting in Port Moresby in October 2005 focused on these initiatives but since these initiatives are largely economic in orientation, their capacity to generate grassroots support is limited. The Plan does include a regional volunteers initiative, a regional sports institute, and a regional congress on youth and leadership, but clearly the Plan's public relations strategy must give these and gender and health initiatives much more attention.

Second, a regionalism of small and relatively similar markets can only stimulate economic growth only so far. In fact it is likely that the costs of integration could outweigh benefits, at least in the short term as we have already witnessed with the implementation of MSG and PICTA. Similar consequences have been experienced by the Organization for East Caribbean States (OECS), CARICOM, and ECOWAS. It is the absence of offsetting benefits that make asymmetrical flows politically unpalatable. Hence the importance of including Australia and New Zealand; after all the FDCs increase the regional market from US$20billion (or $33billion if territories are included) to $700billion and make more possible the opportunity to gain offsetting benefits with popular appeal (ADB-CS, 2005: 159-160).

Third, regionalism must focus on those offsetting benefits that only FDCs provide. Labour mobility presents one opportunity to deliver benefits that reach ordinary people. It already has precedents in the region. PNG youth can work for up to 2 years in the United Kingdom under the Commonwealth Holiday Makers Scheme. The EU has quotas for seamen from Tuvalu and Kiribati for offshore vessels. Taiwan is planning a similar quota scheme for Tuvalu. Fiji nurses currently work in FDCs, EU, US and in FICs. Fiji soldiers have a long record of global peacekeeping service, notably for the UN, and over 1000 Fijians are currently privately employed in Kuwait and Iraq. Remittances to Fiji are worth a conservative US$262 million pa, up 500% since 2000. Tonga earns approximately US$100 million pa in remittances (PacNews, 05a).

In addition migrants form a substantial proportion of FDC labour forces: 20% of New Zealand and Australia's compared with only 12% in the US and 7% in the EU. It is worth noting that both New Zealand and Australia experience low population growth and have ageing populations. They require additional labour in critical areas such as in the health sector, construction, farm work, mines, and armed forces. The 53,000-strong Australian Defence Force loses 1000 personnel pa, and only recruits three quarters of its annual target (Nicholson, 2005). The CEO of Fruitgrowers Victoria estimates that a shortfall of 1000 workers costs the industry $25 million pa in lost fruit (Eastley, 2005).

Unfortunately Australia prefers a 'non discriminatory' policy of permanent migrants (140,000 migrants in 2005-6 with a skilled stream of 97,500). Its 150,000 temporary migrants come from some 18 mostly European and North American countries on 12 month working holiday visas, recently extended to 2 years (Vanstone, 05). Despite its claims, Australia's policies are discriminatory and, unlike Europe, promote a brain gain. Also unlike the EU and US, its ratio of immigrants with tertiary education to native population is higher. These policies do little to assist its nearest neighbours (Dusevic, 2005).

New Zealand's policies are far more liberal. It has a Pacific Access Program, grants open access to Cook Islanders, Niueans, Tokelauns, and has a quota system for permanent migrants from Fiji, Tonga, and Samoa. It also takes in 40,000 working holiday makers (again mostly from Europe and North America) pa (Tait, 2005).

It is also worth noting that neither country restricts the movement of labour between their own countries, yet when it comes to the Pacific Islands both countries fear overstayers and the risk of creating an underclass. But is that fear justified? Or permissible since Helen Clark believes the region needs "to take a quantum leap forward in enhancing cooperation" and sees PACER as the cornerstone for integrating trade in goods and services (*Fiji Times* 2005)? The definition of services under GATS Mode 4, which both countries endorse, includes labour mobility.

Australia's Foreign Minister Alexander Downer has sought to justify his country's reluctance to embrace temporary labour migration on the grounds that the solution to the Pacific's economic problems lies solely in domestically generated growth. He does not believe that labour mobility can play a role, particularly the labour mobility of unskilled labour (PacNews, 2005b). The World Bank says otherwise.

Indeed, a World Bank report (Özden & Schiff, 2006) argues that remittances from migrants should be regarded as an aspect of development. Globally migrants remit $167billion pa, between 2 and 3 times the level of development aid, and the largest source of foreign income for many small countries. The top recipient countries of remittances are China ($21.7billion), India ($21.2billion), and Mexico ($18 billion) (Lamont, 2005).

Growing at 8% pa, remittances boost disposable family income and investment in human capital (education and health), reduce poverty, reduce child labour and raise child education (there are negatives), and have multiplier effects that could make them more important than trade liberalization. Indeed labour migration helps reduce the impact of increasing dependency ratios in developed countries (due to ageing; in US migrants in high skill jobs also boost innovative activity) and generate global welfare gains. If migrants equalled 3% of the OECD workforce, they would generate welfare gains greater than the removal of trade barriers.

Clearly the design of migration policies is important to ensure these results, particularly given the Caribbean experience where 50% of its university graduates lived abroad in 2000, or the Sub-Saharan African experience (excluding S Africa) where 20% of all skilled workers (4% of the workforce) have migrated. The design of temporary migrant strategies is a central argument of Maclellan and Mares' 2005 paper on seasonal work programs. The goal should be to avoid exploitation and maximize mutual benefits. They cite the Canadian Seasonal Workers Program as a model and propose certain requirements:

- Programs must not undercut host country wages and conditions.
- There needs to be an independent disputes mechanism.
- Workers should not be tied to employers.
- Workers must receive training in and work in compliance with occupational, health and safety laws.
- Bilateral agreements should be reached on respective responsibilities and costs, taxes, ethical recruitment practices, the desired targets of programs, and on ways to reduce the costs of remittances. Programs could be trialed with easily monitored small scale projects.
- In addition, workers should receive pre departure training and their families advised on budgeting, the costs of which could be funded by levy on both employers and applicants. A special program could also be established to assist the families of migrants. In addition the development of host community 'sister' linkages with home communities could help cement deeper cross regional relationships.
- Employers should assist migrants by making phone or email services available.
- Trust funds could be established to ensure that the bulk of wages are remitted and tax refunds could be made after workers return.
- Reengagement in programs should be conditional on workers returning home.

Temporary migrant schemes should be seen as means to advance social and economic development, a development opportunity that builds popular confidence in regionalism, provides immediate benefits, delivers directly to families and fosters important inter country relationships that can strengthen Forum regional identification.

At just one per cent of the FDC workforce, temporary migrants could deliver $1 billion to FICs (ADB-CS, 2005: 99). But the role of temporary migration schemes could be far greater if also used to address the brain drain of skilled workers. The Pacific Plan suggests trialling nurses. Half the annual number of nurses trained at the Fiji School of Nursing migrate each year. Temporary migration with the possibility of return after a period of time (like a sabbatical) would reduce loss, ensure upgraded skills are retained, and if done through the University of the South Pacific (USP) would help raise nursing conditions and give USP a new health role in the Pacific.

But the scheme could be extended to include virtually any trade or skill which FICs currently need to upgrade or gain more recruits: construction workers, agricultural and horticultural workers etc. Australian Prime Minister Howard has proposed new technical training institutes in the Pacific. While this might be a useful intervention in some instances, where possible capacity-building will be better achieved if existing facilities are upgraded and the principle of connectivity incorporated for qualifications, trainers and trainees alike. Then we can say we behave as a region and not as a set of disparate countries.

4. Conclusions and Lessons for the Future

If the region is to benefit from such opportunities, it needs to invest more in the health, skills and education of its peoples. This can be assisted by harmonizing and stabilizing development assistance (fallen 40% since 1980) in order to encourage longer term planning (ADB-CS, 2005: 151). It can also be assisted through labour mobility schemes targeted at raising skills in specific areas of need that meet national development goals. However, there is a need to link together confidence-building and governance measures, aid and labour mobility by integrating the Pacific Plan into PACER over the next 5 to 10 years. A formal legally binding agreement would lock in commitments to good governance, economic growth, sustainable development and security in return for development assistance, trade and labour mobility.

Labour mobility is one part of the Pacific Plan that can address national development needs and simultaneously impact directly on the grassroots. Popular support is necessary to sustain regionalism, but popular support also requires accountable and transparent institutions, greater consultation and involvement with civil society, and debate on the future political governance of regionalism. If the Plan raises popular expectations, forces politicians to deliver, and places pressure on FDCs to demonstrate their commitment to regional membership, so much the better.

References

Aryeetey, E. (2001) “Regional Integration in West Africa”. OECD Working Paper 170.

Asian Development Bank (ADB)-Commonwealth Secretariat (CS). (2005) *Toward a New Regionalism*. Manila: ADB.

Brewster, H. (2003) “The Caribbean SME: Is it realistic without commitment to political unity”. St Lucia: OECS.

Casimira, A. (2005) “The Draft Pacific Plan: A Threat to Pacific Peace and Solidarity,” *Fiji Sun*, 2 October: 12.

Dusevic, T. (2005) “Slim Pickings: Should Australia embrace quest workers from the South Pacific islands?” *Time Asia*, 31 October.

Eastley, T. (2005) “National Farmers Federation wants seasonal workers from overseas”, AM News, Radio National, *www.abc.net.au/rn 25 November.*

Eminent Persons Group (2004) *Pacific Cooperation: Voices of the Region.* Suva: PIFS.

Fiji Times (2005) “Clark urges leap in teamwork”. 28 October: 20.

Jayaraman, T.K. (1985a) “Regional Integration in the Pacific”, USP Economics Working Paper 2005/6.

Jayaraman, T.K. (1985b), “The Pacific Plan”. *Fiji Times, 20 August*: 15.

Lamont, N. (2005) "Remittances are an effective weapon against Poverty'. *Financial Times.* 18 November.

Maclellan, N. & Mares, P. (2005) "Labour Mobility in the Pacific: creating seasonal work programs in Australia", paper to State, Society & governance in Melanesia Project's conference on 'Globalisation, Governance and the Pacific islands", ANU, Canberra, 25-27 October.

Malamud, A. (2001) "Presidentialism and Mercosur". http://home.iscte.pt/~ansmd/ Presidentialism%20and%20Mercosur%20(Laursen%20book).pdf

Nicholson, B. (2005) "Military Ranks Dwindling". *Age,* 25 November.

Özden, Ç. & Schiff, M. (eds) (2006) *International Migration, Remittances & the Brain Drain. Washington:* World Bank & Palgrave Macmillan.

Pacific Islands Forum Secretariat (PIFS). (2005) *The Pacific Plan for Strengthening Regional Cooperation and Integration.* Suva: PIFS.

PacNews (2005) "Fiji Remittances", 17 November.

PacNews (2005) "Unskilled labour mobility is not the answer: Minister Downer", 1 December.

Powell, P.T. (1985) "Too Young to Marry: Economic Convergence and the case against the Integration of Pacific Island States", paper to PIAS-DG seminar, 24 August.

Prasad, A. (2006) "Our children are fat, overweight". *Fiji Times,* 8 February: 1.

Tait, M. (2005a) " Australia and New Zealand differ on Seasonal Workers". *Fiji Time,* 25 October: 14.

The Australian (2005) "Human and economic cost of Aids in PNG 'could rival Africa'." 1 December.

United Nations Development Program (UNDP). (2004) *Pacific islands Regional Millennium Development Goals Report.* Noumea: South Pacific Commission.

UNDP (forthcoming) *Pacific Human Development Report 2006: Governance for Human Development.* Suva: PIAS-DG, USP.

Vanstone, A (2005) "Migration (Non Humanitarian) Program". Canberra: Department of Immigration, VPS 052.

In: Development Problems and Prospects in Pacific Islands ISBN: 978-1-60021-793-7
Editors: B. C. Prasad, D. C. Roy, pp. 31-52

Chapter 4

SUPPLY-SIDE CONSTRAINTS TO EXPORT-LED GROWTH IN SELECTED PACIFIC ISLAND COUNTRIES*

Yenteshwar Ram, Biman Prasad and Ron Duncan

1. INTRODUCTION

Economies of the Melanesian group of the Pacific Islands region, namely Fiji, Papua New Guinea (PNG), the Solomon Islands and Vanuatu, are relatively less developed than other island economies sharing similar economic characteristics in other parts of the globe. Over the past two decades, an integral part of their economic policy rhetoric has been export-led economic growth. However, despite the policy and technical support provided by many international organizations and bilateral donors, and an abundance of natural resources, their export sectors remain narrow and, with few exceptions, export industries have experienced little growth.

Therefore, if these countries are to have better economic performance, it is critical to understand the supply-side constraints to an expansion of exports. Hence, the objective of the study was to identify and subsequently analyse the impact of supply-side constraints on export receipts of selected Pacific island countries (PICs), using Linear Programming (LP) models of export receipts.

The study was also designed to provide estimates of the magnitude of increases in export receipts that may be achieved if some of the important constraints are removed. Such findings may help to support the implementation of more effective economic reform programs. The findings will also allow policy makers in PICs to identify and compare the supply constraints faced. This could open up the possibility of formulating solutions for joint implementation by PIC governments, which is of relevance in the context of the ongoing development of the Pacific Plan for increased regional integration of the PICs (PIFS 2005).

---

* This study was conducted as part of implementation of the Asia-Pacific Research and Training Network on Trade (ARTNeT - www.artnetontrade.org) research programme and funded by the United Nations Economic and Social Commission for Asia and the Pacific (UNESCAP).

The rest of the paper is structured as follows. In the next section, we provide an economic overview of the selected PICs, Fiji, Papua New Guinea, Solomon Islands and Vanuatu. In the third section, we review past studies done on this topic. The fourth section discusses the methodology used in this study, while the fifth presents the empirical results and discusses them. The sixth section presents conclusions, including policy recommendations, and discusses possible extensions of the study.

2. An Economic Overview of the Selected Pacific Island Countries

2.1. Fiji Islands

The political crisis of 2000 saw the Fiji economy decline by 2.8 per cent in that year. This contraction was accompanied by substantial job losses and migration of skilled and professional workers; the migration is continuing, although the rate is declining. Since 2000, business confidence and private investment have picked up, but not to a point sufficient to drive sustained growth. Skills shortages affect most sectors of the economy, notably the construction industry, which is trying to keep up with the demand for tourist hotel rooms. The economy recorded reasonable growth around 4.0 per cent in the period 2001-04, driven by a resurgent tourism industry. However, real GDP growth in 2005 was forecast at only 1.7 per cent and at 2.0 per cent in 2006, with the slowdown due principally to the termination of preferential trading arrangements for sugar and garments (affecting principally garment exports to the United States), Fiji's major manufacturing and export industries.[1]

With regard to trade, Fiji has a relatively diversified export base. However, in most years imports have exceeded exports and export growth has been poor. A number of reasons have been given for the subdued growth in exports. The substantial decline in world market prices for primary commodities in recent years, adverse weather conditions, and low productivity in the agricultural sector are some of the factors said to be limiting export growth (Narayan and Narayan 2004). Nonetheless, total exports account for around 40 per cent of GDP. The economy relies heavily on export receipts to finance imports of almost all investment goods used in capital formation. Exports are not only the major source of foreign exchange but also an important source of employment.

Foreign exchange reserves have been low over the past three years (at the end of 2004, reserves totalled \$786.2 million) compared with the levels achieved in 2000 (\$898 million) and 2001 (\$846 million), with the Reserve Bank of Fiji attributing the fall to strong demand for imports as economic activity increased (RBF, Quarterly Review- March 2005).

In pursuit of economic growth and development, Fiji has been implementing economic reforms since the 1980s. Generally, these reforms have taken the following form: deregulation of the economy to bring domestic prices more closely in line with world prices; restraint in the growth of government expenditure (to ensure availability of resources for growth in the private sector); reform of the system of direct and indirect taxation (to minimize

[1] In December, 2006, another military coup, the fourth in 20 years has led to s serious decline in the economy. It is estimated that the economy will decline by about 3.1 per cent in 2007.

market distortions and improve incentives for risk taking and effort); a wage policy that recognizes the paramount importance of maintaining international competitiveness; and the mobilization of all sectors of the community in support of economic expansion (in particular, increased Fijian participation in commerce and industry (Reddy *et al,* 2005). Owing to these economic policies, major reforms have occurred in the political structure, in the trade sector, the labour and goods markets, public enterprises, the civil service, agriculture and land, the financial sector and investment policies (Reddy *et al,* 2005).

The past decade has seen Fiji adopt an export-oriented approach to trade relations. Import restrictions have been largely lifted in favour of export promotion, and as a result Fiji now has a more open economy, with increased volumes of exports and imports. The more open trading approach has led to increased prosperity and opportunities in the economy, creating thousands of jobs in industries such as garments; but it has also led to greater vulnerability to external shocks (Republic of Fiji Islands Ministry of Foreign Affairs and External Trade, n.d.).

2.2. Papua New Guinea

After several years of contraction, the PNG economy grew by 2.8 per cent in 2003, and the PNG government has estimated a growth rate of 2.6 per cent in 2004 and 3 per cent in 2005. Other macroeconomic indicators have also improved, with inflation rates and interest rates at very low levels. The Kina appreciated against the US dollar for most of 2004, but it has been fairly stable in recent months, trading at around 3 Kina to the US dollar. Against the Australian dollar, however, the Kina has weakened from about 2.5 Kina to the Australian dollar in January 2004 to about 2.3 Kina in July 2005 (Bank of Papua New Guinea, *Quarterly Bulletin* – various issues). Despite this more positive outlook, the PNG economy is not growing at rates that yield positive per capita income growth.

Exports of petroleum and agricultural (coffee, copra, cocoa and palm oil), mineral (copper and gold) and timber (logs) exports contribute around 40 per cent of PNG's GDP and account for 90 per cent of its exports. However, the contribution of the mining and petroleum sectors to economic growth is likely to decline appreciably over the next decade as production from existing oil fields and mines declines and new large oil fields and mines are not expected to come on-stream during that time. Even if new projects such as the Highlands gas project, the Ramu nickel and cobalt project, and the Kainantu gold project proceed to development they cannot be expected to deliver sustainable, broad-based economic development because of their enclave nature (Bank of Papua New Guinea *Quarterly Bulletin,* various issues)

Similar to other Melanesian countries, PNG has a dual economy, comprising a formal, corporate-based economy and a large informal economy where subsistence farming accounts for the bulk of economic activity. The formal sector provides a narrow employment base, consisting of workers engaged in mineral production, a relatively small manufacturing sector, public sector employees, and service industries including finance, construction, transportation and utilities. Migration to major urban centres over the past decade has contributed to urban unemployment and social problems. Papua New Guinea's social indicators are well below those of most other lower middle income countries, particularly in rural areas (Bank of Papua New Guinea, *Quarterly Bulletin,* various issues).

PNG has continued to undertake economic reforms over the past five years. Significant achievements have been made in the areas of central bank independence, financial sector prudential supervision, exchange rate flexibility, labour market reforms, tariff reductions, the sale of the PNG Banking Corporation, and recent moves to partially privatise some key utilities. However, fundamental problems remain, including the management of government finances, maintaining law and order, delivering adequate levels of essential services, maintaining national infrastructure, attracting investment and linking traditional methods of agriculture production in rural areas to modern urban and overseas markets. The population continues to grow rapidly, with an increasing number of people living in poverty. These key challenges need to be addressed quickly if PNG hopes to build on the modest gains of the recent years (Bank of Papua New Guinea, *Quarterly Bulletin*, various issues).

2.3. Vanuatu

After negative growth in the early 2000s, the Vanuatu economy experienced real GDP growth in 2004 of 3.2 per cent, building on modest growth of 1.4 per cent in 2003. Buoyant commodity prices, increased tourism, and a focus on economic and budget management have contributed to economic growth. Inflation was stable in 2004 at 0.8 per cent (Reserve Bank of Vanuatu, *Quarterly Bulletin*, various issues).

In 2004, Vanuatu's exports grew by 28.2 per cent to 4.2 billion vatu (A$50.2 million) although they still contribute only about 10 per cent of GDP. Over 80 per cent of Vanuatu's locally-produced exports are agriculture-based, led by coconut oil (31.1 per cent), copra (13.5 per cent), kava (13.4 per cent), beef (8.7 per cent) and timber (7.5 per cent). The transition to cash cropping from subsistence farming is still at an early stage, although it has been growing strongly over the past two years. A resurgence in copra production, an increase in coconut oil prices, a recovery in kava exports following some lifting of European and US bans, and ongoing development in the root crop and beef sectors have all provided a basis for strong growth. In 2004, the value of coconut oil exports increased by 169 per cent (to A$12.3 million), kava by 93 per cent (to A$5.3 million) and copra by 58 per cent (to A$5.37 million). Exports of root crops including taro, cassava and sweet potato are also growing.

Besides agriculture, the tourism sector is a major foreign exchange earner for Vanuatu and has been recognized by the government as a key sector for development, employing an estimated 1,200 people. Continuing growth in Vanuatu's tourism sector will be crucial to providing employment opportunities for Vanuatu's young and rapidly growing population (60 per cent of which is under 25 years). Increasing investment in new boutique-style hotels, refurbishment of larger resorts, stronger interest in locally-owned bungalows, and interest in the backpacker market also point to further growth in this industry (RBV, Quarterly Bulletin, various issues).

Overall, however, private sector investment remains subdued, although real estate development has boomed since mid 2004. Political stability and commitments by government to public sector and economic reforms is needed if investor confidence and growth are to occur. (RBV Quarterly Bulletin, various issues).

In response to the economic and political challenges facing the country, successive Vanuatu Governments have pursued a wide-ranging reform program since 1997, with assistance from the Asian Development Bank (ADB) and international aid donors, including

Australia. This effort has been guided by the Comprehensive Reform Program (CRP) document, which was developed at a national summit in Vanuatu in June 1997. The CRP provides a blueprint for good governance through institutional renewal; improved service-delivery, particularly to rural areas; the development of a redefined role for the public sector and improved public sector efficiency; private sector-led growth; and improved equity between sections of the population.

Some impatience with the CRP sprang from the lack of economic growth prior to 2003, and in particular, little progress in improvements to service delivery. In a move to prioritise activities under the CRP, the Vanuatu Government developed the Prioritised Action Agenda (PAA) in 2003. The PAA is a development framework whose goal is to formulate medium-term development priorities that will guide policy stability and promote reforms. The five-year Australian-Vanuatu Joint Development Strategy, signed on 31 March 2005, is based on the PAA. Another important Vanuatu Government initiative has been the Rural Economic Development Initiative (REDI), which aims to improve service delivery in rural areas and ensure that economic development is a reality for the majority of the population residing in rural areas. REDI plans are developed and administered at the provincial level and supported at the national level. This usefully hands responsibility for development back to the grass roots. REDI plans have shown results in terms of agricultural production and an increase in the number of small-scale tourist operations starting up throughout the islands. The REDI is being supported by a range of donors, including Australia.

Vanuatus economic reform in recent years has led to a major improvement in the management of its public sector finances, with expenditure now more carefully controlled through an accountable and transparent process. Vanuatu adopted a new fiscal format in line with the CRP, part of which was the introduction of a Value Added Tax on 1 August 1998, as well as reform of the tariff structure. A new program budgeting format was also introduced in 1998 and Vanuatu now has an integrated recurrent development budget, incorporating all expenditures funded from domestic and external sources.

The limited revenue base continues to constrain government efforts to deliver services and implement reforms, although the current government is making efforts to increase revenue through tax reform and improvements in tax collection. In recent years, revenue collection has fallen short of projections, making budget management difficult for individual departments and the Government as a whole. A change in revenue forecasting in early 2003 meant that revenue projections for the year were realistic and collections slightly exceeded expectations. Collections improved further in 2004 and predictions are that, with the current Government's reforms, 2005 will see a significant jump in revenue.

2.4. Solomon Islands

The Solomon Islands economy is estimated to have contracted by 14.3 per cent in 2000, by 9 per cent in 2001, and by a further 2.4 per cent in 2002, primarily as a result of the closure of most major industries after June 2000, following severe ethnic conflict since 1999. The long road to economic recovery has, however, begun. Confidence is beginning to return to the local economy due to the improvement in the security environment with the arrival of the Australian Government-led Regional Assistance Mission to the Solomon Islands (RAMSI) and the timely payment by government for goods and services. Local business confidence is also increasing. The Central Bank of Solomon Islands estimates that the economy grew by 5.6 per cent in 2003 and by 5.5 per cent in 2004, the fastest rates of growth since the logging boom of the early 1990s. The Central Bank projects growth of 4 per cent in (CBSI,*Quarterly Bulletin*, various issues).

The violence associated with the ethnic conflict caused extensive damage to property, transport and communication infrastructure, schools, water supply and sanitation systems, electricity supply, government buildings, and the health sector, all of which were already significantly debilitated due to years of institutional neglect, and forced the closure of both large and small businesses. Full recovery will take a considerable length of time. The reopening of the palm oil plantation, now called Guadalcanal Palm Oil Limited and under Malaysian ownership, is an encouraging development as thousands of jobs could be created. The Gold Ridge mine was likely to reopen in 2006 following its purchase by an Australian consortium. Both projects reflect the greatly improved business environment as a result of the return of law and order. The challenge for the Solomon Islands Government will be to ensure long-term and broad-based economic growth by improving the operating environment for business and through investing in infrastructure.

Export earnings fell sharply from 1999 to 2002 as a result of the steep declines in activity in the country's few major export sectors of fisheries, gold and plantation agriculture. This decline in activity was compounded by falling commodities prices. Merchandise exports grew by almost 60 per cent in 2002, and in 2003 some key commodity prices firmed with growth in exports being driven by the agriculture (particularly copra and cocoa), forestry and fisheries sectors. However, current export levels remain below 1999 levels and are overly reliant on unsustainable levels of logging, which were said to be three times above sustainable levels in 2003.

With inadequate controls to reduce the leakage of public funds, the Solomon Islands Government budget for 2002 was significantly overspent and this continued into 2003. But with RAMSI assistance, the Solomon Islands Government has made significant gains in introducing budget discipline, controlling expenditure, enhancing revenue collection and meeting financial obligations. The Solomon Islands Government also produced realistic and credible 2004 and 2005 budgets (CBSI, *Quarterly Bulletin,* various issues).

Government domestic revenue in 2005 is estimated at SBD$550 million, which is a 50 per cent increase on 2003 actual revenue due to increased tax compliance and a growing economy. Budgets are now fully financed without recourse to additional borrowing and at least 15 per cent of revenue is allocated to debt service. RAMSI is now working with the Solomon Islands Government to ensure that future budgets are sustainable, reflect government policies and priorities, and are implemented through effective systems. Other priorities are to strengthen economic policy and planning processes, further strengthen revenue collection, implement a comprehensive debt management strategy, and improve the enabling environment for private sector development.

3. Literature Review

Several studies on supply-side constraints to economic growth have been published over the past decade. While most of these studies pertain to the supply-side constraints faced by developing countries in achieving their growth potential, a few have focused on the supply-side problems faced by developed countries. In the following paragraphs, we provide summaries of some of these studies.

I. In 2002, an African Caribbean Pacific (ACP) Ambassador highlighted that in order to be able to take advantage of trade preferences, ACP countries need to be able to produce competitively and get products to the market at a reasonable cost. As the experience under the Lomé Convention has demonstrated, ACP countries face major problems in producing and supplying goods competitively within an increasingly liberalised trading environment.

Some of these problems and challenges are as follows. With many ACP countries being geographically remote, by virtue of their land-locked or island status, getting products to market is not always easy and can be influenced by factors beyond the control of ACP governments. Climatic factors also play a major role. An example is the devastating setback to Mozambique's development arising from the floods in 2000. To a certain extent, these factors should make one stop and think about the uni-linear vision of development, which underpins so much of Europe's development policy. The sad reality is that things do not always go forward. Setbacks can occur regardless of the best policies pursued by governments. This needs to be taken into account in developing EU policies towards the ACP.

Moreover, there is a need for a realistic assessment of what governments can influence. Within the global economy, there are now only two major assets that government policy can have a bearing on: the stock of physical infrastructure and capital and the stock of human capital. In both of these areas, ACP countries face major constraints on their ability to produce competitively in the context of moves towards free trade with the EU. Indeed, these constraints are , in large measure, the reason for their 'developing country status'. These constraints are: the unreliable provision of public utilities (electricity and water supply); poor public infrastructure (run-down roads and railways); weak institutional and policy frameworks (leading to fluctuating exchange rates and high inflation and interest rates); and low labour productivity (arising from poor education, health and housing provisions).

In many respects, the situation with regard to human capital, particularly in Southern Africa, has become worse in recent years as a result of the impact of the HIV and AIDS pandemic. People are living shorter lives and often dying as they reach their most productive years. This development has profound implications for labour productivity, the competitiveness of the South African economy and its ability to adjust and manage changes. This sad reality needs to be taken on board in the process of trade policy formulation and in the negotiation of future trade arrangements.

II. A 2004 report on supply-side constraints and capacity building by the United Nations Economic and Social Commission for Asia and the Pacfic (UNESCAP) also outlined the major supply-side constraints encountered by developing countries and provided a number of priority areas for ESCAP's future work to assist member countries in removing such constraints through supply-side capacity-building. According to the report, the main supply-side constraints were poor policymaking, ineffective regulatory frameworks, inefficient institutions and poor governance, inadequate energy, poor transport and information and communication technology (ICT) infrastructure, as well as a poor level of general education. The report moved on to describe the two pillars that could address the supply-side constraints faced by the member countries of UNESCAP. These were enhancing productive capacity and reducing the cost of conducting trade.

III. In a study of the economic trends in the Pacific Islands Countries (PICs), Chand (2003) argued that the policy environment in the PICs has generally not been conducive to growth in production. Extensive regulatory controls on prices, exchange rates, the operation of the informal sector, etc., have impeded private investment. Government involvement in private commerce has crowded out private commerce, while drawing resources away from the provision of public services vital for the growth of the private sector. Poor property rights to land, insecurity of debt contracts, unsustainable budget deficits, and political and policy instability have all raised the risk premium on investment, resulting in an increase in the cost of investment in PICs. In addition, poor governance remains a serious problem in several of the PICs.

IV. In a report by the United Nations Conference on Trade and Development (UNCTAD) in 1998, it was stressed that supply-side constraints were the root cause of Less Developed Countries' (LDCs) weak participation in international trade. The UNCTAD Board recommended that the international community should help LDCs to enhance their competitiveness through commodity diversification, improvement of their trade infrastructure, and trade-supporting services and human resource development. Moreover, it was mentioned that LDCs themselves have a responsibility, in the context of formulating and implementing sound macroeconomic policies, to overcome the problems of supply-side constraints.

V. In a study by the Pan-African Productivity Association (2000) on the supply-side constraints that hamper African enterprises from taking advantage of emerging export market opportunities, it was pointed out that Africa has experienced periods of economic development during the past century, but this has clearly not been sufficient to put it on a par with the developed world. The standard of living of Africans increased initially, but for the past 40 years there has been a steady decline. Many factors have contributed to this situation, but low productivity spawned by wrong economic policies and systems lies at the root of the decline. A number of countries have recently started moving away from these systems but it will take many years for them to catch up.

Many factors were said to impair the productivity performance of firms. Economic policy is only one of these. Others are linked to financial factors, lack of foreign direct investment, shortage of high quality human resources that should be delivered by good education and training structures, infrastructure inadequacies, and the basic values of workers. Entrepreneurial and management skills are also scarce. Where these skills are available, the success of the organizations is both dramatic and lasting.

The Pan-African Productivity Association (2000) study recommended that much should and can be done to ensure a more competitive and contributing Africa. At the core is the development of national productivity movements. The notion of productivity improvement should be inculcated in the minds of workers and managers. A change in values should be led by heads of State, who must understand that political and social success depends on economic success, which in turn depends on international competitiveness through productivity. The establishment of productivity centres in itself will not bring about the change required; it will merely create a focal point for guiding the change. Eventually, managers and workers, teachers and labourers will have to be wealth creators rather than wealth seekers.

The report argues that Africa is plagued with unemployment and it is natural that those who have work will do anything to remain employed. For this reason, the underlying philosophy in Africa's productivity improvement endeavours should be to create more wealth with the same or more resources, and not to produce the same with less resources. A throughput growth philosophy is called for with guarantees of no job losses due to higher productivity. Such a philosophy must be supported by wealth-sharing policies.

VI. Finally, D' Acunto et al (2004) endeavoured to model and test the role of demand and supply-side factors in explaining economic growth in 20 Italian administrative regions. This exercise was performed by means of a two-stage econometric approach. In the first stage, estimates for the elasticity of manufacturing output to exports were obtained using regional time-series data from 1963 through to 1996, using the cointegration test advocated by Pearson et al (2001). A significant, long-run relationship between these variables indicated the existence of a demand-constrained growth regime.

The authors then carried out tests to see whether the regional dispersion of supply-side factors had an impact on the regional dispersion of demand-constrained regimes. In other words, a list of supply-side variables was utilised to explain the cross-section dispersion of the causal relationship between exports and manufacturing output. In this case, estimation was carried out by means of a cross-section dummy variable procedure, in which the dependent variable took a value equal to one for regions characterized by demand-constrained growth regimes, and zero otherwise.

The empirical results supported the authors' expectations of strong regional differences. Generally, it was discovered that the more southerly the region, the less likely it exhibited export-led growth or a demand-constrained growth regime and the more likely it was to show signs of a supply-constrained growth regime. Thus, it was confirmed that the regional distribution of demand-constrained regimes was a useful tool for analyzing Italy's regional economic development in the post-World War II period. As for the explanation of these regional differences in growth regimes, the second stage analysis revealed that dominant roles were played by social capital, the state of technology, the average size of establishments in manufacturing, and competition and efficiency in the banking sector. Also influential was the size of regional manufacturing. However, no role was found for labour market rigidities.

The results were useful in defining the conditions under which export-led growth could operate. From a policy standpoint, the results suggested that labour market reforms geared to bringing regional wage differentials more closely in line with regional productivity differentials should not engender drastic changes in the development process of the Southern Italian regions. More importantly, the results highlighted that greater priority should be given to policies designed to encourage innovation and the diffusion of new technologies, development of social capital, and the fostering of efficiency in the financial sector.

4. METHODOLOGY

To address the research question, this study employs the Linear Programming (LP) approach. A LP problem is a special case of a *Mathematical Programming* problem. Under the LP approach, a mathematical programme identifies an extreme; that is, a minimum or a maximum point of a function $f(x_1, x_2, ...x_n)$, which satisfies a set of constraints, e.g., $g(x_1, x_2, ...x_n) \geq b$. The LP approach entails a specialisation of mathematical programming to the case where both function f (called the objective function) and the problem constraints are linear.

From an applications perspective, the LP technique is best described as an optimisation tool, which can allow for the rationalisation of many economic, social and technological objectives pursued by policymakers. A distinct advantage for the applicability of the LP methodology in various contexts is the computational ease of the resulting analytical models. With the advent of modern computing technology, the LP methodology translates to the existence of effective and efficient algorithm procedures that are able to provide systematic and fast solutions to the analytical models. For instance, the Simplex algorithm procedure (developed by Dantzig 1947) provides a powerful computational tool that is able to provide fast solutions to very large-scale applications, sometimes including hundreds of thousands of variables. We used this algorithmic procedure via the LINGO software.

For this study, the general form of the LP problem is as follows. The objective function is an exports receipts function of the form:

$$\max f(X_1, X_2, \ldots X_n) = c_1 X_1 + c_2 X_2 + \ldots + c_n X_n$$

Where: $c_1, c_2, \ldots, c_n$ is the average export price[2] for each of the export commodities of the selected PICs (known as objective function coefficients) and $X_1, X_2, \ldots, X_n$ are the export volumes for each of the export commodities (known as control or decision variables, the values of which are to be derived).

The objective function is subject to a set of supply-side constraints on the export volumes of each of the export products in the objective function. These supply-side constraints take the following general form:

$$a_{i1}X_1 + a_{i2}X_2 + \ldots + a_{in} X_n \, (\geq, =, \leq) \, b_i, \text{ for } i = 1,\ldots,n$$

where: $a_{i1}, a_{i2}, \ldots, a_{in}$ are the technological coefficients of the problem formulation; and b_i is the right-hand side vector of constraints.

In the models solved, we relax some of the supply-side constraints and assess the impact on export receipts. This part of the analysis should provide insights for policymakers in the PICs, as it should inform them of the magnitude of increases in export receipts that can be achieved if some of the supply-side constraints are eliminated.

5. Empirical Results

5.1. Fiji's Islands[3]

Using the LP approach, the objective function specified for Fiji[4] was as follows:

---

[2] In this case, average export prices were used since they are more representative of the entire sample data and hence provide a relatively reliable approximation of export prices that countries have faced over the sample period and are likely to face in the coming years. Use of single year values (e.g. current prices) may not provide policymakers with an accurate picture of the prices that they can expect for their commodities in the future, as current prices will obviously fluctuate over the coming years depending on the social, political and economic factors prevailing in a particularly country at a particular point in time.

[3] Data on Fiji's export values, volumes and prices were provided by the Fiji Islands Bureau of Statistics.

$$ER = 758.4X_1 + 101.7X_2 + 3455.5X_3 + 1024.8X_4 + 589.3X_5$$

Where: ER is the total export receipts from the commodities under study
X_1 is the export volume for sugar (in metric tonnes)
X_2 is the export volume for molasses (in metric tonnes)
X_3 is the export volume for canned fish (in metric tonnes)
X_4 is the export volume for coconut oil (in metric tonnes)
X_5 is the export volume for gold (in metric tonnes)
758.4 is the 11-year (1994-2004) average export price for sugar (in $F)
101.7 is the 11-year (1994-2004) average export price for molasses (in $F)
3455.5 is the 11-year (1994-2004) average export price for canned fish (in $F)
1024.8 is the 11-year (1994-2004) average export price for coconut oil (in $F)
589.3 is the 11-year (1994-2004) average export price for gold (in $F)

The above-mentioned objective function was then subject to the following constraints:

$$230000 \leq X_1 \leq 472000$$
$$96000 \leq X_2 \leq 189000$$
$$600 \leq X_3 \leq 9800$$
$$3200 \leq X_4 \leq 7900$$
$$112600 \leq X_5 \leq 150700$$
$$X_1 + X_2 + X_3 + X_4 + X_5 \leq 808{,}000$$

The first constraint equation restrains sugar export volumes to be within 230000 and 472000 tonnes, whilst the second constraint equation limits molasses export volumes to be within 96000 and 189000 tonnes. The third constraint equation restricts canned fish export volumes to be within 600 and 9800 tonnes, whereas the fourth constraint equation limits coconut oil export volumes to be within 3200 and 7900 tonnes. The fifth equation restraints gold export volumes to be within 112600 and 150700 tonnes. These constraints were put in place as the data on export volumes of the various commodities over the past decade showed that export volumes have been within these ranges. The last constraint equation limits the total export volumes for the five commodities to be less than or equal to 808,000 tonnes. This constraint was put in place because export data over the past decade showed that the total export volume for these five commodities has been less than or equal to 808,000 tonnes. These constraint equations can be regarded as proxies for the various supply-side constraints affecting the export volumes of the five commodities.

The main supply-side factors thought to have caused sugar and molasses export volumes to be within the above-mentioned ranges include the non-renewal of expiring land leases, transportation difficulties, mill inefficiencies, and the high levels of cane burning, which reduces sugar content and quality (Republic of Fiji Islands Supplement to the 2003 Budget Address).

[4] Note that we were not able to include all the export commodities in the objective function as data on export volumes for some commodities (e.g. garments, textiles, footwear, fruits and vegetables, and mineral water) were not available.

The key supply-side constraints believed to have limited canned fish export volumes to be within the above-mentioned range include the lack of air cargo and wharf space, as well as the increasing incidence of illegal fishing by foreign vessels in Fiji waters (RBF *Quarterly Review*, various issues). Common factors believed to have caused coconut oil exports to be within the above-mentioned range include natural disasters and pests, which have imposed severe damage on copra output from which coconut oil is produced (RBF, *Quarterly Review*, various issues).

Gold export volumes have been within the above-mentioned range due mainly to supply-side factors that include the poor quality of gold ore extracted from the mine, as well as the limited extraction capacity of the mine (RBF, *Quarterly Review*, various issues).

Subject to these constraints, the above-mentioned objective function was then solved to obtain values for X_1, X_2, X_3, X_4 and X_5 that would maximize export receipts. It was found that the values of X_1, X_2, X_3, X_4 and X_5 that would maximise export receipts were 472000, 167600, 9800, 7900 and 150700 tonnes, respectively. With these X values, the maximum export receipts that could be obtained would be F$505.8 million.

Hypothetical relaxation of the constraint equations was carried out to see the magnitude of the increase in export receipts that could be achieved. The assumed changes were as follows:

- the upper limits of the first five equations were increased by 5 per cent; and
- the right-hand side value of the sixth equation was also increased by 5 per cent (to incorporate the increases that were made in the preceding five equations).

When the objective function was solved again subject to the relaxed set of constraints, it was found that the maximum export receipts that could be achieved was F$520.7 million, an increase of F$14.9 million or around 3 per cent, when compared with the previous case.

5.2. Papua New Guinea

The objective function specified for PNG was:

$$ER = 2363X_1 + 3574X_2 + 1863X_3 + 450X_4 + 876X_5 + 673X_6 + 1355X_7 + 133X_8 + 6301X_9 + 58X_{10} + 3144X_{11} + 19351X_{12}$$

Where: ER is the total export receipts from the twelve commodities under study

X_1 is the export volume for Cocoa (in metric tones)

X_2 is the export volume for Coffee (in metric tonnes)

X_3 is the export volume for tea (in metric tonnes)

X_4 is the export volume for copra (in metric tonnes)

X_5 is the export volume for copra Oil (in metric tonnes)

X_6 is the export volume for palm Oil (in metric tonnes)

X_7 is the export volume for rubber (in metric tonnes)

X_8 is the export volume for logs (in metric tonnes)

X_9 is the export volume for marine Products (in metric tonnes)

X_{10} is the export volume for crude Oil (in metric tonnes)
X_{11} is the export volume for copper (in metric tonnes)
X_{12} is the export volume for gold (in metric tonnes)

2363 is the 21-year (1984-2004) average export price for cocoa (in Kina)
3574 is the 21-year (1984-2004) average export price for coffee (in Kina)
1863 is the 21-year (1984-2004) average export price for tea (in Kina)
450 is the 21-year (1984-2004) average export price for copra (in Kina)
876 is the 21-year (1984-2004) average export price for copra Oil (in Kina)
673 is the 21-year (1984-2004) average export price for palm Oil (in Kina)
1355 is the 21-year (1984-2004) average export price for rubber (in Kina)
133 is the 21-year (1984-2004) average export price for logs (in Kina)
6301 is the 21-year (1984-2004) average export price for marine Products (in Kina)
58 is the 21-year (1984-2004) average export price for crude Oil (in Kina)
3144 is the 21-year (1984-2004) average export price for copper (in Kina)
19351 is the 21-year (1984-2004) average export price for gold (in Kina)

The above-mentioned objective function was solved subject to the following constraints:

$26000 \leq X_1 \leq 46600$
$40300 \leq X_2 \leq 85000$
$3400 \leq X_3 \leq 9300$
$8400 \leq X_4 \leq 103500$
$15800 \leq X_5 \leq 53200$
$97300 \leq X_6 \leq 339000$
$2300 \leq X_7 \leq 5400$
$990000 \leq X_8 \leq 2943900$
$1000 \leq X_9 \leq 17800$
$1984720 \leq X_{10} \leq 6254161$
$77800 \leq X_{11} \leq 230600$
$19400 \leq X_{12} \leq 72800$
$X_1 + X_2 + X_3 + X_4 + X_5 + X_6 + X_7 + X_8 + X_9 + X_{10} + X_{11} + X_{12} \leq 10161261$

The first constraint equation restricts cocoa export volumes to be within 26000 and 46600 tonnes, whilst the second equation limits coffee export volumes to be within 40300 and 85000 tonnes. The third constraint equation limits tea export volumes to be within 3400 and 9300 tonnes, while the fourth equation restricts copra export volumes to be within 8400 and 103500 tonnes. The fifth equation constrains export volumes of copra oil to be within 15800 and 53200 tonnes, whereas the sixth equation limits palm oil export volumes to be within 97300 and 339000 tonnes. The seventh equation limits export volumes of rubber to be within 2300 and 5400 tonnes, while the eighth equation restricts log export volumes to be within 990000 and 2943900 tonnes. The nineth equation restricts exports volumes of marine products to be within 1000 and 17800 tonnes, while the tenth equation limits crude oil export volumes to be within 1984720 and 6254161 tonnes. The eleventh equation constrains export volumes of copper to be within 77800 and 230600 tonnes, while the twelveth equation limits gold export volumes to be between 19400 and 72800 tonnes. These constraints are in line with the export volume data for each of these commodities over the past two decades. The constraint equations can be regarded as proxies for the various supply-side constraints affecting the export volumes of the twelve commodities.

The last constraint equation limits the total export volumes for the twelve commodities to be less than or equal to 10,161,261 tonnes. This constraint was imposed because export data over the past two decades showed that the total export volume for these eight commodities has been less than or equal to this tonnage.

In PNG's case, the key supply-side factors that have caused export volumes of the various agricultural commodities to be within the above-mentioned ranges include deteriorating infrastructure, particularly roads, due to the inefficient allocation of development expenditure, especially for feeder roads, which are under the authority of Provincial administrations. Additionally, farmers typically do not have much access to credit since they cannot use their land as collateral due to the traditional land tenure system. This practice has undermined the use of more efficient large-scale farming practices. The relatively high cost of plantation labour also presents a supply-side problem (IMF Staff Report on the 2004 Article IV Consultation on PNG).

With regard to the export volume of logs, the main supply-side factors that have caused export volumes to be within the above-mentioned range include the unsustainable and environmentally destructive logging practices stemming from poor governance and uncertain property rights to land (IMF 2004a).

As far as marine products are concerned, the main supply-side factor that has caused export volumes to be within the ranges given above is the high cost of transporting these products to export markets, especially in Asia (IMF, 2004a).

With regard to the production of gold, copper and crude oil, the main problem faced is the geographical isolation of these resources, which gives rise to high extraction cost in addition to the usual capital-intensive nature of mining activity. Foreign companies have financed all of the major mining projects, and there are few downstream linkages, since most mines operate as isolated enclaves. With the violence and collapse of the large copper mine in Bougainville in the early 1990s and the frequent changes in the government's equity and tax policies towards mining, new exploration activity has been significantly reduced. Deteriorating law and order and governance problems, crumbling infrastructure, overdue land reform, and low profitability have hampered the prospects for any large-scale investment activity. Consequently, few projects are expected to be initiated in the years ahead, and fiscal revenues are expected to decline (IMF, 2004a).

Subject to these constraints, the above-mentioned objective function was solved to obtain values for X_1, X_2, X_3, X_4, X_5, X_6, X_7, X_8, X_9, X_{10}, X_{11} and X_{12} that would maximize export receipts. It was found that the values of X_1 to X_{12} that would maximise export receipts were 46600, 85000, 9300, 103500, 53200, 339000, 5400, 2943900, 17800, 6254161, 230600 and 72800 tonnes, respectively. With these X values, the maximum export receipts that could be obtained would be about 3.8 billion kina.

Hypothetical relaxation of the constraint equations was carried out to see the magnitude of the increases in export receipts that could be achieved as a result. The assumptions made were as follows:

- the upper limits of the first 11 equations were increased by 5 per cent; and
- the right-hand side value of the twelfth equation was also increased by 5 per cent (to incorporate the increases that were made in the preceding 11 equations).

When the objective function was again solved, subject to the relaxed set of constraints, it was found that the maximum export receipts that could be achieved was 4.0 billion kina, an increase of 0.2 billion kina or about 5 per cent, when compared with the previous case.

5.3. Vanuatu's[5]

The objective function specified for Vanuatu was:

$$ER = 44517X_1 + 154755X_2 + 301202X_3 + 63166X_4 + 944191X_5 + 45368X_6$$

Where:ER is the total export receipts from the six commodities studied
X_1 is the export volume for copra (in metric tones)
X_2 is the export volume for cocoa (in metric tonnes)
X_3 is the export volume for beef (in metric tonnes)
X_4 is the export volume for timber (in metric tonnes)
X_5 is the export volume for kava (in metric tonnes)
X_6 is the export volume for coconut oil (in metric tonnes)

44517 is the 9-year (1996-2004) average export price for copra (in vatu)
154755 is the 9-year (1996-2004) average export price for cocoa (in vatu)
301202 is the 9-year (1996-2004) average export price for beef (in vatu)
63166 is the 9-year (1996-2004) average export price for timber (in vatu)
944191 is the 9-year (1996-2004) average export price for kava (in vatu)
45368 is the 9-year (1996-2004) average export price for coconut oil (in vatu)

The above-mentioned objective function was solved subject to the following constraints:

$$2500 \leq X_1 \leq 47200$$
$$200 \leq X_2 \leq 1600$$
$$400 \leq X_3 \leq 1900$$
$$3700 \leq X_4 \leq 13500$$
$$100 \leq X_5 \leq 1200$$
$$5300 \leq X_6 \leq 17100$$
$$X_1 + X_2 + X_3 + X_4 + X_5 + X_6 \leq 64000$$

The first constraint equation restrains copra export volumes to be within 2500 and 47200 tonnes, whilst the second equation limits cocoa export volumes to be within 200 and 1600 tonnes. The third constraint equation limits beef export volumes to be within 400 and 1900

[5] Data on Vanuatu's export values, volumes and prices were provided by the Reserve Bank of Vanuatu.

tonnes, while the fourth equation restrains timber export volumes to be within 3700 and 13500 tonnes. The fifth equation constrains kava export volumes to be within 100 and 1200 tonnes whereas the sixth equation limits coconut oil export volumes to be within 5300 and 17100 tonnes. These constraints are consistent with export volume data for each of these commodities over the past decade. The constraint equations can be regarded as proxies for the various supply-side constraints affecting the export volumes of the six commodities.

The last constraint equation limits the total export volumes for the six commodities to be less than or equal to 64000 tonnes. This constraint was put in place because export data over the past decade showed that the total export volume for these six commodities has been less than or equal to 64000.

In Vanuatu's case, the key supply-side factors that have caused export volumes of the various commodities to be within the above-mentioned ranges include the lack of proper infrastructure (particularly good storage facilities, which lowers the quality of output for export purposes), the high cost of credit faced by exporters of all the commodities (which limits their plans to expand production capacity), the high costs involved in transporting their products to export markets, lack of mills and factories that can convert primary products into processed outputs (this is one of the main constraints faced by the timber industry), and a labour force with very limited education and training (making them unproductive). Vanuatu also suffers from a lack of trade facilitation schemes, which could assist the country in boosting their export levels (RBV, *Quarterly Review*, various issues).

Subject to these constraints, the objective function was solved to obtain values for X_1, X_2, X_3, X_4, X_5 and X_6 that would maximize export receipts. These values were 28700, 1600, 1900, 13500, 1200 and 17100 tonnes, respectively. With these X values, the maximum export receipts that could be obtained would be 4.9 billion vatu.

Hypothetical relaxation of the constraint equations was imposed to see the magnitude of the increase in export receipts that could be achieved as a result. The following assumptions were made:

- the upper limits of the first six equations were increased by 5 per cent; and
- the right-hand side value of the seventh equation was also increased by 5 per cent (to incorporate the increases that were imposed in the preceding six equations).

When the objective function was solved subject to the relaxed set of constraints, it was found that the maximum export receipts that could now be achieved would be 5.2 billion vatus, an increase of 0.3 billion vatus or about 6 per cent.

5.4. The Solomon Islands Case[6]

The objective function specified for the Solomon Islands was:

$$ER = 3413X_1 + 325881X_2 + 2616X_3 + 2101X_4 + 1052X_5 + 5395X_6 + 15847X_7 + 41773X_8$$

[6] Data on Solomon Islands export values, volumes and prices were provided by the Central Bank of Solomon Islands.

Where: ER is the total export receipts from the 8 commodities under study

X_1 is the export volume for fish (in metric tones)

X_2 is the export volume for timber (in metric tonnes)

X_3 is the export volume for copra (in metric tonnes)

X_4 is the export volume for coconut oil (in metric tonnes)

X_5 is the export volume for palm products (in metric tonnes)

X_6 is the export volume for cocoa (in metric tonnes)

X_7 is the export volume for marine shells (in metric tonnes)

X_8 is the export volume for gold (in metric tonnes)

3413 is the 20-year (1985-2004) average export price for fish (in SBD$)

325881 is the 20-year (1985-2004) average export price for timber (in SBD$)

2616 is the 20-year (1985-2004) average export price for copra (in SBD$)

2101 is the 20-year (1985-2004) average export price for coconut oil (in SBD$)

1052 is the 20-year (1985-2004) average export price for palm products (in SBD$)

5395 is the 20-year (1985-2004) average export price for cocoa (in SBD$)

15847 is the 20-year (1985-2004) average export price for marine shells (in SBD$)

41773 is the 20-year (1985-2004) average export price for gold (in SBD$)

The above-mentioned objective function was solved subject to the following constraints:

$5300 \leq X_1 \leq 50000$

$300 \leq X_2 \leq 1000$

$600 \leq X_3 \leq 30000$

$50 \leq X_4 \leq 7300$

$0 \leq X_5 \leq 37000$

$2400 \leq X_6 \leq 4500$

$26 \leq X_7 \leq 400$

$0.02 \leq X_8 \leq 1.4$

$X_1 + X_2 + X_3 + X_4 + X_5 + X_6 + X_7 + X_8 \leq 94400$

The first constraint equation restricts fish export volumes to be within 5300 and 50000 tonnes, whilst the second equation limits timber export volumes to be within 300 and 1000 tonnes. The third constraint equation limits copra export volumes to be within 600 and 30000 tonnes, while the fourth equation restricts coconut oil export volumes to be within 50 and 7300 tonnes. The fifth equation constrains export volumes of palm products to be within 0 and 37000 tonnes, whereas the sixth equation limits cocoa export volumes to be within 2400 and 4500 tonnes. The seventh equation limits export volumes of marine shell to be within 26 and 400 tonnes, while the eighth equation restricts gold export volumes to be within 0.02 and 1.4 tonnes. These constraints are in line with the export volume data for each of these commodities over the past two decades. The constraint equations can be regarded as proxies for the various supply-side constraints affecting the export volumes of the eight commodities.

The last constraint equation limits the total export volumes for the eight commodities to be less than or equal to 94400 tonnes. This constraint was imposed because export data over the past two decades showed that the total export volume for these eight commodities has been less than or equal to 94400 tonnes.

In the Solomon Islands case, the key supply-side factors that have caused export volumes of the various agricultural commodities to be within the above-mentioned ranges include high transportation costs, lack of financial services and technical assistance (to help improve the quality of their products and become more productive), and the difficulty in acquiring land, most of which is communally owned and lacks titles (IMF,2004b).

With regards to timber, the main supply-side factors that have caused export volumes to be within the above-mentioned range include the poor governance of this sector, as well as unsustainable forestry practices. Another constraint faced by this industry is the uncertainty in the ownership of the land, which foreign operators exploit by compensating individuals rather than the collective body of owners (IMF, 2004b).

As far as fish and marine shells are concerned, the main supply-side factor that has caused export volumes to be within the ranges give above is the high cost of transporting these products to export markets, especially in Asia (IMF Staff Report on the 2004 Article IV Consultation on the Solomon Islands).

With regards to the production of gold, the main constraint facing mining operations is the uncertain legal status of land. Mining companies cannot buy land, and the profit-share arrangements with landowners are often challenged by other claimants to the land. Moreover, the ethnic conflict experienced by the country from 1999 through to 2003 lowered the production capacity of the mines. The nation's main gold mine, Gold Ridge mine, was closed at the height of conflict in 2000, and its infrastructure and assets were severely damaged (IMF, 2004b).

As far as manufactured products (coconut oil, palm oil and canned fish) are concerned, the main constraint faced includes the uncertain security situation in the country, which has meant very little foreign direct investment and little domestic investment in this sector. Lack of technical and entrepreneurial skills in those who are involved in this sector has also constrained supply to a large extent (IMF Staff Report on the 2004 Article IV Consultation on the Solomon Islands).

Subject to these constraints, the above-mentioned objective function was solved to obtain values for $X_1, X_2, X_3, X_4, X_5, X_6, X_7$ and X_8 that would maximize export receipts. It was found that the values of X_1, X_2, X_3, X_4, X_5 X_6 X_7 and X_8 that would maximize export receipts were 50000, 1000, 30000, 7300, 1198.60, 4500, 400 and 1.4 tonnes, respectively. With these X values, the maximum export receipts that could be obtained would be $SBD622.3 million.

Hypothetical relaxation of the constraint equations was carried out to see the magnitude of the increases in export receipts that could be achieved as a result of these relaxations. The assumptions made were as follows:

- the upper limits of the first 8 equations were increased by 5 per cent; and
- the right-hand side value of the ninth equation was also increased by 5 per cent (to incorporate the increases that were made in the preceding eight equations).

When the objective function was solved subject to the relaxed set of constraints, it was found that the maximum export receipts that could now be achieved was SBD$664.3 million, an increase of SBD$42 million or about 7 per cent, when compared with the previous case.

6. Conclusions and Policy Recommendations

This paper has detailed the wide spectrum of supply-side constraints that Fiji, Papua New Guinea, Vanuatu and Solomon Islands are believed to face in fostering export-led growth. Generally, these include limited and poorly-maintained physical infrastructure, lack of well-defined property rights to land, the absence of a skilled and experienced workforce, natural disasters, man-made disasters (coups, ethnic conflicts, violent crimes, the high cost of conducting trade including geographical isolation, poor trade facilitation, and limited access to trade finance.

Given these constraints, the results obtained using the LP approach showed the maximum export receipts that these four PICs can achieve under present circumstances. It was also shown (through the relaxations of the constraint equations) that if some of these constraints are removed, the increase in export receipts that could be achieved would be substantial.

The issue that arises is how some of these constraints can be removed so that these PICs can realize increases in their export receipts. In the following paragraphs, we provide some policy recommendations, which, if properly formulated and implemented, can help remove some of the above-mentioned supply-side constraints.

The problem of limited physical infrastructure can be addressed by attracting foreign direct investments (FDIs) in these facilities. However, these FDIs can only be attracted if these PICs create a stable macroeconomic and legal environment and have transparent and efficient institutions.

With regard to the problem of insecure tenure and access to land and lack of well-defined property rights, the governments of the relevant PICs should engage in rigorous dialogue with all the relevant stakeholders so that they can arrive at agreed solutions to these problems. At present the insecure land tenure inhibits production efficiency in agriculture. The exports of agricultural products have been declining in these countries and unless efficiency is improved there is little chance that exports will rise.

The problem of the absence of a well-educated and trained workforce can be addressed if business development service providers can act as vehicles for providing short-term professional and vocational training to enhance the capacity of the workers in all sectors of the economy. FDIs can be a very important source of strengthening the skills of the workforce through exposure to new technologies and management methods. However, none of these can totally substitute for deficiencies in the educational and training system of an economy. In the case of Fiji, the emigration of skilled labour has been a major concern and constraint to effective investment in the export sector. Consultations with the private sector regarding their educational needs when developing educational and training curricula are one way to start a process to overcome this obstacle. The provision of job attachments for students completing their tertiary education would also help address this problem.

The creation of proactive, resourceful and disciplined security forces can help address the problem of man-made disasters in these PICs. A security force with such qualities has the potential to track the occurrence of man-made disasters before they take place and to act swiftly in order to prevent these events. It would also have the capacity to respond quickly to man-made disasters in order to minimize, if not eliminate, their impact on the resources (both human and non-human) of the country. However, security forces will only be able to attain the above-mentioned qualities if they are provided with all the modern resources that they need to combat crime and are given appropriate pay and working conditions. An effective partnership between the government, the private sector, and the general public can help ensure that these pre-conditions are met.

Natural disasters in the Pacific Islands are also a major constraint to the development of the export sector. The majority of the PICs are vulnerable to a range of natural hazards such as cyclones, volcanic eruptions, earthquakes, floods, tsunamis, landslides and droughts. Evidence suggests that natural hazards have a considerable economic impact on development in the Pacific. Vanuatu and Papua New Guinea are especially prone to earthquakes and these have caused major damage to infrastructure (Prasad, et al, 2005).

The costs of conducting trade can be broken down into the following components: information and contracting costs; financing costs; transport costs; and administrative and procedural costs (UNESCAP, 2004). Reducing information and contracting costs would require policies that create a healthy level of competition in the telecommunication sector and improve access to information and communication technology (ICT). The development of trade promotion organizations, in partnership with chambers of commerce and other private sector associations, can also help to reduce the costs associated with identifying and reaching foreign markets. Reviewing contract laws and regulations may also be required.

In addition, reducing export financing costs would involve the development of a national or regional trade finance infrastructure able to provide access to a wide array of specialized trade finance and risk management services such as export credit insurance, hedging, and forfeiting. A stable macroeconomic and legal environment and effective and trusted monetary and financial sector regulatory authorities are prerequisites to the development of a comprehensive private sector banking system and the emergence of non-bank financial institutions. The establishment of specialized trade finance institutions such as export-import banks and export credit agencies can then be considered, to further enhance access to trade finance tools and instruments.

With regard to transportation costs, an improvement of the transport infrastructure may help to reduce transport costs by up to 60 per cent, while policies regulating market power in shipping and liberalizing port services may also lead to a reduction in transport costs by up to 30 per cent (Evenett and Venables, 2002).

The issue of the lack of trade facilitation in these PICs can be addressed by the establishment of a national or regional trade facilitation advisory committee composed of representatives of public and private organizations, to identify trade facilitation bottlenecks and recommend changes. The government agency responsible for trade facilitation could head this advisory committee.

Finally, the problem of the lack of access to trade finance can be addressed if the relevant PICs create an environment where contracts are easily enforceable, issues of collateral and security are managed effectively and financial institutions function efficiently and are able to offer a range of financial instruments to the various export industries. Another important measure is to improve the reliability of financial information provided by export businesses by adopting user-friendly accounting and reporting requirements.

The study is limited by testing the impact of supply-side constraints on exports in aggregate. Time limitations prevented development of a means of testing for the importance of individual constraints such as insecurity of land tenure, lack of access to credit, poor and limited infrastructure, etc. Development of effective tests of this nature would lead to LP solutions that would generate shadow prices for the constraints and thereby give policy makers an indication of the importance of each constraint. It is believed that it is possible to carry out such tests by developing proxies for the impact of the constraints on export supply. It is intended to carry out this work in the next stage of the research.

REFERENCES

African, Caribbean and Pacific Ambassador (Anonymous), (2002). "Discussion note on addressing supply-side constraints in African, Caribbean and Pacific Countries" submitted to the informal discussion on the European Union negotiating instructions convened by the Cotonou Monitoring Group of European Development Non-Government Organisations and Networks. Retrieved on June 6, 2005, from http://www. epawatch.net/general/text.php?item ID=53&menuID=17.

Bank of Papua New Guinea. *Quarterly Bulletins P*ort Moresby. CBSI *Quarterly Bulletins* Honiara.

Chand, S., (2003). "Economic Trends in the South Pacific Countries", *Pacific Economic Bulletin*, 18(1), pp. 1-15.

D'acunto, S., Destefanis, S., and Musella, M (2004) "Exports, Supply Constraints and Growth: An Investigation Using Regional Data", *International Review of Applied Economics*, 18(2), pp. 167-189.

Evenett, J. and Anthony J. Venables (2002). "The geographic spread of trade: evidence from twenty-four developing countries", European Research Workshop in International Trade.

Fiji Islands Ministry of Finance and National Planning (2002). *Economic and Fiscal Update Supplement to the 2003 Budget Address*, Government Printery, Suva.

IMF (2004). *Staff Report for the 2004 Article IV Consultation: Papua New Guinea*, Washington, D.C.

IMF(2004). *Staff Report for the 2004 Article IV Consultation: Solomon Islands*, Washington, D.C.

Narayan, P.K and Seema Narayan (2004). "Is there a long-run relationship between exports and imports? Evidence from two Pacific Island Countries", *Economic Papers (Economic Society of the South Pacific)*. Retreived on 26 September, 2005, from http://www. findarticles.com /articles/mi_moPAO/IS_2_23/ai_n6153069.

Pearson, M.H., Shin, Y., and Smith, R.J.(2001) "Bounds testing approaches to the analysis of level relationships", *Journal of Applied Economics*, 16, pp.289-326.

Prasad, B., Mckenzie, E. and Kaloumaira, A. (2005) The Economic Impact of Natural Disasters in the Pacific, SOPAC, USP and AusAID, Suva.

Pacific Islands Forum Secretariat (2005). *Pacific Plan Report*, PIFS, Suva.

Pan-African Productivity Association (2000). "Supply-side constraints that hamper African enterprises from taking advantage of emerging export market opportunities", *International Labour Organisation Action Programme on Productivity Improvement, Competitiveness and Quality Jobs in Developing Countries - Working Paper PMD-5.* Retrieved on June 6, 2005, from http://www. ilo.org/public/english/employment/ ent/papers/pmd-5.htm.

Reddy, M., Sharma, P., Kumar, S., Prasad, B., and Waqailiti, B. (2005). *Understanding Reforms in Fiji (Proposal by Fiji Team).* . Retrieved on October 27, 2005, from http://www.gdnet.org/pdf2/gdn_library/global_research_project/understanding_reforms/Fiji_ proposal.pdf.

Reserve Bank of Fiji. *Quaterly Reviews),* Suva.

Reserve Bank of Vanuatu. *Quaterly Bulletins,* Port Villa.

Reveliotis, S. (nd). The LP formulation and the underlying assumptions. *An Introduction to Linear Programming and the Simplex Algorithm.* Retrieved on February 1, 2005 from http://www.isye.gatech .edu/spyros/LP/node/html.

Republic of the Fiji Islands Ministry of Foreign Affairs and External Trade (n.d). Regional Trade Agreements. Trade Policy. Retrieved October 27, 2005, from http//www. foreignaffairs.gov.fj.

United Nations Conference on Trade and Development (1998). Trade and Investment in LDCs: Opportunities and Constraints in the Multilateral Trading System. Retrieved on June 6, 2005, from http://www.unctad.org/Templates /webflyer.asp?docid = 2774&int ItemID=1958&lang=1.

United Nations Economic and Social Commission for Asia and the Pacific Sub-committee on Trade and Development (2004). Addressing Supply-side Constraints and Capacity-Building. Retrieved on June 6, 2005, from http://www. Unescap.org/ about/CMG/TI/English/sciti_3e.pdf.

In: Development Problems and Prospects in Pacific Islands ISBN: 978-1-60021-793-7
Editors: B. C. Prasad, D. C. Roy, pp. 53-70

Chapter 5

MACRO-STRUCTURAL DETERMINANTS OF DEVELOPMENT BANKING ROLE IN SMALL ISLAND ECONOMIES: A METHODOLOGICAL FRAMEWORK

M. D. Sharma and Uriam Timiti

1. INTRODUCTION

The critical role of financial systems in development has been widely established (Murinde, 1996; Skully, 1997; Levine, 1997; Stiglitz, 1998; Lemo, 2002). Stiglitz (1998) highlights this important role when he likens the financial system to the brain of the economy, performing the task of allocating resources across space and time in an environment of uncertainty. The rapid growth of development banks has been observed with great interest because of their appeal in the context of market failure on the part of existing financial institutions to provide long term loans and accept high levels of risk associated with new and longer term projects (Nicholls, 1997; Aportela, 2001; Sen, 2002).

The weak performance of development banks and the failure of the financial sector to effectively deal with national and global social and economic issues have attracted global attention. While the Monterrey Consensus reaffirmed a common resolve for the eradication of poverty, effective mobilisation of financial resources and the achievement of internationally agreed development goals including those contained in the Millennium Declaration, the International Institute for Environment and Development (IIED) highlighted the importance of the role of financial institutions and other relevant actors in financing development (Banuri, 2002). Among the Pacific Island Countries (PICs), the concern about the weak performance of the Pacific Island Development Banks (PIDBs) has prompted several review studies (Cole, 1990; ADB, 2000, 2001). Skully (1999) and Siwatibau (1998), in particular, pose an important challenge to development banks- the need to reinvent themselves to ensure that they continue to be responsive to the changing circumstances and development needs of PICs. At the global level, such concern about the weak performance of development financing institutions (DFIs) dominated discussions at the 1995 Conference of the World Federation of Development Finance Institutions (WFDFI) as chief executives of DFIs from around the world deliberated on the theme "Reinventing Development Finance Institutions for the 21st Century: The Role of Development Banks Revisited" (Riusanchez, 1999). The issue of role is considered central to this challenge if development banks are to remain relevant.

This exploratory study looks at an alternative methodological framework for identifying the determinants of an appropriate role model of development banking in the context of Small Pacific Islands Countries (PICs). The paper covers four main areas: Firstly, an overview of the contextual setting of the study, including the characteristic features of the Pacific Island economies and the overall performance of Pacific Islands' Development Banks (PIDBs). secondly, description of the macro level SWOT methodological framework adopted in this study; thirdly, analysis and discussion of the main findings of the study and the associated critcal role dimensions of development banks, with specific reference to PICs; fourthly, the conclusions and suggested areas for future research in development banking.

1.1. Setting the Context

The Pacific Island Countries, also known as the Forum Island Countries (FICs) are generally small island countries spread over a vast expanse of ocean. They are diverse in terms of size, resources, political stability, cultures, languages, economic diversification, development opportunities and constraints (UNDP, 2002).

The demographic characteristics of the islands show that the population is rapidly increasing at an average growth rate of just over 2 percent and that between 71 and82 percent of the population live in rural areas, although this pattern has changed since 2001, with more people moving to urban areas. Over 50 percent of the PIC population are under the age of 21 (Siwatibau,1998), and the overall average economically active population (EAP) in 2001 was 56 percent for females and 79 percent for males. The PICs are among the worlds most desnsly populated areas.

1.2. Pacific Island Development Banks (PIDBs)

Although some form of development finance institutions existed in the Pacific since the 1950s, as with Industrial and/or Agricultural Loan Boards, the establishment of fully fledged development banks in the 1970s was prompted by the need in PICs to avail of the services and related facilities of the ADB (Cole, 1990; ADB, 2001). The legal instruments establishing development banks provided sufficient flexibility to engage in a wide range of activities, which can be reduced to the following common functions: i) to promote economic growth and development in accordance with national policies; ii) to provide medium to long term finance for primary production and the establishment of commercial and industrial undertakings; and iii) to provide assistance and support to new and ongoing businesses (Cole, 1990).

As government owned institutions, development banks are expected to play a leading role in bringing accelerated development and they are required to pay particular attention to the underserved sectors of the community including the rural sector and the outer islands (ADB, 2001). Initial funding sources of equity capital have been grants from governments and/or aid money from bilateral donors, supplemented by low cost loan funds and technical assistance grants from the World Bank, ADB, the European Investment Bank (EIB) and other donor agencies. As shown in Table 5.1 total financial assets held by development banks account for only 7 percent of total financial sector assets. This compares with just over 20 percent and almost 50 percent held by National Provident Funds and commercial banks (ADB, 2001).

Table 5.1. Assets of Commercial Banks and Non Bank Financial Institutions (1996-1999)

Type of Financial Institution	Financial Assets Held				
	1996	*1997*	*1998*	*1999*	*Weighted Average*
Commercial Banks	48.6	48.4	48.4	49.5	48.7
Non Bank Fin. Institutions	25.5	25.5	24.9	25.7	25.4
National Provident Funds	20.2	20.5	19.9	21.6	20.6
Development Banks	7.0	7.8	7.5	6.7	7.3

Source: ADB, 2001; ADFIP Country Reports.

The performance of PIDBs has been weak. Most have not been able to grow because they have been burdened with low quality assets and low profitability. Regular loan provisioning and write offs have reduced real growth in the lending portfolio and hence total assets. The review studies and papers by ADB (2000, 2001), Cole (1990), Skully (1997, 1999), and Siwatibau (1998) provide insights into the problems faced by PIDBs and the challenges that need to be addressed if they are to remain relevant. Low profitability has arisen from high operating cost structures, poor loan recoveries and high loan provisions and write offs, narrow interest margins and a slowing down of lending resulting from insufficient funds. Also related to these problems is poor management reflected by a lack of financial plans, poor internal control systems, low quality reporting and a reactive style of management.

Weak governance relating to political interference, inability of the board to provide adequate supervisory checks on management to ensure that appropriate policies are in place in respect of risk management, reporting standards, and loan provisioning, further contribute to the weak performance. Inadequately skilled staff, especially in loan appraisal and supervision, lack of relationship banking or consistent follow-ups on clients and projects, and inadequate business development programs have also contributed to the poor quality of assets (Skully, 1999). At the macro level, there is need to have in place an environment in which development banks can operate effectively, including workable legal systems that allow enforcement of claims on loan securities, sound auditing that encourages responsible reporting on the part of development banks, and adequate regulatory and supervisory mechanisms (ADB, 2001).

2. Methodological Framework

Developing an appropriate role for any institution is synonymous with institutional relevance and effectiveness. A literature review of the genesis and evolution of development banking globally, regionally and across countries, shows that the initially designed role of development banks was to bring accelerated economic growth and development through industrial development. This formed part of a global response to the dual task of post war reconstruction and development of backward economies. The initial aim of development banking was very much influenced by the successes of industrial banking in Continental Europe and neoclassical growth theories that assign critical importance to investment capital in bringing accelerated growth. Consequently the legislative Acts establishing development banks (embodying industrialization and investment led growth strategies) became the defining role of development banks. This, as Diamond et al (1982) noted is grossly inadequate, as the legal charters are generally very broad and often ambiguous. More importantly, over-dependence on such legal documents to define the role of development banks represents a static approach that is not capable of capturing the dynamics of constantly changing environments in which development banks operate.

In the absence of a commonly established methodological framework for determining the role of development banks, this study uses a macro level SWOT analysis to identify national/regional development issues among the PICs; which issues are then converted into corresponding role dimensions for the PIDBs. The exhaustive list of role dimensions (see Appendix II) is then clustered (reduced) into groups, so as to identify the critical/main role dimensions (see Table 5.3). To capture the relative importance of the identified role dimensions, a prioritization matrix is constructed based on the frequency of a role dimension to address each of the development issues identified. As shown in Appendix I, to effectively address a particular identified development issue may require performance of more than one role dimension. On the basis of aggregate frequencies, weights are assigned to each of the main role dimensions to indicate the order of priority and importance. The assignment of weights in the study is therefore not intended to provide any basis for resource allocation. Explanatory notes forming part of Appendix 1 provide more guidance on how the prioritization matrix is constructed and the weights assigned. The application of a macro level SWOT analysis in the study and the associated findings and outcomes are largely a result of a desk review of key documents on the PICs, combined with own knowledge and experiences of the authors.

SWOT analysis is an extremely useful, simple, flexible and low cost planning tool for understanding and decision-making, in respect of all sorts of situations and organizations or entities. It provides a holistic and integrated framework for identifying and analyzing strengths, weaknesses, opportunities and threats, and an impetus to analyze a situation and develop suitable objectives and strategies (Joseph and Sinkey, 1998; Coult, 1992). Through prioritization, SWOT analysis can provide a powerful basis for allocating scarce organizational resources (Boone and Kurtz, 1992). The breadth and scope of SWOT analysis in dealing with the past, present, and future give it an extremely useful ability to capture the dynamics of a changing internal and external environment in which an entity operates (Whyte and Plenderleith, 1992). While SWOT analysis has proven to be one of the commonly used analyses in corporate management, it is evident from a survey of the related literature that very few applied studies have been done at the macro or country level, especially in identifying macro level determinants of the development banking role. In the context, SWOT analysis provides a strategically systematic approach to ensure that the bank roles are continuously aligned to the development needs and aspirations of the people. Further, simplicity and methodological soundness leading to its wide application in management, as well as other disciplines are considered key reasons for using SWOT analysis in this study. In demonstrating the application of a macro level SWOT analysis in development financing, role modeling and performance evaluation, this study aims to make a useful methodological contribution towards creating more relevant and responsive development banks, in the context of constantly changing operating environments.

3. Results and Findings

Using a macro level SWOT analysis, the identified development issues of the PICs, summarized in Table 5.2, are as follows:

Table 5.2. SWOT Analysis - Development Issues

SWOT Dimensions	specific Issues
1.Strengths	strong cultural and community values ; clean environments; abundant human, land, fisheries resources
2. Development Concerns/Weaknesses	
Human Concerns	poverty; disparity; conflict and insecurity
Physical and Environmental Concerns	fragmentation/isolation; inadequate infrastructure; environmental degradation
Institutional Factors	inadequate human resource capacity/skills; poor governance; inadequate policies; inadequate information system poor decision making
Political/Economic Factors	poor governance, oversized public sector; political instability; civil unrest; underdeveloped economic and social infrastructure
Financial Factors	underdeveloped financial infrastructure ; Poor Fiscal management; tax regimes; unsustainable budgets; subsidy dependence
3. Opportunities	human development potential; natural resources potential
4. Threats	natural disasters, epidemics, environmental degradation, poor governance, unhealthy lifestyles

3.1. Lack of Agreement on Development Ideology and Perspective

Lack of agreement on the definition of and the ideological basis for an appropriate development path for the PICs constitutes a fundamental development issue in so far as it affects the detail and nature of development priorities identified, strategies formulated and methodologies used in measuring development performance. A review of the Pacific literature suggests two main development perspectives, namely the economic structuralist view (evident in the ADB reports); and the sustainable human development perspective (UNDP, 1999).

3.2. Strengths

The strategic strengths that the PICs must enhance and take advantage of include the people, strong cultural and community values, as well as clean environments and abundant land and fisheries resources.

3.3. Development Issues/Weaknesses

Human Development Concerns

There is clear evidence of poverty in the Pacific resulting from restricted capabilities, lack of productive/economic assets, and insufficient means of livelihood. Closely related to poverty is the widening disparity between rural and urban communities and also between the rich and poor in the urban sector. Peace and security are increasingly being threatened by a rising incidence of crime and deteriorating traditional and social networks and values (UNDP, 2002).

Physical and Environmental Concerns

The isolation and remoteness of the islands, that leads to costly transportation and limited access to basic infrastructural services, present major physical constraints to development. Environmental degradation caused by high population densities in urban areas and/or the unsustainable use of resources, and unmanaged pollution are seriously threatening the very livelihood of the people (ADB, 2002; UNDP, 2002).

Institutional Concerns

Appropriate institutions can be effective if good policies are in place and the people are adequately and appropriately skilled. Inadequate skill levels in the PICs are a major development concern. Poor governance in terms of frequent abuses of office, corruption and mismanagement have not only wasted public resources but also adversely affected institutional efficiency and productivity. Further, limited capacity to produce reliable and timely information has negatively affected the quality of decision making and hence institutional performance and effectiveness.

Political and Economic Factors

As already mentioned poor governance in governments is seriously undermining national productivity and effectiveness (PIFS, 2002). Oversized public sectors, at the expense of crowding out the private sector, also undermine the allocative efficiency of limited public resources. Political instability and civil unrest, which have brought affliction and conflict leading to the loss of lives, will continue to disrupt national productivity and reduce investor confidence. Underdeveloped economic, social and financial infrastructures will likewise continue to have a negative impact on the effectiveness of national development strategies and programmes.

Financial Factors

Weak fiscal management manifesting itself in excesses, wasteful expenditures, laxity of financial and accounting procedures, politically gainful but sometimes painful tax regimes, and deficits inappropriately financed, will most likely result in a weakening economy and/or macroeconomic instability (Siwatibau, 1995) and resources drawn away from where they are most needed. Underdeveloped financial infrastructures will continue to negatively impact national efforts relating to capital formation resource mobilization and productive investments.

3.4. Opportunities

Opportunities come through full recognition of existing strengths in terms of human, land, and ocean resources and having in place appropriate institutions and policies that together i) create an enabling environment for effective and democratic governance and ultimately ii) promote collective, equitable and sustainable well being of the people. The PICs must open up and learn from the experience of other countries and at the same time develop their capacity to take advantage of related opportunities (Mak and Naya 1995). The availability of funding and technical assistance from bilateral donors and multilateral organizations offers much to the PICs in terms of the needed capital and know-how to develop and harness local human, land, ocean and under the sea bed resources. To translate opportunities into tangible results requires quality decision making for which strong and efficient information systems, capable of producing timely and reliable information, must be in place (ADB, 2000; UNDP, 2002).

3.5. Threats

The major threats facing the PICs can be usefully put into two categories: firstly, uncontrollable threats that are determined by nature, and secondly, controllable threats that are much a product of human device and/or a result of integration into the global economy.

The uncontrollable threats include natural disasters (cyclones, hurricanes, droughts) and epidemics and the rising sea level resulting from global warming. The controllable threats include those that are self-inflicted through poor governance and corruption; political instability and civil unrest; unhealthy lifestyles; unsustainable use of resources and unmanaged environmental and water pollution, especially in the urban areas. The process of globalization is also posing new kinds of threats relating to vulnerabilities from systemic financial crises and changing global economic and market conditions.

4. Development Bank Role Dimensions

The identified development issues summarized in Table 5.2 point to the various role dimensions, which can be clustered under the following headings:

Social Development

The development issues seem to suggest strongly the need for the PIDBs to focus on the social development role. At the institutional level, the PIDBs need to be appropriately structured to address this focus through creation of departments/sections and/or recruiting appropriately skilled staff. Of special importance in this particular directions is the need for active participation of the PIDBs in basic human values promotion and awareness programs, and factoring in social mobilization and community development as component features of their financial products and services. Sustainable banking, giving special regard to environmental issues, mobilization of savings and other financial resources, and the development and enhancement of human development capabilities, is also important.

Equity and Empowerment

Closely linked with social development are equity and empowerment issues. In the context of global poverty and the need to bridge the divide between the rich and the poor, the PIDBs have a critical role in ensuring equal participation in development and the equitable distribution of benefits there-from. This role will require the PIDBs to have the capacity and ability to identify underserved/most vulnerable sectors and segments of society and/or critical bottlenecks to development, and to work out appropriate strategies to address such issues. Of particular relevance among the PICs is the design and delivery of appropriately targeted products and services to address needs of particular social groups, locations, sectors; to develop essential social, economic and financial infrastructure; to enhance entrepreneurial skills and development of the private sector; and most importantly to maintain a functional network of partnership with relevant local and international development agencies. Empowerment strategies by PIDBs will involve broadening opportunities in terms of human skills and capabilities as well as improving access to and equitable distribution of productive assets. Micro financing and entrepreneurship training are also important in this regard.

Policy Development

The PIDBs must be able to contribute to the improvement of broader macroeconomic conditions of the islands and the PIC region as a whole. The extent to which the PIDBs can contribute towards creating an enabling environment in countries where they operate will be a measure of their success. An important aspect of an enabling environment is the existence of an appropriate set of policies, not only to ensure a safe and peaceful physical and social environment, but also to promote a healthy financial sector and attractive investment climate, as well as the maintenance of best practices in governance, fiscal management, trade, development financing and banking. A workable legal framework to safeguard private property, to ensure enforceability of claims as well as the prudent and effective regulation and supervision of the financial system must also be in place. Polices to enhance market efficiency and hence discipline in the business sector, and to guide national practices in technology, trade and industry are also important.

Institutional Development

Central to the issue of institutional quality and development among the PICs is responsiveness. At the macro level, PIDBs must take the lead in promoting an appropriate corporate culture founded on excellence, in terms of manpower skills; professionalism and competence; honesty in terms of high ethical standards; and innovation in the continuing search for novel but more cost effective ways to satisfy the needs of the people, using appropriate technology. At the micro level, PIDBs must ensure that their products and services are appropriately designed and targeted and that delivery mechanisms are cost effective and efficient. Their dynamism in response to changing political and socioeconomic conditions requires putting into place sound information systems capable of producing reliable and timely information, and a competitive edge in information technology. Closely related to this is a strong research and development capability. PIDBs must also aim to achieve financial viability and sustainability if they are to be seen as credible development financial institutions.

Financial Intermediation and Mobilization

The financial intermediation and mobilization roles demanded of the PIDBs relate not only to their ability to attract domestic and international financial resources but also their ability to demonstrate financial competence and institutional efficiency in allocating such resources to where they are most needed. To effectively mobilize financial resources, PIDBs must be able to attain financial credibility through market business discipline and sound financial management practices. The allocative efficiency of PIDBs requires use of best policies and practices in project appraisal and selection as well as an ability to effectively monitor such projects. It is also important that the financial intermediation and mobilization role be carried out in the context of broader national development issues, which in the case of the PICs, call for more social content in terms of social development, equity and empowerment; and improvement of the broader macroeconomic conditions in terms of the best set of policies and appropriate institutions.

5. Discussion

The need to incorporate national development issues in the roles of development banks has long been recognized as a critical design element in the architecture of such institutions. Diamond (1957) and Boskey (1959) for example attribute the diversity of development banks to the different economic, socio-political environments in which they operate. Kongsiri (1999) argues that the future relevance of development banks lies in their ability to understand the environments in which they operate, and Bruck (1999) also argues that the role of development banks must be determined by the nature of society or the development context. In the same vein, Cole (1990) says that development banks must play an important role in overall national efforts to improve the socio-economic conditions of the people faced by the PICs.

The use of a macro level SWOT Analysis in role modeling for development banks provides a simple but powerful and effective methodology to identify national development issues upon which critical role dimensions of development banks can be framed. The identified role dimensions drawn from this study and their relative importance/weightings in the PICs highlighted (see Table 3 below) show that the overriding focus of the PIDBs should be on social development, especially as it relates to equity and social and economic empowerment and hence social fairness and justice. In the Pacific, the current search for an appropriate development path (Emberson-Bain, 1996; Qalo, 2003 and others) generally supports a search for a new 'model for development' that is premised on ideologies other than those of market capitalism. The requirement for more social content in the activities of development banks has long been deeply embedded in the doctrine of development banking, being an institutional device to correct the failure of market financial institutions to provide long term capital, and the consequent neglect of certain sectors and segments of society (Sen, 2002). In addition, the importance of the doctrine of 'lender of last resort' in development banking (Bruck, 1999), and the associated use of cost benefit analysis as a standard project appraisal and selection methodology further highlight the traditionally expected nature of development impact by development banks. But this seemed to have lost significance in the wake of economic and financial liberalization and the associated emphasis on profitability as a bottom line measure of performance.

The current debate about sustainable development and good governance, in addressing poverty and equity issues, further supports the need for the PIDBs to adopt a more socially responsible approach in development financing (Sharma and Timiti, 2003). Further, the World Bank, by incorporating a social development emphasis in its activities, culminating in the creation of the social development unit in 1993, which later became a stand alone Social Development Department (SDD) in 1997; and the commissioning in 2002 of a Sector Strategy Paper (SSP) on social development to guide its work, strongly supports a shift of perspective in the same direction (World Bank, 2004). The dilemma faced by development banks in the Pacific, as they try to meet the dual challenge of being profitable on the one hand, and being sustainable and socially responsible on the other, also confirms the need to revisit the direction of development financing in the Pacific (ADB 2000).

The importance given to the policy and institutional development roles in the study also reflects current thinking on how development banks can be more effective development finance institutions. Siwatibau (1997) strongly argues that the PIDBs must take an active role in the formulation of national adjustment policies and programmes. Bruck (1999) and Ruisanchez (1999), also argue that to improve the macroeconomic context, development banks need, not only to have a deep knowledge of the contextual factors, but also to adopt a broader view in their development financing activities, extending beyond traditional financial objectives (project identification, promotion, financing and monitoring) to making positive contributions towards putting in place an enabling policy and institutional framework. This requires development banks to engage in a continuous dialogue and partnership with government and other relevant development agencies, both domestic and abroad. Bruck (1999) identifies this policy aspect contribution of development banks in their ability to embrace the future and to coordinate and link development efforts, and in providing spirited leadership for the entire financial services community.

The seeming low importance given to the financial intermediation and mobilization role in the study should not suggest that development banks are not relevant in development. It does, however, reflect global and indeed regional and national concern about the failure of development banks to address pressing socio-economic problems. This demands a broader view on the role of development banks, not as mere conduits of financial capital, but more importantly, to ensure that the objective of financing is consistent with broader development objectives (Ruisanchez, 1999). This needed shift in perspective is strongly endorsed by the Monterrey Consensus and the International Institute for Environment and Development (UN, 2002; Banuri, etal, 2002). As indicated in the study, social and economic empowerment and equity issues should underpin the objective of development financing by the PIDBs, so as to promote an all inclusive development (UNCTAD, 2002).

Table 5.3. Prioritization Matrix

Role/ Dimension	Frequency in SWOT Matrix *	Weighting ** %
Social Development	25	36
Human Values Promotion and Awareness, Social mobilization, Community Development, Human Resource Development, Eco lending, Sustainable Banking		
Equity and Empowerment	18	26
Social Lending/projects; Micro finance; Entrepreneurial skills development; Rural/targeted lending; Special assistance programs; Infrastructural Lending; Private sector development; Partnership (local/foreign)		
Policy Development	11	16
Environment; Trade; Financial Infrastructure; Investment Climate; Regulatory and Supervision; Private Sector Development; Market Efficiency; Technology		
Institutional Development	11	16
Product and Services design and development; Business Research and Development; Responsiveness; Financial Viability and Sustainability; Management skills development Information; Technology Transfer; Productivity and Efficiency		
Financial Intermediation and Mobilization	4	6
Total	69	100

* aggregate frequency obtained from Appendix II;

** weightings are calculated as percentage of total frequency.

6. Conclusion

The importance of capturing national development issues and priorities in role modelling for development banks has been well established. In the context of the PICs, the identified development issues, as shown in the study, strongly suggest a need for a shift in focus by the PIDBs to give priority to social development. The associated role dimensions of Equity and Empowerment, Policy and Institutional Development, and Financial Intermediation and Mobilization therefore need to be consistent with the social development focus.

A key challenge to ensure institutional relevance/responsiveness and viability is for development banks to continue to reinvent themselves; which is tantamount to ensuring that their roles are modelled on and consistent with the demands of changing political and socio-economic environments in which they operate. The seeming dependence on legal instruments and charters as guiding documents to define the role of development banks has long been viewed as inadequate as such documents are usually too general and vague. A major contribution of this study therefore is to offer an alternative methodological framework for modelling the role of development banks. By identifying critical development issues and priorities, the use of a macro level SWOT analysis, provides a systematic and dynamic framework to identify an appropriate role model for development banks to ensure that they continue to be responsive to the needs and aspirations of people. Further, the benefits of using SWOT analysis are related not only to the outcome, but more importantly, to the knowledge and understanding gained from the process of doing the analysis.

To the extent that this study is largely a desk review of key documents, punctuated by personal experiences and knowledge of the authors, the findings need to be confirmed by conducting country level SWOT analyses on selected PICs. Suggested useful research in this direction will be in developing an appropriate performance evaluation model for development banks in the PICs that goes beyond traditional financial measures to those that highlight the developmental impact of development banks, in line with national development issues and priorities.

APPENDIX I. SWOT MATRIX

Development Issues and Development Banking Role Dimensions

SWOT Dimensions	specific Issues	Critical Role Dimensions of Development Banks
1.Strengths		
	strong cultural and community values	Social mobilization, and community development, moral development
	clean Environments	Sustainable banking; environmental policies
	abundant Human, land, fisheries resources	Promotional, business research and development Savings mobilization, financial intermediation, entrepreneurial skills development
2. Development Concerns/Weaknesses		
Human Concerns		
	Poverty	target lending, micro credits, entrepreneurial skills development
	Disparity	community development, social services projects, rural/targeted lending
	conflict and insecurity	social mobilization, entrepreneurial skills training savings mobilization/financial intermediation, moral development
Physical and Environmental Concerns		
	fragmentation/Isolation inadequate infrastructure environmental degradation	targeted lending services infrastructural lending environmental policies, social mobilization, community development
Institutional Factors		
	Inadequate human resource capacity/skills Poor Governance Inadequate Policies Inadequate Information System Poor Decision making	Skills development programmes, Institutional development, partnerships Productivity and efficiency, moral development Policy development Products and services Sustainability and Viability Information Technology Transfer Management skills development

Appendix 1. Continued

SWOT Dimensions	Specific Issues	Critical Role Dimensions of Development Banks
Political/Economic Factors		
	Poor governance, oversized public sector, political instability, civil unrest, underdeveloped economic and social infrastructure	Institutional development, moral development Private sector development, promoting market mechanism Social mobilization projects , moral development Investment climate promotion, Business research and development, trade policy development social mobilization
Financial Factors		
	underdeveloped financial infrastructure Poor Fiscal management, Tax regimes, Unsustainable budgets, Subsidy dependence	Financial infrastructure policy and projects Regulatory and supervision Institutional development, human resource capacity building, moral development Policy reform and development Financial skills development , promoting financial sustainability Sustainable banking and Financing
3. Opportunities	Human development potential Natural resources potential	Social investments, community development, entrepreneurial skills development Moral development Foreign partnerships, entrepreneurial skills development Savings mobilization/ financial intermediation
4. Threats	Natural disasters, epidemics, environmental degradation, Poor governance, Unhealthy lifestyles	Special assistance programmes and Social mobilization, eco lending Sustainable banking, moral development and Environmental policies, environmental friendly projects, Community development projects

Appendix II. Prioritization Matrix

Role Dimension[c]	**Frequency in SWOT Matrix**[a]	**Weights (%)**[b]
A. Social Development	*25*	*36*
A.1 Human Values Promotion and Awareness	8	
A.2 Social mobilization	5	

Appendix II. Continued

Role Dimension[c]	**Frequency in SWOT Matrix**[a]	**Weights (%)**[b]
A. Social Development	*25*	*36*
A.3 Community Development	5	
A.4 Human Resource Development	2	
A.5 Eco lending	2	
A.6 Sustainable Banking	3	
B. Equity and Empowerment	*18*	*26*
B.1 Social Lending/projects	3	
B.2 Micro finance	1	
B.3 Entrepreneurial skills development	6	
B.4 Rural/targeted lending	3	
B.5 Special assistance programs	1	
B.6 Infrastructural Lending	1	
B.7 Private sector development	1	
B.8 Partnership (local/foreign)	2	
C. Policy development	*11*	*16*
C.1 Environment	3	
C.2 Trade	1	
C.3 Financial Infrastructure	1	
C.4 Investment Climate	2	
C.5 Regulatory and Supervision	1	
C.6 Private Sector Development	1	
C.6 Market Efficiency	1	
C.7 Technology	1	
D. Institutional Development	*11*	*16*
D.1 Product and Services design and development	1	
D.2 Business Research and Development	2	
D.3 Responsiveness (need driven, delivery, cost effectiveness, technology appropriateness)	3	
D.4 Financial Viability and Sustainability	2	
D.5 Management skills development	1	
D.6 Information Technology Transfer	1	
D.7 Productivity and Efficiency	1	
E. Financial Intermediation and Mobilization	*4*	*6*
	69	*100*

[a] Total frequency scores under each of the main role dimensions are derived by determining the relevant role dimensions to address each of the identified development issues in the SWOT Matrix (Appendix I). For instance, to promote strong cultural and community development will require performance of social mobilization, community development and moral development roles; thus the multiple frequency points of 3 is given to the Social Development Role. This process is repeated for each of the identified development issues to get the total multiple frequency score for each of the main role dimensions.

[b] Weight is calculated by expressing the total multiple frequency score for each main role dimension as a percentage of the overall total multiple frequency of 69. For example the weighting of 6 percent for the Financial Intermediation and Mobilization Role is calculated thus: (4/69)x100).

[c] The nomenclature (A-E) used in the table for the main role dimensions includes the most relevant and directly related dimensions of the identified component roles.

REFERENCES

ADB, 1997. *Kiribati 1997 Economic Report, Pacific Studies Series*, ADB, Manila.

______, 2000. *Annual Report 2000*, ADB, Manila.

______. 2000, *Development Banking in the Pacific- Experience and Alternatives*, ADB, Manila.

______, 2001. *Financial Sector Development in the Pacific Development Member Countries, Volume I, The Regional Report,* ADB, Manila *(http://www.adb.org).*

______, 2001. *Financial Sector Development in the Pacific Development Member Countries, Volume II, The Regional Report,* ADB, Manila , 2002. Outlook 2002, Oxford University Press.

______, 2002. *Outlook 2002, Publication Highlights,* Oxford University Press.

______, 2003. *Outlook 2003, Publication Highlights*, Oxford University Press.

______, 2004. *Outlook 2004, Publication Highlights*, Oxford University Press.

______, 2005. *Outlook 2005, Publication Highlights*, Oxford University Press.

______, 2005. *Outlook 2005 Update, Publication Highlights*, Oxford University Press.

ADFIP (Association of Development Finance Institutions in the Pacific). *Country Reports (1996-2002)*, Suva.

Aportela, F. 2001. *Firms' Financing Costs: The Role of Development Banks in Mexico (http://www.banxico.org.mx).*

Banuri. T, *et al.* 2002. *Financing for Sustainable Development, International Institute for Environment and Development* (IIED), Hertfordshire, UK (*http://www.iied.org*).

Basu, S.K. 1971. *A Review of Current Banking Theory and Practice*, Macmillan Press, Madras.

Boone, L. and D.Kurtz. 1992. *Contemporary Marketing*. Dryden Press, Fort Worth, TX.

Boskey, S. 1959. *Problems and Practices of Development Banks*, International Bank for Reconstruction and Development, John Hopkins Press, Baltimore.

Bruck. N. 1999. 'The Role of Development Banks in the Twenty-First Century' in *Principles and Practices of Development Banking Vol III,* Association of Development Finance Institutions in Asia and the Pacific (ADFIAP), Manila.

Cole, R.V. 1990. *South Pacific Development Banks: Key Issues in Their Future*, Pacific Islands Development Program (PIDP), East West Centre, Honolulu.

Coult, H. 1992. *Management in Banking*, 2nd Ed., CIB Associateship Series, Pitman Publishing, London.

Diamond, W. 1957. *Development Banks*, IBRD, World Bank, John Hopkins Press, Baltimore.

Diamond, W (ed). 1968. *Development Finance Companies; Aspects of Policy and Operation,* INRD, World Bank, John Hopkins Press, Baltimore.

Diamond, W. and V.S. Raghavan (eds). 1982. *Aspects of Development Bank Management*, EDI, World Bank, John Hopkins Press, Baltimore.

Emberson-Bain, A (ed). 1996. *Sustainable Development or Malignant Growth? Perspectives of Pacific Island Women*, Marama Publications, Suva.

Emerson, J (ed). 2000. 'The Nature of Returns: A Social Capital Inquiry into Elements of Investment and the Blended Value Proposition', *Social Enterprise Series No. 17*, Harvard Business School, Boston, MA.

Fairbairn, T.I.J and D.Worrel. 1996. *South Pacific and Caribbean Island Economies: A Comparative Study*, Pacific Island Forum Secretariat, Suva.

Qalo, R. 2003. 'Adjust existing structures to create a unique model of Pacific Governance', in *USP Beat*, Vol. 3, Issue 12, August, 2003, USP, Suva.

Gregory, C.A. 1999. 'South Asian models for the Pacific? The case of micro finance', *Pacific Economic Bulletin*, Volume 14(2), pp81-92, ANU, Canberra.

Houk, J.T.D, 1968. *Financing and Problems of Development Banking*, Frederick A Praeger Publishers, London.

Halapua, S. 1990. *The Role of Institutions in Pacific Island Countries*, PIDP, East West Centre, Honolulu.

Jeucken, M. 2001. *Sustainable Finance and Banking, The Finance Sector and the Future of the Planet*, Earthscan Publications Ltd, London.

Joseph, F and F Sinkey. 1998. *Commercial Bank Management Financial Management* 5th Ed., Prentice Hall, Inc, New Jersey.

Kongsiri. A. 1999. 'The Future Role of Development Banks in the Asia Pacific Region' *Principles and Practices of Development Banking Vol III,* Association of Development Finance Institutions in Asia and the Pacific (ADFIAP), , Manila.

Ledgerwood, J. 1999. *MicroFinance Handbook: An Institutional Perspective,* World Bank, Washington, D.C (http://www.worldbank.org).

Lemo, T. 2002. *The Role of the Financial Institutions in the growth and development of the Real Sector*, Money Market Association of Nigeria *(http://www.expdisc.com /sector.htm).*

Levine, R.. 1997. 'Financial Development and Economic Growth: Economic Agenda', *Journal of Economic Literature*, 35, pp.668-726.

Mak,J and S.F.Naya. 1995. 'Is There a Need for a Pacific Island Development Bank', *Policy Discussion Paper* 1/1995, ANU, Canberra.

McGill, R. 1994. 'Institution Development and the Notion of Sustainability', *International Journal of Public Sector Management,* Vol.7 No.6, pp:26-40.

Mcquire, P.B. 2000. 'South Asian Economic models for the Pacific? The case of micro-finance- a comment', *Pacific Economic Bulletin,* Volume15, 1 p168-171, ANU, Canberra.

Murinde, V.1996. *Development Banking and Finance,* Avebury, Aldeshot.

Nicholls,G.P.1997. *Development Banking in the ECCB Area (http://www.eecb. centralbank.org/Rsch_Papers/Rpann).*

Pacific Islands Forum Secretariat (PIFS). 2002. *Economic Outlook,* Suva *(http://www.forumsec.org.fj).*

Ruisanchez.J, 1999. 'Profitability and Development Banks' in *Principles and Practices of Development Banking Vol III,* Association of Development Finance Institutions in Asia and the Pacific (ADFIAP), Manila.

Sen, B. 2002. *Development Banking – An International Perspective.*

Siwatibau, S. 1995. 'The Pacific Island Countries: Economic development issues and prospects' in R. Grynberg (ed), *Economic Prospects for the Pacific Islands in the 21st Century*, School of Social and Economic Development, USP, Suva.

_______ 1998. *Development Banking in the Pacific: What of the Future*, ADFIP Annual Conference, ADFIP, Suva.

Skully, MT, 1997, 'The South Pacific: Finance, Development and the Private Sector', *International Development Issues* No.48, AUSAid, Canberra.

_______. 1999. *Development Banking in the Pacific: Strategies for the future*, ADFIP Annual Conference, ADFIP, Suva.

Sharma, M.D and T. Uriam. 2003. *Good Governance and the Issue of Subsidization in Development Banking for Small Pacific Island Countries*, Paper presented at the Good Governance Symposium, Foundation for Development Cooperation, October, 2003, Suva.

Stigliz, J. 1998. *The Role of the Financial System in Development*, Fourth Annual Bank Conference on Development in Latin America and the Caribbean, World Bank, Washington.

Tisdell, C. 2000. 'Poverty in the Pacific Islands', *International Journal of Sociology and Social Policy*, Vol. 20 No. 11, pp74-110.

UN. 2000. *Millennium Development Goals (http://www.un.org)*.

UNCTAD. 2002. *The Least Developed Countries Report* 2002, UNCTAD, Geneva.

UNDP. 2002. *Multi-Country Programmes Outline for the Pacific Island Countries* (2003-2007), UNDP, Suva *(http://www.undp.org.fj)*.

USP. 2002. *USP WSSD Team Report: Johannesburg World Summit on Sustainable Development*, Johannesburg, USP, Suva *(http://www.usp.ac.fj/pace)*.

Whyte, I. 1992, *Management in Banking*, Chartered Institute of Bankers, Bankers Book, London.

Woller, G. 2002. *Poverty lending, financial self sufficiency and the six aspects of outreach*, Romney Institute of Public Management Marriot School, Brigham Young University.

Wolfensohn, J. 1999. *Remarks at Conference on Development Banking Institutions into the New Millennium*, Mexico.

World Bank. *2004. An OED Review of Social Development in Bank Activities*. OED, World Bank, New York (*http:www.worldbank.org/html/exteme/dwsp102599.htm)*.

Yunus, M.1999. *Banker to the Poor: Autobiography of Muhammad Yunus*, Aurum Press Ltd, London.

In: Development Problems and Prospects in Pacific Islands ISBN: 978-1-60021-793-7
Editors: B. C. Prasad, D. C. Roy, pp. 71-90

Chapter 6

AID, REMITTANCES AND THE INFORMAL ECONOMY OF PACIFIC ISLANDS: A DEVELOPMENT GOVERNANCE PERSPECTIVE

Cathrin Thodock

1. INTRODUCTION

A common perception of the Pacific is all too often one of island paradises; blue lagoons, 'umbrella drinks' and a carefree life. This view, however, is far from the realities for most Pacific Islanders. The region faces an array of challenges – from providing basic living conditions for the majority of the population, to developing infrastructure and sustainable economies. Poor economic performance and lack of foreign investment have been compensated with massive inflows of aid, but long-term results have failed to appear and the Pacific has become overly dependent on foreign aid. Additionally, aid-funded projects often accommodate the rules and guidelines set by donors or recipient governments, which has led to a remarkable lack of results for those the aid allegedly is intended for. The emergence of an increasingly important informal economy has become vital to poor people's income, but the sector is poorly regulated and the workers are frequently subjected to exploitation. The informal economy does, however, contribute to overall economic growth and poverty alleviation. Migrants' remittances constitute another important partial source of income for disadvantaged people, but they also increase inequalities as non-recipients are made worse off. Recipients' spending of remittances reflects rational decisions, and even if the money primarily is spent on consumption, some is invested; and the overall outcome is increased economic safety for both recipients and their communities. Financial aid from developed countries will still be necessary for a long time, but expansion of the informal economy and the growing flows of remittances show the importance of empowering people instead of making them dependent on others' goodwill and underlying agendas. Sustainable and equitable development is also dependent on the formulation of governance agendas, and the extent Pacific cultural values are taken into consideration.

2. Pacific Economies – Viable, but Underdeveloped

The lack of growth in the Pacific is often explained by the region's geographic position, few natural resources, limited industrial bases, poor governance, and cultural diversity. The region's remote location, small-scale economies and lack of development and infrastructure makes it difficult to compete globally, which has resulted in a collective trade deficit of US$2 billion (Corbel 2004). Small island states also face special problems arising from smallness itself; limited technical capacity, dependence on unstable export markets, and restricted opportunities for comparative advantage in the global economy (Firth 2005). Attempts to encourage economic diversification and import-substitution industrialization have proved insufficient to meet local needs (Connell & Conway 2000). The poor economic performance adds to the Pacific's increased marginalisation; in 2004 Gross Domestic Product (GDP) grew at 2.6 per cent – the region's best year since 2000 – which compares with a growth rate of 7.3 per cent in Asia as a whole (ILO 2005). During the past 30 years, population has grown at more than 3 per cent annually while per capita income has grown at less than 1 per cent and in some islands it has declined; and this discrepancy between population and income growth lies at the core of the Pacific's problems (Hughes 2003). Inhabitants of colonial territories (Guam, the Northern Marianas, American Samoa, New Caledonia, French Polynesia) have the highest standards of living as they are subsidised by foreign economies that have benefited from globalisation; inhabitants of states that are freely associated with metropolitan states (Palau, the Federated States of Micronesia, Marshall Islands, Cook Islands and Niue) benefit from the right to migrate to the rich world; while the large majority in the independent states (Fiji, Kiribati, Nauru, Papua New Guinea (PNG), Samoa, Solomon Islands, Tonga, Tuvalu and Vanuatu) experience much lower standards and less freedom to benefit from globalisation (Firth 2005).

Basic income and resources, and the freedoms to enjoy basic health, education, shelter and physical safety are vitally important; but insufficient economic resources, unstable economic flows and asset losses regularly impair human security (CHS 2003). There are problems with coverage, reliability, comparability and consistency of data in all Pacific developing countries (ADB 2003), but "more than 25 per cent of the population is believed to be living in poverty in Fiji, Kiribati, Micronesia, Papua New Guinea, Solomon Island, Timor-Leste and Vanuatu" (ILO 2005:25). Instead of recognising poverty as a function of economic or political policies, many Pacific communities view it as morally reprehensible and a personal moral failure, and issues of rising poverty are thus perceived as issues of criminality (Connell 2003). The principal assets available to the rural poor tend to be land and water (Sobhan 2004), and more than 90 per cent of the people of the Pacific live in villages (Hughes 2004). Property titling can improve land values and access to credit, as well as provide security for owners, but large tracts of land are not formally registered (UNDESA 2005b). The work of women in traditional agriculture has thus far kept up with population growth so that 'absolute poverty' is not yet present in the Pacific, and a suggestion that an income of less than US$1 a day indicates 'poverty' insults the hard working women who provide food for villages (Hughes 2003).

Development, as outlined in the United Nations Millennium Development Goals (MDGs), includes: eradicating extreme poverty and hunger; achieving universal primary education; promoting gender equality and empowerment of women; reducing child mortality;

improving maternal health; combating HIV/AIDS, malaria and other diseases; ensuring environmental sustainability; and developing a global partnership for development. Most Pacific Islanders are deprived of living standards that millions now enjoy. In Papua New Guinea, Solomon Islands, Vanuatu and most of the small islands, villagers do not have houses with water, power and sanitary facilities or access to transport and communications; and Pacific Islanders wear second hand clothing from charity bins (Hughes 2004). But taken as a whole, rates of improvement in overall life expectancy in the Pacific have significantly outpaced those for comparable Caribbean island states (AusAID 2003). Development within the Pacific states varies, according to the Human Development Index (HDI), which measures achievement of the basic dimensions of human development; poverty/standard of living, literacy/education, and life expectancy. The HDI for 2005 ranks 177 countries (country ranking in brackets); Tonga (54) is found in the 'high development' group, while Fiji (92), Vanuatu (118), Solomon Islands (128) and PNG (137) are classified as 'medium development' countries (UNDP 2005b:220-221). The region's general progress towards the MDGs also varies: although some states have made considerable progress, others struggle to provide a social, economic, physical and political environment that promotes human development, and face escalating difficulties to provide efficient and equitable access to basic social services (ADB 2003). Each country has taken a different approach, but has found the MDGs to be useful for involving sectors of government and civil society that might otherwise not be part of the development planning process (Corbel 2004). Unfortunately, these efforts tend to be somewhat hampered by third parties – namely those who primarily finance the development projects.

3. Aid and Development

The main objective of Overseas Development Assistance (ODA) is to promote economic growth in poor countries and thereby lift people out of poverty, but evidence shows that aid has not fulfilled its goal of promoting development through investment, and money given as aid has often freed government resources for spending on current consumption – which has fuelled corruption as government officials have sought personal benefits from the disbursement of funds (Erixon 2005). ODA also comes with a bewildering array of strings attached. In many cases conditionality undermines country ownership and adds to the unpredictability and volatility of aid; and meeting donor requirements frequently imposes a heavy burden on the recipient ministries (UNDP 2005b). The Pacific is one of the most aid-dependent regions in the world, partially because of its perceived strategic importance to key aid donors and partially because of its smallness (Firth 2005). Aid dependency undermines wealth creation by creating a politicised economy where entrepreneurs see hand-outs from donors as an easy route to wealth, rather than seeing opportunities to produce goods and services more efficiently (Erixon 2005).

Global ODA reached US$78.6 billion in 2004 (Erixon 2005), and the Pacific has received the highest aid inflows per capita in the world by a large margin: Papua New Guinea and Fiji have received comparatively modest amounts per capita because of their relatively large populations, but the aid flows have still been much higher than what equally sized countries in the Caribbean and Africa have received (Hughes 2003). The large inflows of aid have led to stagnation and recession by permitting counterproductive policies to continue, and research shows that in several cases, aid has not even been effective in countries that have adopted pro-growth strategies (Hughes 2003). However, exceptions do exist. The capability of aid to affect growth depends on its form and utilisation; and evidence from Fiji shows that foreign aid, bilateral aid, grant aid, and technical cooperation positively contribute to growth (Gounder & Xayavong 2001). Aid and development in the Pacific is challenging and requires sound understanding of, and sensitivity to, the wide range of cultural and national differences within the region (ACFOA 2002). Thence projects should be carefully selected, as "multiple objectives often work against each other and weaken each other, so that aid may end up serving none of its multiple goals especially well" (Easterly 2003:34).

3.1. The Aid Bureaucracies

Poor nations include an incredible variety of institutions, cultures and histories – from millennia-old civilisations like China to recently created nations like East Timor – and attempts to "aggregate all this diversity into a 'developing world' that will 'take off' with foreign aid is a heroic simplification" (Easterly 2003:40). This is a view common to many providers of bilateral and multilateral development aid, and programmes have tended to be biased by this perception. Development agencies should implement strategies which complement the recipient country's own efforts (Griffith 2004) and take local conditions into account. Thirty years after independence, the Pacific still has little capacity for aid implementation by local contractors, hence inflows have been termed 'boomerang aid' because much of it returns to donor countries in remuneration for consultants and implementing companies (Hughes 2003). Yet the idea that 'aid buys growth' is an integral part of the founding myth and ongoing mission of the aid bureaucracies, who define their final objective as 'poverty reduction' and their immediate output as aid money disbursed (Easterly 2003). Donors are concerned about weaknesses in public expenditure systems, hence multilateral agencies seek to develop potential solutions, but the attempts have so far lacked coherence (AusAID 2003). It should also be noted that donors often have many different objectives for their aid besides poverty reduction (Easterly 2003), such as trade agreements or international terrorism.

Non-Governmental Organisations (NGOs) and community groups may be better able to provide services where they are needed the most – in the poorer segments of society. However, grassroots movements debate whether to engage in dialogue with governments and multilateral agencies, as there is a concern that NGOs will be regarded as only a mechanism to deliver services that the governments cannot or will not provide (ACFOA 2002). Empowerment is essential to reverse impoverishment and promote sustainable development, and local participation is increasingly identified as fundamental to the successful design and implementation of antipoverty programs (Singh & Strickland 1994). But the real value of the community sector, where many internationally connected organisations are long established and well respected, is often overlooked (ACFOA 2002). There is a wide range of women's organisations in the Pacific, working on a spectrum of development issues – from economic rights and income generation to women's participation in development and governance; but as in other regions, the value and extent of women's work is often invisible to development planners and government policy makers (ACFOA 2002). Aid effectiveness can be increased by directing scarce resources from less successful projects, by imposing conditions on loans before they are granted, and evaluating the impact upon completion (Easterly 2003). Some NGOs claim that government-to-government aid concentrates power at the centre and provides fewer resources for successful activities at local levels. For this reason they have called for more community based development to ensure that funds are directly invested where they are intended to serve (Caldwell 2005). It is therefore important that NGOs are involved in policy formulation, planning and advocacy. Some government officials, however, do not appreciate NGOs' ethos, values, or accountability (ACFOA 2002). To counter these tendencies, it would be sensible to scale back levels of ODA, make aid available for strictly limited periods of time (Erixon 2005), and ensure that NGOs and community groups play active parts in the strategic planning.

4. The Informal Economy

When developing countries suffer from 'economic anaemia' – insecure property rights, inflexible commercial capital markets and weak labour markets – economic activity is dominated by personal relationships, which often reflect the weakness of formal markets, mistrust in the public sector, and abuse of official rules and regulations; and much of this activity occurs in the informal sector (Abbot & Pollard 2004). The informal economy is characterised by self-employment; small enterprises employing mostly family members; heterogeneous activities within trade, transport, services and manufacturing; minimal capital investment; low levels of organisation and technology; unwritten, informal relationships between employer and employees; and the activities are carried out outside formal frameworks of laws and regulations (ILO 2000a). It is known to be anti-cyclical - growing and expanding as the economic cycle is downward oriented, and slowing down or shrinking when the cycle turns upward – and has become a means for many countries to cope with population growth, rural-urban migrations, economic crises, poverty and indebtedness (Charmes 2000). It is also a way for households to tackle problems following downsizing, inflation and cutbacks in public services (ILO 2002). The pressures of globalisation are said to boost informal economies (UNDESA 2005b), and rapid growth in the high-technology sector has generated more high-skilled than low-skilled jobs. This means that those who are unable to acquire the necessary skills find that their only option is the informal economy (UNDESA 2005a). Although most of the activities are legal, they rarely comply with official requirements or pay relevant taxes (Charmes 2000), but the outputs from this sector subsidise growth of the economy as a whole (Chen, Jhabvala & Lund 2002), accounting for a significant share of Gross National Product (GNP) and Gross National Income (GNI) in almost all countries, particularly those in the developing world (UNDESA 2005a). A study of the informal economy in 110 countries in 2000 revealed that its average size as a share of official GNI ranged from 18 per cent in developed countries to 38 per cent in transitional countries and 41 per cent in developing countries (UNDESA 2005a). As much as 37 per cent of the economically active Fijian population was engaged in the informal sector in 1996 (Chand cited in Reddy, Naidu & Mohanty 2005). Outside the agricultural sector, informal wage employment comprises 30 to 40 per cent of informal employment in the developing world (ILO 2002), while self-employment accounts for 60 to 70 per cent (UNDESA 2005a).

Taken as a whole, the informal economy helps to resolve employment problems, and reallocates resources from richer to poorer households (Connell 2003), but there are also serious negative aspects. The losers in informal economies are the poor people who sell their produce and labour under severely adverse conditions at the lowest end of the production and marketing chain, which leaves them with little opportunity for value addition to their inputs (Sobhan 2004). The major constraints they face are credit, marketing and insurance, infrastructure and government regulations (Bardhan 2005). The majority of the population in the informal economy is further marginalised and impoverished by standard laissez-faire market-oriented strategies, which serve to reinforce an economy's rigidities and imperfections, thence degrading human capital (Singh & Strickland 1994). In addition, the fact that they often do not have secure property rights restricts or blocks their access to capital and credit, thereby limiting their ability to expand and grow their businesses. They tend to have difficulties accessing the judicial system, leaving them more vulnerable to harassment, exploitation, abuse, corruption and bribery (UNDESA 2005a). Even when countries have laws and regulations to govern the informal economy, they are frequently outdated or inappropriate, and regulations are often enforced selectively or not at all (Chen, Jhabvala & Lund 2002). An employment strategy aimed at promoting decent work under conditions of equality, security and dignity should be a fundamental component of any development strategy, hence it is critical to invest in people; education, skill development, lifelong learning, health and safety (UNDESA 2005a).

4.1. Labour and Basic Rights

The informal economy is highly segmented – by location, sector, status of employment, social groups, and gender – but most workers share a few things in common, low pay, and little or no social protection, rights at work or representation and voice (ILO 2005). Informal employment includes all profitable work – both self-employment and wage employment – that is not recognised, regulated, or protected by laws and regulations, for instance domestic workers, casual labourers, temporary workers, industrial outworkers and unregistered workers (ILO 2002). Street traders, who comprise 30 to 50 per cent of urban informal employment (UNDESA 2005a), are a notable example. Labour market regulations and standards typically apply only to workers in the formal sector, leaving the majority of the workforce in developing countries uncovered, and this reinforces the segmentation between formal and informal employment in ways that are inherently unfair (World Bank 2005). For poor people that are forced to engage in survival activities, the informal economy offers relatively easy entry. They are attracted by the sector's reliance on local resources, and minimum capital investment; but also face greater work-related risks, and typically have fewer mechanisms for dealing with them (Chen, Jhabvala & Lund 2002). Studies in India, South Africa, and Thailand suggest that organising informal workers decreases the workers' invisibility, helps them gain access to information, and gives them voice and self-identity (World Bank 2005). Demands for better security and protection, however, can easily lead to increased vulnerability of employment (Chen, Jhabvala & Lund 2002). Education and skills are usually negligible. This enables poorly educated and untrained workers to enter the workforce, but also makes it easier to replace them. In many cases, low-level skills are learnt at work, where there is little or no appreciation of workers' rights (ILO 2000a). Consequently, informal activities allow disadvantaged people to maximise what is often their only real asset, their labour power (Chen, Jhabvala & Lund 2002). But for a large proportion of the population in developing countries "participation in the informal economy is not a choice but a means of survival" (UNDESA 2005a:34).

Although the informal sector is not readily visible in the South Pacific, self-employment is increasingly the only alternative as neither the public nor the formal private sectors are able to provide enough jobs (ILO 2000a). A large proportion of the labour force in Kiribati, Samoa, Tonga, Papua New Guinea and Vanuatu is engaged in the informal economy (Abbot & Pollard 2004). In the latter two states the unemployed and informally employed are seen as inadequate rather than victims of the labour market (Connell 2003). In Fiji, strong opposition has been directed towards informal economy workers - especially prostitutes, beggars and hawkers - as their presence challenges notions of order, and hints at moral and physical decay (Connell 2003). Women and youth are particularly vulnerable as they have relatively little bargaining power (UNDESA 2005a). Women tend to be underrepresented in the top strata and overrepresented in the bottom, often earning less than men (World Bank 2005). Available data for developing countries is limited, but nevertheless points to the importance of women, who constitute 30-90 per cent of street vendors (except in societies that restrict women's mobility); 35-80 per cent of self-employed and home workers; and 80 per cent of industrial outworkers (ILO 2002). In the Pacific, the proportion of men and women in non-agricultural informal employment is about the same, but when women's participation rate is taken into consideration, informal employment is generally greater for women (ILO 2005). Children and youth also constitute a significant portion of the informal economy. The Asia-Pacific region has about 127 million child workers, which is about 60 per cent of working children worldwide, and in 2003 the number for the Pacific was 5.1 per cent – compared to a world average of 10.1 per cent (ILO 2005). Since 1990, the rates for child workers have declined in many countries, but are still as high as 40 per cent in Timor-Leste and more than 20 per cent in Solomon Islands (ILO 2005).

5. Migration and Remittances

A growing number of migrants are moving to developed countries in search of jobs and better economic opportunities. Few, if any, labour-exporting countries publish accurate records on migration, hence migration flows are estimated by using data from labour-receiving countries (Adams & Page 2003), and it is estimated that 175 million people worldwide – or roughly 1 in 35 – live outside their countries of birth (UNDESA 2005a). Migrants often choose to follow established paths and to work through networks based on family, culture and history (Allen 2003), and support the development of their home countries by transferring remittances to their families, long-term investments, or sending money to charities or community development organisations (ILO 2000b). They rarely cut off relations with their home countries, and most visit regularly (Skeldon 2002). Those who return raise the levels of economic, social and political debate, thus advancing reform where the system is adequately accessible (Hughes 2004), but they may also experience problems finding jobs in which they can use their new skills, or find investment opportunities to put their new knowledge to productive use (Allen 2003). The migrant pools have tended to reflect a bias towards the more skilled workers, but labour shortages and increasing demand in developed countries change this trend, and though not often acknowledged by governments, several countries increasingly tolerate undocumented migration and visa violations (UNDESA 2005a).

The relationship between development, poverty and displacement is intricate and poorly understood, but poverty is often claimed to be the main reason for migration (CHS 2003). Economic analysis of labour migration speaks of 'push' and 'pull' factors exerted on migrants; better prospects 'pull' the better-off migrants, while poorer migrants are 'pushed' because of unemployment, low wages and poverty (Allen 2003). Studies of international migration's statistical impact on reducing poverty shows that on average, "a 10 per cent increase in the share of international migrants in a country's population will lead to a 1.9 per cent decline in the share of people living on less than $1.00 per person per day" (Adams & Page 2003:20). However, the need for capital, or requirements for education and skills, limits the migration opportunities for the poorest segments of society, hence exacerbate inequalities at the local level (Carling 2005).

Generally speaking, there are four kinds of migration in the Pacific; from outer islands and rural areas to urban centres; skilled migration from one part of the region to another; migration to developed countries; and unique to Fiji, the permanent departure of people of Indian descent – most of whom are highly skilled and well educated (Firth 2005). Globalisation pushes labour migration from most Pacific states, a number of which now depend heavily on remittances (Firth 2005), but it also promotes investment in skills acquisition, and literacy rates in Palau, Samoa and Tonga – where emigration is relatively easy – are high compared to Solomon Islands and Vanuatu, where emigration is difficult and internal cultural barriers to mobility exists (AusAID 2003). Samoa and Tonga have been remittance economies since the early 1990s; Fiji is increasingly becoming one; and access to developed labour markets is also available to people from Kiribati and Tuvalu (Firth 2005). Migration is usually a collective decision, as the migrant contributes to the wellbeing of the whole family - often in several generations (Allen, 2003).

5.1. Remittances

Remittances are an important source of finance for developing countries, generally representing a very stable flow of income; largely unaffected by political or financial crises; and tending to be more equally spread than other capital flows (Usher 2005). They can be seen as private family aid that expresses personal commitments at the primordial level, hence it is a kind of moral capital, and migration is therefore not a loss in all respects – but sometimes an asset (Gowricharn 2004), that also can be understood as intra-family obligations being sustained despite geographical separation (Carling 2005). Large remittance flows also influence more widely the local economy through consumption and investment, with the potential for economic development (Allen 2003), and migrants' hometown associations play an increasingly important role in channelling migrants' savings and remittances towards investment and productive use (ILO 2000b). Remittances are considered to be influenced by the number of workers, wage rates, economic activity in importing and exporting countries, exchange rates, relative interest rates between the countries involved, political risk, and level of education and the marital status of the migrants (Puri & Ritzema, n.d.). It is generally believed that these transfers tend to decline after five to ten years, but in many cases emigrants continue to remit to their home countries after several decades (Carling 2005).

Workers' remittances have been growing in absolute terms as well as in comparison to other economic sources, and will continue to be an important and stable source of financing (Rajan 2005). They have surpassed ODA to developing countries, and constitute the second-largest source of financial flows after Foreign Direct Investment (FDI) (UNDESA 2005a). However, data on remittances is incomplete and underestimates the flows of funds through informal channels. But available figures suggest that global remittances amounted to about US$ 69 billion in 1990, and more than US$ 172 billion in 2004 – of which developing countries received US$ 29 billion and US$ 116 billion respectively, which is an annual growth rate of over 8 per cent (UNDESA 2005b). Remittances tend to be negatively correlated with GDP growth, which suggests that they are compensatory in nature, and they do not appear to be intended to serve as capital for economic development, but as compensation for poor economic performance (Chami, Fullenkamp & Jahjah 2005). The flow of remittances provides an additional means of tackling poverty reduction, and also contributes to the MDGs, when the beneficiaries get improved access to health services, schooling, safe water, and housing (UNDP 2005a). They make up a significant portion of the income of receiving households, and are mostly used for basic subsistence needs, such as food, clothing and health care – but are also spent on improved housing, or purchase of land, livestock, or durable consumer goods (Puri & Ritzema, n.d.). Some migrants complain about their relatives' use of remittances, and claim that they spend it carelessly and do not appreciate the effort behind the money, or that remittances are spent in ways that are invisible to other relatives and neighbours - which causes concern for the senders, as they fear that outsiders wrongfully conclude that no remittances are being sent (Carling 2005). Furthermore, evidence suggests that the impact on income inequality is diverse; remittances can have an equalizing effect and lift people out of poverty, but may also increase inequity because better off workers are more capable of paying the costs of migration (Ratha 2003).

The majority of studies on remittance use in the Pacific suggest that they primarily are used for consumption, but also that a significant proportion supports traditional customs and obligations (Connell & Brown 2005). In the smaller Pacific states, remittances far exceed the value of exports (Hughes 2004). In Fiji, the Reserve Bank has reported that incoming remittances rose from FJ$232 million in 2002 to FJ$243 million in 2003 and FJ$266 million in 2004 – which made it almost as important as sugar, and outranking the export value of gold and fish (Firth 2005). The impact is also considered to be significant in Kiribati, Samoa, Tonga and Tuvalu, but the growing flows raise concerns about laziness or over-dependence on others. Hence it is argued that many households are cushioned from their lack of cash employment by remittances, and that this does little to develop the productive base of the economy (Abbott & Pollard 2004). Remittances can and should be seen as a source of capitalisation. To obtain sustainable local development, however, skills, infrastructure and encouraging economic environments are also required (Andrade-Eekhoff 2005). The benefits from remittances generally outweigh the costs of migrating, and even if remittances primarily are used for consumption rather than investment, they are frequently utilised to pay for education or improve the quality of housing for the migrants' families (UNDESA 2005a), which in turn generates income and employment opportunities for informal sector workers, and a multiplier effect takes place (Maimbo 2005). Interestingly, there has been no concerted effort by Pacific governments to offer incentives to remit more through official channels or to induce more investment of remittances in productive activities (Puri & Ritzema, n.d.).

6. Democracy, Governance and Pacific Values

It is widely argued that democracy is a universal value and that good governance is essential to poverty reduction and sustainable development. The conditions for this to occur may be identified as: the empowerment of people that leads to the sharing of democratic values; economic and social underpinnings that uphold and spread the advantages of democracy; partnership and solidarity existing among different actors on both local and national levels; and policies and projects in support of democratic governance being home grown and not imposed by foreign actors (Keuleers 2004). The Pacific governance agenda is more or less completely based on Western political and economic liberalism, and does not take into consideration that liberal democracies increasingly suffer from widening social inequalities, a deficit of political participation, and the vital importance of personal wealth in electoral results (Huffer 2005). Given political and civil rights, citizens have an opportunity to vigorously draw attention to common needs as well as to demand appropriate public action, but the degree to which governments respond depends on the pressure they come under (Sen 1997). Even if most Pacific Islanders have more independence than other groups of similar size in determining domestic policies as well as in international affairs (Crocombe 2001), information on the legislative agenda or draft bills is almost never available in advance, which impedes citizens' participation in the development process. Civil Society Organisations (CSOs) like churches, trade unions and NGOs can be effective in addressing democratic principles and mobilising the general public (Morgan 2005), but recruiting civil society into development planning and activities has proved to be difficult as many governments fail to recognise its value (Holland & Koloamatangi 2004). CSOs are relatively strong in PNG, Fiji, Samoa and Vanuatu, but in other states they hardly exist, except from a few church groups and recently established NGOs while "relations between NGOs and Pacific governments are routinely tense, as are relations between NGOs themselves" (Morgan 2005:9). Democracy and good governance cannot be imposed; and for a successful implementation of democratic ideals, the principles must be relevant and come from within, thence the only form of democracy that will prosper in the Pacific will be home grown (Henderson 2003).

6.1. Governance

Democratic governance relies on strong economic, social and political foundations. There is a need for sustainable growth, skills development, poverty reduction, democratic values, tolerance, a culture of trust and solidarity, protection of human rights, freedom of expression, and parliamentary elections (Keuleers 2004). The Pacific has a diverse record of governance. Lack of institutional capabilities and a legacy of inappropriate colonial structures have seriously impeded internal political integration and nation building, which in many cases has also been affected by absence of political will (AusAID 2003). Hence "good governance has always been a sensitive matter in any discussion on development" (Mellor & Jabes 2004:43).

Many Pacific states operate under systems inherited from England or France, but attempts to convert alien systems to countries with different customs and traditions often fail (Harris 2004). Island governance is very distinctive as islands are intimate communities (Shaw 2004), and great variations in state performance can be explained by enormous contrasts in the internal social structures of the various sub-regions (Reilly 2004). Modern governance structures coexist alongside the traditional governance systems in many Pacific states and the local communities' level of participation in the development process is correlated to "the compatibility of governance structures with local culture and institutions" (Mellor 2002:3).

One measure of states' weaknesses is their inability to reform themselves (Larmour 1996). Nauru and Solomon Islands are categorised as 'failed' states, and the Pacific's most unstable government is undoubtedly that of Nauru, where clan and personal rivalries dominates the political arena (Reilly 2004). However, whether developed or not, every country has weaknesses in governance, and the Western concept of liberal democracy is a relatively new concept and practice – especially in the Pacific, where a suitable model for equitable and effective governance has not had enough time to fully develop (Mellor & Jabes 2004), and evidence suggests that governance, political stability, democratic continuity, internal conflicts, and economic growth explain successes and failures of Pacific states (Reilly 2004). It is argued that the 'Pacific paradox' – why large amounts of aid have not produced the desired development – is due to lack of good governance (Henderson 2003); and the fact that the successors of the 'independence generation' of leaders were, for the most part, financial technocrats with limited political experience prior to undertaking leadership roles (Ross 2003). Poor governance is also commonly considered "a major constraint to economic development and hence poverty alleviation" (Keuleers 2004:3), but economic problems do not automatically lead to significant and desirable political change – even when a government faces international sanctions or denial of development aid (Burnell 2005). The existing practice is nevertheless to place priority on planning the economy, while environment, society, poverty and gender are regarded as secondary in the development process (Sanday, 2003), and a mix of economic, social, and ecological factors is therefore threatening human development in the South Pacific (Shaw 2004). This is resulting in high levels of poverty in several states, which has led to widespread political unrest and civil disturbances (Keuleers 2004). Low quality and quantity of public services is often caused by limited budget allocations that do not reach the needy due to bureaucratic and political corruption (Bardhan 2005, p. 10). A better standard of governance is required, but this need partly arises from a 'disconnection' between traditional and Western structures, hence "to be effective there needs to be a Pacific solution to the governance issue" (Henderson 2003:235).

State power is often diminished and contested at the community level, and many Pacific communities are unacquainted with governance and civic institutions on a national level (Storey 2005; Mellor 2002). Local governance has a crucial role to play in bridging populations with the state, as well as identification and delivery of key services. It therefore needs to be cross-sectoral and collaborative (Storey 2005). Pacific peoples are asserting their right to self-determination (Maclellan 2003), but ordinary citizens in island communities lack understanding of the concept of national governance (Mellor 2002), and have little confidence in the state's competences (Burnell 2005). Expectations of equitable governance are significant at the community level, while experience has kept expectations to central government structures comparatively low, and perceived limitations of superimposed models relate to lack of respect, limited understanding, lack of transparency, and lack of relevance to the beneficiaries (Whyte et al. 2002).

Growth, employment and development can help underpin government legitimacy and national unity, but if governments fail to perform, their domestic legitimacy is questioned and fragmentation pressures can increase (AusAID 2003). Political instability and flawed elections in the Pacific have provoked calls for institutional and procedural changes, and a number of states have passed legislation to encourage integrity in the political arena (Findlay 2003). The region has also taken a big step towards strengthening of the states through greater inter-regional cooperation, and has agreed upon a plan for sustainable development based on Pacific cultures and values. The 'Pacific Plan' is built on the four pillars of enhancing economic growth, sustainable development, good governance, and security through regionalism. Even if security is undertaken within a regional framework, this does not imply any limitation on national sovereignty, and it is not intended to replace national programs (PIFS 2005; for comparative purposes, see ASEAN Security Community, ASEAN 2003).

6.2. Corruption

Several sides of Pacific governance have been critiqued, but the roots and symptoms of corruption demonstrate a key deficiency (Huffer 2005), and lack of political leadership has resulted in reforms being "derailed by short-term political expediency and the self-interest of elites" (AusAID 2003:6). Corruption among politicians and bureaucrats has given the region a negative international reputation; as a centre of pornographic internet sites; money laundering in Vanuatu and Nauru; sales of citizenship in Nauru, Kiribati and PNG (Hughes 2004); fraudulent letters, opening of banking systems to organised crime, and tax evasion; and the resulting impact on national identity and democratic integrity has been strong (Findlay 2003). Further, political and economic instability has led to logging well above sustainable levels in the Solomon Islands (Chand 2002), and the Catholic bishop of Vanuatu claims that "profit has replaced the human condition as the goal for development in the region, with corruption as a consequence" (cited in Findlay 2003:115). The emergence of 'offshore' financial centres is highly significant for the social and economic health of the region, and the 'new economy' of information and communication technology has meant that (a) the region's relatively remote location is of less importance, and (b) the levels of crime-related activities and corruption have increased(Castle 1999).

Politicians and public officials are frequently under strong pressure from community leaders, and accept kickbacks, rank pulling, and misuse of public funds to benefit powerful clans (Mellor & Jabes 2004). Customary gift giving is a tradition within the clan, hence "Pacific Islanders tend to find Western definitions of corruption unconvincing in view of their own societies of communal dependence", and this perception is exploited by foreign interests who expose political leaders to corruption (Findlay 2003:115). On the local level, public officials with powers to issue permits and licences often charge extra. This culture is fast filtering into their work ethics, but applicants are often unwilling to pursue the matter as they fear they will come up against more severe hindrances in future requests (TI 2001). Nepotism is prevalent when officers or management are appointed, contracts for government services are awarded, and public services are outsourced. This means that who you are and who you know could easily become the norm in both public and private sectors – especially in the tight-knit Fijian societies (TI 2001). If politicians perceive their function as being delegates whose responsibility is to channel resources to their own factions, the result will be lower provision of public resources and thence lower development levels for the society as a whole (Reilly 2004).

Corruption undermines democratisation and leads to persistent public distrust, but can be dealt with by imposition of rules that people feel are appropriate and important (Huffer 2005). In many cases, corruption is tolerated because of custom and tradition, and terms like 'the Pacific way' and 'Asian values' are used to argue that corruption is a relatively minor problem and difficult to judge because of the culture of sharing within kin groups and communities (Mellor & Jabes 2004). Studies of 'Asian values' often disclose negative associations with authoritarianism and reduced personal freedom (King 2005:7), but in the context of development 'Asian values' often refers to the principle that democracy remains an unaffordable luxury until prosperity is achieved (Thompson 2001). Much of the contemporary understanding of 'Asian values' focuses on Confucianism, but using these values to justify authoritarianism is not especially Asian (Sen 1997), and the appeal to 'Asian values' should be seen as part of an effort to strengthen national identity (Thompson 2001), and provide equitable development in accordance with the distinct cultural characteristics of the region.

6.3. Culture

Developing countries that score high on governance can have different social structures, as well as substantively different governments; which indicates that even if culture is not necessarily the driving factor of development, a sound understanding of cultural and social values is essential for policy formation (Keuleers 2004). It is generally agreed upon that ethnicity is a construction of 'primordial' and 'created' factors based on clan, tribe and language, as well as social identities formed by colonialism and recent developments (Reilly 2004). Common social principles of the island cultures include: service to the family or clan; strong commitment to customary land ownership; and mutual responsibility amongst leaders and commoners. But the impact of globalisation and trade, aid, debt and investment policies from abroad challenge these values (Maclellan 2003). Western ideas of development fail to incorporate other cultural values and traditions, which is evident "in the emphasis placed on the deliberate construction of a civil society that is unrelated to and often outside Pacific cultural norms" (Huffer 2005:130). The West's emphasis on individual human rights conflicts with the Pacific's traditional concern for collective rights (Henderson 2003), and limited cultural understanding restricts the recognition of indigenous political conceptualisation (Huffer 2005). Indigenous people hold culture, tradition, norms and codes of conduct high, and consider everything born of the land and passed through generations as part of their culture (Gegeo & Watson-Gegeo 2001). Land is a source of livelihood, identity, power, authority and status; and issues of ownership, usage and tenure have led to many conflicts (Maclellan 2003). Traditional Melanesian societies maintained internal order "by a mixture of face-to-face interactions, multi-stranded relationships, common norms and values, self-help retaliation and gossip, shaming and supernatural sanctions" (Larmour 1996:3), and many contemporary Pacific Island constitutions permit the Councils of Chiefs to be in charge of contentious issues of tradition, culture, land and language (Henderson 2003).

Issues of ethnicity permeate the Pacific Islands (Ross, 2003:691), with Samoa, Tonga and Tuvalu being noted as occupying the most ethnically homogeneous end of the spectrum in world terms, and Melanesia at the heterogeneous end of the spectrum with "roughly a quarter of all the world's known languages" (Reilly 2004:480). Additionally, a growing proportion of Pacific peoples has multiple ethnicities and is therefore intimately exposed to new cultures and world views (Gray 2001). In the absence of a strong national identity, most people's primary loyalty is to their clan and kinship group, and such ethno-political groups often attempt to divert public goods towards the exclusive enrichment of their own members (Reilly 2004).

Marginalisation, inequalities and disputes in complex cultural settings challenge prospects for social interdependence and the strengthening of local communities, and without obvious and tangible benefits, societies tend to cling to traditional customs (Storey 2005; Hughes 2003). The political cultures of the Pacific are pervasive and resilient, and identification of cultural influences in national and sub-regional issues is crucial to ensure appropriate reforms (Morgan 2005).

7. Conclusions

Drawing together the various threads of this paper's considerations, a number of conclusions may be advanced. Development and aid are areas with many aspects and an array of 'right or wrong' policies, but in general, the various approaches can be divided into two broad categories; activities funded by external sources, and activities taken up by the people affected by lack of sustainable development and infrastructure otherwise provided by governments. The Pacific region has fallen behind in several areas, and faces many challenges to growth and prosperity, but will achieve higher levels of development if suitable economic and political policies are chosen. Being a major recipient of aid, policies often reflect the donors' agenda rather than accommodating the local needs, which in the long-run leads to dependency instead of innovation and growth. Aid bureaucracies' lack of cultural understanding and local conditions also impedes sound development of the recipient countries' resource base. Poverty is widespread in the Pacific, and as for many other developing countries, policymakers need to pay greater attention to the basic needs of disadvantaged people. This is unfortunately a slow process that often lacks tangible results.

The growth of the informal sector is a clear indicator that selected policies are inappropriate to serve the least developed segments of society, but also that disadvantaged people – given the opportunity – are both willing and able to better their own situation. The informal part of the economy needs regulation and workers' protection. This could be achieved with minimal adjustments of existing policies. By strengthening the informal sector, more people will be better able to financially support themselves, and their economic activities will have a positive effect on the economy as a whole. Another indicator of a poor income-producing domestic economic climate is the increasing number of migrant workers. Generally, they are not from the poorest families, and hence have a certain level of education, but are unable to find suitable work in their home countries. The money they remit to their families provides indispensable financial support, and in many cases both the receivers' spending and potential savings increase the development impact of remittances, hence the local communities can experience a 'trickle down' effect. However, there are also costs of migration to both the migrants' families and society as a whole – especially in the long run. Families experience loss of a loved one, who often is the breadwinner, but in many cases this is only temporarily. Local communities, on the other hand, often lose much needed skills and local knowledge – whether it is in trade, infrastructure or governance.

Growth of the informal economy and increased migration have proven to be effective means of alleviating poverty, but must not be allowed to be an excuse for governments and international aid providers not to implement policies better suitable for sound economic growth and development. Care should also be taken not to overlook the fact that monetary injections derived from informal sector activities and remittances are private transfers; and even if they can add value to a county's economic performance, these transfers can never replace all or parts of a government's responsibility to implement proper pro-growth development strategies. Aid for financing development will be necessary for the coming decades, but the funds should be directed towards sustainable development that empowers local people – an approach that not only places rights and responsibilities with those directly affected by limited growth and poor infrastructure, but also allows disadvantaged people to influence their own future as well as reclaim their dignity.

The main objective of aid is to promote economic growth and thereby lift people out of poverty, but the capability of aid to affect growth depends on its form and utilisation. This is where the efficiency in governance of aid utilisation assumes paramount importance. The Pacific states have received the highest developing country aid inflows per capita in the world, but these inflows have led to stagnation and recession by permitting counterproductive policies to persist. Formulation and implementation of economic policies depend greatly on the structure of political governance (whether democratic or autocratic), on the value system upon which a society is based and the expectations of leaders in such societies. So far, among the developing countries, societies that espouse 'Asian values' are deemed the most successful. It is not clear, however, the degree to which 'Asian values' are responsible for economic development or ethical behaviour. This remains a contested issue. It is also not clear that Asian values can be transplanted to the Pacific. The East Asian governance model is therefore not a suitable solution to improving conditions in the Pacific Islands. If values matter, then it is necessary to ask what is valued and how can this be used by the people themselves to improve their prospects for development and better governance. 'Pacific values' are worth harnessing for better governance through which development may proceed more successfully. Values, like ethnicities, are not static or impervious to change. 'Pacific values' may be subject to consolidation from many directions – including the Pacific diaspora internationally and special interest groups such as women or urban dwellers locally. A culture of positive development governance may grow if properly cultivated.

The picture that emerges from this study and its recommendations is as follows. Confidence in the government and social unity is essential for the functioning of democratic societies, but limited economic growth challenges the positive image of regional development that often is presented by governments and others. Differences in performance among the Pacific states are huge; and political instability, retarded investment, and corruption scandals undermine the peoples' confidence in their leaders, and have led to widespread demands for greater accountability. Governments are increasingly being forced to legitimate themselves by adapting more participatory governance structures, but it is imperative that Pacific governance be based on Pacific cultures and values, as any effort by the international community to force a state to adapt and integrate superimposed international principles to become democratic would be a contradiction of the very meaning of democracy. The international aid community should instead concentrate more on supporting Pacific CSOs – which are important guardians of civil rights but often are weak, lack local legitimacy, and have relatively unsatisfactory scorecards in influencing policy issues. Strengthening the CSOs would also have a positive effect on increasing corruption and cultural tensions. Public office has developed into an attractive opening for personal and group profit, and the result is poor management of public expenditure. Kinship plays a considerable role in all levels of society, and there is a tendency for public servants to exercise power for personal or family gain, or to favour colleagues, friends and relatives. Nevertheless, Pacific political ethics are vital in dealing with corruption and poor governance, as well as in taking into consideration civil, security, economic and social dimensions affecting people. This must be recognised by all parties involved – whether they are local, national, or international.

REFERENCES

Abbot, D. and Pollard, S. (2004) 'Hardship and poverty in the Pacific', Asian Development Bank *(ADB), Pacific Studies Series.* Manila: ADB

Adams, RH. and Page, J. (2003) 'International migration, remittances and poverty in developing countries', *World Bank Policy Research Working Paper 3179/2003,* viewed 28 October 2005, http://www.cfsinnovation.com/managed_documents/ adams_and_ page_2003.pdf

Allen, J. (2003) 'Voices of migrants in Asia: a panorama of perspectives', paper presented at the Regional Conference on Migration, Development and Pro-Poor Policy Choices in Asia, Dhaka 22-24 June, viewed 24 October 2005, http://www.livelihoods.org/ hot_topics/docs/Dhaka_CP_11.pdf

Andrade-Eekhoff, K. (2005) 'The untapped riches of remittances?' *Tracking the Economy,* 38 (4), p. 47.

ASEAN (2003) Declaration of ASEAN Concord II (Bali Concord II), viewed 23 November 2005, http://www.aseansec.org/15159.htm

Asian Development Bank (ADB) (2003) *Millennium Development Goals in the Pacific; relevance and progress.* Manila: Author.

AusAID (2003) *Papua New Guinea and the Pacific – a development perspective*, viewed 28 October 2005, http://www.ausaid.gov.au/publications/pdf/png_pacific_development.pdf Australian Council for Overseas Aid (ACFOA) (2002) *Australia & the Pacific. Update on current trends and issues.* Canberra:

Bardhan, P. (2005) 'Globalisation and rural poverty', *World Institute for Development Economics Research (WIDER), Research Paper No. 2005/30*, viewed 31 October 2005, http://www.wider.unu.edu/publications/rps/rps2005/rp2005-30.pdf Burnell, P. (2005) 'Democracy promotion: the elusive quest for grand strategies', viewed 31 October 2005, http://www.cdi.anu.edu.au/featured_articles/featured-articles_dowloads/CDINews-Jan05_DemocracyPromotion_Burnell.pdf

Caldwell, ZT. (2005) 'Is aid working for the poor?' viewed 31 October 2005, www.globalpolicy.org/socecon/develop/oda/2005/0919aidpoor.htm

Carling, J. (2005) 'Migrant remittances and development cooperation', *International Peace Research Institute Oslo (PRIO) Report 1/2005*, Oslo: PRIO

Castle, A. (1999) 'Money laundering in the Asia Pacific', *International Centre for Criminal Law Reform and Criminal Justice Policy, Asia Pacific money laundering flows and trends, Working Paper No. 2,* viewed 11 November 2005, http://www.icclr.law.ubc.ca/Publications/Reports/Paper2.PDF

Charmes, J (2000) 'Informal sector, poverty and gender; a review of empirical evidence', background paper for the World Development Report 2001, Women in informal employment: Globalising and Organising, viewed 25 October 200 http://www.wiego.org/papers/charmes3.pdf

Chami, R., Fullenkamp, C. and Jahjah, S. (2005) 'Are immigrant remittance flows a source of capital for development?', *The International Monetary Fund (IMF) Staff Papers,* 52 (1), pp. 55-81, viewed 28 October 2005, http://www.imf.org/External/Pubs/FT/staffp/2005/01/pdf/chami.pdf

Chand, S. (2002) 'Managing natural resources in the Pacific Islands', viewed 11 November 2005, http://apseg.anu.edu.au/pdf/ecdev/0802Satish.pdf

Chen, M.A., Jhabvala, R. and Lund, F. (2002) 'Supporting workers in the informal economy: a policy framework', *The International Labour Organization (ILO), Working Paper on the Informal Economy, Employment Sector 2002/2,* viewed 25 October 2005, http://www.wiego.org/papers/ilo_wp2.pdf

Commission on Human Security (CHS) (2003) *Human Security Now*, Washington DC: Communications Development Incorporated.

Connell, J. (2003) 'Regulation of space in the contemporary postcolonial Pacific city: Port Moresby and Suva', *Asia Pacific Viewpoint,* 44 (3), pp. 243-257.

Connell, J. and Brown, RPC. (2005) 'Remittances in the Pacific; an overview', Manila: Asian Development Bank.

Connell, J. and Conway, D. (2000) 'Migration and remittances in island microstates: a comparative perspective of the South Pacific and the Caribbean', *International Journal of Urban and Regional Research,* 24 (1), pp. 52-78.

Corbel, Y. (2004) 'Is the Pacific making progress towards development?' *Islands Business,* November 2004.

Crocombe, R.G. (2001) *The South Pacific*, Suva: Institute of Pacific Studies.

Easterly, W. (2003) 'Can foreign aid buy growth?' *Journal of Economic Perspectives,* 17 (3), pp. 23-48.

Erixon, F (2005), *Aid and development: will it work this time?* London: International Policy Network

Findlay, M (2003) 'The Pacific', *in Global Corruption Report 2003*, viewed 11 November 2005, http://www.globalcorruptionreport.org/download/gcr2003/12_Pacific_(Findlay).pdf

Firth, G. (2005) 'The impact of globalization on the Pacific Islands', briefing paper for the 2nd South-East Asia and the Pacific Subregional Tripartite Forum on Decent Work, Melbourne 5-8 April.

Gegeo, D.W. and Watson-Gegeo, KA. (2001) "How we know": Kwara'ae rural villagers doing indigenous epistemology', *The Contemporary Pacific*, 13 (1), pp. 55–88.

Gounder, R. and Xayavong, V. (2001) 'Globalisation and the island economies of the South Pacific', *United Nations University, World Institute for Development Economics*

Research, Discussion Paper No. 2001/41, viewed 26 October 2005, http://www.wider.unu.edu/publications/dps/dp2001-41.pdf

Gowricharn, R. (2004) 'More capital in Surinamese transnationalism', *Ethnic and Racial Studies,* 27 (4), pp. 607-621.

Gray, A. (2001) 'The definition and measurement of ethnicity, a Pacific perspective', viewed 11 November 2005, http://www.stats.govt.nz/NR/rdonlyres/9022A22E-6094-42AA-9087-7445D2945C6C/0/pacific_main.pdf

Griffith, P. (2004) 'Managing migration: a Southern perspective', *The Foreign Policy Centre,* viewed 10 October 2005, http://fpc.org.uk/articles/291

Harris, I. (2004) 'Activities of the Inter-Parliamentary Union', paper presented at the Conference on political culture, representation & electoral systems in the Pacific, Port Vila, 10-12 July, viewed 12. November 2005, http://www.cdi.anu.edu.au/CDIwebsite1998-004/asia_pacific/asia_downloads/Vila_ElectoralSysConf_paper_Harris_Jul04.pdf

Henderson , J. (2003) 'The future of democracy in Melanesia: what role for outside powers?' *Asia Pacific Viewpoint*, 44 (3), pp. 225–241.

Holland, M. and Koloamatangi, M. (2004) 'Governance, capacity and legitimacy: EPAs, EBA and the European Union's Pacific Regionalism after Cotonou, viewed 10 November 2005, http://www.otago.ac.nz/otagofps/fps2004/pdfs/Holland_Koloamatangi.pdf

Huffer, E. (2005) 'Governance, corruption, and ethics in the Pacific', *The Contemporary Pacific,* 17 (1), pp. 118-140.

Hughes, H. (2003) 'Aid has failed the Pacific', *The Centre for Independent Studies Issue Analysis*, 33 (7), viewed 26 October 2005, http://www.cis.org.au/IssueAnalysis/ia33/IA33.pdf

Hughes, H. (2004) 'The Pacific is viable!' *The Centre for Independent Studies, Issue Analysis,* no. 53, viewed 31 October 2005, http://www.cis.org.au/IssueAnalysis/ia53/IA53.htm

Keuleers, P. (2004) 'Governance in the Least Developed Countries in Asia and Pacific An assessment of the current situation', viewed 31 October 2005, http://regionalcentrebangkok.undp.or.th/documents/reports/GovernanceinLDCsinAP.pdf

King, P.N. (2005) 'Prognosis for sustainable consumption and production in Asia and the Pacific', viewed 19 November 2005, http://www.sages.unimelb.edu.au/research/workingpapers/pdf/wp2-05.pdf

Larmour, P. (1996) 'Research on governance in weak states in Melanesia', *State, Society and Governance in Melanesia,* viewed 12 November 2005, http://rspas.anu.edu.au/papers/melanesia/discussion_papers/larmour96_1.htm

Maclellan, N. (2003) 'Australian neo-colonialism in the Pacific: human rights implications', paper presented at the Castan Centre for Human Rights Law Conference "Human Rights 2003: The Year in Review", 4 December, Melbourne, viewed 12 November 2005, http://www.law.monash.edu.au/castancentre/events/2003/maclellan-paper.pdf

Maimbo, SM. (2005) 'Migrant Labor Remittances in the South Asia region', *Access Finance,* no. 6, viewed 13 October 2005, http://www1.worldbank.org/finance/html/accessfinance/article%202.htm

Mellor, T. (2002) 'Technical assistance for assessing community perspectives on governance in the Pacific', Asian Development Bank, The Pacific Division, viewed 31 October 2005, http://www.adb.org/Documents/TARs/REG/tar_oth36192.pdf

Morgan, M. (2005) 'Cultures of dominance: institutional and cultural influences on parliamentary politics in Melanesia', *State, Society and Governance in Melanesia Project, Discussion Paper 2005/2*, viewed 10 November 2005, http://rspas.anu.edu.au/papers/melanesia/discussion_papers/05_02_dp_morgan.pdf

Pacific Islands Forum Secretariat (PIFS) (2005) 'The Pacific plan for strengthening regional cooperation and integration', viewed 20 November 2005, http://pacificplan.org/artimages/The%20Pacific%20Plan.pdf

Puri, S. and Ritzema, T. (n.d.) 'Migrant worker remittances, micro-finance and the informal economy: prospects and issues', viewed 8 October 2005, http://www.ilo.org/public/english/employment/finance/download/wpap21.pdf

Rajan, RS. (2005) 'Financing development in the Asian and Pacific region: trends and linkages, viewed 14 November 2005, http://www.economics.adelaide.edu.au/staff/rrajan/pubs/financerajan.pdf

Ratha, D. (2003) 'Workers remittances: an important and stable source of external development finance', in Global Development Finance 2003, Striving for Stability in Development Finance, pp. 157-175, Washington: The International Bank for Reconstruction and Development / The World Bank.

Reddy, M., Naidu, V. and Mohanty, M. (2005) 'The urban informal sector in Fiji; results from a survey', Fijian Studies, 1 (1), pp. 127-154, viewed 4 November 2005, http://www.fijianstudies.org/dload/vol1no1/urban_informal_sector.pdf

Reilly, B. (2004) 'State functioning and state failure in the South Pacific', *Australian Journal of International Affairs*, 58 (4), pp. 479–493.

Ross, K. (2003) 'Globalization, governance and guns; some reflections on the South Pacific in the 1990s', *The Round table*, 372, pp. 687-696.

Sanday, R. (2003) 'Good governance the key to sustainable development: a conceptual framework', paper presented at the Development Research Symposium on Governance in Pacific States: Reassessing Roles and Remedies, Suva 29 September – 2 October.

Sen, A. (1997) 'Human rights and Asian values', paper presented at the Sixteenth Morgenthau Memorial Lecture on Ethics & Foreign Policy, New York: Carnegie Council on Ethics and International Affairs.

Shaw, TM. (2004) 'New regionalisms & prospects for sustainable island & ocean governance in the South Pacific at the start of the new millennium, viewed 27 October 2005, http://www.otago.ac.nz/otagofps/fps2004/pdfs/Shaw.pdf

Singh, CN. and Strickland, R. (1994) 'Sustainability, poverty and policy adjustment: from legacy to vision', finings and recommendations of the International Conference on Sustainable Development, Poverty Eradication and Macro/Micro Policy Adjustment, Winnipeg 2-4 December, viewed 16 October 2005, http://www.iisd.org/pdf/legacy.pdf

Skeldon, R. (2002) 'Migration and poverty', *Asia-Pacific Population Journal*, 17 (40), pp. 67-82, viewed 14 October 2005, http://www.unescap.org/esid/psis/population/journal/2002/Jour17-4-p6.pdf

Sobhan, R. (2004) 'A macro policy for poverty eradication through structural change', paper presented at the Expert Group on Development Issues and United Nations University World Institute for Development Economics Research Conference, Unlocking Human Potential: Linking the Informal and Formal Sectors, Helsinki, 17-18 September.

Storey, D. (2005) 'Urban governance in Pacific Island countries: advancing an overdue agenda', *State, Society and Governance in Melanesia, Discussion Paper 2005/7*, viewed

10 November 2005, http://rspas.anu.edu.au/papers/melanesia/discussion_papers/05_07_dp_storey.pdf

The International Labour Organization (ILO) (2000a), 'The informal sector', viewed 8 October 2005, http://www.ilo.org/public/english/region/asro/bangkok/feature/inf_sect.htm

The International Labour Organization (ILO) (2000b), 'Making the best of Globalisation: Migrant Worker Remittances and Micro-Finance', viewed 8 October, 2005, http://www.ilo.org/public/english/employment/finance/download/remitrept.pdf

The International Labour Organization (ILO) (2002), *Women and men in the informal sector: a statistical picture*, Geneva: Author.

The International Labour Organization (ILO) (2005) *Labour and social trends in Asia and the Pacific 2005,* Bangkok: Author.

The World Bank (2005), *World Development Report 2006; Equity and Development,* Washington: Author.

Thompson, M.R. (2001) 'Whatever happened to "Asian values"?', Journal of Democracy, 12 (4), pp. 154-165.

Transparency International (TI) (2001) National Integrity Systems, Country Study Report, Fiji, viewed 11 November 2005, http://www.transparency.org/activities/nat_integ_systems/dnld/fiji.pdf

United Nations, Department of Economic and Social Affairs (UNDESA) (2005a) *The Inequality Predicament; Report on the World Social Situation 2005,* New York: Author.

United Nations, Department of Economic and Social Affairs (UNDESA) (2005b) *World Economic and Social Survey 2005; Financing for Development*, New York: Author.

United Nations Development Programme (UNDP) (2005a), *Voices of the Least Developed Countries of Asia and the Pacific: Achieving the Millennium Development Goals through a Global Partnership.* New Delhi: Reed Elsevier India Private Limited.

United Nations Development Programme (UNDP) (2005b) *Human Development Report 2005*, New York: Author.

Usher, E. (2005) 'The Millennium Development Goals and migration', *International Organization for Migration (IOM) Research Series No. 20,* Geneva: IOM.

Whyte, J., Vatu, C., Kalontano, A. and Siwatibau, S. (2002) 'Gardening good governance in Pacific Island communitie; preliminary insights from Vanuatu', viewed 10 November 2005, http://www.devnet.org.nz/conf2002/papers/Whyte_Jenny_et_al.pdf

In: Development Problems and Prospects in Pacific Islands ISBN: 978-1-60021-793-7
Editors: B. C. Prasad, D. C. Roy, pp. 91-107

Chapter 7

E-GOVERNANCE IN THE PACIFIC ISLANDS: ENTRENCHING GOOD GOVERNANCE AND SUSTAINABLE DEVELOPMENT BY PROMOTING ICT STRATEGIES BASED ON THE RIGHT TO INFORMATION

Indra Jeet Mistry and Charmaine Rodrigues

"We are going through a historic transformation in the way we live, work, communicate and do business. We must do so not passively but as makers of our own destiny. Technology has produced the information age. Now it is up to all of us to build an Information Society."[1] (UN,2005).

1. INTRODUCTION

Many commentators have identified the Pacific Islands countries as being plagued by a diverse range of challenges - political insecurity, ethnic divisions, corruption, economic under-development and social inequality. Making these problems more difficult to tackle is the so-called 'tyranny of distance', the large physical distances and lack of communications infrastructure between the remote communities of the islands and their capitals.

In recent years, Information and Communications Technologies (ICT) have gained prominence for their potential to overcome the tyranny of distance, and in so doing, assist Pacific IslandS Governments to promote their common objectives of good governance and sustainable development, particularly by engaging more effectively with remote and/or rural populations. Indeed, ICTs offer a myriad of ways to connect people in remote locations to their capitals. Although more recent ICTs such as computers are not yet widely entrenched

---

[1] UN Secretary General, Kofi Annan, *Message to World Summit on Information Society*, Tunis 2005. http://www.itu.int/wsis/messages/annan.html.

throughout the Pacific, they are gaining traction and could be effectively coupled with older ICTs, such as radios, to great effect.

Recognising the enormous potential for ICTs in the Pacific – if utilised effectively – this paper seeks to raise awareness at this early stage of the importance of ensuring that any ICT strategy is underpinned by a recognition of the 'right to information' and its potential contribution to good governance and sustainability. By purposefully prioritising strategies that entrench the right to information – in particular, proactive disclosure strategies which use ICTs to put more government information into the public domain – ICTs could be used to bridge the governance divide in the Pacific and bring governments closer to their constituents.

2. What Is the Right to Information?

Different terminology has been used - freedom of information, access to information, the right to know - but fundamentally, the concept remains the same. At the heart of the right to information are three key principles:

- the right of the public to request access to information concerning their government's activities.
- the corresponding duty on the government to meet a request, unless specific, defined exemptions apply.
- the additional duty on the government to provide certain key information proactively - even in the absence of a request.

The right to information has been recognised by the United Nations General Assembly as far back as 1946, when it declared "*Freedom of Information is a fundamental human right and the touchstone for all freedoms to which the United Nations is consecrated*"[2]. Soon after, the right to information was given international legal status when it was enshrined in Article 19 of the International Covenant on Civil and Political Rights.[3] Over time, the right to information has been included in a number of regional human rights instruments, including the African Charter on Human and Peoples' Rights,[4] the American Convention on Human Rights[5] and the European Charter of Human Rights.[6] This has placed the right to information firmly within the body of universal human rights law.

In practice, effective implementation of the right to information requires governments to develop legislation, setting out the specific content of the right - such as who people can access information from, how, when and at what cost - and the duties on relevant bodies to provide information - including when they can legitimately refuse to provide information (see

[2] See UN General Assembly Resolution 59(1), 65th Plenary Meeting, 1946.

[3] This states: "Everyone has the right to freedom of opinion and expression; this right includes freedom to hold opinions without interference and *to seek, receive and impart information and ideas through any media and regardless of frontiers*." [emphasis added]

[4] See *A Right to Information*, Article 9(1), *African Charter on Human and Peoples' Rights*, OAU Doc. CAB/LEG/67/3 rev. 5, 21 I.L.M. 58 (1982), 27 June 1981.

[5] See *A Right to Information,* Article 13(1), *American Convention on Human Rights*, 1969, Costa Rica, OAS Treaty Series No. 36, 1144 U.N.T.S. 123.

[6] See *A Right to Information,* Article 11(1), *Charter of Fundamental Rights of the European Union*, 2000, Nice, Official Journal of the European Communities, C 364/1.

Annex 7.1 for details of best practice law-making principles that constitute an effective right to information law).

The Pacific Media and Communications Facility recently released a report – *Opportunities for Media and Communications in the Pacific* – that summarised the state of the right to information in the Pacific region.[7] Most notably, Papua New Guinea's constitution actually specifically entrenches the right to information,[8] although the Government has yet to develop separate right to information legislation. In Fiji, the Constitution explicitly requires the Government to enact legislation on freedom of information[9], but the then SDL Government had indicated its intention to table a Bill[10] as a priority, draft legislation has yet to be released. The only other Pacific Islands country that appears to have made moves to enact a right to information law is the Cook Islands, which earlier in 2005 had completed the drafting of its Official Information Bill which has since been forwarded to the Cabinet for consideration.

3. The Value of the Right to Information

As noted previously, the right to information imposes a duty on governments to respond to the inquiries of their constituents by providing information on request. It also requires governments to proactively disclose important information to the public, rather than simply conducting its activities in secret. Historically, the right to information was often understood in developing countries as more of an administrative, bureaucratic mechanism. However, experience in many developing countries over the last decade has shown that by empowering citizens with a tool that enables them to scrutinise their government's actions on a day-to-day basis, the right to information is a key mechanism for practically entrenching government transparency, accountability and public participation. Accordingly, an ICT strategy that co-opts the right to information can benefit governance and promote sustainable development in a number of ways.

3.1. Promoting Democratic Governance

The foundation of democracy is an informed constituency that is able to thoughtfully choose its representatives on the basis of the strength of their record and one that is able to hold their government accountable for the policies and decisions it promulgates. The right to

7 For more information see the Pacific Media and Communications Facility website at http://pmcf.muprivate.edu.au/index.php?id=798. See also CHRI's website at www.humanrightsinitaitive.org (click on Right to Information, International, Member States Laws & Papers).

8 Article 51 of the Constitution explicitly recognises the right of reasonable access to official documents, subject only to the need for such secrecy as is reasonably justifiable in a democratic society.

9 Article 30(1) of the Constitution includes the freedom to seek, receive and impart information and ideas as part of the right to freedom of expression. Article 174 explicitly requires that Parliament should enact a law to give members of the public rights of access to official documents of the Government and its agencies, as soon as practicable after the commencement of the Constitution.

10 Minister for Information Marieta Rigamoto announced at the end of September that the Government was drafting a Freedom of Information Bill which, along with the Public Records Act, would give citizens wider access to information held by the Government and its agencies. See http://www.fijitimes.com/story.aspx?id=29425 for more details.

information has a crucial role in ensuring that citizens are better informed about the people they are electing and their activities while in government. Democracy is enhanced when people meaningfully engage with their institutions of governance and form their judgments on the basis of facts and evidence, rather than just empty promises and meaningless political slogans. Where people do not have access to information, as has so often been the case in the Pacific Island states, voters will often fall back on ethnic, religious or geographic affiliations when choosing a candidate.

3.2. Supporting Participatory Development and Effective Service Delivery

In terms of promoting sustainable development, much of the failure of development strategies in the Pacific Islands to date is attributable to the fact that, for years, they were designed and implemented in a closed environment - between governments and donors and without the active involvement of the public. However, if governments are obliged to provide information to the public, then citizens can assess for themselves why they have not benefited from government development activities or even from basic service-delivery initiatives in such areas as health care provision and education. Armed with paper-based documentation, the public are in a better position to effectively lobby governments to ensure that services meet their community-specific needs and that money is spent appropriately.

Information empowers citizens and NGOs

The right to information offers a very practical means for individuals, civil society and even parliamentarians to engage more effectively in development activities and ensure that their rights are protected and their legitimate interests promoted. This has been particularly well-illustrated by environmental action groups, which have been very adept at using access to information legislation to expose and discourage anti-green government and/or donor-driven and/or private sector driven programmes.

For example, in 2002 in Uganda, Greenwatch Limited, an environmental NGO, used the open government clause in Article 41 of the Ugandan Constitution to obtain the release of a key document about a controversial dam project that the Ugandan Government and the World Bank had previously declined to release. The Ugandan High Court ordered the release of the document, whose very existence the Ugandan Government had denied during the court proceedings. A subsequent analysis of the document, commissioned by the International Rivers Network assessed that "Ugandans will pay hundreds of millions of dollars in excessive power payments if the World-Bank-financed Bujagali Dam proceeds according to plan." The project was consequently put on hold by the World Bank.[11]

3.3. Supports State-building and Promotes National Stability

Democracy and national stability are enhanced by policies of openness that engender greater public trust in their representatives. Importantly, enhancing people's trust in their government also goes some way to minimising the likelihood of conflict. In post-conflict

[11] *Ugandan Judge Orders Release of Key Document on Bujagali Dam*, 22 November 2002, http://www.freedominfo.org/ifti1102.htm#1 as at 22 July 2003.

development situations, the right to information can be especially crucial in the state-building process, such as that underway in Solomon Islands because openness and information-sharing contribute to national stability by establishing a two-way dialogue between citizens and the state, reducing distance between government and people and thereby combating feelings of alienation. Systems that enable people to be part of, and personally scrutinise, decision-making processes reduce citizens' feelings of powerlessness and weakens perceptions of exclusion or unfair advantage of one group over another.

3.4. Exposes Corruption

If implemented effectively, the right to information can act as a powerful deterrent of government corruption. In many Pacific states, corruption has eaten away at civil society's trust in the state's political and legal system and has greatly hindered economic development. In particular, corruption can destroy efforts at poverty reduction, creating a vicious circle where funds are often skimmed off by the state, which, in turn, deters crucial foreign investment and growth. However, an effective right to information regime can make it much harder for government officials to cover up their corrupt practices at all levels of government, and also works to expose poor policymaking. Notably, in 2004 of the ten countries scoring best in Transparency International's annual Corruption Perceptions Index, no fewer than eight had effective legislation enabling the public to see government files. In contrast, of the ten countries perceived to be the worst in terms of corruption, only one had access to information legislation in place.

Cracking down on welfare corruption in Delhi, India[12]

In India, poor citizens are given a ration card which entitles them to discounted rice and wheat. This is similar to some of the government subsidy programmes found in the Pacific. In the jurisdiction of Delhi, citizens used their the Right to Information Act to access records held by the private ration shop dealers responsible for administering the programme and found that the shops' owners had been siphoning off rations, while providing false records to the Government Food Department.

Through the right to information applications, citizens could see their ration record held by the Government and compare it to the record in their own ration book. Comparisons showed that the Government's records contained widespread falsifications. The campaign to open up the registers of ration shop dealers and the Government took two years and met with stiff resistance from Government and the private dealers – including death threats and physical attacks. However, at the end of the campaign, the Delhi Government has now agreed to proactively open up ration registers every month to enable citizens to regularly check their ration records. It is expected that this will substantially reduce economic losses to the Government from misdirected welfare and ensure proper benefits to the poorest in the community.

[12] *Look, How Fair Price Shops Clean Up Act*, Indian Express, February 24, 2005. See http://cities.expressindia.com/fullstory.php?newsid=118913.

3.5. Supports Equitable Economic Development and Investment-friendly Growth

In recent years, Pacific Islands states have struggled to attract significant levels of foreign investment in order to accelerate economic growth and development. The benefits from economic development have often not been equitably enjoyed by all citizens. However, a transparent government that is committed to right to information is obliged to provide good-quality economic and social data proactively, which will better inform government economic policy and decision-making. Openness about licensing regimes, awareness of concessions and permits and more accountable government decision-making processes will also bolster private and foreign investor confidence in the economy, encouraging long-term private investment and thereby boosting growth. By empowering smaller stakeholders to more effectively participate in the economy, the right to information can also help to ensure the economy grows in an equitable manner.

4. Pacific ICTs Strategies Should Prioritise the Promotion of the Right to Information

Work on the right to information in the Pacific region has been limited, but already there has been significant interest in utilising ICTs at last to offer to promote good governance and more sustainable and participatory development. ICTs offer an opportunity to finally address the 'tyranny of distance' which has plagued Pacific governance and development strategies for so long, by making geographic constraints redundant, providing remote communities with the means to access the 'information highway' to their capitals and the world beyond.

Nevertheless, although ICTs provide important tools to address the tyranny of distance, if they are to be utilised to maximum advantage in terms of promoting sustainable development and good governance in the Pacific Islands, it is strongly recommended that specific attention be paid at these early stages to ensuring that Pacific ICT strategies properly incorporate the promotion of the right to information.

4.1. A 'Proactive Disclosure' Approach

Ideally, the right to information should be underpinned by comprehensive legislation. However, in the Pacific, legislative processes have proven to be slow and unreliable – Fiji's Constitution *requires* the enactment of legislation but governments have yet to pass a right to information law seven years since the Constitution came into effect! Notably though, this does not mean that ICTs cannot still be used to entrench the right to information in practice to ensure that the benefits of the right can still be enjoyed by citizens of the Pacific Islands.

ICT strategies can be harnessed to prioritise the concept of 'proactive disclosure' – getting governments to routinely disclose and disseminate information into the public domain even in the absence of a specific request for it. Significantly, this emphasis on proactive disclosure would actually draw upon what is becoming an international trend. Early right to information laws – including the access laws passed by New Zealand[13] and Australia[14] in 1982 – focused heavily on the public's right to request specific information from the Government. However, over the last decade, newer right to information statutes have put greater emphasis on the principle of proactive disclosure, in recognition of the fact that if the right is really to be of assistance to the poorest and most disadvantaged, it should place as little burden on them as possible, and instead should actively provide them with information in order to facilitate their re-engagement with government.

Notably, if implemented with public participation objectives in mind, proactive disclosure activities can be a very cheap but effective way of interacting with citizens. The most notable examples of such initiatives are contained in the very strong Mexican *Transparency Law* passed in 2000, and the new Indian *Right to Information Act* passed in 2005 which both include proactive disclosure requirements requiring all public authorities to publish and disseminate more than 15 different categories of information, from basic information about departmental organisation structures and services, to detailed information about public tenders and contracts awarded and recipients of government concessions and subsidies. Most of this information is to be published on government websites – a clear interface between ICTs and the right to information with a view to promoting better governance.

5. Practical Ideas for Implementation

In the Pacific, the right to information has been so overlooked as a governance and development strategy that opportunities exist at all levels to incorporate the right into ICT activities and in so doing, to ensure that the ICTs activities undertaken by Pacific governments are the most appropriate and will most effectively promote good governance and participatory development in both the short and long term. A few areas for work that could be undertaken as an immediate priority are discussed below.

5.1. Developing a Coordinated Information and ICTs Policy

As noted above, although a right to information law is unlikely to be passed in the short term in most Pacific Islands countries, nonetheless, government information and ICT policies that promote proactive disclosure could offer a very good start towards this goal. Information and ICT policies can prioritise proactive disclosure as a means of providing a practical response to the public participation problems identified across the region. It is notable in this regard that many ICT strategies focus on using ICTs to promote better service delivery. While this is an important goal in and of itself, it overlooks the potential for ICT actually to promote broader democratic values and aims – such as transparency, accountability and participation – and instead reduces ICT to promoting only operational ends. This approach should be reconsidered.

---

[13] See http://www.legislation.govt.nz/libraries/contents/om_isapi.dll?clientID=1260365289&hitsperheading=on&infobase=pal_statutes.nfo&jump=a1982-156&softpage=DOC for a copy of the law.

[14] See http://www.scaleplus.law.gov.au/html/pasteact/0/58/top.htm for a copy of the law.

Information and ICT policies need more explicitly to recognise the potential for ICT to promote public participation in governance and development. The public needs to be recognised as not mere passive receivers of government services through web-based mechanisms, but as active partners who should be engaged and supported to interact with the government, most notably through ICT-based dissemination of relevant government information.

Refocusing Pacific ICT and information disclosure policies

In the last year, CHRI has been strongly encouraging many national governments in the Pacific as well as the Pacific Forum Secretariat to promote greater information disclosure, at a minimum via the internet. It was recognised early on that statutory-based information regimes were probably not viable in the short term, but that nonetheless, the people of the Pacific were entitled to have access to more information about who governed them, how and to what end. The Forum Secretariat has been encouraged to include the promotion of the right to information as an objective of the new Pacific Plan. It has also been encouraged to develop a Forum Secretariat Information Disclosure Policy, which would ensure that all except the most sensitive Secretariat documents were published on the Secretariat's website, for download and dissemination within Forum member states.

ICTs can provide effective strategies to deliver government information to remote communities in Pacific countries. However, ICTs have become synonymous with Internet and digital technology while many parts of the Pacific Islands still do not have access to electricity and a telephone line, let alone to a computer. In this context, it is important that ICT and Information Policies recognise the obvious – that ICTs in the Pacific include not only new computer-based e-governance initiatives, but also capture older technologies such as radios. Ideally, these technologies should *all* be utilised, as resources, capacity and geography permit.

In the Pacific, this would necessitate that any ICT strategy clearly recognise the important role that battery powered radios have played in terms of connecting up remote communities. To utilise current radio systems more effectively though, consideration should be given to using the radio more regularly as a cheap but effective method for communicating information on government policies and activities to the public. Special radio programmes updating communities on the development and implementation of key government policies and activities could be run by the government. For example, radio programmes could be developed to update communities on when provincial health service grants have been paid, so that members of the community can then know to question their service providers on what they are doing with the funds. Governments could also use the radio to announce national policies, such as the budget, and explain their specific objectives and likely impacts in simple terms.

Any Information and ICT Policies could also consider the development of community information hubs based around current ICT infrastructure. For example, many rural health clinics contain a radio that is used to link up the clinic with headquarters and other health clinics so that they can get advice from specialists and/or check diagnoses and/or for training purposes. However, health clinics are a community resource more generally and their radios could be considered similarly. Health clinic radios, their noticeboards and possibly even their computer infrastructure, could be utilised as information dissemination points for all members of the community (subject of course, to the needs of the health clinic). Even new ICT infrastructure should be recognised for the potential as information dissemination points. For example, in Solomon Islands the new PFNet system, which is focused on setting up computer-based "information kiosks" in rural areas, could be developed to ensure that those information kiosks allow quick access to key government information, by including sites in the list of favourites and/or by developing a new site – which could be used as the default page when the browser opens – that collects together all key government links.

5.2. Promoting More Participatory Governance

At the moment, there is a dearth of useful, up-to-date information in the Pacific about Pacific governments. Only a very small number of Pacific governments have websites that capture information about all government departments. More commonly, one or two departments may simply set up websites on their own, highlighting only their own work, and even in these cases, the websites are often not updated. This makes it extremely difficult even for citizens in the capital city to engage effectively with their government. Identifying who is responsible for what service or policy can be extremely difficult, while sending a fax or email to that person can be near impossible. Simple forms can be difficult to get hold of, unless a citizen is prepared to actually attend at the relevant department, while it can also be very difficult for people to find out about services and benefits to which they are entitled.

In this environment, ICT clearly need to be harnessed more effectively to promote simple, cheap and user-friendly access to governance information. Ideally, governments should prioritise as one of their first ICT initiatives the collection and dissemination of this information (see the box below for a list of the most essential information). The information could be relatively cheaply published on the internet, although obviously to ensure greater outreach, consideration could be given to using other ICT technologies such as radio, TV and newspapers.

Notably, even if the new governance information is initially provided on the internet, the usefulness of this form of dissemination should not be underestimated simply because many Pacific communities do not currently have good access to the internet. Any ICTs and Information Policies should recognise the importance of developing outreach partnerships so that new technologies can be utilised by existing networks for maximum effect. In the Pacific, the most obvious strategy in this regard is supporting – formally or informally – church and civil society groups who already have strong networks in rural areas to access the information on the web so that they can then disseminate it through their own channels.

Extending the Pacific Portal?

The University of the South Pacific and Institute of Justice and Applied Legal Studies (IJALS) are jointly developing an e-Governance portal. Known as the Pacific Portal, it is understood that the site will focus largely on ensuring the statistical and other data in specific sectors, namely education and health, are comprehensively and consistently collected and placed on the internet.

Notably, however, there is huge potential to extend the scope of the site to include basic government information from across the Pacific, and in so doing, to bring communities across and within Pacific Island Countries closer together. In 2004, CHRI suggested that the Portal could be broadened to include information on the duties, responsibilities and services provided by all levels of government and its departments (see Appendix 7.2 for more). It was suggested for example, that the Portal could include the following information (which of course, ideally should already be collected and published by member country governments):

- *A list of every government department, including:*
  - *the name and contact details of the responsible Minister*
  - *the name and contact details of the CEO/Permanent Secretary*
  - *the physical address and mailing of the department*
  - *a statement of the aims and objectives of the department*
  - *a chart/list setting out the organisational structure of the department and/or a directory of the departments public servants, at least to the level of Section Head (or the equivalent), including the total number of staff in the department broken down by levels and the pay scales applicable to each level*
  - *the services offered, schemes run, subsidy programmes implemented by the department; including any relevant copies of all policies, guidelines and forms*
  - *a description of the powers and duties of senior officers and the procedure to be followed in making decisions*
  - *an explanation of any departmental complaints mechanisms*
  - *a register of the types/categories of information/records the department holds and publishes and the procedure to be followed in obtaining information*
- *If resources permit, a list of every major public authority, such as the Reserve Bank, Office of the Ombudsman, Pubic Service Commission, etc.*
- *The Government's annual budget, including a breakdown by department and further breakdowns by line item if possible*
- *Regularly updated reports (quarterly if possible) about the disbursement of the Budget;*
- *The results of any Government audits and corresponding departmental explanations;*
- *Information about any Government inquiries/commissions, including copies of submissions and draft and final reports;*
- *Mechanisms for citizen participation, where they exist.*

5.3. Supporting More Effective (Decentralised) Service Delivery

A proactive disclosure-focused ICT strategy can also be targeted towards promoting more effective service delivery, in particular by facilitating more informed participation by communities in the operation and oversight of community services. In this context, it is notable that a number of Pacific Islands countries have chosen to pursue devolution or decentralisation strategies, with a view to bringing governance closer to communities. However, these strategies have been fraught with difficulty. Local level corruption is a major problem and effective public participation is still lacking. Making things worse, there is still often considerable confusion, not only among communities but also within government, regarding which department or level of government is responsible for providing what public services. This weakens accountability mechanisms.

As noted previously, however, at a more general level, ICTs could be used as an effective mechanism for proactively disclosing more information about what the government does and who does it. In terms of service delivery specifically, this means that ICTs could be used to disseminate information about how much money is to be spent on a community, what the money is to be spent on, over what period of time and by which department(s). Armed with this information, the public can start demanding more effective service-delivery from the various levels of governments. In fact, ICTs can provide a two-way channel of communication between governments and remote communities that empowers local citizens with real influence over decisions that affect their lives.

Using ICT to promote more effective delivery of education and health services

In the Pacific, health and education services have commonly been developed to local government bodies to implement. Monthly or quarterly grants are sent from the central government to the local/provincial government, which is supposed to administer it and report back on its expenditure. Unfortunately, however, it has been witnessed that that such arrangements have resulted in considerable leakage of funds, with little accountability as the various levels of government blame each other. The public has difficulty knowing who to hold responsible because they have little or no information on when the grant was to be paid, whether it was paid, how much it was for and what services they were supposed to get as a result. All they know is that government – at some or all levels – is not performing.

Using ICTs to proactively disclose more information to communities about government expenditure could be a key way of addressing this problem, as a case study from Uganda shows. In that country, despite the increases in education expenditure during the 1990s, a five-year survey found that 87% of all funds meant for primary schools throughout the country were being pocketed by bureaucrats. Shocked by these findings, the national government began to publicise details of monthly transfers of grants to districts through newspapers and the radio in order to curb the siphoning of funds. Primary schools were also required to display public notices on receipt of their funds.

Empowered with this information, parents could monitor the educational grant programme and make the local government accountable for education provision. In five years, the diversion of funds dropped massively from 80% to 20%, while enrolment more than doubled from 3.6 million to 6.9 million children. In this way, proactive disclosure of information concerning education funding, though a simple and inexpensive strategy, enforced greater local government accountability and ensured the proper use of taxpayers' money.[15]

[15] World Bank (2001), *World Development Report 2000-01: Attacking Poverty*, Oxford University Press, New York

6. Conclusion

ICTs now provide an opportunity to overcome physical boundaries and have been hailed as a solution to the Pacific Islands' chronic problems of governance. What they must do, as a matter of priority, however, is to deliver the immediate benefits of the right to information to Pacific citizens – most easily by helping governments to publish and disseminate a wide range of key government information proactively.

To date, in the Pacific Islands, the paucity of physical infrastructure between governments and their remote communities has made the delivery of government information near impossible. However, if ICT and right to information strategies are developed in a coordinated fashion, together they can be harnessed to open up channels of communication between Pacific Islands governments and their disparate populations, thereby not only narrowing the physical tyranny of distance but also bridging the divide that exists in terms of public trust, transparency and accountability.

Appendix 7.1. Key Principles Underpinning a Good Right to Information Law

Governments can grant access to information through executive orders, administrative guidelines and some have even entrenched Right to Information in their constitutions. Nevertheless, to ensure consistent application of simple, clear, agreed processes, Right to Information legislation is still essential. A number of basic principles that have evolved over time that should be enshrined in all access laws, most of which have been consistently endorsed by the UN, the Commonwealth, the Organisation of American States and the African Union[16]:

1. *Maximum Disclosure*: The value of access to information legislation comes from its importance in establishing a framework of open governance. This means that there should be a presumption in favour of access - bodies covered by the Act have an obligation to disclose information and every member of the public has a corresponding right to receive information. Any person should be able to access information, whether a citizen or not. All arms of Government should be covered – executive, judiciary and legislature – and private bodies should also be subject to the law, at least where the information requested affects people's rights. Bodies covered by the Act should also be required to publish and disseminate documents of general relevance proactively to the public, for example, on their structure, norms and functioning, the documents they hold, their finances, activities, any opportunities for consultation and the content of decisions/policies affecting the public.
2. *Minimum Exceptions:* The key aim of any exceptions to disclosure should be to protect and promote the public interest. The law should therefore not permit non-disclosure in order to simply protect government from embarrassment or the

[16] CHRI (2003), Open Sesame: Looking for the Right to Information in the Commonwealth" Chapter 2. See www.humanrightsinitiative.org.

exposure of wrongdoing. In line with the commitment to maximum disclosure, exemptions should be kept to an absolute minimum and should be narrowly drawn. Blanket exemptions for specific positions (eg. President) or bodies (eg. the Armed Services) should not be permitted. Even where exemptions are allowed, they should still ALL be subject to a blanket "public interest override", whereby a document which is presumed exempt under the Act should still be disclosed if the public interest in the specific case requires it.

3. *Simple Access Procedures:* A key test of an access law's effectiveness is the ease, inexpensiveness and promptness with which people seeking information are able to obtain it. The law should include clear and uncomplicated procedures that ensure quick responses at affordable fees. Applications should be simple and devised to ensure that the illiterate and/or impecunious are not in practice barred from utilising the law. Any fees that are imposed for gaining access should also not be so high as to deter potential applicants and should be limited only to cost recovery. The law should provide strict time limits for processing requests.

   All public bodies should be required to establish open, accessible internal systems for ensuring the public's right to receive information. Provisions should be included in the law which require that appropriate record-keeping and record management systems are in place to ensure the effective implementation of the law.

4. *Independent Appeals Mechanisms:* Effective enforcement provisions ensure the success of access legislation. Powerful independent and impartial bodies must be given the mandate to review refusals to disclose information and compel release. While internal appeals provide an inexpensive first opportunity for review of a decision, oversight by an umpire independent of government pressure is a major safeguard against administrative lethargy, indifference or intransigence and is particularly welcome where court-based remedies are slow, costly and uncertain. The fear of independent scrutiny ensures that exemption clauses are interpreted responsibly and citizens' requests are not unnecessarily obstructed. While the courts satisfy the first criteria of independence, they are notoriously slow and can be difficult to access for the common person.

   As such, in many jurisdictions, special independent oversight bodies have been set up to decide complaints of non-disclosure. They have been found to be a cheaper, more efficient alternative to courts and enjoy public confidence when they are robustly independent, well-funded and procedurally simple. Best practice supports the establishment of a dedicated Information Commission with a mandate to review refusals to disclose information, compel release and impose sanctions for non-compliance.

5. *Penalties:* The powers of oversight bodies should include a power to impose penalties. Without an option for sanctions, such as fines for delay or even imprisonment for wilful destruction of documents, there is no incentive for bodies subject to the Act to comply with its terms, as they will be aware that the worst that can happen is simply that they may eventually be required to disclose information.

   In the first instance, it is important to detail what activities will be considered offences under the Act, for example, unreasonable delay or withholding of information, knowing provision of incorrect information, concealment or falsification of records, wilful destruction of records without lawful authority, obstruction of the work of any public body under the Act and/or non-compliance with the Information Commissioner's orders. Once the offences are detailed, sanctions need to be available to punish the commission of offences. International best practice demonstrates that punishment for serious offences can include imprisonment, as well as substantial fines. Notably, fines need to be sufficiently large to act as a serious disincentive to bad behaviour.

6. *Monitoring and Promotion of Open Governance:* Many laws now include specific provisions empowering a specific body, such as an existing National Human Rights Commission or Ombudsman, or a newly-created Information Commissioner, to monitor and support the implementation of the Act. These bodies are often be empowered to develop Codes of Practice or Guidelines and are also usually required to submit annual reports to Parliament. Although not commonly included in early forms of right to information legislation, it is increasingly common to include provisions in the law itself mandating a body to promote the Act and the concept of open governance. Such provisions often specifically require that the government ensure that programmes are undertaken to educate the public and the officials responsible for administering the Act.

APPENDIX 7.2.

A Proposal to Extend the Pacific Governance Portal

1. The Pacific Governance Portal currently being developed by IJALS provides an exciting opportunity to extend the right to information to the people of the Pacific, despite the absence of a single right to information law in any Pacific country.

Value of the Right to Information

2. *It strengthens democracy*: The foundation of democracy is an informed constituency that is able to thoughtfully choose its representatives on the basis of the strength of their record and that is able to hold their government accountable for the policies and decisions it promulgates. The right to information has a crucial role in ensuring that citizens are better informed about the people they are electing and their activities while in government. Democracy is enhanced when people meaningfully engage with their institutions of governance and form their judgments on the basis of facts and evidence, rather than just empty promises and meaningless political slogans.
3. *It supports participatory development*: Much of the failure of development strategies to date is attributable to the fact that, for years, they were designed and implemented in a closed environment - between governments and donors and without the involvement of *people*. If governments are obligated to provide information, people can be empowered to more meaningfully determine their own development destinies. They can assess why development strategies have gone askew and press for changes to put development back on track.

4. *It is a proven anti-corruption tool*: In 2003, of the ten countries scoring best in Transparency International's annual Corruption Perceptions Index, no fewer than eight had effective legislation enabling the public to see government files. In contrast, of the ten countries perceived to be the worst in terms of corruption, not even one had a functioning access to information regime. The right to information increases transparency by opening up public and private decision-making processes to scrutiny.
5. *It supports economic development*: The right to information provides crucial support to the market-friendly, good governance principles of transparency and accountability. Markets, like governments, do not function well in secret. Openness encourages a political and economic environment more conducive to the free market tenets of 'perfect information' and 'perfect competition'. In turn, this results in stronger growth, not least because it encourages greater investor confidence. Economic equity is also conditional upon freely accessible information because a *right* to information ensures that information itself does not become just another commodity, to be cornered by a few for their sole benefit.
6. *It helps to reduce conflict*: Democracy and national stability are enhanced by policies of openness, which engender greater public trust in their representatives. Importantly, enhancing people's trust in their government goes some way to minimising the likelihood of conflict. Openness and information-sharing contribute to national stability by establishing a two-way dialogue between citizens and the state, reducing distance between government and people and thereby combating feelings of alienation. Systems that enable people to be part of, and personally scrutinise, decision-making processes reduce citizens' feelings of powerlessness and weaken perceptions of exclusion or unfair advantage of one group over another.

The Pacific Governance Portal and the Right to Information

7. The right to information is most commonly understood to refer to the right of the public to obtain access to government information upon request and the concomitant duty of government to ensure that systems are in place to facilitate the efficient exercise of that right. However, over the last decade, the right to information has come to more broadly capture the additional duty of governments to proactively provide the public with important and/or routine information, for which specific requests need not be made.
8. It is the second feature of the right to information – referred to for quick reference as "proactive disclosure" – that the PGP can be developed to address, even in the absence of right to information legislation. The PGP is currently focusing largely on ensuring the statistical and other data in specific sectors, namely education and health, is comprehensively and consistently collected and placed on the internet. However, considering the state of many Government websites in the Pacific, CHRI encouraged IJALS to consider adding an additional section to the PGP - as a matter of priority - which would enable the public to access basic government information.

9. Currently, all Commonwealth Pacific member states except Kiribati have Government Websites[17]. However, their content varies considerably. Solomon Islands for example, only has websites for the PMO and the Commerce Department. Conversely, Tonga has a relatively comprehensive website, with links to all Ministries, including contact details, summaries of their responsibilities and links to some key documents.
10. It would be a major contribution to the Pacific to equalise the access of Pacific people to information about their Governments by ensuring that all Pacific Government websites contain a minimum amount of information. The PGP provides a unique and timely mechanisms for achieving this objective. In keeping with international best practice in terms of proactive disclosure, the new Government Information Section of the PGP could include the following information:
    - *A list of every government department, including:*
        - *The name and contact details of the responsible Minister*
        - *The name and contact details of the CEO/Permanent Secretary*
        - *The physical address and mailing of the department*
        - *A statement of the aims and objectives of the department;*
        - *A chart/list setting out the organisatonal structure of the department and/or a directory of the departments public servants, at least to the level of Section Head (or the equivalent), including the total number of staff in the department broken down by levels and the pay scales applicable to each level*
        - *The services offered, schemes run, subsidy programmes implemented by the department; including any relevant copies of all policies, guidelines and forms;*
        - *A description of the powers and duties of senior officers and the procedure to be followed in making decisions;*
        - *An explanation of any departmental complaints mechanisms;*
        - *A register of the types/categories of information/records the department holds and publishes and the procedure to be followed in obtaining information;*
    - *If resources permit, a list of every major public authority, such as the Reserve Bank, Office of the Ombudsman, Pubic Service Commission, etc.*
    - *The Government's annual budget, including a breakdown by department and further breakdowns by line item if possible*
    - *Regularly updated reports (quarterly if possible) about the disbursement of the Budget;*
    - *The results of any Government audits and corresponding departmental explanations;*
    - *Information about any Government inquiries/commissions, including copies of submissions and draft and final reports;*
    - *Mechanisms for citizen participation, where they exist.*

[17] Fiji - www.fiji.gov.fj, Nauru - www.un.int/nauru; PNG - http://www.pngonline.gov.pg; Samoa - www.samoa.ws; Solomon Islands - www.commerce.gov.sb; Tonga - www.pmo.gov.to; Tuvalu - www.tuvaluislands.com;

11. Although this information will initially require a considerable amount of time to collect properly, the benefits in terms of more transparent and accessible governance in the Pacific would be enormous. Not only local citizens, but also people from throughout the region and even further afield would be able to interact more easily with Pacific governments. This could have particular benefits in terms of foreign investment. Once the initial collection was completed, updating the information would require less effort. Best practice requires updating every 6 months, but common practice sees government providing updates only annually or biennially.

Vanuatu - www.vanuatugovernment.gov.vu.

In: Development Problems and Prospects in Pacific Islands ISBN: 978-1-60021-793-7
Editors: B. C. Prasad, D. C. Roy, pp. 109-120

Chapter 8

ICT-BASED DISTANCE EDUCATION FOR GENDER EQUALITY IN THE PACIFIC ISLANDS

Pramila Devi

1. INTRODUCTION

Information and communication technology (ICT), which refers to the convergence of telecommunication networks and personal computer technology, has the capacity to reach across the globe to those connected to the Internet. The increasing use of ICT in different sectors is seen as having impact on all spheres of life. The use of ICT is also seen as opening up "new opportunities for developing countries to harness these technologies and services to serve their development goals" (Mansell & Wehn 1998, 1). In order to take advantage of the ICT, developing countries are encouraged to exploit the potential of ICT by investing in their infrastructure and training (Mansell & Wehn, 1998; and Khan 2005). If harnessed appropriately by developing countries, ICT posseses potential for narrowing the divides, including gender gap, threatening our communities. Recent international conferences and summits on gender issues, for example, also acknowledged the potential of ICT and encouraged women to use ICT to reap the benefits ICT has to offer. The ability of women in developing countries to take advantage of ICT to a large extent depends on access to ICT and women's educational and/or skills level to use ICT.

Education generally and distance education in particular are seen as one of the foundations of development, for developing countries to exploit the potential of ICT for learning (Mansell & Wehn 1998; Khan 2005). With the use of ICT-based modes of communication, distance education has potential to help the most marginalized to take part in development through its community-based knowledge networks (Khan 2005). In most developing countries, women are predominantly marginalized in terms of access to ICT infrastructure and skills levels. Distance education, however, with its capacity to reach out and provide a flexible learning environment, has huge potential for empowerment of women in developing countries.

While literature on the use of ICT in distance education has increased rapidly in the past decade, gender-based analysis in the field remains under researched. Though it has been substantiated that the use of ICT has a major role to play in bridging the gender gap, there is a need for more gender-based studies to determine the extent to which women use ICT in comparison to men. This paper, therefore, attempts to examine how females compare to male distance learners at the University of the South Pacific, in the use of email, WebCT-based homepages and discussion boards.

2. University of the South Pacific

The University of the South Pacific (USP) is a regional university governed by its 12 member countries scattered across 33 million square kilometers of the Pacific Ocean. These countries are Cook Islands, Fiji, Kiribati, Marshall Islands, Nauru, Niue, Samoa, Solomon Islands, Tokelau, Tonga, Tuvalu and Vanuatu. USP was established in 1968 and its distance education programme commenced only a few years later in 1971. Distance education at USP has since been seen as fulfilling USP's mission of serving its regional member communities. Distance education has always played a key role in the growth of the USP as a regional institution. The increase in the percentage of distance students at USP from 19% in 1971 to 59% in 2003 itself is a robust indication of the significance of distance education at USP. From its inception till early 2000, distance education at USP has been delivered predominantly through print mode. Since the implementation of USPNet in 2000, USP has also been using video broadcast to deliver courses to its regional student body. Video broadcast courses are supplemented by other ICT-based modes such as audio conferencing, video conferencing, email and the Web. WebCT, which supports homepages, mail, discussion boards and text chat facilities, is used as the computer conferencing tool to supplement video broadcast courses. With the use of such ICT modes, the distance education structure at USP is changing along with the global transformation in distance education.

3. Distance Education

Distance Education refers to education where instruction and communication between the teacher and learners are mediated through a mode of communication other than face-to-face. Due to distance education's sole reliance on modes of communication enabled by technology, distance education has always been in a stage of transition. Since ICT is used for creation, dissemination, storage and management of information, which is central to distance education, ICT is making a huge impact on distance education (Blurton 1999). The increasing use of ICT in distance education is seen as transforming distance education and leading it towards sustaining a more flexible learning environment. Based on the use of various modes of communication, Taylor (2001:40) categorized distance education into five generations or models. These are correspondence model, multimedia model, telelearning model, flexible learning model and intelligent flexible learning model.

The modes of communication studied in this paper fall within the framework of the fourth generation of distance education, the flexible learning model.

4. Flexible Learning Model

The flexible learning model or the fourth generation of distance education is seen as causing changes to distance education and it refers to the use of asynchronous modes of communication such as computer conferencing tools and email. Modes used in the flexible learning model allow distance learners to interact and communicate with their lecturer and peers, and access course materials and external resources at a place, time and pace convenient to them. While both synchronous and asynchronous modes allow distance learners flexibility in terms of place, only asynchronous modes provide flexibility in terms of time and pace. Flexibility in terms of place is a central concept in distance education regardless of the mode of communication used. Flexibility in studying from own place allows distance learners to carry on with their education without having to go to classrooms for face-to-face education. Though flexibility in terms of place is enabled by all modes of communication, including print, the use of ICT-based modes of communication enables synchronous/live delivery, which is a major structural change in distance education. In the case of communication between the lecturer and students and amongst students, a synchronous mode such as video conferencing enables live interaction, and email and computer conferencing tools, on the other hand, enable time-delayed interaction. Both the modes provide spontaneous and faster communication than in the print-based correspondence model.

Flexibility in terms of time and pace is fostered by the use of asynchronous ICT-based modes of communication. Flexibility in terms of time allows distance learners to access course materials and external resources, and communicate with their lecturer and peers at a time convenient to them (Blurton 1999; Harasim 1990). Flexibility in time also allows distance learners the time to read; understand; and refer to the original information before providing their response (Collis 1996; Harasim 1990; Harasim et al 1996). Similar to flexibility in time, flexibility in terms of pace also allows distance learners to read, understand, respond and study at their own pace. Studying at own pace is also seen to have advantage for learners with special needs and non-English speakers (Harasim, et al 1996, Mason 1998). It allows learners with special needs time to respond at their own pace. An ICT-based mode such as computer conferencing encourages and allows flexibility in terms of time and pace.

5. Learning Environment

In addition, flexibility in terms of time and pace enabled by the use of ICT-based asynchronous modes also create provision for a more customized and personalized learning environment. Individuals learn differently. Since learners think and perceive differently, learning styles and theories can incorporate ICT-based modes to design instructions for a flexible learning environment. One of the learning styles is the experiential learning model developed by Kolb (1984, 1993), which is based on cognitive constructivism and characterizes learners into four types; divergers, assimilators, convergers and accommodators. Kolb's claim that the four types of learners learn differently can duly be embedded into course design for ICT-based modes of communication to provide a more personalized learning environment for distance learners based on the types characterized by Kolb.

One of the commonly used models for ICT-based learning environment is constructivism, which refers to active construction of meaning/knowledge either individually or socially. With the use of ICT, information to verify original source is faster and more accessible. An individual learner, for example, reads information on the discussion board and/or email, which he/she does not agree with, searches for more information and may even check the original source of the information before responding to it. Learning is faster and information is more accessible with the use of ICT-based modes. ICT-based modes with provision for synchronous and asynchronous interaction applied to constructivist principles would foster a flexible learning environment in terms of accessing information at a place, time and pace convenient to the individual learner. Secondly, social constructivism places emphasis on interaction between "changing social conditions and the biological substrata of behavior" (Vygotsky 1978, 123). The concept of zone of proximal development developed by (Vygotsky 1978) refers to the importance of interaction with others. By zone of proximal development, Vygotsky means the distance between the "actual developmental level as determined by independent problem solving and the level of potential development as determined through problem solving under adult guidance or in collaboration with more capable peers" (Vygotsky 1978, 86).

ICT can play a crucial role in learning if the principles of learning styles and theories are embedded into the mode of communication being used. ICT allows creation of an environment of conflict such as group discussions and debates, which also reflects the principles of constructivism. According to constructivism, learners learn by constructing knowledge, which takes place as a result of sharing ideas and debating with others. Secondly, attempts have been made to create more personalized curriculum using the social inquiry teaching model based on social cognitive theory of Vygotsky. Design to suit students' needs based on students' social characteristics, communication styles, personality, cognitive ability, linguistic styles and academic background can be created. Therefore, a flexible learning environment can also accommodate the needs of women learners.

6. Gender and Distance Education

Gender difference among distance education students is a global issue (Taplin & Jegede 2001) and the South Pacific region is no exception. A study by Bolabola and Wah (1995) also shows the existence of gender disparities. They found that in a Melanesian society like Fiji, the enrolment number of women in distance education was low and the rate of attrition was high. This study further supports the view by Tavola (2000) and Leckie (2000) that gender disparity exist from the primary school level. Gender disparity is even embedded into school curriculum, which is reflected in the type of subjects studied by boys and girls. Girls predominantly study subjects, that lead them towards service providing careers such as nursing and teaching. Girls' enrolment numbers in subjects such as science and technology have predominantly been low. Whether the use of ICT will change this pattern is debatable: few studies in developing countries compare the use of ICT by male and female learners.

A recent paper by Williams (2001) claimed that the use of ICT in the South Pacific revealed that if available ICT made a positive impact on the welfare of women and the greater community. Williams's study, therefore, "dispelled the view that women might feel uncomfortable using new technology" (Williams 2001, 10). Though the Williams study revealed access to ICT as one of the drawbacks, it also revealed a positive attitude towards the use of ICT by women. This leads to the research question to be posed in this study *to what extent do female distance learners use email and WebCT compared to male distance learners at USP?*

7. Research Design

The number of female students at USP has recently been increasing. Table 8.1 shows that the percentage of female students at USP has increased from 43% in 1994 to 52% in 2003. This indicates a significant increase.

With the increase in the percentage of female students at USP, as shown in Table 1, the percentage of female distance students also shows a constant increase. The percentage of female students studying through distance increased from 47% in 1997 to 55% in 2003 (table 8.2)

Table 8.1. Percentage of Female Students at USP from 1994 to 2003

	1994	1995	1996	1997	1998	1999	2000	2001	2002	2003
Female %	43	44	44	45	46	47	48	49	50	52

Table 8.2. Gender Breakdown of USP Distance Students between 1998 and 2003

	Female	Male	Total	Percentage Female
1998	2395	2722	5117	47 %
1999	1834	1895	3729	49 %
2000	2145	2059	4204	51 %
2001	2209	2088	4297	51 %
2002	2540	2182	4722	54 %
2003	4991	4118	9109	55 %

Table 8.3. Gender breakdown of Fiji-based distance students between 1998 and 2003

Fiji	Female	Male	Total	Percentage Female
1998	1447	1461	2908	50%
1999	1351	1338	2689	50%
2000	1481	1370	2851	52%
2001	1468	1290	2758	53%
2002	1777	1467	3244	55%
2003	3096	2162	5258	59%

Table 8.4. Gender breakdown of Fiji-based respondents

	Male	Female	Total
Number	72	77	149
Percentage	48%	52%	100%

Furthermore, Table 8.3 shows the percentage of females studying through the Fiji-based Centres. While the reason for a high percentage of female distance learners enrolled through Fiji-based centres is not clear, Table 8.3 apparently states that more female than male students enrolled through distance mode.

The data used in this paper is derived mainly through a survey questionnaire and supplemented by data compiled from interviews. Six out of ten video broadcast courses offered in Semester I, 2003 were selected for this study. The survey was distributed to 292 distance students across the 12 USP member countries. A total of 195 students responded and 149 (76%) of the respondents were enrolled through the three Fiji Centres. For the purpose of this paper, only responses from 149 Fiji-based respondents are analysed. Table 8.4 provides the female (52%) and male (48%) breakdown of Fiji centre based survey respondents.

In addition, a total of 59 Fiji-based distance learners was interviewed of which 29 were females. Most of the interviews were focus group based with semi-structured interviews. The interviews were transcribed and analysed according to the thematic analysis technique.

8. Survey Respondents Profile

The data in Table 8.5 reveals that computer science and physics courses have fewer female respondents than male. This pattern of a high percentage of males than females in computer science and physics courses can be explained by the fact that these courses traditionally represent a male dominated field of study.

Table 8.5. Gender breakdown of Fiji-based respondents per course

	Total (N)	Male (N)	Female (N)	Female (%)
Computer Science	41	24	17	41%
Education	67	25	42	63%
Geography	14	7	7	50%
Physics	20	14	6	30%
Sociology	7	2	5	71%

In A similar manner, a high percentage of female respondents in the education course can be explained by the fact that education courses are compulsory for the teacher training programme and teaching has been one of the professions with a high percentage of females. The geography and sociology courses also show a similar pattern. Though the numbers in geography and sociology courses are smaller compared to other courses, geography is also a teaching subject in Fiji schools. Sociology, on the other hand, is not a teaching subject but normally attracts more females than males. The pattern shown in Table 8.5 is also reflected in the course-based analysis and discussion of the study findings, which is discussed according to the two ICT-based attributes, flexibility and interaction.

9. Study Findings

The analysis of survey and interview data suggests the emergence of four themes; flexibility, interaction, limited access to the Internet and inappropriate pedagogical design.

Table 8.6 shows that 83% of male and 82% of female respondents from the computer science course used email to contact their lecturer. The data does not show any significant difference between the extent to which males and females used email to contact their lecturer. In the case of the use of email to peers, the percentage of female respondents in the computer science course shows the same 82% as email to lecturer but more males (88%) used email to contact peers than to contact lecturer. Unlike the use of email to the lecturer and peers, email to friends/relatives shows an opposite pattern. All 17 (100%) female respondents used email to communicate with friends/relatives while only 83% of the males used email to contact friends/relatives. Results for the computer science course clearly suggest that despite computer science being traditionally a male dominated field, females not only equally used email to contact the lecturer, peers and friends/relatives but a high percentage of women respondents used email for the three purposes. Unlike the overall high percentage of usage of email by computer science respondents, the percentage of education respondents is not only low but below 50%. The response rate for the education course was low for a couple of reasons. First, the education course students mostly viewed recorded lectures on Saturdays during a 3-hour session. The face-to-face meeting on Saturdays may be one of the reasons for low interest in the use of email for interaction. Secondly, a majority of education students were mature working (teachers) students who only attended the Saturday sessions. Access to the Internet could also be one of the reasons. Despite that the education course had low response and had more females than males, the data shows that a higher percentage of female than male respondents used email to contact the lecturer, peers and friends/relatives. Geography course, which had an equal number of male and female respondents, shows that higher percentages of males than females used email to communicate with their lecturer and peers. Physics, which has traditionally been a male dominated field like computer science, shows higher percentage of females than males used email to contact their lecturer, peers and friends/relatives. This pattern could be explained by predominantly younger and full time students enrolled in the Physics course. Full time students accessed the Internet during the day and obviously had more access hours compared to working students who booked for limited available time after hours. Sociology course results show the same percentage of male and female respondents used email to contact their lecturer but more females than males used email to communicate with peers and friends/relatives. Results suggest female respondents used email equally to if not higher than males.

Table 8.7 provides a gender breakdown of the use of WebCT homepages per course. Computer science course results show that the percentage of female respondents for the use of WebCT-based homepages is the same as the use of email. The percentage of male respondents, however, is much higher (96%) for the use of WebCT-based homepages.

Table 8.6. Gender breakdown of the use of email per course

Use of email either 'always' 'usually' 'sometimes'			Email to lecturer	Email to peers	Email to friends/relatives
Computer Science	Male	24	20 (83 %)	21 (88 %)	20 (83 %)
	Female	17	14 (82 %)	14 (82 %)	17 (100 %)
Education	Male	25	4 (16 %)	5 (20 %)	8 (32 %)
	Female	42	16 (38 %)	15 (36 %)	19 (45 %)
Geography	Male	7	6 (86 %)	4 (57 %)	3 (43 %)
	Female	7	4 (57 %)	2 (29 %)	3 (43 %)
Physics	Male	14	9 (64 %)	8 (57 %)	8 (57 %)
	Female	6	5 (83 %)	5 (83 %)	6 (100 %)
Sociology	Male	2	2 (100 %)	0	1 (50 %)
	Female	5	5 (100 %)	5 (100 %)	5 (100 %)

Table 8.7. Gender breakdown of the use of WebCT-based homepages per course

Use of WebCT-based homepages either 'always' 'usually' 'sometimes'			WebCT-based homepages
Computer Science	Male	24	23 (96 %)
	Female	17	14 (82 %)
Education	Male	25	11 (44 %)
	Female	42	25 (60 %)
Geography	Male	7	7 (100 %)
	Female	7	5 (71 %)
Physics	Male	14	8 (57 %)
	Female	6	5 (83 %)
Sociology	Male	2	2 (100 %)
	Female	5	5 (100 %)

The education course also shows a difference in the male and female percentages, female respondents being more (60%) than males (44%). The relatively high percentage of respondents in the education course for the use of WebCT-based homepages than the use of email reflects flexibility in access to course materials, and course related information and tips on the WebCT-based homepages. The data from the geography course shows that all seven male respondents used WebCT-based homepages and five of the seven females. Though the percentage of female respondents (71%) who used WebCT-based homepages is less than males (100%), it is more than the percentage of female respondents' use of email to contact their lecturer, peers and friends/relatives. Unlike other courses, responses from physics show an opposite pattern. Though the physics course had more males than females, the percentage of female respondents (83%) is much higher than males (57%) for the use of WebCT-based homepages. In the sociology course, all seven (2 male and 5 female) respondents used WebCT-based homepages.

The WebCT-based homepages created flexibility by making course materials and other course related information available to distance learners. This is further supported by the interview data. Results clearly reveal that female students interviewed used WebCT-based homepages to retrieve notes and course related information:

> "I download notes and email. I read messages on discussion boards but never replied. I check for assignment due and other related notices and tips."
> "I mostly use it for lecture notes. It is useful but sometimes the access is slow.
> "I have also used WebCT for downloading notes, assignments and about tests. But I have not sent email to the lecturer. I have sent email to other students in Suva on campus regarding solution for problems.
> "We get exercises through WebCT. There are good tips too about assignments.

Results in Table 8.8 show a higher percentage of female respondents (82%) than males (79%) used WebCT-based discussion boards for reading messages. The percentage of females who used WebCT-based discussion boards to read messages is the same as those who used WebCT-based homepages. This suggests that female respondents use technology more to retrieve or access information rather than for interaction purposes. This is also supported by the high percentage of male respondents' use of WebCT-based discussion boards to respond to their lecturer and peers, and post new messages.

Table 8.8 Gender breakdown of the use of WebCT-based discussion per course

Use of WebCT-based discussion boards either 'always' 'usually' 'sometimes'			Read messages	Respond to messages by lecturer	Respond to messages by peers	Post new messages
Computer Science	Male	24	19 (79 %)	15 (63 %)	16 (67 %)	16 (67 %)
	Female	17	14 (82 %)	8 (47 %)	8 (47 %)	9 (53 %)
Education	Male	25	7 (28 %)	4 (16 %)	4 (16 %)	3 (12 %)
	Female	42	24 (57 %)	12 (29 %)	10 (24 %)	7 (17 %)
Geography	Male	7	6 (86 %)	2 (29 %)	1 (14 %)	1 (14 %)
	Female	7	4 (57 %)	2 (29 %)	1 (14 %)	1 (14 %)
Physics	Male	14	9 (64 %)	7 (50 %)	8 (57 %)	7 (100 %)
	Female	6	6 (100 %)	5 (83 %)	5 (83 %)	5 (71 %)
Sociology	Male	2	2 (100 %)	1 (50 %)	1 (50 %)	1 (50 %)
	Female	5	5 (100 %)	5 (100 %)	5 (100 %)	4 (80 %)

Results from the education course also show a similar pattern. Female respondents had an edge over males in the use of WebCT-based discussion boards to respond and post new messages but females show significantly higher percentages in the use of WebCT-based discussion boards to read messages. While the percentage of females in the geography course for the use of WebCT-based discussion boards to read is the same as that of the education course, a higher percentage of males in the geography course used WebCT-based discussion boards to read messages. The use of WebCT-based discussion boards to respond to the lecturer and peers, and post new messages does not show any gender-based differences. Similar to the use of WebCT-based homepages, for the use of WebCT-based discussion boards for all purposes except to post new messages, females have a higher percentage use than males. However, though lower than male respondents, females had 71% usage for posting new messages. Sociology course results too show that percentage of females using WebCT-based discussion boards to read, respond and post new messages is higher than or equal to males. Therefore, the data clearly suggest that females do use WebCT to the same extent as males.

The fact that students normally used WebCT for accessing information and not for interacting and communicating with their lecturer or peers is also supported by the interview data. Some of the interview responses were as follows:

> "I normally read the messages but do not post myself
> "I do read other information on the WebCT but do not get enough time to use WebCT-based discussion boards. We teach and can come here only after school and in the weekends."
> "We just access WebCT for notes and tips. Access at the Centre is not available all the time. We get limited time so it is not possible to spend time writing on it.
> "If they opened in the evenings and on Saturday afternoons, we would access WebCT.

These responses suggest that female distance learners faced the problem of limited access to WebCT and/or personal computers at their regional centre. Some even mentioned that they would have made more use of the WebCT-based modes if access was not a problem. Secondly, the sociology course, which allocated marks for online participation, had a higher percentage of participation than other courses. Some felt that they had to contribute because their participation was assessed:

> "I have not posted an original one but responded to others. I did in almost every unit. There is 10% mark for that so you have to do it.
> "We have to read messages and send as well because there is mark for that".

Sociology students were also given topics to discuss through WebCT-based discussion boards and their lecturer and tutor occasionally made comments to generate discussion and debate. In other courses, students used WebCT-based discussion boards voluntarily.

10. Conclusion

The study findings indicate that there is no significant difference between the extent to which female and male distance learners at USP use email, and WebCT homepages and discussion boards. Results suggest that both, female and male distance learners found ICT modes created a flexible and interactive learning environment for them. The data also suggest that the extent to which ICT modes enhanced flexibility and interaction for distance learners varied from course to course. Two key factors seen to be influencing this pattern were limited access to the Internet and the lack of appropriate pedagogical design. Since a majority of distance learners accessed Internet through their regional centres, they felt restricted by the limited hours of access to the Internet at their centres. Secondly, sociology course which had assigned online activities for students shows that students used ICT modes more for productive interaction. Students in other courses used ICT-based modes on a volunteer basis for social and other course related interaction.

Despite the drawbacks, female student response shows a positive attitude towards the use of ICT-based modes. The findings also strengthens Williams's (2001) study that if available ICT makes a positive impact on the welfare of women. The ability of female students to use email and WebCT tools to the same extent as male students suggests that ICT fosters a flexible and interactive learning environment for female distance learners, which further suggest that with access to ICT and appropriate design women can benefit from a more customized and personalized learning environment.

Apart from providing a suitable learning environment, ICT-based distance education provides and opportunity for the empowerment of women by upgrading their education and skills level. The use of ICT by female students revealed in this study and the claim that distance education has the capacity to reach out to most marginalized (Khan 2005), not only confirm that ICT has potential for the development of women but also that women have the ability to use ICT. The findings, therefore, support the view that if used appropriately, ICT has potential to narrow the gender gap.

REFERENCES

Anderson, T. (2003). Modes of Interaction in distance Education: Recent Developments and Research Questions. In M. Moore & W. Anderson (Eds.), *Handbook of Distance Education*. New Jersey: Lawrence Erlbaum Associates.

Bates, A. W. (1995). *Technology, Open Learning and Distance Education*. London: Routledge.

Blurton, C. (1999). New Directions in Education. In UNESCO (Ed.), *World Communication and Information 1999-2000 report UNESCO*. Paris: UNESCO.

Bolabola, C & Wah, R., (1995). *South Pacific Women in Distance Education*. Suva: University of the South Pacific and the commonwealth of Learning.

Collis, B. (1996). *Tele-learning in a digital World: The Future of Distance Learning*. London: International Thomson Computer Press.

Harasim, L. S. (1990). Online Education: An Environment for Collaboration and Intellectual Amplification. In L. Harasim (Ed.), *Online Education: Perspectives on a New Environment*. New York: Praeger.

Harasim, L. S., Hiltz, S., Teles, L., & Turoff, M. (1996). *Learning Networks: A Field Guide to Teaching and Learning Online*. Cambridge: MA. MIT Press.

Johnson, R., Kemp, E., Kemp, R., & Blakey, P. (2002). From Electronic Textbook to Multidimensional Learning Environment: Overcoming the Loneliness of the Distance Learner. Paper presented at the International Conference on Computers in Education, Auckland.

Kaye, A. (1990). Computer-Mediated Communication and Distance Education. In R. Mason et al (Eds.), *Mindweave: Communication, Computers and distance Education*. Oxford: Pergamon.

Khan, A. W. (2005). Distance Education for development. Keynote address delivered at ICDE International Conference on Open Learning and Distance Education, Indira Gandhi national Open University, New Delhi.

Leckie, J. (2000). Women in Post-Coup Fiji: Negotiating Work Through Old and New Realities. In A. H. Akram-Lodhi (Ed.), *Confronting Fiji Futures*. Canberra: Asia Pacific Press.

Mansell, R. & Wehn, U. (Eds) (1998) *Knowledge Societies: Information Technology for Sustainable Development*. Oxford: The UN Oxford University Press.

Mason, R. (1994). *Using Communications Media in Open and Flexible Learning.* London: Kogan Page.

Mason, R. (1998). *Globalising Education: trends and Applications.* London: Routledge.

Mason, R. & Kaye, T. (1990). Toward a New Paradigm for Distance Education. In L. Harasim (Ed.), *Online Education: Perspectives on a New Environment.* New York: Praeger.

Peters, O. (2000). Digital Learning Environment: New Possibilities and Opportunities. *International Review of Research in Open and Distance Learning,* 1(1).

Peters, O. (2003). Learning with New Media in Distance Education. In M. Moore & W. Anderson (Eds.), *Handbook of Distance Education.* New Jersey: Lawrence Erlbaum Associates.

Tavola, H. (2000). The Education of Women and Girls. In *Learning Together: directions for Education in the Fiji Islands*, Suva: Ministry of Education, Fiji.

Taylor, J. (2001). Fifth Generation Distance Education. *Higher Education Series,* Department of Education, Canberra, 40.

Williams, E. (2001). Women and ICTs in Open and Distance Learning in the South Pacific. Paper read at a symposium on the Barriers to Access to Information and Communication Technologies Encountered by Women in the Pacific Region for Open and Distance Learning, Wellington.

In: Development Problems and Prospects in Pacific Islands ISBN: 978-1-60021-793-7
Editors: B. C. Prasad, D. C. Roy, pp. 121-136

Chapter 9

PACIFIC ISLANDS PARLIAMENTARY WEBSITES: A PRELIMINARY SURVEY*

Graham Hassall

1. INTRODUCTION

This paper surveys the current stage of development of parliamentary websites of Pacific IslandS parliaments, in order to assess how well, or how closely, they are following globally accepted best practices. Parliaments play a vital role in democratic systems of government, as the principal law-making body and as principal body responsible on behalf of the citizenry for oversight of the executive branch of government. These fundamental roles are supplemented by others which are no less important in the steering of a society – particularly as the site of dialogue and debate amongst political leaders about future directions for society, reflective of peoples' hopes, concerns, and aspirations. A great deal of information management and communicative capacity is required by any parliament to fulfil these functions, and the new "Information and Communication Technologies" (ICTs) provided by computers and the internet have created powerful techniques for the provision of information, for information and knowledge management, and for assisting in decision-making processes in matters of law and public policy. Online parliaments are part of online Governments. As Kingham (2003) points out, ICTs have the potential to transform "representative democracy" into "participatory democracy".

A global survey published by the Inter-Parliamentary Union (IPU) in 2000 indicated that 29% of the Pacific Parliaments had websites – a proportion lower than in any other region. By November 2005, when the current survey was conducted, this figure had increased to approximately half of the parliaments in the Pacific region.[1] They have joined the rapidly

* The author acknowledges the research assistance of Amrita Nand.

[1] In addition to sites of national parliaments the regional organization Asia-Pacific Parliamentary Forum has a site (http://www.appf.org.pe/). Pacific Island members are Papua New Guinea, Fiji, Marshall Islands and Federated States of Micronesia: of these parliaments, only Fiji has a working link (as tested 8 October 2006).

emerging field of "eGovernance", or "Computer mediated information, services or dialogue between the Government and citizens". The IPU survey suggested that:

> Parliaments are well placed to take advantage of the Internet's ability to disseminate electronic documents quickly, cheaply and efficiently. Moreover, as new communication technologies make it possible to establish a closer relationship between citizens and their representatives, it is increasingly likely that the Internet's role in the political process will evolve beyond the mere dissemination of Information ...Information technology looks set to provide an electronic boost to democracy as unconstrained access to legislative information and the interactive nature of parliamentary Web sites make the legislative process and parliamentary proceedings more transparent and subject to closer public scrutiny". [2]

Globally, the rapid emergence of ICTs, with associated ideas about "the information society" and "the knowledge society" is also associated with preparations for, and outcomes of, the World Summit for the Information Society (Geneva 2003 and Tunis 2005). In the Pacific region these global processes are reflected in the Pacific Plan, and more specifically, the "Pacific Digital Strategy".[3]

ICTs are particularly suited to the needs of the island states through their ability to overcome the barriers of distance, and through such innovations as websites for Pacific parliaments hold considerable potential for enhancing governance processes and increasing public trust, particularly by increasing the transparency and accountability of this important democratic institution. Most fundamentally, websites can become an essential element in developing relations between the legislature and constituencies. In one sense, parliamentary websites simply continue traditions of parliamentary broadcasting (through radio and to a lesser extent through television). They have the potential to strengthen democratic processes by increasing access to public information, and facilitating public interest and debate, and increasing the potential for progress toward deliberative democracy. In particular, Parliamentary websites can do this through interactivity and public submissions. Websites can also promote better functioning of Parliament, through their assistance to MPs, administrative and research support staff, and parliamentary committees. They also promote greater interaction between parliament and other organs of state, particularly the government. In addition to the desirable outcomes referred to above, effective functioning of parliaments

---

[2] Inter-Parliamentary Union (2000). *Guidelines for the Content and Structure of Parliamentary Web Sites*. Geneva, Inter-Parliamentary Union. As expressed by Senator Cantero of the Republic of Chile: Societies once centralised are now configuring themselves as networks, closed systems are being prised open, time and space are becoming virtual, and diversity and pluralism enjoy new status. Wherever people live, connectivity and access to digital media are indispensable guarantees of equity and equality of opportunity for the citizen, who is clamouring for a new development ethos. Above and beyond digital infrastructure, it is time to change society's culture and mentality, to create a positive organisational environment which instills life into endogenous collegiality. The parliaments and geopolitical blocs that are quick to comprehend and unravel this process, converting passive awareness into active know-how, and which can extrapolate from individual and collective experiences for the good of society, as the philosopher and pedagogue Jean Piaget taught, are the ones that will stand to gain the most from the opportunities offered by the Information and Knowledge Society and its new paradigms." Cantero, C. "Parliaments in a Knowledge-Based Society." *Inter Parliamentary Union: http://www.ipu.org/english/pressdoc/news/13%2D3.htm.*

[3] www.pacificplan.org

and information sharing through enhanced use of ICTs in particular, can be regarded as a peace-building activity.[4]

2. Assessment of Pacific Parliamentary Websites

A number of initiatives are underway to improve the functioning of Pacific Island Parliaments. In 2001 the 1st Pacific Islands Speakers forum, meeting in Nuku'alofa, agreed on a set of 'best practices for Forum Island Countries Legislatures". Although these guidelines were mostly focused on the internal functioning of legislatures, Part V, which concerns law making processes, states that "Procedures for the preliminary examination of issues in proposed legislation should be adopted and published so that: (a) there is public exposure of issues, papers and consultation on major reforms including draft bills."[5] International agencies such as the Commonwealth Parliamentary Association and UNDP are also interested in fostering the progress of Parliaments.[6]

Table 9.1: urls for Pacific Island Parliaments

1. Commonwealth of the Northern Mariana Islands
   Legislature: http://www.cnmileg.gov.mp/
   senate: http://www.cnmileg.gov.mp/index.cfm?pageID=8
2. Federated States of Micronesia
   Congress - http://www.fsmcongress.fm/
3. Fiji - http://www.parliament.gov.fj/parliament/main/index.aspx
4. Palau: *House of Delegates* - http://oek.palaunet.com/HouseofDelegates/Househome.html
   House of the Senate http://oek.palaunet.com/Senate/senatehome.html
5. Papua New Guinea - http://www.parliament.gov.pg/
6. Tokelau - http://www.tokelau.org.nz/Government/governance.htm
7. Tonga - http://www.parliament.gov.to/
8. Samoa - http://www.parliament.gov.ws/
9. Guam - http://www.guamlegislature.com/

To date, the systematic development of websites by Pacific Parliaments has not been considered. The "Legislative Needs Assessment" project undertaken by UNDP to assist the development of the Parliaments of Fiji, Kiribati, Solomon Islands, Tonga, Tuvalu, and Vanuatu in 2000 did not include website development in its various country specific reports and recommendations.[7] A UNESCO survey of e-Government preparedness of Pacific Island

[4] Stauffacher, D., W. Drake, et al. (2005). *Information and Communication Technology for Peace: The Role of ICT in Preventing, Responding to and Recovering from Conflict.* New York, United Nations Information and Communication Technologies Task Force.

[5] 1st Pacific Island Speakers' Forum (2001). Guiding Principles of Best Practices for Forum Island Countries' Legislatures. Nuku'alofa, Tonga.

[6] See, for instance, United Nations. Department of Economic and Social Affairs (2003). *World Public Sector Report 2003: E-Government at the Crossroads*. New York, United Nations.

[7] See the reports online at http://regionalcentrepacific.undp.org.fj/HTML%20docs/Reports.html

Countries completed in 2002 does not make any reference to parliaments.[8] Pacific judicial institutions, in contrast, already collaborate extensively online through the Pacific Islands Legal Information Institute.[9] While UNESCO's "Information For All Programme" holds promise for great digital activity in the Pacific, there is as yet little policy development or scholarship concerning the digital presence of constitutional institutions in the Pacific region.[10]

As this scholarship does emerge, it will no doubt consider whether the introduction of parliamentary websites contributes to or ameliorates the "digital divide": do they bring all citizens closer to the democratic process? Or are they a technology that widens the gap between those with access to knowledge and power and those without? Spenneman has identified a "digital divide" not only between Pacific Island countries and more developed regions, but *between* and *within* them.[11]

In considering the contribution being made to enhanced democratic processes by parliamentary websites, a number of questions arise. Firstly, it is necessary to note which parliaments have websites and which do not. Additionally, it is useful to learn when websites were established, what features they support (whether they provide hansard, bills, acts, records of committee meetings, press releases, MP information, Rules of parliament, and a history of the parliament); what links they provide (such as to the Parliamentary library, to the other Pacific parliaments, to government sites, and to other parliamentary organizations), what level of interaction they offer to stakeholders (such as through a newsletter to subscribe to, an information service, or parliament's future calendar), and their level of sustainability (Who is the webmaster? Who is financing the site? How many "hits" are they getting? When were they last updated? How responsive are they to inquiries?). Additional questions need to be asked about which parliaments provide their members with email accounts, and which provide training for members to enhance their ITC skills.

By the end of 2006 nine Pacific Parliaments had an online presence in some form. These are: CMNI, Federated States of Micronesia, Fiji, Palau, Papua New Guinea, Tokelau, Tonga, and Samoa. Although Papua New Guinea is included in this list because a URL has been established (at http://www.parliament.gov.pg), it should be noted that no additional steps have been taken for the past several years. At least four other parliaments (Solomon Islands, Tuvalu, Vanuatu and New Caledonia) are known to also have website development projects.[12]

The Inter-Parliamentary Union,[13] the global peak organization for Parliaments, has in recent times established guidelines for the content and structure of parliamentary websites,[14] while a number of national and even sub-national parliaments have undertaken their own

---

[8] Zwimpfer Communications (2002). *Internet Infrastructure and e-Governance in Pacific Islands Countries. A Survey on the Development and Use of the Internet.* Wellington, UNESCO.

[9] www.paclii.org

[10] At search at http://www.austlii.edu.au/au/other/CompLRes/ yelded just three items concerning the digitization of law in the Pacific: "Computerizing the Law of PNG", "How to Sustain the Laws of FSM on the Net" and "Putting the Law of the South Pacific States on the Web".

[11] Spenneman, D. (2004). "Digital Divides in the Pacific Islands." *IT and Society* **1**(7): 46-65.

[12] The site for New Caledonia has been publicized (http://www.congress.nc) but was not in operation by the end of 2006.

[13] http://www.ipu.org

[14] Inter-Parliamentary Union (2000). *Guidelines for the Content and Structure of Parliamentary Web Sites*. Geneva, Inter-Parliamentary Union.

extensive evaluations of best practice.[15] The IPU guidelines recommend seven "Essential Elements" for parliamentary websites:

- general information on structure of parliament
- electoral system, party groups
- legislative processes and documents
- presiding officers
- members of parliament
- parliamentary bodies
- publications

Although the Pacific websites do not indicate whether they follow "best practices" articulated by the IPU, a preliminary survey suggests that most have incorporated the "essential elements" to some degree. A full assessment of the content of Pacific Parliamentary websites as at November 2005, in the context of IPU Parliamentary website guidelines, is provided in an appendix. In summary, the following observations are made about the current state of development of these sites.

3. Country Perspectives

3.1. Federated States of Micronesia

The FSM Congress website is well maintained, and currently provides information on members, bills, resolutions, public laws, and committees. It provides a vibrant "Congressional Photo Gallery" to supplement the text information elsewhere on the site. Of historical interest is a photo-gallery of the 1971 Congress of Micronesia.[16] Given the size of this small state, this is a well maintained site.

3.2. Fiji Islands

The Fiji parliament site is one of the best developed in the region. It shows current bills, committee reports, and legislation. It also provides current contact information for members of parliament but not for the webmaster or parliamentary services such as library, or secretary-general. A photo gallery has been established but yields just five images. The website is equipped with a calendar that allows for search of news on a daily basis, but little activity has been uploaded. Its strengths are its appearance, and its provision of current bills, committee activity notification, Hansard, legislation, and contact details for members of parliament and senate. It has little interactivity.

---

[15] *See, for example, The Scottish Office, "Telematics and the Scottish Parliament: Transferable Democratic Innovations", online at* http://www.scotland.gov.uk/government/devolution/tdi-04.asp; *Parliament of Victoria. Scrutiny of Acts and Regulations Committee (2005). "Victorian Electronic Democracy, Final Report."* online at http://www.parliament.vic.gov.au/SARC/E-Democracy/Final_Report/ToC.htm accessed 6 October 2006.

[16] http://www.fsmcongress.fm/COMHistory%202.htm

3.3. Palau

The website was created in 2003, but there have been minimal developments over the past two years, as the most recent update appears to have been made in 2005. Links to the webmaster are not active. In general, the site is poor.

3.4. Papua New Guinea

A URL has been established but there has been no subsequent development of the site. Given the size of this parliament, in the biggest democracy in the Pacific Islands region, this result is poor.

3.5. Tokelau

The site provides current information on the Council of Elders, the General Fono and the Council for the Ongoing Government of Tokelau. It provides no interactivity and no additional documentation. Given the small population size of Tokelau it can be presumed that citizens are able to get information about legislative matters from their representatives or the Fono.

3.6. Tonga

As at December 2006, the Tongan parliamentary website had not been updated for a period of fifteen months. While it provides information on the position of the parliament within Tonga's constitutional system, it does not include the parliament's legislative program, nor does it introduce individual members. The "news" section provides links to other Tongan publications, but provides no news about the activities of parliament. The "database" of legislation provides a link to Paclii (the Pacific Islands Legal Information Institute)[17] But not yet to the "Legislation of Tonga" website launched in early 2007.[18] Given interest at the current time in constitutional developments in Tonga, the website could be considered underdeveloped.

3.7. Samoa

The site of the Samoan parliament is among the most comprehensive of all Pacific Island parliamentary websites. It is bilingual (English and Samoan). It lists acts of the Parliament dating to 1920 through to 2006; and provides information on all members of parliament; a calendar of sitting dates; and reports of all parliamentary committees. Together with the Fijian and Guam sites it ranks as the best maintained in the region.

---

[17] www.paclii.org

[18] http://legislation.to/cms/home.html

3.8. Guam

The Guam legislature website is one of the most interactive of the Pacific parliamentary websites. It provides full text of all legislation and resolutions, and a record of voting patterns. It includes a "guestbook" in which constituents can record comments and make requests for action. The website provides links to the personal websites of those members of the legislature who maintain one.[19]

4. CONCLUSIONS

The small size of Pacific Islands Countries must be considered when assessing the scope of their parliamentary websites, and indeed whether they require a website at all. It could be argued, for instance, that small states such as Niue and Nauru hardly require a parliamentary website – certainly not as a priority in the context of their national development goals. It could be argued, on the other hand, that citizens and stakeholders in even the smallest polities desire information and deserve the most efficient forms of communication possible. One can leave open, therefore, the possibility that democratic dialogue even in these small states could be best served through some form of digital parliamentary presence.

Having surveyed the current status of Parliamentary websites of parliaments in the Pacific region a number of conclusions are possible. Firstly, it has to be noted that Pacific parliamentary websites are a recent phenomenon, with those of Fiji and Samoa appearing in 2003 and others being of even more recent origin. These sites are a promising vehicle for access to information about legislative processes and for enhancing the participation of constituents. The slow implementation of some sites points to the significant resource implications for small states that seek to establish and maintain adequate sites for their parliaments – as indeed for any and all institutions of state. In some cases, resources are currently deployed in such traditional activities as printing of parliamentary papers: some parliaments may prefer to maintain paid positions through sales of parliamentary papers rather than provide them over the internet for free. Finally, the question as to "who drives" websites is important: is demand coming from members of parliament, who wish to reach out to their constituencies, or from administrators seeking to make their activities more accessible? Or is it government, citizens, or donors? In the short term, website development will only be encouraged if sufficient demand for this is expressed by one or other of these actors in the democratic process, and if sufficient resources continue to be supplied for this purpose. The development of informative websites could add to the efficient flow of information between the legislature and the electorate. This would add to improved governance in the Pacific Islands countries.

APPENDIX 9.1. SURVEY OF WEB CONTENT USING IPU CRITERIA

1. GENERAL INFORMATION	Fiji	Tonga	PNG	Guam	FSM	Palau	Tokelau	Marshall Is.	Samoa
RECOMMENDED ELEMENTS									
Overview of Composition and Functions of Parliament	✓	✓			✓	✓	✓		✓
Full Texts of Standing Orders / Rule-setting Documents	✓	✓			✓	✓			✓
Text of Constitution		✓		✓				✓	✓
International and Regional Parliamentary Assemblies	✓								
OPTIONAL ELEMENTS									
Overview of Parliamentary Procedure	✓	✓			✓		✓		✓
Order of Parliamentary Business					✓	✓			
Statistics on current Legislature		✓							✓
History of Parliamentary Institutions	✓								✓
Texts of Official Press Releases	✓				✓				
'Guided Tour" of Parliamentary Building	✓	✓							
Diagram of Seating Arrangements									
Organisation chart of Secretariat of Parliament and Information on Secretary General/Clerk to Parliament									
Information on access to Parliament building, Library and Archives	✓	✓							

2. ELECTORAL SYSTEM, PARTY GROUPS	Fiji	Tonga	PNG	Guam	FSM	French Polynesia	Palau	Tokelau	Marshall Is.	Samoa
RECOMMENDED ELEMENTS										
Explanation of the election procedure (voting system, electoral divisions/constituencies, who votes, who can be elected, nomination requirements, who conducts the election, etc.)										✓
Results of the last elections by party affiliation and constituency										
OPTIONAL COMPONENTS										
Current composition of party groups and coalitions		✓							✓	
Results of last elections by age, gender and profession										
Texts of relevant election laws										

[19] For instance, the site of Ray Tenorio at http://www.raytenorio.com/main/?sec=home

3. LEGISLATIVE PROCESS AND DOCUMENTS	Fiji	Tonga	PNG	Guam	FSM	French Polynesia	Palau	Tokelau	Marshall Is.	Samoa
RECOMMENDED COMPONENTS										
Schematic explanation of the legislative process	✓									
Legislative agenda and schedule of the current session		✓		✓						
Searchable database of legislative acts enacted by the current legislature	✓	✓		✓			✓			✓
Status of current parliamentary business by bill number, topic, title, date, document code, parliamentary body, etc.	✓			✓	✓		✓			
OPTIONAL COMPONENTS										
Searchable database of committee reports, records, hearings, votes and other parliamentary documents pertaining to the current legislature	✓				✓		✓			✓
Searchable database of legislative acts and other parliamentary documents pertaining to at least immediately preceding legislatures	✓	✓		✓						✓
Special section on budget and financial legislation				✓		✓				
Summary or complete records of parliamentary debates/sessions	✓									
Special section devoted to parliamentary questions and inquiries addressed to the executive branch										
Glossary of parliamentary procedure										
Audio and video Web telecasting of parliamentary sessions										
RECOMMENDED CONTENT										
Biodata of the current Presiding Officer of the parliament or parliamentary chamber		✓			✓					
Brief description of the Presiding Officer's powers and prerogatives										
Names of Deputy- and/or Vice-Presidents (if applicable)										
OPTIONAL ELEMENTS										
Presiding Officer's public agenda (upcoming meetings, events)										
Collection of the Presiding Officer's important speeches and public addresses										
List of past Presiding Officers		✓			✓					
Feedback page or similar mechanism for sending questions and comments to the Presiding Officer										

Appendix 9.1. Continued

4. PRESIDING OFFICERS	Fiji	Tonga	PNG	Guam	FSM	French Polynesia	Palau	Tokelau	Marshall Is.	Samoa
5. MEMBERS OF PARLIAMENT										
RECOMMENDED MINIMUM										
Up-to-date alphabetical list of all members of Parliament (current legislature) [with information about each MP's constituency, party affiliation and membership in parliamentary committees and/or commissions, and with hyperlinks to MPs' personal Web sites (where applicable)]	✓	✓			✓		✓			✓
Similar to the above but with the list of members grouped by constituency	✓									✓
Similar to the above but with the list of members grouped by party or political affiliation	✓	✓								✓
Contact information for each member of Parliament including his or her e-mail address (where applicable)	✓	✓								✓
List of former members of parliament who have resigned from the current legislature or whose membership ceased for any other reason										
OPTIONAL ELEMENTS										
Biodata of each member of Parliament		✓					✓			
Automatically generated index of references to instances of participation in parliamentary debate sorted by member's name, date and topic of discussion										
Public record of voting by individual members of parliament (when applicable)										
Basic information concerning the status of a member of Parliament, such as parliamentary immunity, salaries and allowances, inviolability,etc.										
Alphabetical list of members of Parliament of the legislature immediately preceding the current one with clearly specified dates										

6. PARLIAMENTARY BODIES	Fiji	Tonga	PNG	Guam	FSM	French Polynesia	Palau	Tokelau	Marshall Is.	Samoa
RECOMMENDED DATA										
Complete list of non-plenary parliamentary bodies with hyperlinks to separate pages devoted to each body in that category										✓
Description of the mandate and terms of reference of each parliamentary body										
Membership and names of presiding officer(s) of each parliamentary body										✓
Information on current business and data on upcoming meetings										
Relevant contact information (addresses, telephone and fax numbers, e-mail) of each body										
Composition and other relevant information concerning the National IPU Group, parliamentary friendship groups as well as national delegations to international and regional parliamentary assemblies of which the parliament is a member										
OPTIONAL DATA										
Schedule of meetings and hearings held by each parliamentary body					✓					
Press releases and other relevant material pertaining to the work of each body										
Historical data on the National IPU Group										
7. PUBLICATIONS	Fiji	Tonga	PNG	Guam	FSM	French Polynesia	Palau	Tokelau	Marshall Is.	Samoa
RECOMMENDED INFORMATION										
List of publications and documents currently available from the Parliament (indicating their prices)	✓									
Information on how this material can be obtained by traditional means and (where applicable) through the on-line order service										

APPENDIX 9.1. CONTINUED

7. PUBLICATIONS	Fiji	Tonga	PNG	Guam	FSM	French Polynesia	Palau	Tokelau	Marshall Is.	Samoa
RECOMMENDED INFORMATION (continued)										
OPTION										
Direct on-line order service allowing users to select their publications and pay for them with the help of electronic commerce tools										
Electronic versions of those publications that can be downloaded from the site free of charge, for example, in *.PDF format	✓									

8. EXTERNAL HYPERLINKS	Fiji	Tonga	PNG	Guam	FSM	French Polynesia	Palau	Tokelau	Marshall Is.	Samoa
RECOMMENDED LINKS										
Web sites of the country's Presidency, Government, Constitutional and Supreme Courts (when applicable)				✓					✓	
Official Web site of the country (usually maintained by the Ministry of Tourism or similar governmental services)	✓			✓					✓	
Web site of the other chamber in a bicameral parliament (when applicable)										
Web sites of state/provincial legislatures				✓						
Inter-Parliamentary Union										
Other international, regional and sub-regional parliamentary organisations	✓									
Web sites of national political parties	✓									
Web sites of individual members of Parliament (where applicable)										

8. EXTERNAL HYPERLINKS	Fiji	Tonga	PNG	Guam	FSM	French Polynesia	Palau	Tokelau	Marshall Is.	Samoa
OPTIONAL LINKS										
Web sites of individual ministries and other national agencies	✓	✓					✓		✓	
Web sites of national parliaments of other countries (as this information is constantly changing, it might be easier to establish a link with the relevant page at the IPU site	✓									
Global Internet search engines (such as Yahoo! etc.)				✓						
National Internet search engines (when applicable)										

9. FEEDBACK AND OTHER INTERACTIVITY TOOLS	Fiji	Tonga	PNG	Guam	FSM	French Polynesia	Palau	Tokelau	Marshall Is.	Samoa
RECOMMENDED TOOLS										
A feedback utility that allows users to send their comments and questions directly to the Webmaster by means of forms (i.e. without resorting to e-mail services which might be unavailable in some situations)										
Preconfigured electronic mail for sending messages to parliamentary bodies and individual officers directly from the pages of the Web site										
OPTIONAL TOOLS										
Discussion forums where users can take part in on-line discussions on specific issues, usually related to current debates in the parliament; members of parliament often act as moderators for such forums						✓				

APPENDIX 9.1. CONTINUED

9. FEEDBACK AND OTHER INTERACTIVITY TOOLS	Fiji	Tonga	PNG	Guam	FSM	French Polynesia	Palau	Tokelau	Marshall Is.	Samoa
Mailing lists which allow users to subscribe to automatic e-mail delivery of parliamentary information, such as legislative texts										
Electronic opinion polls which allow users to express their views on a given subject through multiple choice questions										
CONTACT INFORMATION										
RECOMMENDATION										
All sections of the site (from the home page down to pages devoted to individual members of parliament) should contain relevant contact information placed at visible spots throughout the site	✓									

10 LANGUAGES	Fiji	Tonga	PNG	Guam	FSM	French Polynesia	Palau	Tokelau	Marshall Is.	Samoa
RECOMMENDED COMBINATION										
For countries with two or more official languages, the entire content of the parliamentary Web site should be available in at least one of the official languages of the country						✓				✓
A complete or partial version of the site should also exist in one of the languages of international communication, usually English	✓	✓		✓	✓	✓	✓	✓	✓	✓

11. SEARCH AND INTERNAL NAVIGATION TOOLS	Fiji	Tonga	PNG	Guam	FSM	French Polynesia	Palau	Tokelau	Marshall Is.	Samoa
RECOMMENDED TOOLS										
Quick search utility - this standard intra-site search tool is based on automatic indexing of documents and allows free-text search for words and word combinations throughout the site				✓					✓	✓
"What's New" page - a sort of announcement board with direct hyperlinks to the newest documents on the site	✓	✓								
Site map - textual or graphical visualization of the site's overall structure containing hyperlinks to individual documents	✓	✓		✓	✓	✓	✓		✓	✓
OPTIONAL TOOLS										
"Frequently Asked Questions" page - a traditional Internet method of providing a one-stop place for answers to questions that are asked most frequently		✓							✓	
Keyword index - a special page (usually generated automatically) from which all documents are accessible directly through their respective keywords	✓									✓
Parliamentary staff vacancies page		✓								

REFERENCES

Cantero, C. "Parliaments in a Knowledge-Based Society." *Inter Parliamentary Union:* http://www.ipu.org/english/pressdoc/news/13%2D3.htm.

First Pacific Island Speakers' Forum (2001). Guiding Principles of Best Practices for Forum Island Countries' Legislatures. Nuku'alofa, Tonga.

Inter-Parliamentary Union (2000). *Guidelines for the Content and Structure of Parliamentary Web Sites.* Geneva, Inter-Parliamentary Union.

Kingham, T. (2003). e-Parliaments. The Use of Information and Communication Technologies to Improve Parliamentary Processes, World Bank Institute.

Parliament of Victoria. Scrutiny of Acts and Regulations Committee (2005). "Victorian Electronic Democracy, Final Report." online at http://www.parliament.vic.gov.au/SARC/E-Democracy/Final_Report/ToC.htm accessed 6 October 2006.

Spenneman, D. (2004). "Digital Divides in the Pacific Islands." I*T and Society 1*(7): 46-65.

Stauffacher, D., W. Drake, et al. (2005). *Information and Communication Technology for Peace: The Role of ICT in Preventing, Responding to and Recovering from Conflict.* New York, United Nations Information and Communication Technologies Task Force.

United Nations. Department of Economic and Social Affairs (2003). *World Public Sector Report 2003: E-Government at the Crossroads.* New York, United Nations.

Zwimpfer Communications (2002). *Internet Infrastructure and e-Governance in Pacific Islands Countries. A Survey on the Development and Use of the Internet.* Wellington, UNESCO.

In: Development Problems and Prospects in Pacific Islands ISBN: 978-1-60021-793-7
Editors: B. C. Prasad, D. C. Roy, pp. 137-155

Chapter 10

PUBLIC FINANCE MANAGEMENT IN FIJI : ISSUES OF GOVERNANCE AND GROWTH

Mahendra Reddy and Monovi Amani

1. INTRODUCTION

Bad governance practices by governments in developing countries have been noted as one of the leading causes of poor economic performance and rising poverty (Kantha, 2005; Kaufmann and Kraay, 2002). At the national level, the effect of bad governance on the economy is evident from measures of national economic and fiscal indicators. It is visible from low GDP growth rates, poor export growth, low investment and large fiscal deficits.

Pacific Island Countries (PICs) are plagued with various issues of bad governance that have affected their economic, social and fiscal position. The poor performance of the PICs economies have challenged them to re-examine their domestic economic policies. There have also been strong pressure from lending institutions such as the IMF and World Bank on PICs to undertake market oriented reforms. The reforms suggested and pursued are in areas of trade, goods market, factor market, labour market, financial market and public sector. While most PICs began reforming their economies since the mid 1980's, the economies have yet to deliver a consistent economic growth record. Some economists argue that difference in institutions and governance structures are one of the leading causes of not only the poor performance of PIC economies, but also the variations in growth levels amongst the PICs.

A recent meeting of the Forum Economic Ministers identified the prevalence of bad governance as a cause for concern for policy makers. Statements from the meeting included the following (Forum Secretariat, 2004:3):

i. good governance is essential to economic growth and should be supported by effective laws and institutions.
ii. that even a perception of corruption, lack of accountability and poor transparency could have harmful social and economic effects.

iii. that stakeholders are well informed on their respective roles, rights and responsibilities.
iv. that robust systems are needed for detection and their enforcement a discouragement for corrupt behavior. a
v. that governments must be committed to increase efforts and strengthen institutions and laws to prevent corruption, including its causes, and to improve public sector economic governance through action at the national level.

In this paper, the broad issue of governance is examined. The paper begins with defining governance and follows through to provide examples of bad practices of governance in Fiji. These bad practices are examined to illuminate areas that give rise to these practices and how these deficiencies can be overcome.

2. Governance Defined

Governance is in general, a decision making and implementation process. The IMF defines good governance as measures that will contribute towards macroeconomic stability, external viability, and orderly economic growth in member countries (IMF, 1997). The World Bank defines governance as the process by which authority is conferred on rulers, by which they make the rules, and by which those rules are enforced and modified. The Australian government, while acknowledging that the term 'governance' is used to describe a range of phenomena, proposes that a broad definition would include:[1]

i. the management of public resources, or public administration
ii. the activities of government or the system of governing
iii. government's interaction with civil society and citizens in general. This definition introduces actions directed towards government as well as by government. This includes the constraints and accountability mechanisms under which parliamentarians operate
iv. the interaction of traditions, values, institutions and processes that shape society. In this definition, government is less central. While still an important player in some interactions, it may be marginal or absent in others. A similar approach views governance as the exercise of power in society.

The notion of good governance requires adherence to some basic principles such as the respect for rule of law and judicial independence, respect for human rights, the control of corruption, use of public funds and public policy measures. These measures are aimed at reducing and ultimately eradicating poverty, creating security, improving the overall standard of living, political accountability, reliable and equitable legal frameworks. An appropriate legal framework should include judicial independence, bureaucratic transparency, effective and efficient public sector management, participatory development and the promotion and protection of human rights.

---

[1] (http://www.aph.gov.au/library/pubs/rn/2001-02/02RN11.htm)

In its 1999 Human Development Report, UNDP draws attention to two aspects in particular: on the one hand the benefits of a 'way of conducting world business' which, by setting up coalitions between government, the private sector and representatives of civil society that extend beyond geographical borders and traditional political circles, can deliver on the aspirations of a world citizenry, and on the other hand the need to guide markets rather than reject them.[2]

An academic definition of public sector governance put forward by Kaufmann et al. (2002) is that governance refers to traditions and institutions by which authority is exercised, which tend to include:

i. the process by which governments are selected, monitored and replaced
ii. the capacity of the government to formulate and implement policies effectively
iii. the respect of citizens and the state for the institutions that govern economic and social interactions among them.

All these definitions form the basis of how governments and their institutions should conduct their business in pursuit of the ultimate objective. On the basis of these definitions, we may derive the following summary of characteristics measuring governance:

Participation: An attempt should be made to ensure all men and women have a voice in decision-making.

Transparency: There should be a free flow of information.

Responsiveness: Institutions must respond to their stakeholders.

Consensus orientation: The consensus approach allows ownership and no dissent.

Equity: There should be equal opportunity for all, irrespective of their background, ethnicity, race, gender or religion.

Effectiveness and efficiency: The scarcity of the resource requires that it be used for the best possible alternatives and that these alternatives be matched with the needs of the society.

Strategic vision: For effective and sustained development, long-term planning is essential. This will require, amongst other things, good knowledge of the historical, cultural and social complexities.

Rule of law: There should be a good legal framework respected by all.

Accountability: By the very nature of elections, the policy makers must be accountable to stakeholders.

[2] NZAID has also offered its criteria for governance, which include; (i) improving institutional frameworks for democratic processes and respect for human rights; (ii) assisting countries to implement international agreements on human rights; (iii) capacity building for sustainable institutional development and for the promotion and protection of civil and human rights, including relevant media training; (iv) promoting fairness and justice and strengthening the advocacy role and capacity of civil society organisations; (v) promoting gender equitable participation and access; (vi) directly contributing to enhancing the quality of government, particularly in promoting accountability, participation, predictability (legal frameworks) and transparency; (vii) improving decision-making processes; (viii) encouraging participatory policy-making processes; (ix) public sector administration/management reform; and enhancing the business and regulatory framework and environment. (source: http://www.nzaid.govt.nz/programmes/global/goodgovernance/ggpguidelines.html)

3. THE GOVERNANCE–GROWTH NEXUS

There is widespread consensus that insufficient domestic resource mobilisation and wasteful public expenditures are at the root of adjustment and growth problems faced by many countries, in particular, the transitional economies (Bardhan, 1997; Chand and Moene, 1999; Gradstein, 2004; Vinod, 1999, 2003). Good governance encompasses all spheres of an economy, the political, economic, social and the private sector. The role of the private sector and civil society is crucial in the quest for good governance, especially in the corporate and economic realms. The private sector's role is significant in the harnessing and distribution of resources for wealth creation and sustainable development. Wealth creation is largely dependent on trade and investment. Almost all the growth theories emphasise the importance of investment in promoting growth including Adam Smith's classical theory, in which he notes that the supply side model of growth has capital as one of the independent variables. This was later picked up the neo-classical theorists. The Keynesians, though, arguing that demand creates supply, do talk about the public sector's role in raising aggregate demand from capital and consumption expenditure.

The creation of capital, as espoused by these theories, requires market-friendly policies, whose development and implementation are made by the political process. The values, ethics and parameters within which this political process operates to develop policies, implement these policies and enforce the regulations determine to a large extent whether we end up in a situation of 'capital deepening' or 'capital shallowing', thus determining the level of growth in the country.

The process of waste and abuse of public sector resources by individuals working in the public sector is called rent seeking behaviour. The resources that these individuals use are of no social value, that is, it is a private gain made at a cost to others. The cost of this behaviour on the society can also be illustrated using Figure 10.1. Assume a competitive market with a constant marginal cost (MC). Therefore, the MC curve is also the industry supply curve. With a barrier to entry by the rent seekers, price increases and output are restricted. This is depicted by a new price, P_M, and a new quantity, Q_M. Therefore, the welfare loss is represented by the triangle abc, a loss caused by increased price and a reduction in quantity produced.

Rent seeking behaviour can be observed at all levels of the public sector, ranging from politicians to lower-level employees. The existence of corrupt practices in the top echelons of government could lead to a contagion effect on the lower levels (Andvig and Moene, 1990). This effect could be more evident if it is generally perceived that the administrative structures are being used to promote the self interest of their management rather than the mandated objectives (Chand and Moene, 1999). The lower-level employees would be more compelled to cooperate in such practices when they view their own career progression as being dependent on the extent to which they compromise with the top echelons (Chand and Moene, 1999).

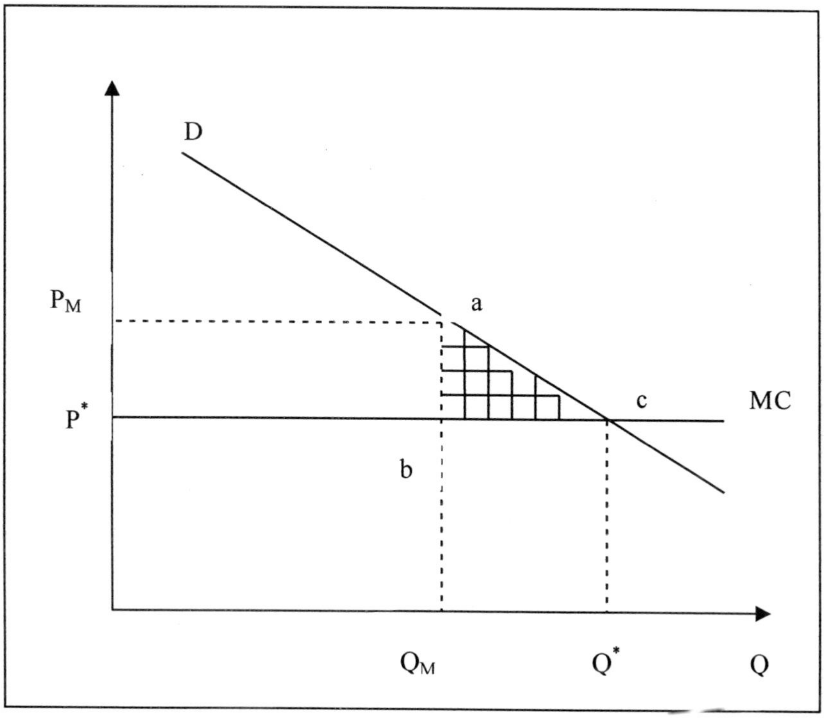

Figure 10.1. Welfare Cost of Rent Seeking.

Mauro (1998:263) suggests that "in a world in which governments do not always act in their citizens' best interest, corrupt politicians may be expected to spend more public resources on those items on which it is easier to levy large bribes and maintain them secret". Krueger (1974) suggests that for rent seeking behaviour to occur, rents must exist. That is, large bribes will be available on items produced by firms operating in markets where the degree of competition is low and on goods whose exact value is difficult to monitor (Mauro, 1998).

Three key factors contribute to corruption or rent seeking behaviour (Rose-Ackerman, 1978:22):

i. the overall level of potential benefits from corrupt behaviour. Benefits here could be payoffs for facilitating tax evasion or excessive billing of government expenditures. The higher the tax rate, the higher the potential benefits from evasion
ii. the cost of bribery, or the penalties and sanctions applicable to bribed and bribe. Past records of poor application of sanctions/penalties lower the costs of being corrupt
iii. bargaining power of officials, or the extent of exclusive discretionary powers in the hands of individual bureaucrats.

Calderon and Chong (2005) also argue that there is a possible link between democracy and rent-seeking behaviour. According to them, not only do democracies reduce rent-seeking behaviour, but they also improve the quality of a country's institutions over time. In addition, they suggest that the more transparent the laws and regulations within democracies, the less likely the presence of bad institutions; likewise, the less opaque the political process, the better the property rights in the country and the lower the rent-seeking behaviour in the society.

Some studies suggest that red tape[3] and corruption occur together and are the most ancient and widespread disease of bureaucracy (Guriev, 2004). Guriev states:

> corruption in one part of a hierarchy may stem from corruption in another part; excessive red tape may emerge due to potential corruption; bribes may be extorted because of potentially high red tape. When trying to make public bureaucracy more efficient, one should keep these interdependencies in mind in order to fight causes rather than consequences (Guriev, 2004:489).

De Soto (1989) and Brunetti et al., (1997) comment that in a large number of countries, red tape ranks very high as an obstacle in doing business, ranking it as an even greater obstacle than financial constraints (EBRD, 1999; Johnson et al., 2000). The excessive use of red tape not only creates more opportunities for corruption (Bardhan, 1997) but also has an adverse effect on growth and development (Mauro, 1995).

An area where corrupt practices are often found is in the assessment and collection of taxes (Galtung, 1995). A number of studies on developing countries reveal that half or more of taxes that should be collected cannot be traced by government treasuries, as a result of corrupt practices and tax evasion (Alm, Bahl and Murray, 1991; Bird, 1990, 1992; Krugman, et. al., 1992; Richupan, 1984). Governments of various countries have embarked on tax reform programs to curb these problems (Fjeldstad and Tungodden, 2003). However, if strategies are to be comprehensive, the programs must ensure that both the demand and supply sides of issues surrounding such practices are addressed.

4. The Public Finance Management in Fiji

Public Finance Act and Accountability

Governments in democracies are accountable to the taxpayers for the manner in which they use the funds at their disposal. Furthermore, they are also accountable to the public with respect to the performance of all their institutions (Lodhia and Burritt, 2004). The democratic way in which these governments are elected is the basis for this accountability. The democratic base also explains the fact that government's resource allocation is vetted by the elected parliament (the representatives of civil society) before a bill becomes an act, i.e. before it becomes a piece of legislation. Thus the issue of accountability lies at the heart of democratic governments.

The cycle of accountability begins with Parliament, the legislature, approving the use of various resources in a particular program and specifying the expected outcomes, and ends with reporting back to Parliament on the utilisation of the resources and the results achieved. The executive arm of the government, the Ministries and the staff, are entrusted with public resources on a stewardship basis and have a responsibility to use them economically, efficiently and effectively. They discharge their accountability role by preparing reports,

[3] Red tape can be defined as 'unnecessary' or 'excessive' official routines, rules, or procedures resulting in delays.

including financial reports, to show the results of their administration of public funds and use of resources. Public sector auditors assist in the accountability process by providing assurance as to the credibility of management's reports and making assessments of management's performance. However, the ultimate responsibility of accountability for public finances rests on the shoulders of the Minister of Finance. The Constitution provides that all revenues or other monies raised or received for the purpose of the government shall be paid into the Consolidated Fund. No money should be withdrawn from the Consolidated Fund except to meet expenditure either charged upon the Fund by the Constitution or by an appropriation for the expenditure as approved by the House of Representatives (Reddy, et. al., 2007).

The Finance Act amplifies in detail the method of control and management of public monies and property. The Act prescribes in detail the functions and responsibilities of the Minister of Finance and by extension, to its accounting officers, specifying the various accounts to be kept, the procedure for reporting on the year's results, borrowing powers and other related matters.

In accordance with the Public Finance Management Act, the Finance Minister must prepare the following accounts on an annual basis and submit them for audit:

- Statement of Financial Assets and Liabilities
- Consolidated Fund – Statement of Balance
- Operating Fund Account – Statement of Receipts and Expenditure
- Borrowing Fund Account – Statement of Receipts and Expenditure
- Lending Fund Account – Statement of Receipts and Expenditure
- Revolving Fund Account – Statement of Receipts and Expenditure
- Contingencies Fund Account – Statement of Receipts and Expenditure
- Consolidated Trust Fund – Statement of Assets and Liabilities
- Consolidated Trust Fund -– Statement of Receipts and Expenditure.

These statements are prepared by the Finance Ministry on an annual basis. A summary of the above accounts for the years 1985–2002 is presented in Appendix 10.1.

The Borrowing Fund Account consists of Government's total public debt liability, which has been steadily rising over the years. This remains a cause for concern. The Lending Fund Accounts, in a number of years, reveal that expenditure has been in excess of the budgeted appropriation as at 31 December each year. This then is regularised in the following year by a Supplementary Appropriations bill tabled in parliament. This is certainly not a good funds management procedure. Under section 57 of the Finance Act, The Minister of Finance has the authority to set aside $18m for operation of the twenty-five main revolving accounts, with authorised limits for each account. This limit was later (in 2002) reduced to $16.4m. However, excess drawing on these revolving fund accounts seems to have set in as a trend. This problem could be easily curbed if monthly reconciliation statements of each account were submitted to the Finance Ministry. Government's investment position also saw a sudden surge in late-2000 due to an investment of $212,5448,974 in Amalgamated Telecom Holding (ATH) Limited, amid a lot of controversy surrounding the deal, in particular about the investment figure (it has been noted publicly that the second highest bidder was 1/3rd the bid of Government). In 1999, government made further investment of $30m in Airports Fiji Limited, $4.9m in the Colonial National Bank and $525,000 in the *Daily Post*, a print media company. Furthermore, returns on government investment have been particularly promising in recent years (Table 10.1).

Office of Auditor-General and Audit Findings

The watch dog on Government finances, by law, is the Office of the Auditor-General (OAG). The OAG is established under Section 166 of the Constitution (Amendment) Act 1997. OAG conducts the audits of the accounts and the finances of the Fiji Government's Ministries and Departments and its statutory bodies in accordance with Section 167 of the 1997 Constitution of the Republic of the Fiji Islands and the Audit Act (which states that the Auditor-General shall, on behalf of the Parliament inquire into and audit the accounts of all accounting officers. Section 167(1) of the 1997 Constitution states that at least once in every year, the Auditor-General must inspect and audit, and report to the Parliament on:

1. the public accounts of the state
2. the control of public money and public property of the State
3. all transactions with or concerning the public money or public property of the state.

The primary objectives of the audits conducted by the OAG are based on Section 6(2) of the Audit Act, which states that the Auditor-General shall satisfy himself/herself that:

1. the accounts have been faithfully and properly kept
2. all reasonable precautions have been taken to safeguard the collection of public monies and that the laws, directions or instructions relating thereto have been duly observed;
3. expenditure has been properly authorised and applied to the purpose for which funds were appropriated by the Parliament and otherwise has been properly accounted for, and that the regulations and procedures applied are sufficient to secure an effective control over expenditure, and that it has been incurred with due regard to economy and avoidance of waste and extravagance
4. adequate stores regulations and procedures have been made to ensure proper receipt, issue and custody of stores and other property of whatsoever nature, and that such regulations have been duly observed
5. the provisions of the Constitution and of the Finance (Control and Management) Act, and of any other law relating to money or stores subject to the audit have been in all aspects complied with.

(Source: Report of the Auditor-General of Fiji, 1985, 1990, 1995, 2000 and 2002).

In accordance with the Constitution, the Auditor-General submits to Parliament, in the following year's sitting of parliament, detailed reports on these areas for all Ministries for a particular year. Appendix 1 provides a brief summary of the findings for the years 1999–2002. The findings reveal that common practices of bad governance are evident every year. These include disregard of rules, regulations and procedures by public servants, including the staff of the Ministry of Finance. Furthermore, as a result of such practices, significant amounts of public funds are misused, abused and lost, whose effect in generating sustained growth rates are lost. This lost money could also have been used to lower public debt directly, while indirectly, it would have boosted growth, and thus increased government revenue for financing of expenditure and servicing debt.

This summary report indicates that rules and regulations have been blatantly disregarded and this behaviour has led to loss of millions of dollars of public money. The Finance Act clearly stipulates that no monies of the consolidated fund must be used unless the Parliament has formally appropriated it. However, this has been violated. Fiji government's finances in the year 2001 and 2002 demonstrated several cases of expenditure use over and above the budgeted amount thus forcing the Auditor-General to provide a qualified report on the state of finance management. The following two excerpts are examples:

On Government Finances for 2001

Without qualification to the opinion expressed above, attention is drawn to the following matters:

i. Ineffective cash management was evident in that despite sufficient cash holdings, the Ministry continued to raise Treasury Bills, thus increasing the debt burden of the Government. Furthermore, although the actual deficit as at 31 December 2001 was $100,410,000, Government had raised loans totalling $239,248,000.
ii. The Ministry of Finance was unable to furnish explanations on debit balances amounting to $26,739,539 in the Unpresented Cheques, as reflected in Appendix 3 Statement of Cash and Bank Balance of the Accounts and Finance Report. Moreover, the Ministry of Finance could not provide breakdown for $6,509,162 shown as 'bank adjustments' in Appendix 25 Statement of Cash flows.

On Government Finances for 2002

Without further qualification to the opinion expressed above, attention is drawn to the following matter:

i. The Ministry of Finance was unable to furnish explanations on debit balances amounting to $20,500,836, reflected as Unpresented Cheques in Appendix 3: Statement of Cash and Bank Balance of the Accounts and Finance Report. (AOG, 2002:20).

The above cases reveal that laxity on the part of executive arm of the government has also contributed to additional borrowing, thus creating further debt burden on the taxpayers.

Furthermore, these issues raised by the Auditor General also tie in with number of complaints being received by the Interim Government on corrupt practices in public service. In a recent article in one of Fiji's leading daily newspaper, the Chief Executive Officer in PM's office stated the following:

> "...the unit had received many allegations and complaints but they would have to be categorised so those that can be dealt with procedurally can be sorted out straight away. The rest of the files would be subject to further investigation by the proposed Anti-Corruption Commission. The allegations were received from individuals as well as organisations and the nature of the allegations ranged from underhand dealings to mismanagement. They range

from various issues like the provision of government services. Some people have been complaining that they have had to pay a sum of money for certain services and that someone has been deprived the first opportunity because they were not in the good books of some people. They range from individual complaints, organisational level complaints and complaints pertaining to management and even to some extent boards, but these are just some of the complaints that I mentioned that is subject to further investigation" (The Fiji Times, 2007:3).

These cases, though yet to be examined in detail do raise questions on the nature of governance practices within Fiji's public sector.

Table 10.1. Return on Investment, 1993–2002

Year	Total Government Investment ($)	Dividends on Investment	Rate of Return on Investment (%)
1993	156,535,696	7,557,687	5
1994	156,566,986	10,909,601	7
1995	155,732,425	18,548,150	12
1996	155,752,425	13,754,684	9
1997	170,415,528	9,033,912	5
1998	346,231,329	16,040,333	5
1999	375,988,519	8,814,120	2
2000	215,956,469	19,257,619	9
2001	213,289,008	11,000,480	5
2002	545,789,484	21,563,220	4

Source: Report of the Auditor-General of Fiji, 2002.

5. Wastage of Government Resources and Supplementary Budgets

Apart from the above stated cases of bad governance practices and the loss of growth opportunities, the waste of public sector resources also makes the government vulnerable. The loss of resources via bad governance practices deprives of government of its ability to meet important and crucial obligations, and defaulting on those would not only compromise on important government objectives, but also create further economic crisis. One way out, to which the government has often resorted, is to make supplementary appropriations. The government has tabled supplementary budget(s) in the parliament every year, either to move funds from one ministry to another or to raise further money to finance existing expenditure (see Table10.2 for allocations for years 1997-2004). Supplementary budgets are not uncommon. They can arise if the budgeting practices have been incorrect, the government is faced with unforeseen circumstances such as natural disaster, or existing allocations have been misused or misallocated. In Fiji, it seems, it has mostly been the latter two: government budgeted funds have been misused and therefore, fall short to run the affairs of the government till the end of the year.

Table 10.2. Supplementary Appropriation by Government, 1997–2003

Year	Amount Appropriated (F$m)	Ministries /Department Allocated To
1997	42.5m	Thirteen Ministries; Office of the President; PM's Office; Attorney-General; Labour and Employment Relations; Legislature; Miscellaneous Services
1998	58.1m	Various other ministries and departments
1999	14.0m	Ministry of Agriculture, Fisheries, Forest and ALTA; Miscellaneous Services. These expenditure are for normal expenses
2000	N.A	N.A
2001	48.2m	Home Affairs and Immigration; Regional Development and Multi-Ethnic Affairs; Agriculture, Fisheries, Forest and ALTA; Miscellaneous Services
2002	67.7m	Two supplementary appropriations were made; which were channelled to various ministries for normal expenditures
2003	75.1m	Various ministries for normal expenditures
2004	57.2m	Various ministries for normal expenditures

Source: Ministry of Finance, Appropriation (Supplementary) Act, (various years).

Note: In addition to these appropriations, the Government also engages in re-deploying funds from one Head to another.

N.A: Data not available.

A startling revelation was made regarding 1999 (which may be the same for the other years) audited accounts and the commentary provided by the Auditor General's Office regarding bad practices such as order splitting, virements, over-expenditure and misappropriation.

A review of this shows that more than 80% (some Ministries 100%) of these occurred in the last quarter of the Budget year and the goods acquired in most instances are office equipment and furniture. Performance of Ministries during this period was based on inputs which meant Heads of Ministries that did not use up their allocated funds would be subjected to disciplinary action. This scrambling in the last quarter by ministries to use remaining funds and transfer funds to busted expenditure accounts is a reminder that input-based budgeting systems can contribute to corrupt and bad practices.

The data presented in Table 10.2 make it apparent that supplementary appropriations have become a normal practice of the government to make discretionary spending. Apart from the 1997–98 period, when a significant proportion of the supplementary appropriation was channelled towards natural disaster relief (drought), in all the other years the appropriation was to meet regular expenditure, which could have been easily budgeted for with some foresight. The failure to do so either reveals poor and inadequate budgeting skills on the part of the Ministry of Finance staff or is a deliberate attempt to keep net deficit as a percent of GDP low in the initial budget presentation by making lower than normal appropriation (in which the case the shortfall will be picked up by the supplementary appropriations in the following year). However, whatever the reason may be, it seems the practice of making a minimum of two appropriations for a year is becoming a normal feature of Fiji government. This does not increase the confidence of the private sector with regard to the credibility of the government.

The question that remains is how this situation can be improved to ensure that this practice does not re-occur as of right and that public sector resources are put to their best use. To answer this question, one needs to understand the mechanism by which these activities that lead to waste and abuse of resources take place. OECD (2004) states that these practices can be categorised as corrupt practices. While corruption is generally defined as exploitation of public office for personal gain, it can take many forms, including (Grabosky and Larmour, 2000):

- Bribery: where an official accepts money or some other consideration to engage in a particular course of action or inaction
- Extortion: where an official demands money or some other consideration to engage in a particular course of action, or inaction
- Embezzlement: where an official misappropriates public assets for personal use
- Fraud: where an official makes a false claim for benefits for which he or she is not entitled, or in order to avoid liability for payment such as tax or customs duty
- Conflict of interest: where an official stands to profit incidentally from an official act. This could involve a planning decision that has the effect of increasing the value of property owned by the official, or the awarding of a government contract to a company in which the official has a financial interest.
-

A detailed explanation of how three factors—contributory factors, systemic characteristics and contextual variables—contribute to corrupt practices in the public sector are provided in OECD (2004). A summary of the complex interplay is provided in Table 10.3.

Table 10.3. Factors Potentially Relevant to Addressing Corruption Risk

Contributory factors	Systemic characteristics	Contextual variables
– Inadequate compliance with accounting and reporting rules – Patronage in appointments – Weak oversight of arm's-length public bodies – Secretive and unaccountable officials – Weak internal and external controls – Weak safeguards for awarding government contracts	– Lobbying and party funding system – Incentives and accountability of officials – Accounting and reporting standards among officials – Senior civil servant system (élite/non-élite, permanent or politically appointed) – Official information disclosure regime – Effectiveness of external invigilators	– Power of organised labour to resist change – Capacity of the legislature to constrain Executive action – Balance of power between head of government and ministers – Constitutional autonomy of lower levels of government – Citizens' interest in and expectations of official behaviour – Independence/assertiveness of judiciary – Political capacity of Executive for difficult decisions

Source: OECD (2004:45).

The issues outlined in table 10.3 provide a clear picture on the areas that need to be scrutinised and dealt with if leakage of public sector resources through wasteful practices is to be minimised. However, the above measures deal only with reducing supply of avenues for bad governance (preventive measures). To achieve effective control, demand side issues must also be addressed. Government must begin by exercising "fiscal transparency" defined as:

> openness toward the public at large about government structure and functions, fiscal policy intentions, public sector accounts, and projections. It involves ready access to reliable, comprehensive, timely, understandable, and internationally comparable information on government activities – so that the electorate and financial markets can accurately assess the government's financial position and the true costs and benefits of government activities, including their present and future economic and social implications. (Heald, 2003:726).

Fiscal transparency may not be sufficient to combat deeply rooted corruption, thus, we must curb the demand for such practices as well. One of the ways this could be addressed is to ensure that the full brunt of the law falls on those who have committed such activities. The Auditor–General's report recommendations must be implemented and those implicated should face the law. Failure to do so will increase the probability that these practices of bad governance continue, with misuse of large sums of public sector resources.

Fiscal corruption of the nature described above could seriously undermine government trustworthiness and thus the legitimacy of the government, where legitimacy refers to citizens' approval of the government, which in turn justifies citizens' obedience (Fjeldstad and Tungodden, 2003). Diminishing legitimacy of government may in turn lead to citizens not obeying laws of the government, thus leading to a vicious circle where distrust breeds distrust (Fjeldstad and Tungodden, 2003).

6. Fiji's Efforts to Prevent Corruption

Corruption is an enveloping and complex phenomen and its presence in the public sector threatens countries all over the world including Fiji. Public institutions are being threatened daily sometimes in the guise of efficiency and or expediency and other non-purposeful influences of improper use of public resources and power and by the undermining of the confidence of its people in the legitimate activities of state. In a survey[4] of 15 OECD country's measures to protect their public institutions against corruption, countries were invited to describe the corruption mechanisms they have in place. Results reveal that whilst there are similarities in their efforts most are employing multiple methodologies to do so. Among the initiatives against corruption reported by countries, moves to increase administrative transparency stood out as the most popular. In particular, obliging public officials to declare financial and other interests incompatible with public duty was most frequently cited. Fiji in this regard has legislation that already exists requiring this information to be tabled. However, despite this, there have been numerous accusations about

---

[4] This survey provides an overview of the measures that 15 OECD Member countries (Belgium, the Czech Republic, France, Germany, Greece, Hungary, Ireland, Italy, Japan, Korea, Mexico, Poland, Spain, Sweden and Switzerland) are currently using against corruption. OECD, 1999 'Public Sector Corruption: An International Survey of Prevention Measures, PARIS, OECD.

corruption being rife in the public sector. In November, 2006, the Republic of Fiji Military Forces (RFMF) overthrew the ruling government citing a number of reasons and corruption was one of them. Three months into its tenure, the Interim Government led by the Commander of the (RFMF) established an Anti-Corruption Unit to hear complaints and investigate cases of corruption. The regime also stated that the drafting of legislation is in progress to establish a much wider and more powerful corruption commission, named the Fiji Independent Commission against Corruption. While announcing the commission, the Interim Prime Minister and Commander of RFMF said:

> "…..to ensure the independence of the commission, the commissioner was to report directly to the President and be accountable to him alone. The commission would also be able to conduct prosecutions on its own. The creation of the Fiji Independent Commission against Corruption begins an unprecedented chapter in the eradication of corruption from Fiji. The widespread instances of corruption both in government and private sector have denied ordinary citizens of this country the opportunities for fair play and improved standards of living. The rich, powerful and the deceitful have oppressed the chances of the poor and downtrodden to come out of poverty and also the young and talented ones have been denied the opportunities to excel and be successful." (The Fiji Times, 2007:3).

While the establishment of the anti corruption unit and the proposal to establish an independent commission with more powers to root out corruption is a bold step in the right direction, the effectiveness of this committee in undertaking that task will only be evident in few years time.

7. Summary

Poor governance of public sector resources and institutions is becoming the leading obstacle for growth and development in small developing economies. Fiji is no exception to this. Appropriate macroeconomic policies may not be able to deliver targeted growth if public sector resources are mismanaged, public servants' morale is low, transaction costs are high and required infrastructure for private sector development is either absent or underdeveloped. These are the basics and fundamentals that must be addressed for sustained growth and development.

The long term solution to curb bad governance practices is to ensure control or eradication of demand and supply of corrupt practices. There should be strengthening of the financial management system so that supply of avenues for corrupt practices with regard to financial management is not available. To curb the demand for such practices, offenders should be severely dealt with so that would be offenders are deterred from engaging in such practices. The establishment of an Anti-Corruption Unit by the Interim government will certainly send the right signals to the public any planned rent seeking behaviour and thus may discourage it.

The public must also be educated on resource allocation and delivery of the resources to allocated areas. The public must ask for transparency and accountability. The media has an important role to play by highlighting issues of bad governance, which could be then picked up by other watch dogs to examine the issues more deeply and take appropriate actions. The issue ensuring that taxpayer resources are used for the best endeavour rests on all in the society and collective effort will provide best results.

APPENDIX 10.1: HIGHLIGHT OF KEY ISSUES RAISED BY AUDITOR-GENERAL'S REPORT, 1999–2002

1999 A-G Report

a) Management and use of public funds a cause for concern
b) Evidence of misuse of powers by public servants
c) Rules and regulations concerning purchase of goods and services ignored
d) Revolving Fund Account drawn beyond the limit
e) Accounting officers in Ministry fail to furnish basic information on money owed to government, thus ineffective monitoring and poor recovery
f) Contractual works by certain Ministries have not followed proper procedures
g) Hiring of consultants and payments made were riddled with errors, leading to major financial loss to government
h) Weak payroll system resulting in overpayment of salaries
i) Ministries continue to ignore rules, regulations and procedures governing the use of motor vehicles
j) Management of trust funds was considered unsatisfactory
k) Trust Fund Accounts have been overdrawn. The reports indicate that public servants are not following good governance practices and as a result, are not only setting the wrong example for other institutions, but also indulging loss of massive amounts of public funds that could have been utilised to generate growth.

2000 A-G Report

a) Ministries continue to ignore Transport Rules and Regulations governing the use of motor vehicles
b) Revolving Fund Account overdrawn
b) Salary payment not properly controlled and overpayments continue to occur.
c) Standing regulations covering purchase of goods and services continued to be ignored; purchasing authority exceeded, approvals for purchases by tender Boards were ignored, competitive quotations were not obtained and unauthorised purchases were made
d) Revenue collection procedures not being followed and as result, cases of misuse and frauds continue to surface in some Ministries and Departments
e) Debt recovery procedures employed by Ministries and Departments are not effective
f) FMF signed a six-year MOU for supply of a product, with concurrence of the Ministry of Finance and Major Tenders Board
g) Finance Ministry gave loan to Fiji Hardwood Corporation Limited without a feasibility study. The loan was later converted to a grant

h) Ministry of Agriculture conducted the financing of Affirmative Action Plan for Indigenous Fijians and Rotumans without specific criteria. Massive expenditure was incurred without calling for tenders
I) Budgets for some Ministries were not adhered to
j) Government commercial companies and statutory authorities did not always submit annual reports and audited financial accounts
k) Ministry of Works violated rules, regulations and procedures resulting in financial loss
l) Major Tender Board was also brought under scrutiny by the AG.

The reports indicate that public servants are not following good governance practices and as a result, are not only setting the wrong example for other institutions, but also indulging loss of massive amounts of public funds that could have been utilised to generate growth.

2001 AG Report

a) Ineffective cash management was evident as despite sufficient cash holdings, Ministry continued to raise Treasury Bills, thus increasing the debt burden of the Government. Actual deficit as at 31 December 2001 was $100,410,000. Government, however, raised loans totalling $239,248,000
b) Anomalies in unpaid cheques and lack of explanation for "Bank Adjustment" figure
c) Numerous defects in the operation of the revolving fund account, including overdrawing of the Revolving Fund Account
d) Absence of effective internal control systems
e) Ministries and departments continue to ignore transport rules and regulations
f) Department annual reports not submitted on time and reports on projects not submitted by Ministry of Regional Development
g) Salary overpayment continues and recovery of advances has been poor
h) Grants have been given out by some Ministries without contractual obligations on method of utilisation.
i) FMF refuses to take PSC directive on a case
j) Some Ministries do not follow the recruitment procedure
k) Delays in transactions for release of stock have resulted in thousands of dollars of loss for Government Pharmacy
l) Overpayment of salaries and inability to recover
m) No criteria for administration of Poverty Alleviation Grants
n) Poor planning on projects results in substantive financial loss
o) The audit was not about accounts for $34.8m in respect of trust monies, with the Cash at Bank documents

The use of T Bills will have an implication on the debt burden of government. The Finance Ministry inability to provide explanation on its own account raises serious questions on their ability and accountability. The lack of effective internal control has led to uneconomical, inefficient and ineffective operations and exposes government resources to fraud, waste, abuse and mismanagement.

2002 AG Report

a) Procurement procedures continued to be abused by some Ministries and Departments
b) Ministry of Finance and Ministries/Departments have not maintained their ledgers satisfactorily
c) Ledgers have been riddled with errors and expenditures have been charged haphazardly to the accounts
d) Numerous misallocations were noted
e) Effective cash management was generally found to be lacking
f) Excessive use of Treasury Bills to meet the operations of government during the year
g) Use of overnight loan facility of the Reserve Bank
h) Trust monies held by Government have been used for the purposes of government
g) Revolving Fund Account (RFA) exceeded the financial ceilings
g) Ministry of Finance not able to recover salary deductions for overpayment and excess payment
h) Government Supplies Department demonstrated huge profits because all operating expenditure had not been accounted for
i) Transport rules and regulations are continuously being ignored
j) Certain Island Councils are recipients of grants. However, they are supposed to provide acquittals and audited annual financial statements in order to secure further grants. These have not been furnished, while grants continue to be released
k) Immigration Department did not follow correct procedures covering granting of work permits, extension of visitors and work permits and training of locals to replace expatriates
l) FMF not following procedures in procurement of goods and services
m) Salary overpayment, payment without LPOs, lack of cost–benefit analysis for major payments, payment of sitting allowances for meetings that were never convened and not collecting rent for government quarters
n) Lack of controls in processing of building grants, thus leading to defrauding of Government
o) Advancement of farming assistance without any specific criteria
p) Tender procedures not followed properly
q) An amount of $41.7m in respect of trust monies was not supported by Cash at Bank documents
r) Poor budget monitoring and control had resulted in the Government incurring unauthorised expenditure of $14.8m

Source: Report of the Auditor-General on the Accounts of the Government of Fiji (various years), Parliament of Fiji.

REFERENCES

Auditor General of Fiji (1986-2003) *Report of the Auditor General on the Accounts of the Government of Fiji*, Parliament of Fiji, pp. ~1200.

Alm, J., R. Bahl and M. N. Murray (1991) "Tax Base Erosion in Developing Countries", *Economic Development and Cultural Change*, 39(4):849-872.

Andvig, J. C and K. O. Moene (1990) "How Corruption may Corrupt", *Journal of Economic Behavior and Organisation*, 13(1):63-76.

Bardhan, P. (1997) "Corruption and Development: a Review of Issues", *Journal of EconomicLiterature*, 35(3):1320-1347.

Bird, R (1990) *Expenditures, Administration and Tax Reform in Developing Countries,* International Bureau of Fiscal Documentation: Bulletin (June), pp. 340.

Bird, R (1992) *Tax Policy and Economic Development, Baltimore/London,* The John Hopkins University Press, pp. 322.

Brunetti, A., G. Kisunko and B. Weder (1997) "Institutional Obstacles to Doing Business: Region-by-Region Results from a Worldwide Survey of the Private Sector", World Bank , *World Bank PRD Working Paper*, No. 1759, pp. 75.

Calderon, C and Chong, A. (2005) "Do Democracies Breed Rent-seeking Behavior", *Working Paper* #534, World Bank

Chand, S K. and K. O. Moene (1999) "Controlling Fiscal Corruption", *World Development*,27(7):1129-1140.

De Soto, H. (1989) *The Other Path: The Invisible Revolution in the Third World,* Harper and Row, N.Y, pp. 325.

EBRD, (1999) *Transition Report: Ten Years of Transition*, European Bank for Reconstruction and Development , London, pp. 320.

Forum Secretariat (2004) *Forum Economic Action Plan*, Forum Economic Ministers Meeting, Rotorua, New Zealand, 9-10 June, pp3.

Fjeldstad, O and B. Tungodden (2003) "Fiscal Corruption: Vice or a Virtue?" *World Development*, 31(8):1459-1467.

Galtung, F. (1995) "Current Strategies for Combating Corruption: A Study of Corruption in the *Tax* Administration", *Occasional Working Paper*, 8/95. Berlin: Transperancy International, pp. 85.

Grabosky, P and P. Larmour (2000) "Public Sector Corruption and its Control", *Trends and Issues in Crime and Justice,* No. 143, pp. 1-6.

Gradstein, M. (2004) "Governance and Growth", *Journal of Development Economics*, 73(2):505-518.

Guriev, S. (2004) "Red Tape and Corruption", *Journal of Development Economics*, 73(2):489-504.

Heald, D. (2003) "Fiscal Transparency: Concepts, Measurement and UK Practice", *Public Administration*, 81(4):723-759.

IMF (1997) *Good Governance: The IMF's Role*, IMF, pp. 20.

Johnson, S., J. McMillan, and C. Woodruff (2000) "Entrepreneurs and the Ordering of Institutional Reform: Poland, Slovakia, Romania, Russia and Ukraine Compared, *Economics of Transition*, 8(1):1-36.

Kantha, S (2005) "Good Governance Key to Development in PNG", http://archives.pireport.org/archive/2005/November/11-22-com.htm, pp. 3.

Kaufmann, D and A. Kraay (2002). *Growth without Governance,* World Bank, pp. 56.

Kaufmann, D., A. Kraay and P. Zoido-Lobaton (2002) "Governance Matters II: Updated Indicators for 2000/01", *Policy Research Working Paper*, No. 2772, Washington: World Bank, pp. 64.

Krugman, P.R., J. Alm., S. M. Collin and E. M Remolina (1992) Transforming the Philippine Economy, Quezon City: APO Production Unit, Inc., pp. 356.

Krueger, A (1974) "The Political Economy of the Rent Seeking Society", *American Economic Review*, 64(3):291-303.

Krueger, A. (1974) "The Political Economy of the Rent Seeking Society", *American Economic Review*, 64(3):291-303.

Lodhia, S. K and R. L. Burritt (2004) "Public Sector Accountability Failure in an Emerging Economy", *The International Journal of Public Sector Management*, 17(4):345-359.

Mauro, P. (1998) "Corruption and the Composition of Government Expenditure", *Journal of Public Economics*, 69(2):263-279.

Mauro, P. (1995) "Corruption and Growth", *Quarterly Journal of Economics*, 110(2):681-712.

McAfee, R. P and J. McMillan (1987) "Auctions and Bidding", *Journal of Economic Literature*, 25(3):699-723.

OECD (2003) "Public Sector Modernisation", *Observer*, October, pp. 1-8.

Reddy, M., G. Chand and R. Singh (2004) "Public Finance Management in Fiji: The Institutional Environment and the New Finance Management Bill" Fiji Institute of Applied Studies, Research Report 6, pp. 64.

Richupan, S. (1984) *Income tax Evasion: a Review of the Measurement of Techniques and some estimates for the Developing Countries*, Departmental Memorandum No. DM/84/46. The International Monetary Fund, Fiscal Affairs Department, Washington, DC, pp. 45.

Rose-Ackerman, R. (1978) Corruption: A Study in Political Economy, Academic Press, New York, pp. 355.

The Fiji Times (2007) "Army Sets Up Anti –Corruption Unit", *The Fiji Times*, Thursday, 1st February, pp. 3.

The Fiji Times (2007) "Anti –Corruption Unit sets up System", *The Fiji Times*, Friday, 2nd February, pp. 3.

Vinod, H. D. (2003) "Open Economy and Financial Burden of Corruption Theory and Application to Asia", *Journal of Asian Economics*, 13(1):873-890.

Vinod, H. D. (1999) "Statistical Analysis of Corruption data using the Internet to reduce Corruption", *Journal of Asian Economics*, 10(2):591-603.

In: Development Problems and Prospects in Pacific Islands ISBN: 978-1-60021-793-7
Editors: B. C. Prasad, D. C. Roy, pp. 157-166

Chapter 11

MANAGEMENT OF PUBLIC DEBT AND ECONOMIC GROWTH IN FIJI: AN EMPIRICAL STUDY ON DEBT GROWTH NEXUS

S. Ajay Chandra and T. K. Jayaraman

1. INTRODUCTION

Focusing special attention on public debt in emerging market economies, the International Monetary Fund (IMF)'s *World Economic Outlook* (2003), noted that debt levels in emerging economies at the prevalent levels at around 70 percent of their gross domestic products (GDPs) were higher than those in industrial countries and observed that a large public debt hampered economic activity. Higher taxes, which are required to service the growing debt, are seen to exercise upward pressure on real interest rates crowding out private investment, thereby affecting long-term growth.

According to IMF, the prevailing levels of public debt in emerging economies were not currently sustainable-that is, continuation of past fiscal policies would not be sufficient to enable the debts to be repaid in the future. The sustainable level of debt for a typical emerging economy, based on the past fiscal performance, has been estimated by IMF at 25 percent of GDP, while estimates of fiscal policy reaction functions indicated that emerging market economies as a group have failed to respond in a manner consistent with ensuring fiscal solvency once the public debt exceeds 50 percent of GDP (IMF 003).

With excess liquidity in the system in Fiji's economy, which was reflected by low interest rates, including the 91-day treasury bill rate, domestic borrowing by government in the past five years for financing its rising annual fiscal deficits was not felt to be difficult. However, the burden imposed by growing debt would give rise to annual interest payments and cause distortions in the economy created by inflationary tendencies, ultimately affecting growth. The objective of the paper is to examine whether public debt during the last 34 years (1970-2003) led to economic growth in Fiji. The remainder of the paper is organized as follows. The second section presents trends in Fiji's public debt over the last three decades, the third section outlines the methodology adopted for the study; the fourth section presents the results; and the final section offers some conclusions of policy implications.

2. Trends in Public Debt in Fiji

In Pacific Island countries (PICs), external grants in aid in the past were financing capital expenditures to a substantial extent (Table 11.1). In some PICs, external aid in the past had also been financing their current budgets, by providing support for wages and salaries. Fiji annually receives external grants only to the extent of 2% of GDP, the least in the region, with the result its annual fiscal deficits in recent years have to be increasingly financed by resorting to public borrowing.

2.1. Debt Levels in Fiji

Fiji's total debt, comprising domestic and external debt, during the past two decades was low. In fact, the country made conscious efforts during the late 1980s and early 1990s to reduce the external debt by early retirement of loans from international agencies. Fiji was not allowed the facility of concessional loans at an annual 1% rate and long maturity period, which were available to other PICs. With the then prevailing comfortable international reserves equivalent to six-month imports of goods and nonfactor services, Fiji felt appropriate to retire the external debt in advance, rather than continue paying loan installments and interest from future export earnings. With budget deficits also being close to yet another benchmark of 3% of GDP, it was possible to maintain low levels of domestic debt in the 1990s at around 45 % of GDP (Table 11.2).

From 2000 onwards, Fiji stepped up its domestic borrowing to finance its annual fiscal deficits, the major lender being the National Provident Fund. There has been another justification as well. Investor confidence was very low soon after the 2000 coup. Expectations that the private sector would soon recover did not materialize. It was, therefore, considered appropriate to boost investment by incurring fiscal deficits for a while, which were financed by public borrowing. In 2003, Fiji's public debt, including contingent liabilities, was a little above 60% of GDP (Narube 2004).

2.2. Fiscal Deficits and Debt

A recent study (IMF 2004) on *Fiscal Adjustment in IMF Supported Programs* acknowledged that misplaced optimism about private sector recovery would lead to "an understatement of the need for a more countercyclical fiscal stance that is too tight" (Selowsky 2004). Taking the cue from the above, one would conclude that in retrospect, Fiji's fiscal deficits for the last four years were part of countercyclical measures to compensate the loss of fall in private investment.

Table 11.1. Selected indicators of pacific island countries

Country	Land Area sq.km	Population ('000) (2002)	Exclusive Economic Zone ('000 sq.km)	Total GDP (US$ mill) (2001)	Per capita GDP (US$) (2001)	Aid per capita (US$) (2000)	Aid as % of GDP (2000)	Human Develpt Index (1999)	Global HDI Rank (1999)
Cook Islands	240	19	1,830	51	2,651	420	15.9	0.822	62
Fiji	18,272	799	1,260	1,605	2,008	46	2.3	0.667	101
Kiribati	690	85	3,550	45	530	203	38.4	0.515	129
Marshall Islands	170	51	2,131	102	2,008	1,438	49.3	0.563	121
Micronesia	701	114	2,978	213	1,864	1,010	54.1	0.569	120
Nauru	24	12	320	81	7,017	183	2.6	0.663	103
Niue	259	2	390	7	4,773	2,720	58.6	0.774	70
Palau	487	19	601	129	6,989	2,168	31.1	0.861	46
Papua New Guinea	3,120,000	5,099	468	4,232	830	82	8.5	0.314	164
Samoa	2,857	175	120	177	1,004	208	20.6	0.590	117
Solomon Islands	28,446	418	1,630	300	720	102	14.4	0.371	147
Tonga	699	98	700	173	1,763	252	14.3	0.647	107
Tuvalu	26	11	757	4	345	471	130.0	0.583	118
Vanuatu	12,189	183	680	241	1,319	223	16.8	0.425	140

Source: US General Accounting Office(2001); Australian Agency for International Development (2001); Asian Development Bank (2003).

Table 11.2. Overall Fiscal Balance, Growth, Debt and Inflation: 1996-2003

	1996-1999 (Average)	2000	2001	2002	2003	2004 (Revised)	2005 (Revised)	2006 (Budget)
Annual GDP Growth Rate(%)	2.1	-3.2	3.0	4.1	5.0	4.1	1.7	2.0
Fiscal Balance (% of GDP)	-3.5	-3.4	-6.6	-5.6	-6.1	-3.2	-4.3	-4.0
Total Debt (% of GDP)	46.1	41.2	45.5	47.8	50.4	50.3	52.6	53.4
Domestic Debt (% of GDP)	39.2	35.4	40.1	42.9	46.3	46.2	48.0	48.4
External Debt (% of GDP)	6.9	5.8	5.4	4.9	4.0	4.1	4.6	5.0
Inflation (%)	3.2	1.1	4.3	0.8	4.1			

Source: Reserve Bank of Fiji, Quarterly Economic Review (Various Issues); Budget Estimates.

This raises an important question about the nature and composition of public expenditure. While the current budget is nothing but housekeeping expenditure dominated by wages and salaries, the capital budget relates to asset creating investment activities. The ratio of current expenditure to capital expenditure in PICs, including Fiji, has been around 80 to 20. Further, procedural delays involved in the approval of projects through finalization of tenders and contracts along with traditional time lags, would often render fiscal policy at best a blunt tool (Treadgold 1992). Whether public expenditure was undertaken purely as a countercyclical measure to meet the projected fall in demand or simply as a political commitment to step up growth through state sponsored schemes, the resultant rise in public debt due to fiscal expansion given the slow growth in revenue, is a matter of concern.

2.3. Three Reasons

A recent World Bank study (Gill and Pinto 2005) identifies three reasons why public debt might be better than taxation. The three reasons are categorized as (i) tilting; (ii) smoothing; and (iii) stability. Under the first, it would be more equitable if a country can finance projects of long gestation nature through debt, as such projects benefit future (richer) generations than through taxing the current (poorer) generation. The second reason is raising and lowering taxes frequently might entail efficiency losses and generate economic uncertainty and hence, debt allows a more efficient manner for conducting countercyclical polices and for meeting emergency spending needs. The third reason is ensuring stability, since debt avoids reliance on printing money. The latter involves high and volatile inflation, obscuring information content of relative prices and thereby hurting investment. However, as Gill and Pinto (2005) remind us, debt is nothing but postponed taxation since it has to be re-paid; and returns from every infrastructure project for future growth funded by debt, regardless of whether it be physical or social infrastructure, have to include not only user fees but also higher future taxes.

A growing domestic debt level is of concern, because of the growing annual interest burden it would impose on the government. Interest payments have to be made out of primary balance defined as surplus of current revenues over current expenditure, excluding interest payments. A study (Sahay 2004) on the island countries in the Caribbean, with which PICs have been sharing many commonalities, has shown that during 1991-2002, the highly indebted countries in the Caribbean, except Jamaica, were failing to generate primary surpluses. The result has been further deterioration in their overall fiscal balances, leading to further rise in debt levels, as interest payments have to be financed by recourse to additional public borrowing. Therefore, the only way to justify the past public debt in retrospect is to convince the nation that it has contributed to growth.

3. THE METHODOLOGY

For examining the relationship between economic growth and public debt, we resort to the cointegration technique. This technique allows an analysis of the long run equilibrium. By taking into account the properties of time series, we also utilize the vector error-correction model (VECM), which incorporates the error-correction term from the cointegrating equation to capture the long-term deviation from the equilibrium relationship between economic growth and debt.

The cointegration technique requires that time series in the system should be non-stationary in their levels. Further, all time series in the cointegrating equation should have the same order of integration. Accordingly, we begin first by ascertaining the time series properties of the variables, say X and Y by utilizing the augmented Dickey-Fuller (ADF) test for stationarity. The equation to be estimated for the ADF test is given by

$$\Delta X_t = \alpha_0 + \beta_1 X_{t-1} + \delta_t + \sum_{i=1}^{m} \theta_i X_{t-1} + \varepsilon_t \tag{1}$$

where, Δ is the first difference operator, t is the time trend, ε_t is the stationary random error and m is the maximum lag length. The null hypothesis is that the series has a unit toot which implies that β is zero. The null hypothesis is rejected if β is negative and statistically significant.

A time-series is integrated of order d, denoted by $I(d)$, if the series can achieve stationarity after differencing d times. An $I(0)$ series is thus by definition stationary, while $I(1)$ series is random walk, which contains a unit root and non-stationary. Non-stationary series may drift apart from each other in the short-run but a linear combination of the series may be stationary which share a long-run equilibrium relationship. This property is referred to as cointegration. If two series, X_t and Y_t, are both $I(1)$, their linear combination

$$Z_t = X_t - \alpha Y_t \tag{2}$$

is generally also $I(1)$. However, if Z_t is stationary or $I(0)$, then X_t and Y_t are said to be cointegrated. The cointegrating relationship $X_t - \alpha Y_t = 0$ represents a long-run equilibrium relationship between two variables, and Z_t measures the deviation from this long-run relationship for some time-period t.

Existence of cointegration enables us to model both the short-run and long-run relationships simultaneously. If X_t and Y_t are cointegrated, then by Granger representation theorem (Engle and Granger 1987), there exists an error correction representation of the following form:

$$\Delta X_t = \beta_1 Z_{t-1} + \sum_{i=1}^{k} \pi_i \Delta X_{t-i} + \sum_{j=1}^{k} \pi_j \Delta Y_{t-j} + u_{1t} \tag{3}$$

$$\Delta Y_t = \beta_2 Z_{t-1} + \sum_{i=1}^{k} \phi_i \Delta X_{t-i} + \sum_{j=1}^{k} \delta_j \Delta Y_{t-j} + u_{2t} \tag{4}$$

where u_{1t} and u_{2t} are independent white noises. In these two equations, the series X_t and Y_t are cointegrated when at least one of the coefficients β_1 or β_2 is not zero. In this case, the two series will display long-run relationships. If $\beta_1 \neq 0$ and $\beta_2 = 0$, then series Y_t will lead X_t in the long-run. On the other hand, if $\beta_2 \neq 0$ and $\beta_1 = 0$, series X_t will lead Y_t. If both β_1 and β_2 are nonzero, the conclusion then is that there exists a feedback relationship between the two series.

Besides the long-run relationships, short-run relationships between the two series, X_t and Y_t, are signified by the coefficients τ_j's and φ's. If τ_j's are not all zero, movements in the Y_t will cause X_t in the short-run. If φ_i's are not all zero, movements in the X_t will cause Y_t in the short-run. According to Engle and Granger (1987), if α can be obtained so that Z_t can be constructed, the remaining parameters in equation (3) and (4) can easily be estimated. Engle and Granger (1987) propose a two-step procedure. The first step involves ordinary least squares (OLS) regression of X_t on Y_t and yields a consistent estimate for α. The next step involves OLS estimation of equations (3) and (4) with Z_t replaced by $Z_t = X_t - \alpha Y_t$.

The short-run as well as long-run dynamic relationships between X_t and Y_t can be assessed by forming hypotheses and testing them on the estimated coefficients in the equations (3) and (4). In general, six possible testable hypotheses concerning the short-run and long-run influence of X_t on Y_t ($X_t \to Y_t$) and Y_t on X_t ($Y_t \to X_t$) can be formulated. These can be described in the following ways:

(1) $H^{ST}_{Y_t \to X_t}$ *(No ST linkage)* $: \tau_j = 0 \quad (j = 1,\ldots,k);$

(2) $H^{LT}_{Y_t \to X_t}$ *(No LT linkage)* $: \beta_1 = 0;$

(3) $H^{NO}_{Y_t \to X_t}$ *(No ST or LT linkages)* $: \beta_1 = 0$ *and* $\tau_j = 0 \quad (j = 1,\ldots,k)$

(4) $H^{ST}_{X_t \to Y_t}$ *(No ST linkage)* : $\phi_i = 0 \quad (i = 1, ..., k)$;

(5) $H^{LT}_{X_t \to Y_t}$ *(No LT linkage)* : $\beta_2 = 0$;

(6) $H^{NO}_{X_t \to Y_t}$ *(No ST or LT impact)* : $\beta_2 = 0$ *and* $\phi_i = 0 \quad (i = 1, ..., k)$

These individual hypotheses can be tested using standard *F*-tests on the estimated coefficients of the error-correction model. The hypotheses deal with both short-term and long-term relationships between real GDP and stock price index.

Testing for cointegration and performing six causality tests thus involve four steps. First, determine if the level of series are non-stationary and their differences are stationary by employing either Dickey-Fuller (DF) or the augmented Dickey-Fuller (ADF) unit room tests [Dickey and Fuller, 1979, 1981].

The second step involves estimating the following cointegrating regression by OLS:

$$Y_t = \alpha_0 + \alpha X_t + u_t \tag{5}$$

The null hypothesis of no cointegration is tested against the alternative hypothesis of cointegration. The cointegration test involves examining whether the estimated time series of the residuals from the cointegrating regression has a unit root. This cointegration test can either be based on the standard Durbin-Watson (DW) statistic or augmented Dickey-Fuller (ADF) test. The calculated value of DW is obtained from the OLS regression estimate of equation (5). Based on simulation, Engle and Yoo (1987) provide critical values for cointegration tests. If DW test statistic is greater than its critical value, then the null hypothesis of no cointegration is rejected. But a statistically more powerful ADF test can be performed by estimating the following regression:

$$\Delta\hat{U}_t = a\hat{U}_{t-1} + \sum_{i=1}^{m} b_i \Delta\hat{U}_{t-i} + g_t \tag{6}$$

where U_t's are the estimated residuals from equation (5). The optimal lag length can be determined by examining at what lag length the error term g_t becomes a white noise. The ADF test statistic is a pseudo *t*-value associated to test the null hypothesis of no cointegration. The null hypothesis is rejected if the calculated ADF test statistic is greater than its critical value provided by Engle and Yoo (1987).

The third step involves the estimation of error correction model by following the two-step procedure prescribed by Engle and Granger (1987). Finally, the sixth hypotheses regarding lead-lag and feedback relationships among time series are tested using standard F-tests.

4. Empirical Results

The study on Fiji's debt and growth covers a 34-year period (1970-2003). We resort to a simple bivariate model. In view of (3) and (4), the VECM equations to be estimated are given by

$$\Delta LRGDP_t = \beta_1 Z_{t-1} + \Sigma\pi_1 \Delta LRGDP_{t-i} + \Sigma l_1 \Delta LRTD_{t-j} + \mu_{1t}, \tag{7}$$

$$\Delta LRTD_t = \beta_2 Z_{t-1} + \Sigma\pi_2 \Delta LRGDP_{t-i} + \Sigma l_2 \Delta LRTD_{t-j} + \mu_{2t} \tag{8}$$

where $\Delta LRGDP_t$ is the *log* of real Gross domestic product in F$ (millions) and $\Delta LRTD_t$ is the *log* of real total debt in F$ (millions).

4.1. Unit Root Tests

It is well-known that in the time series study, with a view to avoiding spurious regression, we have to ensure stationarity property of the data. Thus, we employ unit root tests to ensure the robustness of our results in determining the univariate properties of the data. The ADF unit root tests results are presented in Table 11.3. The optimal lag length for the ADF test was chosen based on Schwarz Information Criterion (SIC). Tests clearly show that all data are stationary in their first differences, indicating they are *I(1)* processes. These results also imply that the analysis should be conducted in the first difference series rather than in levels. The unit root tests results satisfy the condition that all data should have the same order of integration for them to be cointegrated.

Table 11.3. Unit Root Tests Results

Variables	Level	First Difference
LRTD	-2.3297	-4.0449*
LRGDP	-.0.5663	-3.6286*
Sig. Level	Critical Values	
5%	-3.5867	-2.9750

* Indicates significance at the 5% level.

4.2. Bivariate Cointegration Test

Once the order of integration of each time series is determined, the next step is to test for the cointegration relationship among the variables in the model. The Johansen maximum likelihood method due to Johansen and Juselius (1990) is utilized to examine the number of cointegrating vector(s) in the model. Table 11.4 reports the Johansen-Juselius bivariate cointegration test results. The optimal lag length for the VAR is chosen as 2. As shown in Table 11.4, the null hypothesis of zero cointegration (r = 0) is rejected on the basis of the

Trace test. However, we cannot reject the null hypothesis for at most one cointegrating vector. This implies that there is a single cointegrating vector in the model, and consequently there is a long run stable linear equilibrium relationship between economic growth and debt.

Then the normalized cointegrating regression with t values in the brackets is given by

$$LRTD = -1.8764 + 1.175\, LRGDP$$
$$\qquad (-0.258) \quad (1.347)$$

Table 11.4. Johansen and Juselius Cointegration Test Results

Endogenous Variables: LRTD, LRGDP		
H_0	H_1	λ_{max}
$R=0$	$r=1$	23.2627*
$R\leq 1$	$r=2$	8.3136

Note that r is the number of cointegrating vector and * indicates significance at the 5% level.

4.3. Estimation of Error-correction Model

The next step is to examine the VECM equations (7) and (8) to determine the direction of bivariate causality between economic growth and debt. The estimated VECM equations for log real debt and for log real GDP are as follows:

$$\Delta LRTD_t = -0.144 * Z_{t-1} - 0.414\,\Delta LRGDP_{t-1} - 0.034\,\Delta LRTD_{t-1}$$
$$(-3.760) \qquad (-1.387) \qquad\qquad (-0.206)$$
$$\Delta LRGDP_t = -0.548 * Z_{t-1} + 0.006\,\Delta LRGDP_{t-1} + 0.0002\,\Delta LRTD_{t-1}$$
$$(-2.145) \qquad (0.031) \qquad\qquad (0.002)$$

where * indicates significance at the 5% level and the figures in brackets denote t values.

In the two equations none of the coefficients except those of the respective error correction terms are found significant, indicating the absence of any short-run causality running either from debt to growth or growth to debt. Since only the error terms in both the equations are found statistically significant at the 5% level, the existence of bi-directional causality (feed back) between debt and growth is highlighted.

5. Conclusions

This paper utilized the cointegration procedure to investigate the nexus between debt and growth data for Fiji during 1970-2003. Specifically, the study employed the Johansen cointegration procedure to determine the rank of cointegration space spanned by the stochastic process of economic growth and rise in the nation's total debt. The VECM was estimated to ascertain the direction of causality.

The results show that there is no short-term relationship between debt and economic growth, either from debt to economic growth or economic growth to debt. The relationship between the two has been only in the long term and it happens to be bi-directional. That is, while the causality runs from debt to growth, we also have the causality running from growth to debt. Debt in the long run contributes to income creating and growth supporting assets for ultimate rise in GDP. In addition, economic growth itself leads to conditions for sustaining public debt in the future so that it gives rise to further increase in debt. In other words, we have a statistically significant feedback relationship in this case.

Although the study results indicate the existence of a long-term relationship between debt and growth, there is insufficient evidence to suggest the absence of any adverse effects of rising public debt in the short run. Further research is needed and the ongoing research by the present authors into the monetary implications is expected to fill in the gap.

References

Asian Development Bank (ADB). (2004). *Key Indicators of Asian and Pacific Developing Countries 2004,* Asian Development Bank, Manila.

Gill, I. and B. Pinto (2005). "Public Debt in Developing Countries: Has the Market Based Model Worked?", *Working Paper Series 3674,* Washington D.C.: World Bank.

International Monetary Fund (2004). *Fiscal Adjustment in IMF Supported Programs* Washington D.C.: International Monetary Fund.

International Monetary Fund (2003). *World Economic Outlook* 2003, Washington D.C.: International Monetary Fund.

Narube, (2004). "Fiji Economic Update: Can We Sustain Our Economic Performance?" *Reserve Bank of Fiji Symposium on Towards Prosperity for All*, Suva: Reserve Bank of Fiji: 55-61.

Sahay, R.(2004). "Stabilization, Debt and Fiscal Policy in the Caribbean", *Paper presented at the Seminar on Developmental Challenges Facing the Caribbean,cosponsored by the Central Bank of Trinidad and IMF*, Port of Spain, June 2004.

Selowsky, M. (2004). "IMF Book Forum: Fiscal Adjustment in IMF- Supported Program", quoted in *IMF Survey*, June 28:188.

Treadgold, M. (1992). *The Economy of Fiji: Performance, Management and Prospects*, International Development Issues No.62, Canberra: Australian Agency for International Development.

United Nations Economic and Social Commission for Asia and the Pacific (2004). *Economic and Social Survey 2004.* Bangkok: UNESCAP.

In: Development Problems and Prospects in Pacific Islands ISBN: 978-1-60021-793-7
Editors: B. C. Prasad, D. C. Roy, pp. 167-188

Chapter 12

TRANSITION TO A MARKET ECONOMY IN FIJI: THEORY, POLICY AND EVIDENCE

Rukmani Gounder

1. INTRODUCTION

Just as every country is concerned with its level of economic and social development and its overall performance, many developing countries have a higher degree of concern for their sluggish performance. The political and economic history of the nations, the differential effects of the traditional factors of production along with the political-institutional-social determinants of growth note several experiences and lessons for developing countries. For many developing countries, transition to a market economy has been a means of attaining a higher level of economic growth. These countries have utilised various theories and approaches to enhance growth. Transition reform policies include macroeconomic and microeconomic elements (i.e. fiscal and monetary policies, as well as trade and social policies). Fiji has adopted polices to move towards transition to a market economy. This paper examines the transition economy literature and key factors that contribute to higher growth prospects, particularly in the case of Fiji. The narrow economic resource base, policy options and cultural factors are crucial in understanding Fiji's development goals. Being one of the most affluent South Pacific island nations Fiji's case has special interest, as political instability consequently reflects the dilemma where global challenges merged with concerns of social malaise and racism.

Transition describes a system change where the primary focus is a move to a market based economy. The allocation of resources, thereby, changes from state controlled plan targets to a response to price signals. Two main methods of change include reallocation and restructuring for economic development. The economic, social and institutional mechanisms bring rapid improvements in the standard of living. The interplay of these mechanisms concerns efficient resource allocation, the steady state growth in aggregate output and appropriate public policies for long term growth. Along with economic factors that explain growth include attitude, social capital and social capability thus, culture influences economic outcomes. In order to set the stage for the analysis, it is necessary to understand growth determinants, sectoral impacts, and policy trends and changes that have taken place in Fiji. Although Fiji is an open economy, the political and economic decisions taken by the government in the last 15 years have marked, at the outset, an extended stagnated growth. In considering economic growth there are two important questions that emerge from Fiji's history. First, how did Fiji achieve such fast growth before the 1987 coups despite some of the detrimental effects of rapid population growth, balance-of-payment constraints and pervasive government intervention with import substituting growth policies? Second, why has economic growth remained stagnant despite the implementation of various economic reform policies?

Fiji's economic performance, management and maintenance of stability started with its multi-ethnic composition and its greater passion for economic achievement. The historical perspective of the nation also suggests that other factors (e.g. ethnic diversity, cultural cooperation) and, in addition, government policies and cultural change can be targeted to achieve some non-economic end (i.e. fostering national unity) and create a culture more conducive to economic growth. Fiji's institutional structures were well developed at the time of independence, thus economic achievement until 1986 was remarkable. The military coups of 1987 led the economy to the brink of collapse. Including economic factors with different social structures, development policies, and integration of cultural studies, civic education and the community is a necessary condition to enhance growth and avoid deep differences as well as social strife. Along with these factors the government needs to link political stability, economic policies and its timing and sequences to address various concerns about dangers of slow growth. Timing and sequencing of economic policies, continuing economic and political instabilities, structural changes and social implications have contributed to the dangers of slow growth. The concern therefore is how Fiji has fared in the turbulent years and what are the growth prospects in the next decade.

2. Economic Growth, Transition Economy and Development: An Overview

The basic question asked in the development literature is how people live and what are the processes of improving the quality of life of all human beings. Economic development in a nation is concerned with economic and political factors for impacting rapid structural and institutional transformation to efficiently provide the fruits of economic progress to all segments of the populations. Since the late 1950s, the literature has comprised different approaches to achieving growth. A variety of growth models applied by developing countries can be traced back to the early 1950s with the linear stages theory (i.e. Rostow and Harrod-Domar growth models). In the immediate years following World War II, the prevailing view was "export pessimism" amongst the development economists, with an accompanying emphasis on "import replacement", "domestic industrialization" or "balanced growth". In the late 1960s and 1970s economies transformed their domestic economic structures from the traditional agriculture sector to modern urbanized industries (i.e. manufacturing and services). The Neoclassical Counterrevolution model in the 1980s noted privatization and free markets as relevant and asserted that market price allocation does a better job then state intervention.

The New Growth theory in the 1990s advanced to include the dynamic forces of productivity increase for economies of scale, increasing returns, meeting imperfect competition, have positive spill-over effects, human capital, and research and development (R&D). These factors have become crucial components for the growth process for countries adopting market orientated.[1]

Currently, the emphasis is on transition to market economies and the multi-sector models, which distinguish between the public and private sectors; consumer and producer sectors; domestic and foreign sectors. So to increase resources and opportunities in the private sector led to raising benefits from trade. Key factors have been noted that contribute to growth. Temple (1999) explains why some countries have become rich while others remain poor and notes various aspects of growth - such as world income distribution, steady state paths, returns to inputs like physical capital and the lack of inputs - that developing countries face.[2] Market efficiency, effective communication, transport and power infrastructure can have a positive effect on growth rates where increasing the rate of return on investment through lower transport costs, increased service quality, lower information gathering costs and increased access to technology are growth enhancing. Accordingly, a change to a market based economy is undertaken through allocation of resources and restructuring, thereby, changes from state controlled plan targets to a response to price signals (Blanchard, 1997; Lavigne, 1999; Pomfret, 2002).

Two schools of thought have been identified regarding the speed of transition efforts (Wolf, 1999). First, the conditions/distortions in the economy and the structural-adjustment problem are considered. Consequently, prices and trade are to be liberalized rapidly and comprehensively through fiscal and monetary policies. Most countries have adopted reforms known as 'big bang' reforms (Lavigne, 1999). The second school emphasizes that both market institutions and market-supporting structures are taken where the change must include the creation of an institutional framework that must precede the liberalization of prices together (Wolf, 1999). These reforms are gradual changes and are characterised by more microeconomic focus. Pomfret (2002) notes that there is no clear parting line between the two schools as not everything can be done overnight and that the implementation periods are long. For example, macroeconomic changes for the foreign trade liberalisation often lead by a devaluation of the domestic currency and the microeconomic reforms include reforms and policies applied to sectors, industries or enterprises (Lavigne, 1999; Pomfret, 2002). Enterprise reforms focus on a shift in ownership from state-owned to private and self-financed. Therefore, two possibilities distinguished are the change in structure, production organisation and ownership of the state companies.

Achieving long-term sustainable economic growth, therefore, is crucial for nations to raise capacity to supply increasingly diverse goods to their population through growing capacity based on industrialization, role of agriculture, changing patterns of trade, increasing application of human capital and knowledge to production and the institutional and advancing

[1] This theory is similar to the Neoclassical Counterrevolution theory but differs in assumptions (i.e. diminishing returns of capital and labour, increasing returns to scale in aggregate production, role of externalities in the rate of return on capital).

[2] Importantly, he also points out the empirical issues of models, data, cross-country growth accounting and the problems associated with empirical framework. Another very important development in this study is the inclusion of the proximate sources of growth and the wider influences on growth. This has led to the criticism that the inferences drawn from the new growth empirics are 'fragile' (Levin and Renelt, 1992).

technology. Superior accumulation that accounts for growth in many developing countries in the Asian region has been through institutional efficiency and supporting private domestic investment, and rapidly growing human capital. Manufactured exports grew rapidly by absorption of foreign technology, population growth declined much faster leading to growth in per capita consumption and larger surplus for reinvestment, better allocating of resources to high-return activities, high productivity growth and change in total factor productivity. In moving towards transition to market economies the sustainable growth achieved in the East Asian region has been linked to government's role in provision of infrastructure and good policies to foster economic growth. Thus, benefits were to trickle down to the poor with economic growth and development (Toye, 1993). An explanation through the neoclassical framework is that society becomes forward-looking, motivated and achievement-orientated.

Lack of endogenous factors (i.e. savings and investment) and inefficient and poor institutional structures intensify constraints and impede growth in many developing countries.[3] Poor institutional infrastructures in many developing countries decrease foreign investment flows as well. Even if institutions in place are inefficient there is often little incentive for those in power to change since the private gains for those in power are often under inefficient institutions (Todaro and Smith, 2003). Efficiency, openness, capital mobility, and government policies therefore get distorted as institutions become dysfunctional in reaction to by political instability. Flow of investment is deterred by political instability in those nations where the Institutional Investor Risk Ratings indicators show high levels of risk and uncertainty and low rates of return on capital. Gounder (1999, 2005) highlights the concern over political instability and its impact on investment and growth in Fiji. Many governments suffer from lack of credibility and capability, so even when growth-inducing policies such as increase in openness to trade and incentives for foreign investment are announced does not result into high growth as investors are wary of policy reversal and high capital risk. Enforcement of contracts and rule of law are necessary to attract foreign direct investment (Temple, 1999), but the law is often not enforced, especially in Africa, Asia and the Pacific, so there is a high rate of contract defaulting.

Development of capital markets in many countries has been impeded by lack of institutional infrastructure where nations are hampered by poor and/or lack of property rights (Ghatak, 2003). Property rights (i.e. land property rights, patents etc.) need substantial institutional support in terms of administrative procedures in order to be enforced to attract foreign and domestic investment. Also, lack of security in the capital markets in developing countries and lack of a formal financial sector limit investment. Imperfect goods market often lowers growth, due to the small number of external markets, inefficient cost of production and the low returns on investment. In the global market, if capital accumulation is not supported by economic freedom, good governance and policies then it does not contribute to sustainable growth. But in developing countries lack of support for capital-accumulation-led growth and imperfect goods market structures have hampered growth (Berthélemy and Söderling, 2001). Studies show that countries utilising the structural adjustment policies require a multiple integrated approach to development, including macroeconomic policy, institutional and

[3] In the case of Tanzania, decentralization has led to tax collection by the local governments, so that increased tax burdens have greatly affected the rural farmers. This lowers the growth since increased taxes lower cash levels and thus saving levels, leaving only ill-liquid assets of livestock and sometimes land (Ellis and Mdoe, 2003).

infrastructure reform, and an open economy to enhance growth (Kalter and Khor, 1990; Collier and Gunning, 1999; Butkiewicz and Yanikkaya, 2005).

Globalisation of the world economy saw many developing countries implementing changes to various policies in the 1980s and 1990s to move towards an open market economy. But to a large extent economic growth in these countries has been impeded by imperfect capital and goods markets. Six variables identified to explain slow African economic performance include lack of social capital, lack of openness to trade, deficient public services, geography and risk, lack of financial depth and high aid dependency (Collier and Gunning, 1999). These countries have implemented various reforms over the last decade to overcome the limitations and provide necessary factors for growth. In the case of Sub-Saharan African countries Gounder and Xayavong (2002) find that growth in GDP in over achieving countries has been attributed to the practice of democratic system and adoption of liberal economic regime while the under performing economies lack democratization and free economic system. While it requires market signals emanating from policy reforms and deliberate policies to stimulate growth determinants, political stability is a basic requirement for successful integration into a global economy. Economic freedom, political configuration, and institutional structures based on a democratic system are crucial for resource allocation, production and efficiency.[4] So transition to a market economy has been regarded as enhancing economic performance.

The main implication of the discussion on growth theories is that it is obvious that developing countries' economic performances have greater variation over time due to differences in the effects of various factors (i.e. economic, political, social, institutional and cultural values) in determining economic growth and development. Landes (1998) points out that if we learn anything from the history of economic development it is that culture makes all the difference. Reflecting on the cultural aspect of influence on economic growth, the key characteristics noted by Weil (2005) are openness to new ideas, hard work, saving for the future, trust, social capital and social capability. Characteristics from the economic perspective can be explained in terms of differences in per capita income among countries, which leads to accumulation of physical capital, technology and efficiency in production. The preceding analysis notes how growth factors and development are important for welfare. These issues are examined in the case of Fiji below. The historical literature of Fiji's colonisation and land issues, and the constitutions are examined briefly followed by the trends in output and factors of production are considered.

3. Key Factors of Production in Fiji

An intriguing issue in development economics in recent times has been the impasse faced by several developing economies, whereby they are, despite the fulfilment of most if not all of the traditional pre-requisites for growth, locked into a slow-growth or no-growth steady state. But, it is now increasingly recognised that the cardinal missing link has actually been the absence of a favourable politico-institutional milieu.[5] Fiji could easily be mentioned as a

[4] Economic freedom is an important conditioning factor which promotes activities, therefore contributing to higher economic growth and attaining improved standards of living (Wu and Davis, 1999 and Gounder 2002).

[5] See M.Olson jr. (1996) for a discussion on why some nations are rich and others poor.

typical example reflecting such a dilemma where issues of global challenges, economic vulnerability, security concerns, and moral hazards have emerged. In its efforts towards development, Fiji moved with the time and adopted strategies and policies, that had been in vogue and internationally recognised, yet the economy remains sluggish posing serious challenges to policy makers.

The fundamental reason for the failure lay not in the pursued policies but more in the inability to marry these policies with compatible socio-economic, cultural and political management for desirable outcomes. Elster's (1994) contention is that the constitution of a country forms a key component of its economic performance and it should promote stability, accountability and credibility. Fiji's 1997 Constitution requires imbuing a common perspective across the socio-economic plurality for resource allocation and utilization in the production function, so that land ultimately combined with capital can enhance long-term growth. Land, natural resource endowments and agricultural productivity without doubt are vital growth determinants. A serious impediment to increase productivity from the land in Fiji is the system by which land is held and farmed.

The structure of land property rights at the time of Fiji's independence did not ring any alarm bells. Even in the drafting the 1970 Constitution it was never an issue: displacing non-Fijian ethnic communities least occupied the minds of its framers. In the 1990s, though it affected both the renewal of land leases and land utilisation. Issues on land leases are well documented in Prasad and Tisdell (1996), Lal et al., (2001) and Prasad (2006). The sugar industry, agriculture, tourism and peoples' livelihood rely on land leases; however, the system by which the land is held and farmed is a serious impediment to increasing productivity, due to insecurity surrounding lease renewal and the charging of management fees at various levels. To enhance economic growth and development land reforms are vital. Poorer communities in the capital market would face barriers due to lack of income earning capacity that would increase poverty, and reduce society's potential for productive investment and innovation. In explaining the factors for growth, particularly land and the role of the Constitution, the challenges remains how resource allocation and reforms can be implemented through economic, institutional and social policies for wellbeing and higher economic performance. Besides enhancing national wealth an appropriate role of the state is to assimilate culture, freedom and rights, and use of resources to engage in exchange; and these aspects are constitutionally guaranteed. The penultimate section examines economic growth trends and key conditioning factors necessary to attain sustainable growth.

3.1. Trends in Output

As a young independent nation Fiji was on the path of achieving a relatively high-level economic growth in the 1970s. Using Rostow's (1960) stages of growth theory, Fiji had set targets with an emphasis on the "take-off" to "self-sustaining" growth. The main emphasis was on capital formation, more specifically an increase in the rate of investment, and at the same time several structural changes and human capital aspects were being expanded to meet its development goals. Basic strategies for development were based on import substituting industrialisation, i.e. the promotion of industries orientated towards the domestic market by using restrictions, or even import prohibition, to encourage replacing imports by domestic products.

An initially successful beginning of economic growth has been due to increased activities of most sectors of the economy; Figure 12.1 depicts the Gross Domestic Product (GDP) growth rates for the period 1961 to 2003. Fiji achieved preconditions to take-off in the mid-1970s due to higher domestic savings and investment and also via increase in flows of foreign capital. Higher growth outlook in the early 1970s has been boosted by increased business and high consumer confidence and investment, strong labour market growth and an increase in Fiji's major trading partner countries and preferential trade agreements under the Lome convention. From 1970 until the mid-1980s, Fiji primarily relied on tourism and resource-based industries, the most important of which was sugar. There was a greater reliance on market forces and increasing manufactured exports volumes. In the agriculture sector sugar was the main commodity, and fishing and the tourism sectors also provided a positive impetus to growth. The manufacturing sector was developed (so improved technology) with clothing and textile industries that gathered momentum in the 1980s increasing the exports to the countries in the Asia-Pacific region. Agriculture productivity rose and the industrial employment grew with urbanization of the economy.

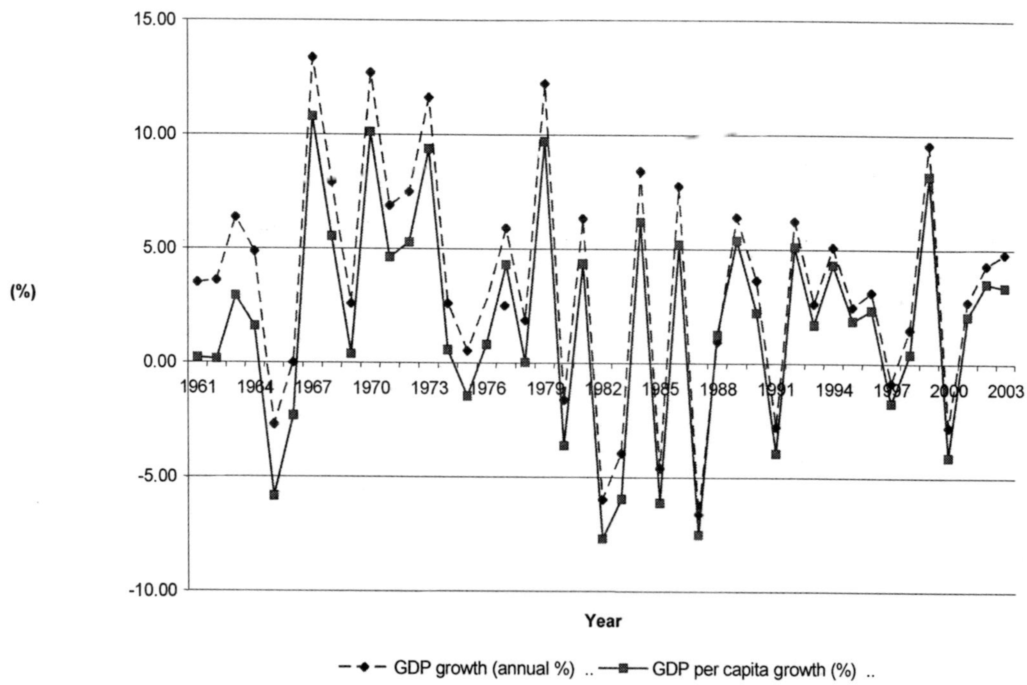

Source: World Bank (2005).

Figure 12.1. GDP Growth Rate and GDP Per Capita Growth Rate, 1961 to 2003.

Foreign capital flows, in terms of foreign aid and foreign direct investment (FDI), became important sources for economic growth. In the early 1980s when economic performance experienced negative impact many of the determinants that had performed well in the past deteriorated immensely. Recessionary phases were due to protracted world recession, slump in commodity prices and high international interest rates. Natural disasters and climatic conditions also adversely affected the economy, thus agriculture and tourism sectors and other export industries suffered the repercussions affecting the supply shocks. It no doubt worsened the economic situation that affected long run growth. Real GDP trend in Figure 12.1 shows that economic growth recorded double-digit growth in 1970, 1973 and 1979. While the period 1970-79 maintained positive growth of at least above 5% for some years, fluctuated growth rates in the early 1980s these were weather-induced setbacks in agriculture and the oil crises, therefore growth in several industries' output were low.

The largest decline in growth that stands out as a crucial turning was in 1987 due to two military coups, the growth rate declined by -6.8%. Volatility in several of the factors of production occurred that felt an immediate adverse impact. Contributions of the agriculture and industry sectors declined drastically since than, impacting per capita GDP significantly. In 1989 the large increase in growth rate (i.e. 13.5%) has been through the contribution of the sugar cane sector (benefits arising from the higher price of world market sugar) and boosting industrial expansion in the building and construction sector. While the 1980s was dubbed the "lost decade" domestic political crisis added to Fiji's troubles together with poor progress in export diversification. Narayan and Prasad (2003) note that larger declines in exports and problems in export diversification hindered output and growth. As political instability in the 1990s continued economic growth declined and per capita income fluctuated and rose much more slowly than GDP in the latter period. Without the establishment of policies for competition and the structural reforms Fiji was unable to compete with foreign industries the reform policies failed to revive the economy. But Fiji experienced the failure of the reform policies to revive the economy.

The political instability and economic crisis following the military coups and implemention of the racially-biased 1990 Constitution, non-resolution of the land leases and with no past tradition of laissez faire policies meant that private sector development was not sufficient due to low sectoral output growth along with lower output from the traditional agriculture sector. Domestic economic activities weakened due to deterioration in the textile, clothing and footwear industry. The mining sector was affected by lower ore quality, fragile corporate and consumer confidence, sluggish investment and a weak labour market that contributed to slow growth (Reserve Bank of Fiji (RBF), 1997). High indebtedness and deterioration of the fiscal balance position certainly played adversative roles, including the engine of growth determinants being affected by rent-seeking problems in the post-1987 coup period (Chand, 2001). This became the root of the trouble, as the rent-seeking devices have created interests that made their overhaul difficult.

From early to mid-1990s growth in output remained low even with the implementation of various economic policy reforms. Reasons for this impact in addition to the lack of factors, included poor economic policies, macroeconomic instability and poor management of funds, and lack of accountability led to increased corruption. Fiji embraced the IMF recommended structural adjustment policies. Emphasis was placed on diversifying the export base while the service sector also emerged as the leading sector for growth. But resource distortions, lower economic growth rates and lack of a number of crucial economic factors provided shortages to export diversification. Besides this, private investment was at low levels, lack of skilled labour also affected the labour markets and a narrow economic resource base, lack of finance, and political instability caused severe risk and uncertainties (Gounder, 1999; Narayan, 2001). Interventionist restrictions, inefficient state enterprise and bureaucratic red tape harmed industries and entrepreneurship as the government supported few interested groups and not broad development. High growth of 9.6% in 1999 by the newly elected government in 1998 was shattered by the May 2000 coup. Growth declined by 9.3% in the third quarter of 2000, while the overall growth declined by almost 3 percent in 2000. Lifting the monetary restrictions (i.e. lower interest rates and sufficient liquidity for loans) by the RBF and the government's support for key sectors through fiscal policy response after the crises protected the financial position to enhance growth. Disaggregated GDP components are analysed below to measure the individual impact of each factor, sectoral performance and its impact on growth.

3.2. Trends in Labour Force and Capital Stock

The influence on capital accumulation with central planning playing the key role for growth maximisation via the investment sector has been pivotal. This section examines two main influences of growth determinants, namely labour and capital. The question that arises is whether capital and labour increased over time and what is the likely impact on growth due to the availability (or lack) of these factors of production. A large population essentially means a large market so long as people have sufficient means to demand the output produced. Also, a higher educated population can supply ample skilled labour, in theory an important factor in the growth process. The labour force is about half of the population aged 15 to 64. About 50% of the population are in the communal and rural based subsistence sector.

The basic growth determinants focus on two types of inputs, namely labour and capital stock. The contribution of skilled manpower in the production process is most important for GDP to grow. Table 12.1 presents the data of labour and capital stock for the period 1970 to 2002. Fiji's population growth decreased from almost 2.4% in the 1970s to 1.8% in the late 1980s and 1990s. The population in 1999 was 1.54 times and the labour force 2.07 times the 1970 levels. A severe problem in the labour market has been that uncertainty in the political and economic environment caused high unemployment. The number of newly registered taxpayers with the Inland Revenue Department, a partial number indicator of employment, fell between 20 and 30% in the post-coup period. Redundancies have continued to rise, mainly in the manufacturing sector (i.e. garments and timber industries) but also there has been an increase in the closure of businesses/firms (mainly entering into receivership). Improvement in the employment situation can only be envisaged if there is an increase in economic activities in the future but political stability and economic certainty are the basic requirements to gain business confidence and employment generation.

The situation in the labour market has been exacerbated by a large number of Fiji residents emigrating since 1987, categorised as mainly professional or skilled workers (Mohanty, 2001). Decline in the skilled labour contribution affected productivity growth as there has been a consistent outflow of skilled workers, which surged following the 2000 coup.[6] Decline in skilled manpower and economic activities led the government to implement structural adjustment policies to give greater prominence to export-led industries. Initially,

[6] Between 1987 and 2001, skilled emigrants of all ethnic backgrounds has been estimated to be 70,660 of which almost 90% were Indo-Fijians, while the number of emigrants in 2000 was 5,275 and 6,316 in 2001 (Kumar and Prasad, 2002, pp.10-11). Skill categories of these emigrants are architects, accountants, teachers, medical workers, transport workers, clerical and supervisors, administrative and managerial workers, sales personnel, agriculture, animal husbandry and forestry workers, fishermen as well as service workers (RBF, 1997). Cumulative to May 2001 the number of professionals leaving the country increased by 32 percent (RBF, 2001, p. 15), and around 5,800 left in 2003 which represents a 5 percent increase from 2002 (RBF, 2004, p. 17).

marginal increase in the labour force has been in the garment sector. Narayan and Prasad (2003, p. 4) note that "early signs from Fiji's export-led strategy for growth were encouraging, for it saw the emergence of labour-intensive garment industry, which in its peak employed some 18,000-20,000 people, of which 79% were female workers". But the garment workers faced loss of jobs due to closure of the garment factories in the post-2000 coup period. While the number in total employment increased in the 1990s in some sectors what is crucial is that sectors where skilled labour are employed (i.e. Agriculture, Fisheries and Forestry; Mining & Quarrying; Electricity, Gas & Water; Finance, Insurance, Real Estate, Business Services) declined in the late 1990s. The post-2000 crisis period does not show higher expansion in employment at a level necessary to enhance growth.

Table 12.1. Labour Force and Capital Stock, 1970 – 2002

Year	Total Population	Population Growth Rate (%)	Total Labour Force	Total Population Aged 15-64	Gross Fixed Capital Formation (%)			
					Govt.	Public	Private	Total
1970	520,000	2.33	153,920	280,505	-	7.3	13.3	20.6
1975	576,000	1.98	177,408	333,998	-	8.7	11.4	20.1
1980	634,000	2.07	203,514	368,029	5.0	7.8	14.9	27.7
1985	697,000	1.59	232,101	408,817	3.5	3.2	13.6	20.3
1986	714,000	2.41	239,190	418,612	3.3	2.0	11.0	16.2
1987	721,000	0.98	243,698	422,538	2.5	3.9	10.9	17.3
1990	736,000	1.37	253,920	430,781	3.1	6.5	5.5	15.0
1995	770,000	0.59	287,210	469,353	2.4	6.0	4.1	12.5
2000	811,900	1.35	323,298	514,000	2.9	5.4	3.1	11.5
2001	817,000	0.63	329,398	522,000	3.5	6.7	3.5	13.7
2002	823300	0.77	336,038	529,000	-	-	-	-

Source: World Bank (2005) and Reserve Bank of Fiji (2004).
Notes: not available.

Analyses of the next factor of production, i.e. physical capital, have long noted that physical capital stock has played an important role through mechanization process to increase productivity in developed nations. Mechanization and capital resources have made substantial contributions to rapid growth in Fiji, particularly since the encouragement of the manufacturing sector in the 1980s. Domestic investment in Fiji's post-independence period was rather modest the increased substantially ranging between 20 to 25% of GDP between 1970 and 1985 (Table 12.1). Initially, private investment share to total investment made up over 50%, but this began to decline drastically to less than 30% of total investment share in the post-1987 period. Private investment started to decline from the mid-1980s and it reduced substantially in the post-coup period where it declined to the single digit composition that remains very low, totalling to less than 5 percent of GDP in the late 1990s. Public and Statutory Bodies investment rates have been low and has also not increased to the 1970s level. Investor confidence will be further distorted affecting growth in the medium and long term. Rao (cited in Duncan, 2004) points out that an investment to GDP ratio of around 25 percent is needed to achieve a sustained GDP growth of 5%.

Fiji's domestic investment rates ranged between 10 and 15% of GDP during the 1990s, a level much lower than the rates experienced in other Pacific Island countries during the period. Of particular concern is the fact that productivity growth rates achieved from these levels of investment have been relatively low. Chand (2004) suggest that this low level of productivity of investment can partly be explained by natural constraints imposed by size, isolation, political instability, and the consequential lack of consumer confidence. Fiji's lack of capital accumulation suggests that technological progress can not be maintained to increase productivity in the associated sectors as imports of machinery and equipment have also declined due to low demand and weak economy. This effect implies that decrease in investment reduces the predominant role it played in the growth process. Uncertainty in the political environment caused high risk to capital and lowered the rate of return, which ultimately affected the constant returns of scale. Moreover, lower productivity affects under-capacity utilization owing to the constraints on output. The uncertain political environment, caused a bleak economic environment which affected capital formation and outflow of skilled labour, retarded economic progress as social development suffered. Fiji's ranking of HDI has slipped from 44th in 1996 to 66th in 1998 to 92nd in 2003 (UNDP, 2001, 2005).[7] Outcomes of such situations are seen in terms of vertical and horizontal inequality, larger number of households living in poverty, high drop out rates in primary and secondary schools, increased crime rates, destitution and depression.

The economic purpose of capital flows in the form of FDI and foreign aid are crucial in meeting the resource needs for development. Both FDI and foreign aid are seen as a way of filling in gaps between the domestically available supplies of savings, foreign exchange, government revenue and human capital skills and the desired level of these resources necessary to achieve growth and development targets. Table 12.2 presents Fiji's 5-year average values of FDI and foreign aid flows and its various components for the period 1970/74 to 2003. The FDI flows declined substantially immediately after the 1987 coups, also between 1995 and 1999 and in the post-2000 political crisis period. Instability and uncertainty has led to lower FDI flows in 2003, i.e. FDI to GDP ratio declined to 0.98%. It is seen that FDI contributes substantially to gross capital formation amounting to over 32% between 1990 and 1994. The decline in 2000 by -8.22% is significantly higher, which reduces the number of capital projects and the funds flowing to those projects.

The contribution of foreign aid towards capital formation and imports of goods and services have been substantial over time, but with political instability these flows have declined. Due to lack of these investment funds a range of projects funded via FDI and aid would therefore take longer to complete or may not be finished. Higher deficits would also result in the balance of payments problems owing to lower availability of funds towards good and services. Essentially, as the domestic capital is scarce, development projects (i.e. infrastructure and industrial investment programmes) are affected and given the decline in FDI and aid flows domestic consumption would also get affected. Fiji needs to provide a stable environment to attract FDI for long-run economic investment for plants, equipments and other capital flows thus it can not afford temporary or speculative capital, as it brings high levels of risk. Higher FDI flows can be achieved by improving the time taken for FDI

[7] In comparison with other South Pacific Island nations Tonga and Samoa are ranked way ahead of Fiji, with Tonga in 54th place and Samoa at 74th place in 2003 (UNDP, 2005).

approval, improving protection of property rights, reducing the brain drain and reducing the costs of telecommunications (Duncan, 2004).

Table 12.2. Capital Flows to Fiji, 5-Year Average 1970/74 to 1995/99 and 2000 to 2003

Year	FDI, net inflows (% of GDP)	FDI, net inflows (% of gross capital formation)	Aid (% of GDP)	Aid (% of gross capital formation)	Aid (% of imports of goods & services)	Aid per capita (constant US$)
1970-74	3.09	13.90	3.58	15.46	..	3.45
1975-79	1.57	6.86	3.10	13.20	5.67[a]	11.71
1980-84	2.76	10.84	3.03	11.74	5.45	23.16
1985-89	1.41	9.22	3.45	21.77	6.71	33.69
1990-94	4.60	32.71	3.51	23.62	5.27	55.05
1995-99	1.69	12.81	5.50	16.82	3.39	48.85
2000	-0.91	-8.22	1.75	15.21	..	35.87
2001	2.42	17.62	1.59	10.97	..	33.13
2002	1.46	..	2.04	..	..	43.48
2003	0.98	..	2.61	..	..	67.01

Source: World Bank (2005).

Notes: .. not available, [a] value shown is for 1979 only, as data for 1975-78 was not available.

Aid programmes also contribute substantially to capital investment projects that consist of a wide variety of resource transfer activities including multi-year projects (usually involving technical and material/equipment inputs); human capital development; economic and social infrastructure development; and commodity support (i.e. grants given to meet the cost of importing goods required for development purposes). As the economy has been impeded by poor infrastructure, inefficient resource allocation, and imperfect capital and goods markets, therefore aid is utilised to finance imports of capital and intermediate goods. Aid as a source for gross fixed capital formation is larger than FDI share of the contribution. Essentially, aid has been used for public sector investment (Jayaraman, 1998; Gounder, 2001; Narayan, 2004). Aid assists the public sector and supports the balance of payments linked to public expenditure for social and economic services. While aid may not promote faster growth as seen in many developing countries, but if aid is reasonably well designed and allocated it can be effective in helping a variety of programmes and the poor. Gounder (2001) finds a positive impact of the aid-growth nexus for Fiji. There is a need to increase savings for capital formation (Reddy, 2000). Savings to GDP ratio was over 20% in the pre-1987 coup period and has declined to lower than 15% of GDP in the post-coup period. Low savings rates can be problematic in that they reflect a high propensity to consume, shallow financial systems and the narrowness of the monetized portion of the economy.

3.3. The Sectoral Focus of Growth

Particularly in that it is a small open island economy, trade is pivotal for Fiji's growth process. Since adopting market polices the country has faced the global conditions of competition. However, the smallness in size, lack of capital resources and political instability led to major constraints in various sectors. Fiji relies heavily on imports for domestic consumption and production, thus both exports and imports are crucial for growth from the perspective of both demand and supply side.

The 1970s trend in imports to GDP ratio has been over 50 percent until 1984 with export shares trending closely to import ratios. Import substitution was significant in the 1970s but the economy was dependent on import of non-durable consumer goods, intermediate products, capital goods and raw material. The period 1985 to 1988 is the only period when exports to GDP share exceeded import ratios. Decline in imports essentially has been due to fall in domestic demand of import of investment goods like machinery, chemicals and electrical goods reflecting a weak economy and investment climate, besides imports costing more since the devaluation of the currency in 1988. Export growth suffered major set backs due to political uncertainty and policies not conducive for exports. Even an increase in the volume of garment products did not result in higher export earnings due to price fluctuations. While the sugar exports share and sugar prices fell drastically, the share of manufactured exports increased but it was not large enough to offset the decline in sugar revenue to increase total export earnings. Export sector performance was inferior despite implementing export-orientated policies where price fluctuation, low agricultural export earnings, dependent on few primary products, and uncertainty (created by expiry and non-renewable of land leases) affected export productivity and output.

A major cause in Fiji's balance of payments constraint resulted from insufficient foreign exchange to finance the growth of imports for realising full capacity of the economy. The severity of this problem was felt during the political crisis of 1987 extending to 1990s. Thus the terms of trade (TOT) deteriorated, i.e. the price of imports was much larger than relative price to exports. Constraints of price fluctuations of the agricultural commodities were badly hit by decline in prices of those exports. Performances of agriculture, industry and service sectors have been adversely affected. As the annual growth in value added of these major sectors declined severely in 1996 and 1997, real GDP per capita level deteriorated to real value of 1973 level (See Figure 12.1). Problems in the agriculture sector reflected most drastically on the sugar industry while receipts from tourism declined significantly. Since the mid-1990s there has been a perpetual decline in both the sectors due to falling productivity and expiring land leases. As seen in Figure 12.2 the performance of the agriculture sector has been low and erratic. Annual growth in agriculture value added does not indicate any likely improvements due to low agricultural earnings and non-renewal and resolution of land leases. The tourism sector was negatively impacted but it recovered with higher tourist arrivals and tourist receipts. Garments exports were stimulated with the introduction of in-bound manufacturing sites and creation of tax-free zones, but it has been adversely affected by closure of several garment firms. Manufacturing sector employment increased substantially to cater for the changes in the structure of this sector.

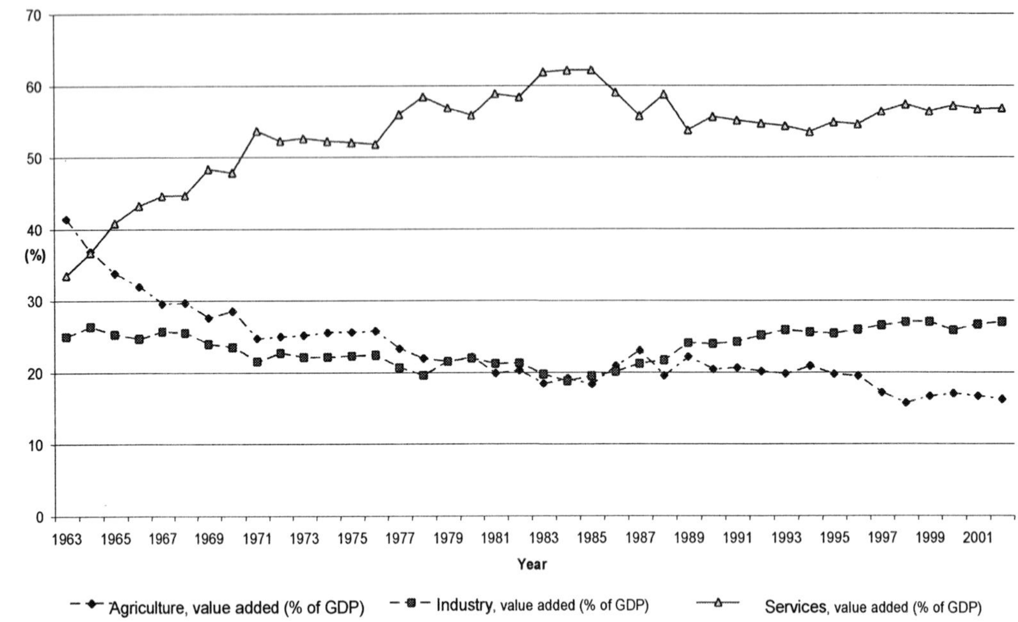

Source: World Bank (2005).

Figure 12.2. Agriculture, Industry and Service Sector Contributions as a % of GDP, 1963 to 2002.

Of the three sectoral contributions to GDP the service sector out-performs the agriculture and industrial sectors. What is interesting here is that annual growth in the service sector was much higher in the 1970s (between 8 to 16% annual growth), its contribution to GDP is substantially higher in the pre-1987 coup period but the value added does not exceed 5% between 1990 and 1999. This is not surprising as following the implementation of reform policies there have been major cuts in employment in the tourism and garment industries. As the business and consumer confidence declined the service sector experienced a low rate of expansion in the value added. Based on the theory of economic development the service output growth is much faster than growth in GDP when compared with other sectors performance and it is considerably higher and contributes to overall economic growth. However, service sector growth is marginal in Fiji. Also, outflow of highly skilled labour adversely impacted the private sector development and most of the expansion has been in the public sector and is closely tied to government budget. The private sector on the other hand has not performed to its capacity and the tourism sector has not expanded to the extent of rapid service sector growth, which could have been achieved independent of the government sector. Moreover, fluctuations in the tourism industry, lack of business services and the May 2000 political crisis do not give much confidence that this sector could be the engine of growth.

The GDP by activity is presented in Table 12.3. Substantial structural changes have occurred in the economy in the 1980s. The share of primary sectors (i.e. Agriculture, Forestry, Fishing) have fallen sharply from 22.2% in 1985 to 19.72% of GDP in 1995. Decline in sugar, forestry and fisheries output has not improved, thus its share to GDP contribution declined to less than 15.5% in 2002. Mining and Quarry activities also fluctuated over time. The manufacturing sector's share increased marginally between 1985 and 1992, but since than it has remained almost unchanged at around 14% of GDP in the late 1990s and 2002. The share of Electricity, Water, Building and Construction to GDP declined considerably in 1999 to almost the level of 1985, largely due to a decline in the building and construction industry. The Trade, Restaurant and Hotel activities and the activities of the Transportation and Communications sector have risen over time. Other Services activities of Finance, Insurance, Real Estate and the Business Services share to GDP declined between 1996 and 2002, with increases noted in the Community and Social Services sector. The trends in GDP activities show substantial decline in the performance of various sectors which led the government to shift the economy from a primary-based to a service-oriented structure. Given the adjustments over time it is vital to evaluate economic policies and structural changes to enhance the growth performance.

Table 12.3. GDP by Activity (Constant 1989 Prices) Selected Years, 1985 to 2002

Year	Agriculture Forestry Fishing	Mining & Quarry	Manufac-turing	Electricity Water Buildg. Const.	Trade, Restaurant Hotels	Transport & Communi-cation	Other Services[a]	Total
1985 $M	156.2	0.8	79.3	46.5	124.8	90.3	205.9	703.7
%	22.20	0.11	11.27	6.61	17.73	12.83	29.25	
1990 $M	329.7	55.3	218.5	112.7	271.1	170.7	455.6	1613.6
%	20.43	3.42	13.54	6.98	16.80	10.58	28.23	
1995 $M	362.8	46.7	267.7	152.9	299.4	222.7	487.9	1840.1
%	19.72	2.53	14.55	8.31	16.27	12.10	26.51	
2000 $M	342.1	51.1	295.9	176.0	382.0	270.0	515.1	2023.2
%	16.83	2.51	14.56	8.66	18.80	13.29	25.35	
2001 $M	326.90	52.0	330.1	180.0	395.5	279.1	520.2	2084.7
%	15.68	2.49	15.83	8.63	18.97	13.39	24.95	
2002[b] $M	334.0	50.1	316.9	195.9	414.3	314.0	544.7	2170.1
%	15.39	2.30	14.60	9.02	19.09	14.47	25.10	

Source: Reserve Bank of Fiji (1998, 2004).

Notes: [a] Other Services less imputed services charges. [b] Provisional. Percentages may not add to 100 due to rounding errors.

4. Economic Policy and Structural Changes

The issue of which government policies can maximize growth is one of the oldest questions in economics. Association of the political economy with material welfare has been through a systemic inquiry where the policies for regulating production, distribution, consumption, exchange of commodities, labour, capital etc. are to enhance growth and development. Over centuries nations have on the basis of the principles of economics and political economy utilized public economic policies for the production of wealth and welfare to satisfy human wants. States have implemented laws to govern the civil society but over time it has created class and modern bourgeois society. Nations characterized by diverse ethnic groups are confronted with the question of meeting ends and means. Therefore, in an environment of modernization, scarcity, resource allocation problem, population growth, employment, inflation, technology, globalization, the role of the state and economic policies are crucial for overall welfare, growth and development.

Fiji's economic policies and structural changes undertaken to accommodate growth and overcome the problems through policy instruments in the pre- and post-coup period have been considerable. The successive five-year Development Plans (DP) in Fiji focussed on economic growth with equitable distribution of the benefits of development, generation of increased employment opportunities, diversification of economic base, greater self-reliance and regional development (Central Planning Office, 1985). Medium-term and long-term strategies are formulated given the macroeconomic targets, the fiscal framework and the sectoral focus. These targets set the direction of government's policy framework to contribute to economic and financial stability and ultimately improve the standard of living. In the 1970s and early 1980s the inward-looking strategy of import substitution was one way to accelerate growth. Changing the requirements for the economy was addressed by shifts in the type, direction and distribution of growth as the objectives in these plans placed greater emphasis on strengthening and further diversifying the economic base via export promotion policies. Fiscal and monetary policies, trade and balance of payments policies and price and income policies were formulated to address the changes.

In 1984 Fiji signed the IMF structural adjustment programme. Real shift in industrial policy, i.e. a move towards trade liberalization, occurred in 1986 with the announcement of creating in-bound manufacturing sites with the provision of various investment incentives. It offered both local and foreign investors customs exemptions and tax concessions in exchange for a commitment to export at least 95% of the output. Fiji responded to both economic liberalization and export-oriented industrialization and to specific advice from international agencies (Chandra, 1989). It maintained a regulatory regime consisting of relatively high tariffs and various non-tariff barriers such as licensing and import quotas. Fiji pursued the program of import substitution, however "the manufacturing sector was small so the limited industrial development that did occur... was still largely based on import substitution policies (Akram-Lodhi, 1996, p. 262).[8] This policy initiative was a decisive step in a shift in industrial policy away from import substitution toward export promotion which was intensified following the 1987 military coups. Outward-looking development strategy could not achieve the level that a market based system does to promote exports due to loss of competitiveness of Fiji's products, adverse international price movements of major export commodities, sluggish investment levels and lower consumer demand.

Immediately after the drastic and adverse economic consequences of the 1987 coups the military-backed interim government to enhance the industrialization process, implemented an export-oriented model of development that became central to Fiji's future economic development (Chandra, 1989, p 170). In addition to setting up in-bound manufacturing sites the approval processes for FDI were simplified, Fiji largely removed import licensing and progressively reduced tariff levels. In a speech in 1991 (the late) Ratu Sir Kamisese Mara (the former Prime Minister and Interim Prime Minister of Fiji) stated that "[O]ur economic policies indicate that we have woken up to the challenges of competing in the international

[8] See Sturton and McGregor (1991), and Elek et al., (1993) for the economic policies in the post-coup period.

environment. We are no longer content to hide behind high tariff barriers" (Mara, 1991, cited in Akram-Lodhi, 1996, p.265). Comprehensive development planning was substituted by a document highlighting policies and strategies in the medium term (Government of Republic of Fiji, 1993). The (then) Minister of Finance and Economic Planning in 'introduction' of this document states that "the strategic approach to planning ...differs essentially from the traditional 'comprehensive' approach to planning in that it emphasises the primacy of effective policy formation and concentration on specific issues relating to the implementation of policy" (Manueli, 1993, p.v).

Following the introduction of policy change several macroeconomic policies implemented were to improve economic performance. But the economy was operating under the 1990 Constitution which created a volatile and unstable political and economic climate while all economic sectors including non-economic activities were affected by the policies stated in this Constitution. International pressure to review the 1990 Constitution provided some assurance for its growth factors.[9] Although the government instituted economic policies for sustainable economic growth it neither achieved sustained recovery nor sustainable growth in the 1990s. This can be attributed to a mixture of poor economic policies, non resolution of land leases and political instability. Policy reforms alone have been insufficient to stimulate export-led growth as private investment and FDI flows did not increase despite government's assurance and policies to support private sector development. Kumar and Prasad (2002, p. 3-4) sum up the views of many critics that "policy switch from import substitution to export-oriented strategy pursued vigorously after the coups of 1987 led to modest economic recovery in the period 1991-1996 and 1996-2000. However, this policy shift has not as yet delivered a higher average annual growth".

The failure of policies has been because the changes were undertaken in isolation and not integrated with those policies that linked the economy. For example, trade liberalisation policy has occurred against a backdrop of political instability and ongoing uncertainty about land property rights that deterred investment (Prasad and Tisdell, 1996; Chand, 1998). Recently expired land leases displaced a large section of farming community that leading to rural-urban migration. As these displaced tenants seek alternative employment in urban areas it has caused large squatter settlements without basic needs. Given the rural-urban push factors there is now a wider recognition that the agricultural sector was downgraded too early in the structural reform program (Akram-Lodhi, 1997). Siwatibau (1997) noted several economic policies necessary to meet the challenges for the 21st Century. The changing direction of politics has not been helpful in achieving its growth targets, thus contributing to an increase in the number of people living in poverty. In addition, the process of consolidating democratic government and embracing a market-oriented growth strategy has been affected by the 19 May 2000 coup.

As economic activities did not recover faster in the 1990s the Reserve Bank of Fiji introduced an export credit ratio to complement the monetary policy measures to assist the nation's economic rebuilding program (RBF, 2001). Devaluation of the currency (by 20%) in January 1998 was to boost tourism, improve the competitiveness of exports, promote FDI, increase demand for goods and therefore raise employment and thus income. Further

[9] The new 1997 Constitution came into force on 27 July 1998. The then President, (the late) Ratu Sir Kamisese Mara, addressed the nation to support the Constitution, saying that "it safeguards the basic rights and freedoms of individuals and ethnic groups. ...The new document contains a bill of rights, removes discriminatory provisions introduced after the military coups of 1987" (EIU, 1998, p. 14).

exchange control relaxations were introduced in January 2002 targeting the investment sector with offshore investments, foreign exchange loan pre-payments, repatriation of profits and withdrawals of investments to promote economic growth (RBF, 2004). Problems contributing to weak economic performance besides political instability include inadequate protection of property rights, inadequate growth impulses in the export sector, absence of strong backward linkages in the export and manufacturing sectors, outflow of skilled labour and very low private sector investment. Good policies are vital for growth.[10] To inject some adroit ways to enhance growth an investment-led growth would be crucial through public investment expenditure, fiscal policy, encouragement of private investment and creation of an enabling environment. Government's commitment to building business and investor confidence, political and civil liberty, economic freedom, and stable and good governance are crucial factors to stimulate domestic business and FDI flows.

The deleterious impact of poor economic performance on the society and the nation in the post-1987 coups and 2000 political crises period point to various factors that can be noted to what government's part of the causes that are bad for growth. Non-maintenance of the rule of law, inefficiency in planning, poor policies, corruption, dictatorial regimes, sub-optimal degree of income redistribution and the cultural factors in a segregated manner are more detrimental to growth. Holden *et al.*, in the Asian Development Bank (2004) publication *Swimming Against the Tide* note some of these factors of the state as the main issues faced by the private sector in the Pacific. Fiji's population diversity, cultural cooperation and economic growth through government policy and cultural change can be targeted to achieve some non-economic end (such as fostering national unity) and create a culture more conducive to economic growth. As culture influences many of the decisions that people undertake, the main aspects of these decisions are generally economically related, where parents/elders decide, for example, the motivation of work (how hard they work), what they want for themselves and their children, how much education they give their children, respect, regard and cooperation for elders at home as with their peers. The economic success of the individuals in Fiji's multi-cultural society shows that attitude, values and beliefs are prevalent in a society. Therefore, it is possible that cultural differences amongst the groups of people in Fiji can be utilized for better economic outcomes. The issue is that as growth affects culture it raises the possibility that the association between particular cultural attributes and the level of income per person may involve income affecting culture, so building trust and reassurance as a matter of policy is in the best interests of the nation.

5. Conclusion

Development theories over time show that many factors are relevant to achieve sustainable growth. Problems of development are not just insufficient resources and inefficient use of resources but markets, domestic institutions, structures and socio-cultural values and factors have to be sufficient for economic values to increase growth. In Fiji's case sluggish economic performance due to political instability increased economic costs in that inadequate infrastructure, capital and goods markets affected economic development at

[10] Generally, the performance of the economy in terms of efficiency, innovativeness and growth largely depends on the economic and political institutions, and policies adopted by that country (Bernholz, 1992).

various levels differently. In the climate of globalization the new growth theory reconfirms the traditional theory that strong linkages between growth factors are required for sustainable economic performance.

At independence Fiji's economic performance, management and maintenance of stability started with its multi-ethnic composition and people's greater passion for economic achievement. All sectors of the economy have been adversely impacted by political crises whilst economic policies have not been appropriate to reduce uncertainties and poor performance. Increase in foreign and domestic capital and the policies that intensify and stimulate agriculture and non-agriculture production remain crucial to create economic opportunities. Inclusive policies for all social groups are important to attain benefits of growth rather than just globally vogue policies. The institutional framework has to be adequate to meet the governance needs and address global challenges, economic vulnerability, security concerns and moral hazards. Empowering all citizens to participate is relevant to strengthen economic, cultural, institutional environment and facilitate distribution of benefits.

What are the implications of the findings for Fiji's development policy? As cultural attributes promoted growth in the post-independence period Fiji fell victim to the patterns of growth in the post-1987 period. Investment, land property rights, skilled manpower, capital flows, efficient services, macroeconomic stability and financial management were obstructed. Liberalization and privatization programs have not shown the signs of improvements, thus causing deterioration in the standard of living (low human development index), particularly more so after the political crisis of 2000. With lack of land resources several communities have been affected by the policies where hard work, trust and social capability have been distorted. Accumulation of wealth is extremely important for social development, but moral issues however unjust are seen in the policy framework. High-quality growth will not be achieved in the absence of "bold reformism" - severe disequilibria and inappropriate structural adaptation must be addressed promptly, and on all fronts, and the public must know the hard facts about the scope of the problems and the policies chosen. Let us not be mistaken – rational economic policies and programs are not cheap so greater national solidarity is needed. Rapid growth is central to meet domestic demands and avoid social crises, so patterns of growth will be important to focus on future policies.

REFERENCES

Akram-Lodhi, A.H. (1996) "Structural Adjustment in Fiji Under the Interim Government, 1987-1992", *Contemporary Pacific*, 8: 259-290.

____ (1997) "Structural Adjustment and the Agrarian Question in Fiji", *Journal of Contemporary Asia*, 27: 37-57.

Asian Development Bank (2000) *Republic of the Fiji Islands 1999 Economic Report*, Manila: ADB.

____ (2004) *Swimming Against the Tide? An Assessment of the Private Sector in the Pacific*, Manila: ADB.

Bernholz, P. (1992) "Efficiency, Political-Economic Organisation, and International Competition Among States", *International Journal of the Unity of the Sciences*, 5: 443-83.

Berthélemy, J. and Söderling, L. (2001) "The role of capital accumulation, adjustment & structural change for economic take-off: Empirical evidence from African growth episodes", *World Development, 29*: 323-343.

Blanchard, O. (1997) *The Economics of Post-communist Transition*, Oxford: Clarendon.

Butkiewicz, J.L. and Yanikkaya, H. (2005) "The effects of I.M.F. & World Bank lending on long-run economic growth: An empirical analysis", *World Development,* 33: 371-391.

Central Planning Office (1985) *Fiji's Ninth Development Plan 1986-1990, Policies, Strategies and Programmes for National Development*, Suva: Central Planning Office.

Chand, G (2004) "Overview of Current Economic Conditions in Fiji". Paper submitted to Global Policy Network,

Chand, S. (1998) 'Current Events in Fiji: An Economy Adrift in the Pacific', *Pacific Economic Bulletin*, 13: 1-17.

____ (2001) "Lessons for Development from Pacific Island Countries", *Pacific Economic Bulletin*, 16: 95-108.

Chandra, R. (1989) "The Political Crisis and the Manufacturing Sector in Fiji", *Pacific Viewpoint*, 30.

Collier, P. and Gunning, J.W. (1999) "Explaining African Economic Performance", *Journal of Economic Literature*, 37: 64-111.

Duncan, R. (2004) "The Fiji Economy – Needing a Better Investment Environment", University of the South Pacific, Pacific Institute of Advanced Studies in Development and Governance, Working Papers. Retrieved 8th Sept., 2005. http://www.usp.ac.fj/index.php?id=piasdg_downloads_governance.

Economic Intelligence Unit (1998) *Country Profiles: Pacific Islands*, London: EIU.

Elek, A., Hill, H. and Tabor, S. (1993) "Liberalization and Diversification in a Small Island Economy: Fiji Since the 1997 Coups", *World Development*, 21: 749-769.

Ellis, F. and Mdoe, N. (2003) "Livelihoods & Rural Poverty Reduction in Tanzania", *World Development,* 31, 1367-1384.

Elster, V. (1994) The impact of constitutions on economic performance, in M. Bruno and B. Pleskovick (eds.) *Proceedings of the World Bank Annual Conference on Development Economics*, Washington D.C.: World Bank, 209-26.

Ghatak, S. (2003) *Introduction to development economics (*4th ed.). London: Routledge.

Gounder, R. (1999) "'The Political Economy of Development: Empirical Evidence From Fiji", *Economic Analysis and Policy*, 29: 133-50.

___ (2001) "Aid-Growth Nexus: Empirical Evidence from Fiji", *Applied Economics*, 33, 1009-19.

____ (2002) "Democracy, Economic Freedom, Fiscal Policy and Growth: Findings and Reflections for Fiji", *Contemporary Economic Policy,* 20: 234-45.

____ (2005) "Fiji's Public-Private Sector Investment And Economic Growth: Evidence From Time Series Data", *Fijian Studies A Journal of Contemporary Fiji*, 3: 87-110.

Gounder, R. and Xayavong, V. (2002) "Globalization and the Island Economies of the South Pacific", In S. Mansoob Murshed (ed.) *Globalization, Marginalization and Development*, London: Routledge, 203-16.

Government of Republic of Fiji (1993) *Opportunities for Growth: Policies and Strategies for Fiji in the Medium Term*, Government of Republic of Fiji, Suva.

____ Jayaraman, T. (1998) "Private Investment in Fiji: 1977 – 1994. Did Investment have any Crowding-Out Effect?" *South Pacific Study*, 18, 57-67.

Kalter, E. and Khor, H.E. (1990) Mexico's Experience with Adjustment. *Finance & Development,* 27: 22-25.

Kumar, S and Prasad, B. (2002) "Fiji's Economic Woes: A Nation in Search of Development Progress", *Pacific Economic Bulletin,* 17: 1-23.

Lal, P., Lim-Applegate, H., and Reddy, M. (2001) "The Land Tenure Dilemma in Fiji – Can Fijian Landowners and Indo-Fijian tenants Have Their Cake and Eat it Too?", *Pacific Economic Bulletin,* 16: 106-119.

Landes, D.S. (1998) *The Wealth and Poverty of Nations: Why Some Are Rich and Some So Poor,* New York: W.W. Norton.

Lavigne, M. (1999) *The Economics of Transition: From Socialist Economy to Market Economy* (2nd ed.), Houndmills: Macmillan.

Levine, R. and Renelt, D. (1992) "A Sensitivity Analysis of Cross Country Growth Regress", *American Economic Review,* 82: 942-63.

Manueli, P.F. (1993) "Introduction", In Government of Republic of Fiji, *Opportunities For Growth, Policies And Strategies For Fiji In The Medium Term,* Suva: Government Printers.

Mohanty, M. (2001) "Contemporary Emigration from Fiji: Some Trends and Issues in the Post-Independence Era", *Current Trends in South Pacific Migration,* Asia-Pacific Migration Research Network, Wollongong: University of Wollongong, 51 73.

Narayan, P. (2001) "Fiji's Garment Industry: An Economic Analysis", *Journal of Economic and Social Policy,* 6: 35-55.

Narayan, P. (2004) "Do Public Investment Crowd Out Private Investment? Fresh Evidence From Fiji", Journal of Policy Modeling, 26: 747-53.

Narayan, P.K. and B.C. Prasad (2003) 'Fiji's Sugar, Tourism and Garment Industries: A Survey of Performance, Problems and Potentials, *Fijian Studies,* 1: 3-27.

Olson, M. Jr. (1996) "Big Bills Left on the Sidewalk: Why Some Nations are Rich and Others Poor?", *Journal of Economic Perspectives,* 12: 3-24.

Pomfret, R. (2002) *Constructing a Market Economy: Diverse Paths from Central Planning in Asia and Europe.* Cheltenham: Edward Elgar.

Powles, C. G. (1996) "Constitutional Reforms in Fiji", *Pacific Economic Bulletin,* 13: 73-5.

Prasad, B.C. (1998) "The Woes of Economic Reform: Poverty and Income Inequality in Fiji", *International Journal of Social Economics,* 25: 1073-1093.

Prasad, B.C. (2006) "Resolving the Agricultural Land Lease Problems in the Fiji Islands: Current Discussions and the Way Forward", *Public lecture, University of the South Pacific, Suva,* 27 February, 2006, *mimeo.*

Prasad, B.C. and Tisdell, C.A. (1996) "Getting Property Rights 'Right': Land Tenure in Fiji", *Pacific Economic Bulletin,* Vol. 11, pp. 31-46. Reddy, M. (2000) "Trends and Determinants of Capital Formation in Fiji", *Pacific Economic Bulletin,* 15: 104-12.

Reserve Bank of Fiji (1997) *Quarterly Review December 1997,* Suva, Reserve Bank of Fiji.

____ (1998) *Quarterly Review June 1998,* Suva: Reserve Bank of Fiji.

____ (2001) *Reserve Bank of Fiji Annual Report,* Suva: Reserve Bank of Fiji.

____ (2004) *Quarterly Review,* Suva: Reserve Bank of Fiji.

Rostow, W.W. (1960) *The Stages of Economic Growth,* Cambridge: Cambridge University Press.

Siwatibau, S. (1997) "Pacific Island Economic Management Challenges for the 21st Century", *VIII Pacific Science Inter-Congress Conference,* 13-19 July, USP, Suva.

Sturton and McGregor (1991).

Temple, J. (1999) "The New Growth Evidence". *Journal of Economic Literature,* XXXVII: 112-156.

Todaro, M.P. and Smith, S.C. (2003) *Economic Development,* 8th Edition, New York: Addison Wesley Longman.

Toye, J. (1993). *Dilemmas of Development: Reflection on the Counter-Revolution in Development Economics.* Oxford: Blackwell.

UNDP(1990) *Human Development Report 1990,* New York, OUP.

____ (2001) *Human Development Report 2001,* New York, Oxford University Press.

____ (2004) *Human Development Report 2004,* New York, Oxford University Press.

____ (2005) *Human Development Report 2005,* New York, Oxford University Press.

Webster, A. (1990) *Introduction to the Sociology of Development.* London: Macmillan.

Weil, D.N. (2005) *Economic Growth,* New York: Pearson Addison Wesley.

Wolf, H.C. (1999) *Transition Strategies: Choices and Outcomes,* Princeton, NJ: International Finance Section.

World Bank (2005) *World Development Indicators,* Data on CDROM, Washington, D.C.

Wu W. and Davis, O. (1999) "Two Freedoms in a Growth Model", *Journal of Private Enterprise,* 14: 115-43.

In: Development Problems and Prospects in Pacific Islands ISBN: 978-1-60021-793-7
Editors: B. C. Prasad, D. C. Roy, pp. 189-195

Chapter 13

MODELLING ELECTRICITY CONSUMPTION FOR THE FIJI ISLANDS

Paresh K. Narayan and Baljeet Singh

1. INTRODUCTION

The relationship between energy consumption and economic growth has been debated quite extensively in the literature, yet the direction of the causality relationship remains unresolved. The debate has focused on whether energy consumption causes economic growth or economic growth causes energy consumption, or whether a two-way relationship exists. From a policy viewpoint, the direction of causality between these variables has important implications (Narayan and Smyth, 2005; Asafu-Adjaye, 2000; Ghosh, 2002). For instance, a finding in favour of a positive unidirectional causality running from GDP to electricity consumption is a strong justification for energy conservation policies, such as electricity rationing, for this finding implies that a country is not dependent on energy for growth and development. However, if unidirectional causality runs from electricity consumption to GDP, then reducing electricity consumption could lead to a fall in income. This is because a finding confirming evidence in favour of energy positively causing GDP implies that (1) the country in question is energy dependent, and (2) negative shocks to energy, such as shocks leading to higher energy prices or energy conservation policies, will negatively impact GDP.

Like other developing countries, Fiji requires large volumes of energy for producing goods and services, and as in most non-oil producing countries its energy demand is met by large quantities of imports. Electricity is a crucial input in the production of goods and services in Fiji. It is a major input component for several sectors, including manufacturing, communication, education, commercial, entertainment, and construction. Table 13.1 shows the growth of electricity consumption and real GDP for Fiji. The average growth in electricity consumption over 10-year intervals has outpaced the growth in real GDP. Both electricity consumption and real GDP growth have generally shown a downward trend and similarly the electricity consumption growth to GDP growth ratio has also declined over the same period.

For instance, over the periods 1970-1980, 1981-1990 and 1991-2000 electricity consumption growth to GDP growth ratio was 6.4, 3.7, and 1.8, respectively.

Table 13.1. Growth of real GDP and electricity consumption, 1970-2002

Year	Real GDP growth rate	Electricity consumption growth rate	Electricity consumption growth to GDP growth ratio
1970-1980	4.8599	31.5222	6.4861
1981-1990	2.4534	9.2780	3.7817
1991-2000	2.4117	4.4773	1.8565
2001-2002	2.1837	5.4476	2.4946

Source: Fiji Electricity Authority Annual Reports (various issues), Asian Development Bank Key Statistics and International Monetary Fund Database.

The aim of this chapter is to examine the long-run relationship between real GDP and energy consumption for the Fiji islands using time series data for the period 1971-2002. We test for a possible long-run relationship between real GDP and electricity consumption through using Johansen's (1988) cointegration technique. We then estimate the long-run impact of electricity consumption on real GDP through using four different estimators, namely the ordinary least squares (OLS), fully modified OLS, autoregressive distributed lag model (ARDL) and the maximum likelihood (ML) procedure. Apart from investigating the correlation between real GDP and electricity consumption, we also examine causality among the variables using the Granger F-test.

The reminder of the paper is organized as follows. In the next section, we provide a brief overview of the literature on the nexus between electricity consumption and GDP. In section 3, we explain the econometric methodologies and results, and in the final section we provide some concluding remarks.

2. An Overview of the Related Literature

The causality relationship between electricity consumption and economic growth has important policy implications, as explained earlier. Hence, several studies have attempted to establish the relationship between electricity consumption and economic growth. A general observation from these studies is that the results have been mixed: that is, while some studies find causality running from economic growth to electricity consumption, others find causality running from electricity consumption to economic growth. The purpose of this section is to provide a brief overview of the findings of studies that model the nexus between electricity consumption and economic growth.

In a recent study, Narayan and Smyth (2005) examined the relationship between electricity consumption, employment and real income for Australia using multivariate Granger causality tests. They found a unidirectional causality running from employment and electricity to income and consumption. They found that in the long run electricity consumption Granger caused GDP and GDP Granger caused electricity consumption, and in the short-run only electricity consumption Granger caused GDP. Similarly, Jumbe (2004) examined the relationship between electricity consumption and economic growth for Malawi.

His finding showed a two-way causal relationship between electricity consumption and economic growth. Lam and Shiu (2004) examined the causal relationship between electricity consumption and economic growth for China. They also found evidence of unidirectional Granger causality running from electricity consumption to economic growth. Glasure and Yu (1997) examined the relationship between GDP and electricity consumption for Korea and Singapore, and found evidence of unidirectional causality running from electricity consumption to GDP; however, no evidence of causality was found in the case of Korea. In a recent study for Turkey, Altinay and Karagol (2005) found evidence of unidirectional Granger causality running from electricity consumption to income. On the other hand, Ghosh (2002) examined the causality relationship between electricity consumption and economic growth for India. He found evidence of unidirectional Granger causality running from economic growth to electricity consumption.

3. Methodology and Results

3.1. Data and Unit Root Test

The two variables used in this study, namely real GDP and electricity consumption contain annual observations for the period 1971-2002. All data were obtained from the *Asian Development Bank Key Statistics*, The Fiji Electricity Authority annual reports, the Department of Energy Statistics and the *Current Economic Statistics* published by the Fiji Bureau of Statistics. Our first aim is to investigate the unit root properties of the data series.

We perform the conventional augmented Dickey and Fuller (ADF) test for a model without a time trend, which is based on the following regression model:

We find that the ADF test statistics for real GDP and electricity consumption exceed the 5 per cent level critical value. The computed ADF test statistics for the real GDP and electricity consumption are -0.2018 and 0.2759, respectively, while the 5 per cent level critical value is -2.96. However, when we subject the first difference of these variables to the ADF test, we find test statistics smaller than the 5 per cent level critical value. The computed ADF test statistics for the first difference of the real GDP and electricity consumption are -8.1399 and -6.9454, respectively, leading us to conclude that $[Y_t, E_t]$ are integrated of order one or $I(1)$.

3.2. Cointegration Test

We use Johansen's (1988) approach, which uses the maximum likelihood procedure to determine the presence of cointegrating vectors. This procedure is based on the following vector autoregressive (VAR) model:

$$\Delta Y_t = C + \sum_{i=1}^{k} \Gamma_i \Delta Y_{t-i} + \Pi Y_{t-1} + \varepsilon_t \qquad (1)$$

Here, Y_t is a vector of I(1), non-stationary in level form, variables and C is a constant. The information on the coefficient matrix between the levels of the stock price series is decomposed as $\Pi = \gamma\delta'$, where the relevant elements of the matrix are the adjustment coefficients and the δ matrix contains the cointegrating vectors. Johansen and Juselius (1990) recommend the trace test and the maximum eigenvalue test statistics to determine the number of cointegrating vectors.

Before undertaking the Johansen test for cointegration, we must first perform the lag specification tests. In other words, the first step in our cointegration analysis is to determine the number of lags, k, of our VAR model. Using the Schwarz Baysian Criterion and the Akaike Information Criterion, we find that 1 lag is the optimal for this exercise.

We report the results for cointegration based on the maximum eigenvalue statistic in Table 13.2. We find that according to the maximum eigenvalue statistic, when testing the null hypothesis of no cointegration ($r = 0$), it turns out to be 16.87, which exceeds the 5 per cent critical value of 15.89. Thus, we can conclude that there is one cointegrating relationship among the variables.

Table 13.2.Cointegration with restricted intercepts and no trends in the VAR

Cointegration LR Test Based on Maximal Eigenvalue of the Stochastic Matrix				
Null	Alternative	Statistic	95% Critical Value	Prob.
r = 0	r = 1	16.8749	15.87	0.0350
r<= 1	r = 2	2.10256	9.16	0.7572

3.3. Long-run Elasticities

In this section, we present the long-run coefficients on the electricity consumption on national income in order to gauge whether or not the electricity consumption causes economic growth for the Fiji Islands. In other words, we estimate following specification:

$$Y_{it} = \alpha_{0i} + \alpha_{1i} E_{it} + e_t \tag{2}$$

Our approach here is as follows. In order to estimate equation (2), we depart from the extant literature through using 4 different long-run estimators. More specifically, we estimate equation (2) using the ordinary least squares (OLS) estimator, the fully modified OLS (FMOLS) estimator, the autoregressive distributed lag (ARDL) estimator, and the maximum likelihood (ML) estimator. For such a crucial hypothesis, we believe that it is imperative that researchers apply more than one estimator to unravel the relationship between electricity consumption and national income, for the application of more than one estimator allows one to gauge the robustness of the results, and thus draw firm conclusions. Our results are presented in Table 13.3. We find that all the 4 estimators provide very consistent results on the electricity consumption on national income. The coefficient ranges from 1.81 to 1.97, implying that a one unit increase in electricity consumption leads to a \$1.81-1.97 increase in national income.

Table 13.3. Long-run elasticities

	E_t
OLS	1.96***
	(21.2057)
FMOLS	1.92***
	(11.7405)
ARDL	1.82***
	(6.4313)
ML	1.81***
	(7.4833)

*** denotes statistical significance at the 1 per cent level.

3.4. Granger Causality

Given that in section 3.2 we established that real GDP and electricity consumption shared a cointegrating relationship, in testing for Granger causality we need to model the two variables within a vector error correction (VEC) framework. In other words, we need to augment the Granger-type causality test model with a one period lagged error correction term. This is an important step because Engle and Granger (1987) caution that if the series are integrated of order one, in the presence of cointegration, vector autoregressive estimation in first differences will be misleading. Thus, after taking into account this modification, we arrive at the following equations for Granger causality.

$$\Delta Y_t = \upsilon + \sum_{i=1}^{p} \vartheta_i \Delta Y_{t-i} + \sum_{i=1}^{p} \kappa_i \Delta E_{t-i} + \pi_1 ECT_{t-1} + \varepsilon_{1t} \tag{3}$$

$$\Delta E_t = \upsilon + \sum_{i=1}^{p-1} \kappa_i \Delta E_{t-i} + \sum_{i=1}^{p} \phi_i \Delta Y_{t-i} + \pi_2 ECT_{t-1} + \varepsilon_{2t} \tag{4}$$

In addition to the variables defined above, ECT_{t-1} is the lagged error-correction term derived from the long-run cointegrating relationship, and ε_{1t} and ε_{2t} are serially independent random errors with mean zero and finite covariance matrix.

The existence of a cointegrating relationship among GDP and electricity consumption suggests that there must be Granger causality in at least one direction, but it does not indicate the direction of temporal causality between the variables. We examine both short run and long run Granger causality within a VEC model. The short run causal effects can be obtained by the F-test of the lagged explanatory variables, while the *t*-statistics on the coefficient of the lagged error-correction term in Equations (3) and (4) indicate the significance of the long-run causal effect.

The results are reported in Table 13.4, and are organised as follows: Columns 2 and 3 contain the F-test statistics for short-run causality, while the last column contains the t-test statistics for long-run causality. Beginning with the short-run effects, there is absence of any causality running from real income to electricity consumption. However, at the 5 per cent level we find causality running from electricity consumption to real GDP.

Table 13.4. Results of Granger causality test

Dependent variable	ΔY_t	ΔE_t	ECT_{t-1} [t-statistics]
ΔY_t	-	4.4367** (+) [0.0443]	-0.1779** [-1.9190]
ΔE_t	0.0005 (+) [0.0005]	-	-0.2058 (-1.5958)

Note: *** (*) denote statistical significance at the 1 per cent and 10 per cent levels, respectively. The probability values are in square brackets while the estimated signs are in parenthesis.

Turning to the long-run results, the coefficient on the lagged error correction term is significant with the correct sign in the national income equation at the 5 per cent level, which confirms the results from the Johansen test of cointegration. This implies that changes in national income are a function of disequilibrium in the cointegrating relationship. Thus, in the long run electricity consumption Granger cause national income, meaning that causality runs through the error correction term from electricity consumption to national income.

4. Concluding Remarks

In this chapter we investigated the time series relationship between real GDP and electricity consumption for the Fiji Islands over the period 1970-2002. We achieved this goal by undertaking a bi-variate modeling strategy, which involved four steps. In the first step, we subjected the data series –real GDP and electricity consumption – to the ADF test in order to ascertain the unit root properties of the variables. The ADF test, which tests the null hypothesis of stationarity, revealed that all variables were integrated of order one. In the second step, we investigated evidence for any cointegrating relationships among the variables by using the Johansen (1988) test for cointegration. We found that there was one cointegration relationship among the variables. In the third step, having established a long-run relationship, we estimated long run coefficients on the impact of electricity consumption on GDP. This goal was achieved through using four long run estimators, namely the OLS, the FMOLS, the ARDL, and the ML procedures. We found similar results from these estimators: that electricity consumption had a positive and statistically significant impact on Fiji's real GDP. In the final step, we investigated the direction of causation among the variables using the Granger causality testing procedure. We found unidirectional causality running from electricity consumption to GDP in both the short-run the long-run.

Our findings that in both the short-run and long-run electricity consumption Granger causes economic growth suggests that Fiji is an energy dependent country. This implies that energy conservation policies, such as rationing electricity consumption, are likely to have an adverse effect in the long-run.

REFERENCES

Altinay, G and Karagol, E., (2005) Electricity consumption and economic growth: Evidence from Turkey, *Energy Economics*, 27, 849-856.

Asafu-Adjaye, J., (2000) The relationship between energy consumption, energy prices and economic growth: time series evidence from Asian developing countries, *Energy Economics* 22, 615-625.

Chang, T., Fang, W., Wen, L. F., (2001) Energy consumption, employment, output and temporal causality: evidence from Taiwan based cointegration and error correction modeling techniques, *Applied Economics*, 33, 1045-1056.

Dickey, D.A., and Fuller, W.A., (1979) Distributions of the estimators for autoregressive time series with a unit root, *Journal of the American Statistical Association*, 74, 427-31.

Dickey, D.A., and Fuller, W.A., (1981) Likelihood ratio statistics for autoregressive time series with a unit root, *Econometrica*, 49, 1057-72.

Engel, R.F. and Granger, C. W. J., (1987) Cointegration and Error Correction Representation, Estimation and Testing, *Econometrica*, 55, 251-276.

Ghosh, S., (2002) Electricity consumption and economic growth in India, *Energy Policy* 30, 125-129.

Glasure, Y.U and Yu, A.R (1997) Cointegration, error-correction, and the relationship between GDP and electricity: the case of South Korea and Singapore, *Resource and Electricity economics*, 20, 17-25.

Johansen, S., (1988) Statistical Analysis of Cointegration Vectors, *Journal of Economic Dynamics and Control*, 12, 231-254.

Johansen, S., and Juselius, K., (1990) Maximum Likelihood Estimation and Inference on Cointegration with Applications to the Demand for Money, *Oxford Bulletin of Economics and Statistics*, 52, 169-210.

Jumbe, C.B.L., (2004) Cointegration and Causality between electricity consumption and GDP: empirical evidence from Malawi, *Energy Economics* 26, 61-68.

Lam, P. and Shiu, A., (2004) Electricity consumption and economic growth in China, *Energy Policy*, 32, 47-54.

Narayan, P.K and Smyth, R., (2005) Electricity consumption, employment and real income in Australia evidence from multivariate Granger causality tests, *Energy Policy*, 33, 1109-1116.

In: Development Problems and Prospects in Pacific Islands ISBN: 978-1-60021-793-7
Editors: B. C. Prasad, D. C. Roy, pp. 197-213

Chapter 14

ESTIMATING THE SIZE OF THE FIJI ISLANDS AGRICULTURAL SECTOR

Phillip Hone, Henry Haszler and Apenisa Tuicakau

1. INTRODUCTION

These days government is everywhere and follows us from the cradle to the grave. Governments register our births and deaths, both of which might occur in a public hospital. On our path through life they insist we attend school, certify our school results, restrict our access to alcohol before a specified age, issue our driver's licences, register our marriages – and divorces – and nominate the currency we shall use. Governments also legislate shopping hours, tell us how to label our foods, subsidise the production of some goods, impose tariffs on imports, and – depending on where in place and time we are – may conscript us to miserable, painful deaths in battle on foreign soil against people against whom we may have no personal grudge at all.

All the while, governments tax us so that they can pay for all the ways they impinge on our lives. Citizens and taxpayers tolerate government involvement in their lives because of the common judgement that – in democratic societies at least – governments generally intervene to promote the "common good.". Pursuit of the common good makes it sensible for at least some things to be done or organised or overseen by government.

However, there is no clear consensus – even within any single country or community – on the acceptable or proper role of government. At a perhaps cynical extreme, government has been defined as "that group of individuals which has, for the time being, usurped the power of ultimate punishment – death." An ignoble definition if ever there was one. A less extreme attitude to government might be summarised in the observation that "One person's tax is their own and/or another person's Medicare rebate, or yet another person's farm adjustment assistance, or yet again the newly sealed road to 'my' village." Clearly, there are good reasons to consider criteria under which government intervention in the economic and other dimensions of our lives might be justified. That consideration must be broad ranging.

In addition to having criteria that are accepted as justifying intervention, it is essential for good governance that government actions are monitored and evaluated. For the purpose of this paper it is convenient to consider government activity in two broad dimensions. First, there is the 'political' dimension which in our taxonomy covers voting systems or other mechanisms for choosing the form of legislature(s) and the politicians who will sit in the legislature(s), including those who will make up the government for the time being, In our classification this political dimension, also includes the rules that govern the legislature(s) and the legislators and the system of laws they introduce and support.

Our second dimension of government is the economic dimension, which we define as concerned with the particular economic decisions of government that is, matters related to taxes, tariffs, subsidies, social security payments and so forth.

In both cases good governance requires that taxpayers and citizens have access to good information by which to judge government actions and their outcomes. For the political dimension of government activity the information might be of a rather qualitative or descriptive type. But for the economic dimension the information needs to be much more quantitative and of the kind we normally define as economic statistics,

The regular publication of reliable data on the performance of the economy tends to add to the accountability of public decision makers. Repeated poor economic management decisions show up in the long run as reduced national income and a low rate of economic growth. The publication of reliable data on these measures provides some basis for both indicating the nature of problems and assessing the performance of government decision makers in responding to these issues. Therefore, to the extent to which reliable economic data make decision makers accountable, they also tend to improve governance in the public sector.

2. Relevance to Agricultural GDP in Fiji

Why is all this relevant to agricultural GDP in Fiji? The Fiji Islands are relatively resource rich. The environment is attractive to tourists, there are extensive fishing grounds and, relative to population, there is considerable arable land with soil types and a climate suited to many agricultural and forestry pursuits. And by developing country standards, Fiji's workforce has a wide range of skills. Despite these advantages, Fiji's growth potential does not seem to have been realised and the prospects for a sustained improvement in the standard of living are not as strong as they might be. This poor performance results partly from problems in agriculture, which accounts for around 16 percent of *official* GDP, probably a larger proportion of the *actual* economy, and for 44 percent of Fiji's merchandise exports. (including sugar and food processing).

The disappointing growth in the agricultural sector itself has been due at least partly to the slow growth in the commercial agricultural sector. The sugar industry has been under severe market pressure, copra production has declined, and other more recently introduced tree crops such as cocoa – once seen to offer great potential – have virtually disappeared. Also, the outlook for horticultural exports has not met earlier optimistic forecasts. For example, exports of kava have suffered recently because of "health scares" in Europe and the USA.

In the case of sugar, proposed policy changes in the EU will effectively withdraw output price support for Fiji's sugar. The high prices previously paid for sugar in Fiji have sustained a relatively large industry, accounting for 45 percent of the value of official farm output and around 25 percent of the nation's exports. Recent disruptions to land tenure arrangements in the sugar industry are likely to aggravate the disruption from the change in EU policy.

The potential outcome of these problems is an increase in poverty. Concerns about poverty have been highlighted by Fiji's recent drop from 81st to 92nd place in the UNDP Human Development Index (UNDP 2005). Poverty is widespread with claims that about 25 percent of the population lived below the poverty line in 1990-91 (ADB MFNP 2003). All major elements of the population are affected but, significantly, 60 percent of the heads of poor households are employed in agriculture. The differential increases in the CPI and wages since 1990-91 suggest the extent of poverty may have increased.

The development literature makes it clear that a key determinant of the ability of countries to shift to rapid development and poverty alleviation has been increasing productivity in the agricultural sector. As the British Department for International Development says:

> 'All recorded rapid reductions in widespread poverty started with livelihoods being enhanced through agricultural transformation.' (DFID 2005 p.6)

Fiji is a middle ranking developing country and already has a sizeable commercial agricultural sector. But Fiji also still has a substantial subsistence agriculture sector which can be described as "traditional" in the sense used by Schultz (1964) to categorise the Guatemalan Panajachel Indians described by Tax in his *Penny Capitalism* (1953). The Panajachel Indians were capitalist and economically very efficient, but also poor. They were efficient but poor because they had reached an equilibrium based on traditional agricultural methods undisturbed by new ways of doing things. This may be a reasonable approximation of subsistence agriculture in Fiji and other Pacific Island countries. The relevance of this ancient history for Fiji today is that Schultz describes the transformation of traditional agriculture as '*a relatively cheap source of economic growth*'. (Schultz, p 102).

So *it is important* to improve the efficiency of the policy process and get agricultural policy right. Unfortunately, the chances of developing and implementing an appropriate agricultural policy regime in Fiji to deal with these problems are currently constrained by a lack of the fundamental economic information required for making informed policy decisions.

3. Data Availability

A number of organisations in Fiji collect agricultural and food sector data linked to the national accounts. The Fiji Islands Bureau of Statistics (FIBoS) publishes annual data on the contribution of agriculture to GDP (see Table 14.1), and on employment, trade, etc. The Bureau also conducts Fiji's Household Income and Expenditure Surveys (HIES) covering both urban and rural residents. The rural sector national accounts rely partly on data provided by the Ministry of Agriculture Sugar and Land Resettlement (MASLR). The Ministry conducts the national agricultural census and also collects quarterly production data. The

National Food and Nutrition Centre (NFNC) compiles Fiji's food balance sheets which are effectively annual supply–utilisation tables based on production and trade data by commodity from FIBoS and MASLR. The NFNC also conducts national nutrition surveys.

Table 14.1. Agriculture Related Components of Real GDP at Factor Cost: Fiji Islands

Item	1995	2000	2001	2002	Change 2001	Change 2002
	– $F million at 1995 prices –				– percent –	
Agriculture, Fishing & Forestry GDP	*476*	*462*	*436*	*454*	*- 5.8*	*4.3*
Agriculture	371	341	329	343	- 3.6	4.1
Sugar	*179*	*132*	*122*	*125*	*- 7.5*	*2.4*
Fishing	66	85	71	81	-16.1	14.0
Forestry	39	36	35	31	-2.7	- 13.2
Of which Subsistence Production	*155*	*163*	*164*	*166*	*0.6*	*1.3*
Agriculture	113	119	120	122	0.6	1.3
Fishing	26	27	28	28	0.6	1.3
Forestry	16	17	17	17	0.6	1.3
Total Gross National Product	*2,373*	*2,610*	*2,680*	*2,795*	*2.7*	*4.3*
	– percent –					
Agriculture, etc Share of National GDP	*20*	*18*	*16*	*16*		
Subsistence Share of Agriculture, etc	*32*	*35*	*38*	*37*		
Agriculture	30	35	36	36		
Fishing	39	32	39	34		
Forestry	40	45	47	55		
Subsistence Food Share of Total Food	*54*	*50*	*53*	*50*		

Note: Data for agriculture include public sector production from experiment stations etc. Food equals total agriculture less sugar and forestry. Source: FIBoS (2005), *Key Statistics*, March – from www.statsfiji.gov.fj

Unfortunately there are limitations to the basic agricultural data that do exist – such as seemingly significant discrepancies between alternative sources for some data as shown in Table14.2. The table is based on the 1999 agricultural survey by MASLR, and on food balance sheets produced by FAO and Fiji's National Food and Nutrition Centre.

Table 14.2. Comparisons of Selected Agricultural Statistics by Source

Item	Production				Consumption	
	1999		2002		2002	
	FAO	MASLR	FAO	NFNC	FAO	NFNC
	– '000 tonnes –					
Cereals[a]	12.3	18.1	9.7	13.5	123.6	91.2
Rice (Milled)	11.5	9.7	8.6	12.9	35.4	40.6
Maize	0.7	8.4	1.1	0.6	0.8	0.1
Starchy Roots	63.4	409.7	86.2	89.9	82.7	91.7
Cassava	26.9	307.8	33.0	41.4	23.2	38.3
Sweet Potatoes	5.1	15.0	6.2	7.2	6.0	6.9
Yams	2.2	11.3	5.2	4.5	5.0	4.3
Sugar & Sweeteners	364.1	na	317.1	333.0	29.6	32.1
Pulses	1.2	0.4	1.2	0.7	8.1	7.6
Oilcrops[b]	170.8	392.5	160.2	113.6	50.1	29.8
Vegetable Oils	8.3	na	9.1	11.3	8.6	0.0
Coconut Oil	8.3	na	9.1	11.3	1.0	0.0
Vegetables	20.0	59.3	21.2	15.7	35.3	27.9
Fruits[c]	18.2	44.4	22.8	9.4	27.6	11.3
Bananas & Plantains	4.0	12.4	6.5	3.6	5.6	3.2
Pineapples	2.4	na	3.7	1.9	3.6	1.7
Alcoholic Beverages	18.5	na	20.0	21.6	20.8	21.3
Meat	22.0	na	22.3	14.7	32.4	27.6
Bovine Meat	8.6	na	8.6	2.4	9.3	3.7
Pigmeat	4.1	na	3.9	0.7	4.1	0.7
Poultry Meat	8.4	na	8.8	10.6	9.1	10.9
Eggs	3.1	na	2.7	2.7	4.7	3.0
Fish, Seafood	37.5	na	43.8	56.9	27.6	41.3

a) Excluding beer. b) Mostly coconuts. c) Excluding wine. na not applicable.
Sources: FAOStat, 2005 accessed 12 October 2005; Otanez *et al* (2000); Vatucawaqa (2002).

Some of the discrepancies shown in table 14.2 will be due to differences in reporting units – for example carcase and dressed weight for meat – and so will be more apparent than real. The significant differences that do exist – production of starchy roots in 1999 – are likely to arise at least partly from the lack of reliable information on the production, sales and consumption of smallholder-subsistence farmers and fishermen (Walton, 2002). Given the apparent importance of the smallholder sector in Fiji, this means there is no basis for reliably estimating either the present size of the agriculture, fishing and forestry sectors individually or as a whole, or the impact that policy changes will have on them. This lack of information on the informal components of the "rural" sector in turn reduces the reliability – and hence policy relevance – of any estimates of levels of, or trends in, national household incomes and of food consumption and the nutrition status of the population.

Therefore, there is no reliable basis for estimating either the true magnitude of the problems in the agriculture, fishing and forestry sectors, or the impact of policy changes on them. This reduces the scope for designing appropriate poverty alleviation strategies and other policies.

4. Economic Policy and the Need for Information

The demand for national economic statistics has been government driven from the beginning. Indeed the word "statistics" is ultimately derived from the Latin phrase for "council of state" and the Italian for "statesman" or "politician". Its first use in German (1749) described the analysis of information about the state (Wikipedia, November 2005). There is little doubt the Roman Emperors – to take just one example from earlier times – took a keen interest in statistics on grain harvests and trade because these influenced their income and so their capacity for world conquest.

The word statistics has moved well beyond its original definitions, but a primary reason for collecting economic statistics is *still* to help determine – and judge – government activities.

There is considerable debate on where government intervention is appropriate and on its degree and form(s). For its part, economics proposes clear rules based on the proposition that – in the absence of market failures and given the distribution of income – free competitive markets will deliver Pareto efficient outcomes. The case for intervention then rests on market failure. The practical value of this well-known and elegant edifice of primary theory and its derived rules for intervention rests on there being good information on which to judge market outcomes. And as Sachs says:

> '... good development practice requires monitoring and evaluation, and especially a rigorous comparison of goals and outcomes', (2005, p 80).

These requirements cannot be met without reliable statistics which, paradoxically, are probably more important in developing countries where the stakes are higher than elsewhere.

While there are any number of potentially policy relevant pieces of information, we focus on estimates of Gross Domestic Product (GDP) for agriculture, fishing and forestry and particularly on the estimates of subsistence production from these sectors. As is well-known, GDP represents the total market value of production of all final goods and services in the economy in a specific period. In principle, this total includes ***all*** marketed output – reported, unreported and illegal – plus production used for home consumption.

We recognise that, even within its definition, GDP is essentially an indicator rather than a precise measure of the economic or even the market sales value of what is produced. Reported values can be distorted through evasion and survey error. The difference between the size of the actual economy and the measured economy at any time depends on the size of the "black economy" and of the informal economy. The former represents evasion of public regulations and controls. Empirical evidence suggests that it is growing and its expansion is positively related to rising taxes, increased regulation and a decline in respect for the public sector. The black economy is a significant element in all countries but tends to be more substantial in lesser developed economies. For example, Schneider and Enste (2000) estimate that the black economy could represent 12 per cent or more of GDP in OECD countries, 23 percent in transition economies and on average 39 percent for developing countries – the percentage exceeds even this high average in some countries.

GDP estimates that do not include measures of non-marketed agricultural, fisheries and forest production in an economy like Fiji's will underestimate the true size of the "rural" sector and provide a misleading impression of the nature and extent of economic changes in the sector over time. However, actual practice on what home produced consumption is included and whether it is specifically identified seems to be based on the pragmatic issue of just how important subsistence production is in the national scheme of things.

These days the Australian accounts incorporate estimates of farm production consumed on farm (ABS 1990 p 6) but these estimates do not appear to be separately identified in the published data. By contrast, estimates of backyard or subsistence egg production by *all households* were included along with commercial output in the egg production statistics for many years. The estimates were based on a consumer survey in 1949, which showed that backyard egg production was quite a large proportion of total supply. The same backyard quantity was included in the egg data for twenty years or thereabouts and, therefore was also included in the national accounts. The backyard egg series was eventually abandoned after commercial output had expanded considerably.

In Fiji, home produced foods, etc. are more significant than in more developed countries and are identified as separate line aggregates in the national accounts.

The issue in this paper is how well subsistence rural GDP is currently measured.

a) Absolute Contribution of Agriculture to the Economy

GDP and its growth rate are among the most common headline statistics used to describe national economic performance and wellbeing. Like so many newspaper headlines, GDP does not tell the full story. The conventional national accounting approach to the economic contribution of agriculture and other sectors measures the size of each sector effectively in terms of the level of its gross market value of production.

The concepts involved here can be clarified from an examination of the very familiar hypothetical market shown in Figure 14.1. From a welfare economics perspective, the total economic value of production is reflected in the value consumers are willing and able to pay. The total gross economic value of the sector is equivalent to the sum of the three shaded areas (OQ_2EP_4). This area can be further decomposed into three parts:

- the area OQ_2EP_1 represents the opportunity cost of the resources used in production
- the net surplus to the owners of these resources is the area P_1EP_2
- the surplus from the sector flowing to domestic consumers is the area P_2EP_4.

The overall net contribution of the production process is given by the sum of the producer surplus (P_1EP_2) and the local consumer surplus (P_2EP_4). That is, the economic contribution of the sector is equal to the gain that producers get over and above their returns in other enterprises plus the residual value domestic consumers derive from the consumption of the product after they have paid for it.

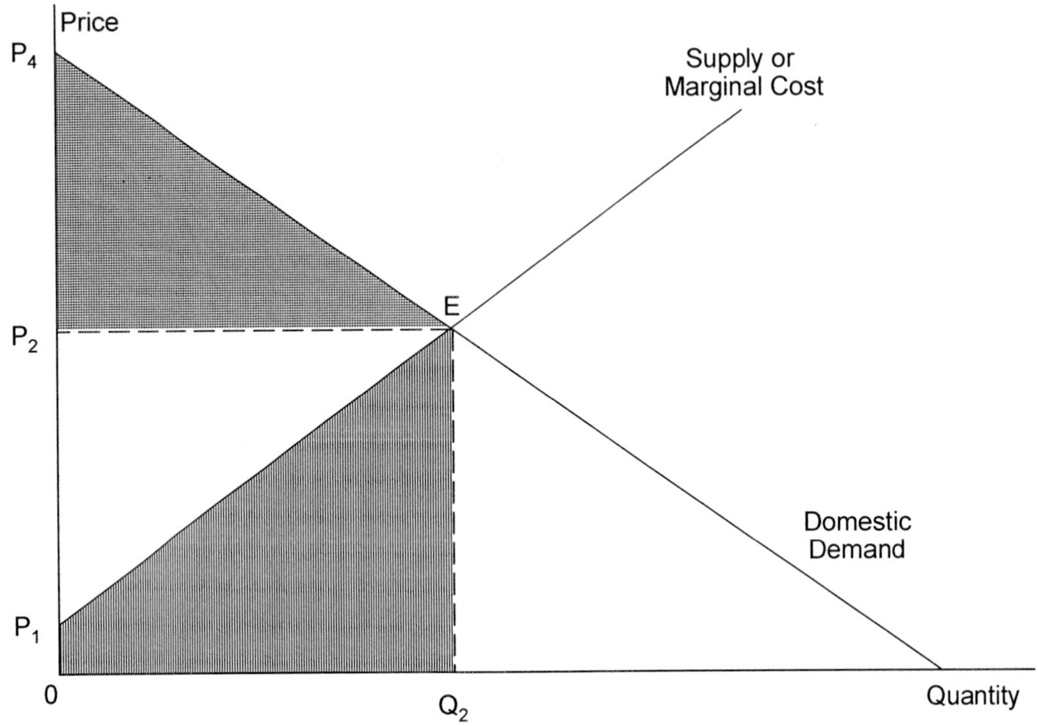

Figure 14.1. Standard Hypothetical Market.

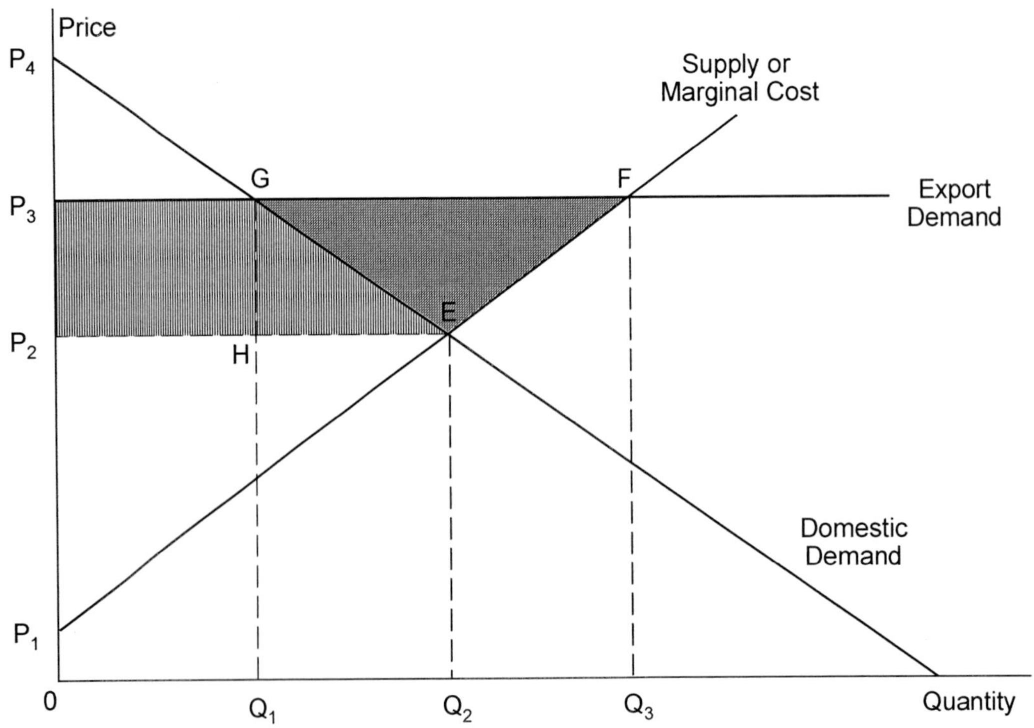

Figure 14.2. Impact of Exports.

Now consider the case where some part of production is exported, either directly or indirectly in the form of being consumed by overseas tourists and visitors. The more overseas visitors there are, the greater will be the gains to producers – at least to the extent to which greater demand for output drives up food prices. Of course, if overseas demand advantages producers through higher prices, it disadvantages domestic consumers. The net impact of overseas demand is shown in Figure 14.2.

The demand from overseas consumers is such as to increase the quantity produced and sold from Q_2 to Q_3. This has the impact of driving up food prices from P_2 to P_3 and as a result domestic sales fall to Q_1. Overseas sales are assumed to be Q_3-Q_1. The gain to producers from overseas sales is then equal to the value of the area P_2EFP_3. So producers gain from a higher price on the original Q_2 sold and from the additional Q_3-Q_2 output sold due to overseas demand. However, there is a loss to domestic consumers from reduced consumption equal to the area HEG and higher prices on the residual consumption given by P_2HGP_3. The net gain to Fiji from overseas sales equals the value of the area GEF.

b) Relative Size of Agriculture in the Economy

If the objective of the exercise is to compare the size of the agricultural sector with the overall economy the situation is different. The calculation of producer and consumer surplus values is not undertaken as part of the national accounts system so national aggregates are not available in this form. In this context, comparison of the GDP from agriculture with national GDP may be relevant. That is, GDP is still useful as a broad-brush indicator partly because it is based on a systematic framework for collecting economic statistics known as the System of National Accounts (SNA) developed under United Nations auspices (UN, 2003). Fiji's national accounts are based on the first SNA issued in 1968. A revised SNA was issued in 1993. Another revision is underway. In terms of the case portrayed in Figure 2, GDP would be measured by the area OQ_3FP_3.

Agriculture, fishing and forestry clearly account for a significant slice of Fiji's GDP, and subsistence production is an important component of these sectors (Table 14.1). The official data indicate that agriculture, fishing and forestry together contribute around 16 percent of total GDP while subsistence activities produce approximately 37 percent of the total output in the combined sectors. Consequently about 50 percent of the food (fish plus agriculture excluding sugarcane) produced in Fiji is produced and consumed within the same household.

This conclusion is based on the results of Fiji's Household Income and Expenditure Surveys (HIES) and supported by the national nutrition surveys (NFNC 1995) and a survey by Owen *et al* (2002). However, the subsistence data are derived from a population based extrapolation of survey estimates from the 1990 HIES. That explains why the growth rates of subsistence production are identical and equal the rate of population growth. The implication of the extrapolation method is that an important part of the latest official estimates of aggregate agricultural GDP is benchmarked on data from 15 years ago.

Table 14.3. Sources of Selected Foods

Food	Fijians				Indo-Fijians			
	Rural		Urban		Rural		Urban	
	Bought	Home	Bought	Home	Bought	Home	Bought	Home
	– percent of food consumed –							
Breadfruit	3.1	96.9	30.0	60.0	34.0	52.2	41.7	45.8
Cassava	2.9	97.1	61.3	38.7	34.8	34.8	66.7	29.6
Dalo	8.6	91.4	74.2	25.8	52.2	39.1	92.6	7.4
Green Vudi	6.3	93.8	59.3	33.3	27.3	36.4	80.0	10.0
Kumala	21.1	78.9	81.8	9.1	88.9	11.1	92.0	8.0
Yams	6.1	90.9	48.0	28.0	63.2	15.8	94.1	0.0

Note: Totals may not add as details shown exclude gifts.
Source: Owen *et al* (2002).

In an economy where rural sector production is less important this procedure may not raise concern, but in a country where agriculture, fishing and forestry are important production activities this approach means the official data need to be treated with extra care.

5. Determinants of Household Production

The nature of the bias or error that the existing extrapolation procedure might introduce into the GDP data set is unclear.

Any bias due to the current extrapolation method depends on the accuracy of the 1990 HIES estimates of subsistence production and on the stability of the relationship between subsistence production and population *per se*. However, both the 1993 national nutrition survey (NFNC 1995) and the 2001 survey (116 households) by Owen *et al* show (Table 14.3) that the extent of home produced consumption varies widely according to the household's ethnicity and whether it is a rural or urban household. For example, Fijian and rural households are generally more reliant on home production than urban or Indo-Fijian households.

Therefore the marked urbanisation of Fiji's population since 1986 and the decline in the Indo-Fijian population are potentially significant developments in the context of Fiji's subsistence GDP. The importance of these types of changes is examined through a regression analysis of the 2001 household survey by Owen et al. The estimated models test the hypothesis that the importance of household production in total consumption in Fiji depends on cultural factors, income levels, and production opportunities – all of which are changing. The variables used are defined in Table 14.4.

The basic estimation model is:

Dependence = f(Urban, Fijian, Div1, Div2, Div3, Employment, Unemployment, Prof, Trade, Manual, House, Age).

Table 14.4. Definition of Regression Variables

Variable Labels	Definitions
Dependent Variables	
All Crops	Proportion of value of all fruit, vegetables and cereals consumed in and produced by the household.
Root Crops	Proportion of value of all root crops (e.g. dalo, cassava) consumed in and produced by the household.
Greenleaf Vegetables	Proportion of value of all greenleaf vegetables (eg cabbage and rou rou) consumed in and produced by the household
Explanatory Variables	
Urban	Dummy variable – 1 for households in urban areas.
Fijian	Dummy variable – 1 for ethnic Fijian households
Employment	Proportion of adults in the household who are not unemployed.
Age	Average age of adults in the household.
Div1	Dummy variable – 1 for households in Division 1.
Div2	Dummy variable – 1 for households in Division 2.
Div3	Dummy variable – 1 for households in Division 3.
Unemployment	The number of unemployed people in the household
Prof	Dummy variable – 1 for households with at least one member in a professional or administrative job.
Trade	Dummy variable – 1 for households with at least one member in a trades job.
Manual	Dummy variable – 1 for households with at least one member in a manual labouring job.
House	Dummy variable – 1 for households with at least one member in household duties.

The equation was estimated separately for three food groups: “All Crops” (excluding sugar), “Root Crops” and “Greenleaf Vegetables”. The base for the regression is an Indo-Fijian family living in a rural location in Division 4 with at least one farmer in the family. The coefficients on the dummy variables represent the departures from this base case.

The regressions were estimated using a Tobit approximation given the substantial number of respondents who reported zero values for the dependent variables. The data are effectively truncated at zero on the lower bounds so OLS estimations are probably unreliable. The final models (see Table 14.5) were derived from the base models by deleting variables that were clearly insignificant.

The results in Table 14.5 are fairly consistent across all three models and support the initial hypothesis. The Adjusted R^2 values show a substantial extent of the variation in dependence on home production can be explained by cultural differences (the significant positive coefficient on Fijian), income (negative coefficients on Employment and Prof) and opportunity to produce food at home (negative coefficient on Urban). These are promising results because the survey was not designed for this particular application. For example, it would have been useful to have direct income data as well as the occupational data that were collected.

Table 14.5. Determinants of Home Production Dependence

Variable	All Crops		Root Crops		Greenleaf Vegetables	
Constant	0.08	(0.08)	0.37	(0.03)	0.53	(0.00)
Fijian	0.62	(0.00)	0.94	(0.00)	0.62	(0.00)
Urban*Fijian	-0.49	(0.00)	-0.52	(0.00)	-0.80	(0.00)
Div1			-0.39	(0.01)		
Div2			-0.32	(0.06)	-0.35	(0.03)
Div3			-0.46	(0.00)	-0.38	(0.00)
Prof	-0.14	(0.05)	-0.34	(0.03)		
Employment	-0.79	(0.00)	-1.57	(0.00)	-1.70	(0.00)
Employment^2	0.64	(0.02)	1.42	(0.02)	1.54	(0.03)
Adjusted R^2	0.78		0.67		0.50	
Akaike IC	0.40		1.11		1.50	
Dependent Variable Mean	0.24		0.40		0.47	

Note: Values in parenthesis are p-values. Values less than 0.05 indicate the coefficient is significant at the 5 percent level. Regression coefficients derived from Tobit estimations.

The final All Crops equation explains nearly 80 percent of the variation in dependence on home production. While coming from an ethnically Fijian family tended to increase the consumption of home produced food relative to purchased food, this influence was moderated in urban areas as urban Fijians depended less on home produced crops than Indo-Fijians. After adjusting for all other factors, there was no statistical difference between rural and urban Indo-Fijians. Incomes – proxied by job category – appear to be a significant explanator of dependence as the coefficients for the proportion employed within the household and the presence of a household member with a relatively highly paid job in a professional or administrative role were all clearly significant. However, the impact of income on dependence may not be a simple linear one as the coefficient on Employment is negative while the coefficient on the squared term is highly significant and positive. This is consistent with increasing incomes reducing the consumption of home grown food but with the size of the negative impact falling as incomes rise.

The picture is similar for Root Crops and Greenleaf Vegetables, except that regional differences were evident – residence in Division 3 reduced dependency relative to residency in Division 4 by 115 percent for Root Crops and 81 percent for Greenleaf Vegetables. Also, note that Fijian ethnicity had less impact on Greenleaf Vegetable home dependency than was the case for either All Crops or Root Crops. In the urban context, the average ethnic Fijian household had a nearly 40 percent lower dependence on home produced Greenleaf Vegetables than Indo-Fijians of similar occupational and employment status.

The significance of these results can be interpreted through the relevant impact measures or "elasticities" (Table 14.6). Fijian ethnicity increases dependence on home production by 260 percent in rural areas and 54 percent in urban areas. A 10 percent increase in the proportion of adult family members in employment reduces home production dependence by around 8 percent while the presence of a family member in a relatively highly paid professional job reduced dependency by nearly 60 percent.

Table 14.6. Impact Estimates

Variables	All Crops	Root Crops	Greenleaf Vegetables
	– elasticity of column with respect to row –		
Fijian – Urban	0.54	1.05	-0.38
– Rural	2.58	2.35	1.13
Employment	-0.76	-0.88	-0.8
Div1		-0.98	
Div2		-0.8	-0.74
Div3		-1.15	-0.81
Prof	-0.58	-0.85	

Note: Estimates derived with dummy variables equal to 1 and with Employment, All Crops, Root Crops and Greenleaf Vegetables all at data means.

6. APPLICATION

These regression results can be combined with guesstimated time series values for the explanatory variables (see Figures 14.2 and 14.3) to generate estimates of the value of subsistence production that are more information-rich than the current population based extrapolations. In the pilot example below it is assumed for illustrative purposes that the final All Crops model results are applicable to all subsistence agricultural, fisheries and forest production and that sugar is not a subsistence crop.

Given that assumption and annual data for the explanatory variables, the preparation of alternative estimates of subsistence agricultural, fisheries and forest GDP is in principle a relatively straightforward three step arithmetic task:

- calibrate the estimated equation to base year data – 1992 when the current published data put the dependence ratio for agricultural, fishing and forestry GDP at 0.56;
- calculate annual values of the ratio using annual values of the explanatory variables;
- derive the estimates of subsistence agricultural, fishing and forestry GDP using identities based on the ratio and the value of marketed rural production.

The revised subsistence estimates (Figure 14.3) are based on interpolations between, and extrapolations from, available data that reasonably approximate the definitions of the explanatory variables Fijian, Fijian*Urban and Prof. Due to difficulties in constructing a proxy variable, the published subsistence estimates are not adjusted for variations in the Employment variable.

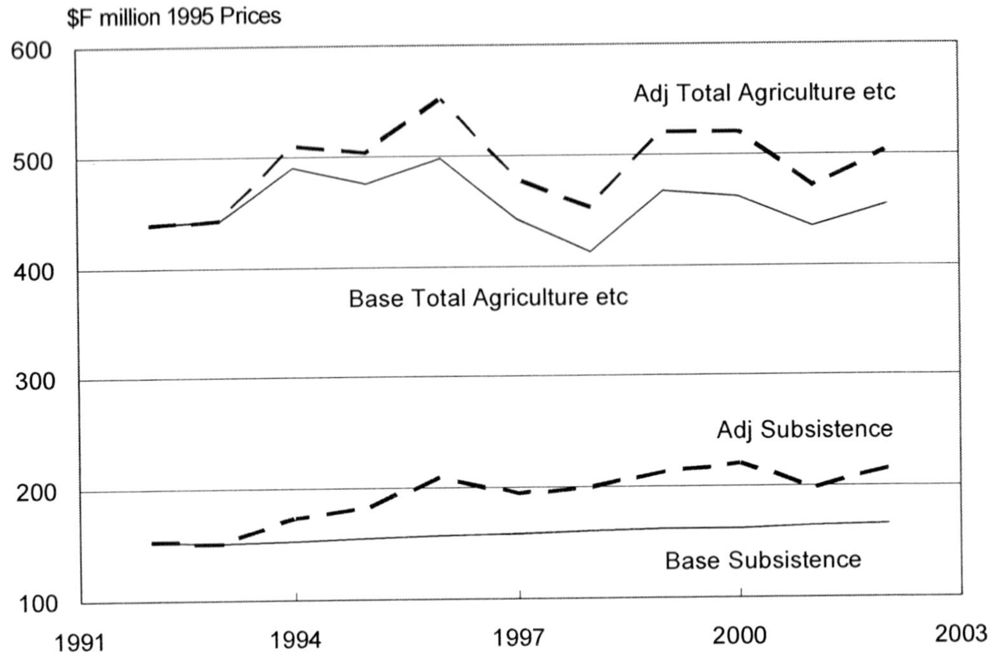

Figure 14.3. Base and Adjusted Subsistence and Total Rural GDP (Real 1995 $F).

Due to the 0 – 1 specification of household attributes, the explanatory variables in the All Crops equation are expressed in a probabilistic sense. So the Fijian variable is given by the ratios of ethnic Fijians to the total population and indicates the chance of a randomly chosen person being an ethnic Fijian. The ratio of ethnic *Fijians* is used as a proxy for the ratio of *Fijian households* in all households. The hard available data – indicated by the markers in Figure 3– are limited to census information for 1986 and 1996 and estimates for 2004 from the FIBoS website[1]. The equations shown in the body of Figures 14.4 and 14.5 are the time trend functions (where x = 1,2,3...n) used to generate the time series values of the explanators applicable to the estimated All Crops home dependence equation. In the equations "y" represents the dependent variables, Fijian, Fijian*Urban and Prof.

The Prof variable (Figure 14.5) is defined as the ratio of the numbers of Salaried Personnel to the total of employed Wage Earners and Salaried Personnel and so does not account for self-employed people. However, with the calibration of the All Crops equation to the base year, it is the *variations* in the explanators, not their *levels* that matter.

The results of these procedures (Figure 14.4), indicate that the current population based extrapolations understate the value of subsistence agricultural, fishing and forestry GDP in 2002 by about thirty percent, equal to an eleven percent understatement of total rural GDP.

Overall, the dependency ratio is projected to increase only marginally because a substantial increase in the proportion of ethnic Fijians in the population offsets the effects of their increasing urbanisation and some decline in the relative numbers of professionals. The understatement of subsistence and total agricultural GDP in 1996 is about the same as in

[1] www.statsfiji.fj

2002. Since the 1996 estimates are based on census data, they strengthen the overall conclusions of the analysis.

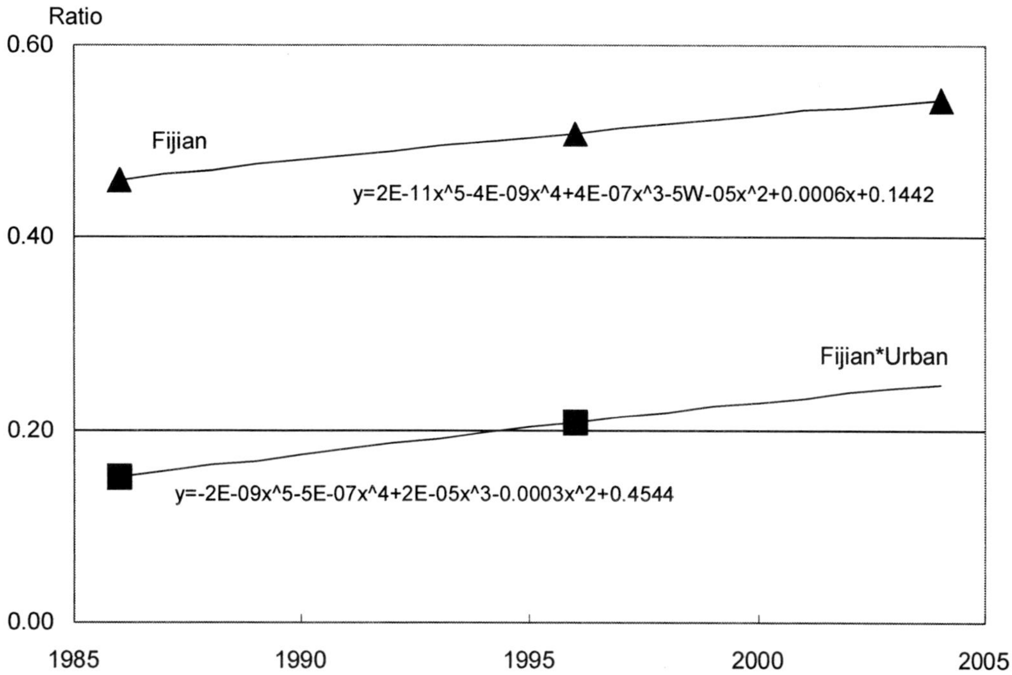

Figure 14.4. Extrapolated and Interpolated Fijian Variables.

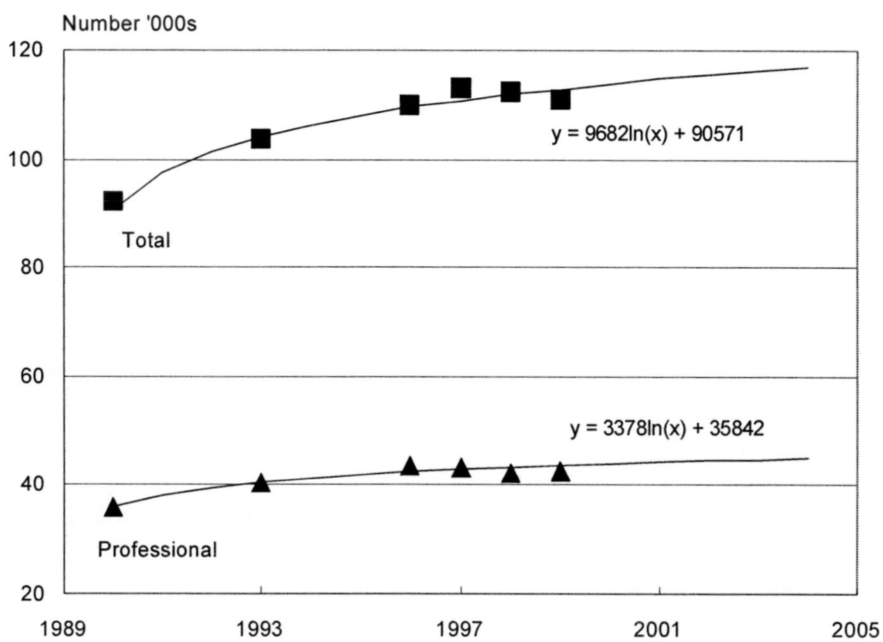

Figure 14.5. The Prof Variable.

Based on the adjusted values of subsistence GDP, the subsistence sector expanded on average at around 3.5 percent per year compound over 1992 to 2002 compared with an annual growth rate of under 1 percent according to the population based extrapolations. The adjustments to subsistence production lift the annual growth of total rural GDP between 1992 and 2002 from under 0.5 percent to 1.4 percent.

Even with the adjustments made here, subsistence and total rural GDP may still be understated for two reasons. First, the published value for the 1992 base year used here may be too low because it includes two years of population based subsistence extrapolations from the HIES year of 1990. Second, the rural to urban movement of Fijians may have contributed to some unemployment. So inclusion of proxies for the Employment variable would likely have caused some increase in the adjusted value of agricultural, fishing and forestry subsistence GDP.

7. Conclusions

Clearly, this pilot study has its limitations. After all, the underpinning econometric model is based on the serendipitous application of data collected for a survey with different aims. Furthermore, the annual values of the explanatory variables used to derive the alternative estimates of subsistence GDP rely on very few firm data points. That said, the key points to note are:

- It should be obvious even to casual observers that subsistence rural production in Fiji is substantial and represents an appreciable component of total rural production;
- This casual observation is supported by a number of more analytically formal surveys;
- Therefore, marketed rural GDP *alone* will considerably understate rural and national GDP – so *it is necessary* to allow for subsistence production in the annual national accounts;
- It seems the currently used population based extrapolations considerably understate the economic contribution of the subsistence sector.

Compared with the population based extrapolations, the estimation method outlined here is more analytically grounded and information-rich and so should in principle be the better performer. The full results of the latest HIES will provide a near term test of the two methods. The new HIES will also provide a very much richer data set for analysis. Therefore, it should be possible to improve significantly on the present results, for example through more robust results for the constituent components of aggregate subsistence production.

Ultimately, the indirect method outlined here should be supplemented, or even replaced, by the use of formal economic models of the subsistence sector. Such modelling is one of the components of the project for which this paper represents a start.

Meanwhile, we believe the present analysis is sufficiently robust to support the maintained hypothesis that the current population based extrapolations of subsistence rural GDP understate the true size of the subsistence sector in Fiji. These conclusions have potentially important policy implications related to assessing the resilience and capacity of subsistence producers, for judging the nutritional status of the population and in relation to poverty assessments, especially in relation to rural poverty, just to name a few issues.

REFERENCES

(ABS) Australian Bureau of Statistics (1990) *Australian National Accounts: Concepts, Sources and Methods*, ABS Catalogue No 5216.0, May.

(ADB, MFNP) Asian Development Bank and Ministry of Finance and National Planning (2003) *Fiji: Poverty Status Discussion Paper: Final Report as Presented to Government*, ADB TA 6047-REG, 4 June.

(DFID), Department for International Development (2005) *Productivity Growth for Poverty Reduction: An Approach to Agriculture: Draft for External Feedback*, July.

Owen, K, P. Vatucawaqa and J. Chand (2002) "Understanding Protein Choices in Fiji". Paper presented to the Fiji Food Choice Workshop, Suva, 4-6 June 2002.

Otanez, G., J. Ratuvuki and M. Ledua, (2000) *Fiji National Agricultural Survey – 1999*, Ministry of Agriculture, Fisheries and Forests, Suva, April.

Sachs, J. (2005) *The End of Poverty: How We Can Make it Happen in Our Lifetime*, Penguin: London.

Schneider, F. and Enste, D.H. (2000) "Shadow Economies: Size, Causes and Consequences, *Journal of Economic Literature*, 38(1):77-114.

Schultz, T.W. (1964) *Transforming Traditional Agriculture*, Yale University Press.

Tax, S. (1953), *Penny Capitalism A Guatemalan Indian Economy*, Smithsonian Institution Institute of Social Anthropology Publication No. 16, USGPO, Washington.

UN (2003) *National Accounts: A Practical Introduction*, ST/ESA/SER.F/85, UN, New York.

UNDP (2005), *Human Development Report 2005: International Cooperation at the Crossroads: Aid, Trade and Security in an Unequal World*, http://hdr.undp.org,.

Vatucawaqa, P. (2002) *Food Balance Sheet Fiji 2002*, National Food and Nutrition Centre, Suva, May.

Walton, P. (2002) *Collection, Access and Use of Agricultural Statistics in the Pacific Islands: Report of Study*, Working Paper IAP – WP45, ACIAR, Canberra.

In: Development Problems and Prospects in Pacific Islands ISBN: 978-1-60021-793-7
Editors: B. C. Prasad, D. C. Roy, pp. 215-228

Chapter 15

TOTAL FACTOR PRODUCTIVITY GROWTH IN PACIFIC ISLAND ECONOMIES: CASE STUDY OF FIJI, PAPUA NEW GUINEA AND SAMOA

Mahendra Reddy, Nilesh Kumar and Yogesh Karan

1. INTRODUCTION

The economic performance of the Pacific Island Countries (PICs) economies over the last two decades has been below the potential for a developing country standard (see Table 15.1 for GDP growth data). There have been years during which the economies have done well, while there have also been periods when there was marginal or negative growth.

The poor performance of the PICs economies has challenged policy makers to re-look at their domestic policy making. There has also been strong pressure from lending institutions such as the IMF and World Bank to undertake market oriented reforms. The reforms have been mainly in areas of trade, and in the goods market, factor market, labour market, financial market and public sector. Reforms in the goods market involved the dismantling of barriers to trade, as in the removal of licences and reduction or elimination of tariffs and quota. Reforms of the financial sector involved the removal of restrictions on entry and exit of financial institutions and relaxation on the movement of capital. Labour market deregulation has been aimed at making it more flexible.

The market oriented reforms have their origins linked to classical economist Adam Smith, who wrote in his famous book, *An Inquiry into the Nature and Causes of the Wealth of Nations*, that trade can be seen as a vent for surplus production and widening the market and improving the division of labour. Leading on from the classical theory, the neo-classical economics proposes that an economy left to the market with minimum intervention will allocate resources efficiently and generate growth. The neo-classical theory of growth assumes that markets are working perfectly and that economies are functioning in line with their comparative advantage (Solow 1956; Swan 1956). Therefore, the theory essentially assumes that all the appropriate institutions for markets to function efficiently are in place and that there are no price distortions and no resource misallocation.

Table 15.1. GDP Growth Rates (%) of Pacific Island Economies and East Timor, s1986-2004

Year	FSM	Cooks Islands	East Timor	Fiji	Kiribati	Marshall Islands	Nauru	PNG	Samoa	Solomon Islands	Tonga	Tuvalu	Vanuatu
1986	2.0	--	--	--	--	--	--	--	--	--	--	--	--
1987	6.0	-1.5	--	-6.3	-3.1	13.2	3.1	2.8	1.0	2.3	3.2	--	6.0
1988	0.7	1.8	--	0.4	18.2	9.4	1.3	2.9	-0.2	5.4	-1.8	--	-0.4
1989	4.1	4.5	--	...	-8.6	0.8	-0.5	-1.4	1.3	6.9	-0.3	-1.9	3.3
1990	6.2	7.9	--	3.6	2.1	7.0	-2.1	-3.0	-7.5	--	2.0	15.4	0.0
1991	3.6	7.1	--	-2.7	-5.4	1.1	-3.8	9.5	-2.4	--	2.4	3.6	13.3
1992	6.8	6.0	--	6.1	-0.2	0.0	-7.3	13.8	-2.3	--	3.2	2.8	4.7
1993	2.0	3.9	--	2.6	2.3	4.1	-7.3	18.2	2.4	--	-0.4	4.1	6.0
1994	1.7	3.9	9.9	5.1	8.9	2.8	-7.3	5.9	--	--	--	10.3	9.6
1995	-5.1	...	9.5	2.5	5.6	2.7	-7.3	-3.4	6.6	--	4.6	-5.0	0.0
1996	-6.1	-0.3	10.8	4.7	3.1	-15.9	-7.3	6.6	7.3	1.9	0.2	-7.1	2.5
1997	-0.7	-2.3	4.1	-2.3	4.6	-9.4	-7.3	-6.3	0.8	-0.9	-3.0	5.6	8.6
1998	-3.5	-0.8	--.	1.2	15.8	3.0	-1.9	4.7	2.4	1.4	3.6	19.7	4.3
1999	9.3	2.7	-35.5	9.2	8.7	0.8	-1.9	10.1	2.2	-0.5	2.3	-0.5	-3.2
2000	0.5	13.9	15.5	-2.8	-0.7	-2.0	-1.0	0.0	6.1	-14.3	5.6	13.4	2.7
2001	0.9	4.9	14.6	2.7	2.9	-1.5	-0.8	2.7	6.8	-8.7	2.5	5.9	-2.7
2002	0.1	3.9	3.0	4.3	-1.2	4.0	0.9	2.0	1.2	-2.1	2.6	1.2	-4.9
2003	-3.3	3.1	-2.7	5.0	3.5	2.0	2.5	2.8*	3.5	5.7*	3.1	2.0*	2.9
2004	019	--	1.0	4.1	3.5	--	--	2.6*	3.9	5.5*	1.6*	3.0*	--

Source: ADB Database, 2005.

Note: -- Refers to no data.

This theory has provided the conceptual basis for policies to induce rapid growth in all the developed countries. The forces of globalisation led to a push in developing countries to adopt similar policy agenda. This includes government playing a complementary role rather then directly intervening into areas where market could allocate resources efficiently. While there has been some degree of disagreement on a consistent policy package given the differences between countries, the IMF's *World Economic Outlook* for May 1997 provided a "new Washington consensus" which seeks to summarise the current state of economic policy making:

> A key lesson seems to be that the pressures of globalisation, especially in the past decade or so, have served to accentuate the benefits of good policies and the costs of bad policies. Countries that align themselves with the forces of globalisation and embrace the reforms needed to do so, liberalising markets and pursuing disciplined macroeconomic policies, are likely to put themselves on a path of convergence with the advanced economies, following the successful Asian newly industrialised economies. These countries may expect to benefit from trade, gain global market share, and be increasingly rewarded with larger private capital flows.

> Countries that do not adopt such polices are likely to face declining shares of world trade and private capital flows, and to find themselves behind relative terms (IMF, 1997:72).

The last two decades of reform have still not delivered the desired growth rates in some PICs. The low growth could be that the underlying institutional factors, the macroeconomic environment and the lack of economic fundamentals have affected efficiency and technological change in the economy. These two factors are the two sources of total factor productivity change in any economy. In this paper, the aggregate macro data is analysed to see the movement in TFP and how efficiency and productivity contribute to this change.

The second section of the paper provides an overview of PICs economies. The third section of the paper examines methodology of TFP. The fourth section provides results and discussion while the last section provides summary and conclusion.

Fiji's economy had negative growth rates in 1987, 1991, 1997 and 2000. The years 1987 and 2000 were the two years in which the country was racked by coups and political instability and 1997 was the year of massive drought.

Fiji's sugar and garment industries seem to be winding down while tourism has picked up to become the foremost foreign exchange earner. The government has responded positively to develop the required infrastructure for the industry to grow. This indicates that strategies to diversify an economy are important to withstand shocks. Both expiring land leases and the loss of preferential prices are responsible for the decline of the sugar industry whilst the garment industry has been affected by the expiry of the trading agreement, SPARTECA, that facilitated free access of Fiji's garment products into Australian and New Zealand.

Papua New Guinea has also emerged from long drawn out civil unrest that has affected its economy and governments fiscal position. In the mid 1990s, PNG's economy had performed very poorly and then began positive growth since 1997. PNG has a good natural resource base and the petroleum and gold exports have brought major foreign exchange to keep the economy afloat. The country's agriculture sector, including the coffee industry has lot of potential to support PNG's economy. However, the land tenure system needs to be re-examined to ensure that it does not become an obstacle to PNG's growth.

Solomon Islands similarly has a large stock of natural resources, particularly fish and timber. However, the 2000 law and order crisis caused significant infrastructure destruction and tarnished investor confidence in the country, thus affecting growth. The growth in that year fell by 14.3% and the economy was in recession till the end of 2002. However, it has begun to show a positive trend since then.

Vanuatu's economy has also been growing slowly and in fact had suffered negative growth in the 2001-02 period. One of its major exports, kava, had a major set back when several European countries imposed an import ban for medical reasons. While copra is one of the other major industries providing rural income, falling world prices have had a significant impact on its export income. Vanuatu also derives a significant amount of its foreign exchange from tourism. The economy bounced back in 2003 with a significant growth rate of 2.9%.

Tonga's economic performance has not been very strong. However, despite being a small economy with an agricultural export base, particularly squash, vanilla and kava, which are the main exports have been consistent with respect to growth levels.

Samoa is one country in the region that has been quite consistent with its growth performance. With poor performance up till early 1990s, it has been on a positive growth trend since then. Its tuna industry targeting the Japanese market has been very successful. Its agricultural sector has not made any significant progress and continues to be stagnant but the growth in tourism has supplemented this decline.

The economies of Kiribati, Micronesia and the Marshalls have performed poorly over the last decade. They have a very narrow resource base and aid and remittances have played a important role in propping up these economies (see Appendix 15.1 for Aid data and Appendix 15.2 for Remittance data).

The economy of East Timor is one that has great potential. The limited GDP growth data indicates that GDP growth rates for East Timor in 1994-1997 ranged from 4.1% to 10.8%. With a major fall in GDP in 1999, resulting from massive damage to economic infrastructure by Indonesian troops and ant-independence militias, the economy started to bounce back immediately with positive growth rates in the years that followed. However, the extensive drought and the gradual winding down of the international presence saw negative growth in 2003.

The PICs are gradually moving towards an export oriented growth strategy. Examining the export performance of PICs provides mixed results (see Table 15.2 for data). For the years 1993-95, Kiribati, Marshall Islands, FSM, PNG, Samoa and Solomons did very well. However, this configuration has changed in the forthcoming years. In 1996-00, Cooks, PNG, Samoa and Tuvalu fared well. For the period 2001-03, PNG, Solomons, Tonga and Tuvalu had good export growth rates. These trends reveal that only PNG has been consistent as far as export growth rates are concerned.

Table 15.2. Export Growth rate as a % of GDP, 1993-2003

Country	Growth Rate (%)		
	1993-95	1996-2000	2001-2003
Cook Islands	3.9	41.7	-6.0
Fiji Islands	8.4	8.2	0.9
Kiribati	25.1	5.8	--
Marshall Islands	45.2	-9.2	--
Micronesia, Fed. States of	22.5	-48.1	--
Palau	-9.4	-5.4	--
Papua New Guinea	21.7	12.3	10.8
Samoa	64.0	18.8	0.4
Solomon Islands	23.8	-7.7	24.9
Tonga	2.5	2.7	40.4
Tuvalu	-28.9	17.2	387.9
Vanuatu	6.6	3.8	-1.5
East Timor	--	--	636.7[a]

Source: ADB database, 2004.

[a] The figure refers to 2002-2004 average.

-- Refers to data not available.

The structure of the PICs economies is also changing as there is a gradual shift away from the agriculture sector towards manufacturing and service. Agriculture's contribution to total GDP has declined for all the PICs over the last ten years. Tonga's contribution of agriculture is 29% of the total GDP while Marshall Islands is least dependent on agriculture. This trend is also confirmed by examining the data on Industry value added as % of GDP, which has been increasing for all countries except for Vanuatu. The highest industrial component for GDP is for PNG (40.7%) while the lowest is for Vanuatu (9.4%). For East Timor, the agricultural sector still accounts for a very high proportion of the overall GDP, with the average for 2001-03 being 27.9%.

Table 15.3. Savings and Capital formation as a % of GDP

Country	Savings as % of GDP			Capital formation as % of GDP		
	1990	2000	2003	1990	2000	2003
Fiji Islands	10.9	5.1	9.7	14.1	12.6	14.8
Papua New Guinea	16.1	23.7	11.7 [a]	24.4	21.3	19.8
Solomon Islands	11.5	...	...	20.1	...	...
Tonga	-12.7	-14.6	-23.7 [b]	18.5	21.8	20.9
Vanuatu	5.7	19.3	16.7 [a]	34.9	22.2	20.9
East Timor	--	-52.6	-32.4	--	32.9	27.4

[a] Refers to 2002.

[b] Refers to 2001.

Note: Data for other countries not available.

Source: ADB Indicators, 2004.

Table 15.4. Inflation (%) in PICs, 1992-2003

Country	1992-95	1996-00	2001-03
Cook Islands	3.4	0.8	4.7
Fiji Islands	3.3	3.0	3.1
Kiribati [a, b]	4.8	1.8	3.7
Marshall Islands [a]	7.3	4.0	1.7
Micronesia, Fed. States of	4.7	2.3	0.3
Nauru	-7.1	5.2	
Papua New Guinea	7.4	11.9	11.9
Samoa	4.9	3.1	4.0
Solomon Islands [a]	10.7	9.5	9.0
Tonga	2.6	3.4	9.6
Tuvalu [a]	3.0	2.0	3.1
Vanuatu [a]	3.3	2.4	2.9
East Timor	--	--	5.1

Source: ADB database, 2004.

[a] Data refer to capital city

[b] Data refer to the rate of change of retail price index.

-- Refers to no data.

The savings and investment levels have also been low in most of the PICs (Table 15.3). However, the level of both savings and capital formation is worrying. Generally developing countries, which have had reasonable real growth rates of 5% and above, have had a savings to GDP ratio of over 30% and investment to GDP ratio between 20 and 25 percent. Most of the Pacific island countries lag far behind these ratios for savings and investment. For East Timor, while the negative savings rate has declined, the level of capital formation as a percentage of GDP has declined from 32.9% in 2000 to 27.4% in 2003.

nflation in most of the PICs was modest but in PNG, Solomons, Tonga and Cook Islands it was higher then normal. The high inflation in PNG is due to persistent large budget deficits financed by borrowing thus putting pressure on currency and interest rates. The high inflation in Solomons is due to the twin effects of supply constraints and capital inflow. The civil conflicts led to supply constraints and external assistance for reconstruction has led to capital inflow, which has exerted pressure on currency demand. Similarly, Tonga's inflation has also been fueled by a number factors including remittance inflow and high budget deficit and borrowing. The negative impact of remittances and tourism earnings on the purchasing power of the dollar is also felt in Cooks and Fiji. These two countries have to monitor the monetary sector, in particular the exchange rates and fiscal policy, to fight off any demand driven inflation. East Timor also has a very high inflation rate, which could become a problem for the economy if not controlled immediately.

2. The DEA Method and the Malmquist Index of Productivity Measurement

This study uses the Data Envelopment Analysis (DEA) method to estimate an index of productivity change and decomposes the productivity change into two effects: the efficiency change effect and the technological change effect. In this article, we use Malmquist productivity index to estimate productivity changes. The major advantages in using the Malmquist index are as follows:

a) it is a useful way of estimating total factor productivity when inefficiency in production exists;
b) estimation does not require price or cost share data, only quantity data;
c) it is a useful tool to analyze productivity of public services, i.e., where inputs and outputs are not marketable (e.g., schools, hospitals, and utilities);
d) it can be decomposed into changes in efficiency and changes in frontier technology;
e) technical change is not constrained to be Hicks-neutral even under constant returns to scale, since the estimation is not constrained to a specific functional form;
f) the distance function and thus the Malmquist index does not require behavioural assumptions such as profit maximization, cost minimization, or revenue maximization; and it is a useful application for cases where data are limited, and the assumptions of profit maximization and efficiency in production are not appropriate (Reddy, 1998).

The Malmquist productivity index has not been widely applied in the agricultural literature. However, a large number of non-agricultural studies (banking, hospitals, etc.) have used this measure. Recent studies of productivity growth in the banking industry using the Malmquist index approach include Neal (2004), Borger and Kerstens (2000) Avkiran (1999),

Walker (1998), Elyasiani and Mehdian, (1995), Fukuyama, (1995), Berg *et al.* (1993), Berg *et al.* (1992) and Berg, *et. al.* (1991). The approach has also been applied to the analysis of productivity changes in Swedish pharmacies by Fare *et al.* (1989).

Three recent studies that have applied the approach to productivity analysis in the agricultural sector are Arnade (1994), Umetsu (1996), and Fulginiti and Perrin (1997). Arnade (1994) applied the Malmquist index approach to measure international agricultural efficiency and productivity. Results from his study show that the multi-factor productivity of the agricultural sector has risen in most developed countries and fallen in many developing countries over the 20-year period since 1974. He suggests that adoption of input-intensive technology by developing countries may have offset productivity gains from improved yields and labour productivity. Umetsu (1996) applied the approach to productivity analysis of the Philippine rice sector. Her results showed that technical regress occurred in the Philippine rice sector over the period 1971-90, primarily due to input-biased intensification. Umetsu's study also pointed out that factors affecting productivity, efficiency, and technological change varied depending on the agro-ecological characteristics of each region in the Philippines. Fulginiti and Perrin (1997) applied the Malmquist approach to an examination of agricultural productivity in 18 developing countries over the period 1961-85. The primary purpose of their study was to compare their results with the results from other studies that have reported a declining trend in agricultural productivity in less developed countries (LDCs) using methods other than the Malmquist index. The authors' findings using the Malmquist index approach confirmed the earlier findings of a declining trend in agricultural productivity in LDCs. The authors also found that countries that tax agriculture heavily had negative growth rates in productivity.

The Malmquist index was developed by Fare *et al.* (1989), following the work of Caves *et al.* (1982). The index is based on the Farrell measure of technical efficiency (Farrell, 1957) and Shephard's (1970) distance function. The output distance function for a given output vector y and input vector x for a period t technology is defined as:

$$d^t(y,x) = \min_{d>0}\{d:(y/d,x) \in S^t\} \qquad (1)$$

where S^t represents technology in period t. The distance function can be defined as the smallest factor by which output can be deflated so as to be feasible with input vector x. This concept of distance function can be illustrated using Figure 15.1.

Observations can lie above (y) or below (y*) with given technology S^t. δ is greater than one for "y" and less then one for "y*", given the same input vector x. Since y_t is assumed to be optimal for x_t in S^t (technology in period t), $d^t(y_t,x_t)=1$. Equivalently, if y_s is optimal for x_s, then $d^s(y_s,x_s)=1$.

The Malmquist output index, based on technology in period t is defined as

$$Q^t(y_s, y_t, x) = \frac{d_t(y_t, x)}{d_t(y_s, x)} \text{ for an arbitrarily selected input vector.} \qquad (2)$$

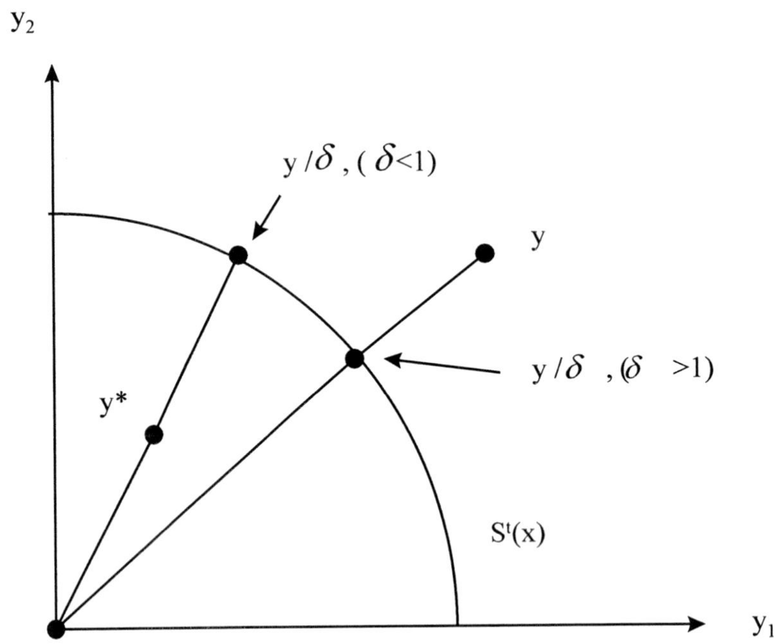

Figure 15.1. Illustration of Distance Function.

The output index number defined above simply measures the growth in output and does not distinguish between the contribution of the growth of inputs and the contribution due to technical progress. To determine what portion of output growth is due to technical progress and what portion is due to input growth, productivity indices are computed. This requires the use of panel data. Given the availability of panel data, one may use Data Envelopment Analysis (DEA) such as linear programming or a (input- or output-based) Malmquist TFP index to measure productivity change. DEA is a non-parametric mathematical programming approach to frontier estimation. Detailed discussion of the DEA methodology is provided in Seiford and Thrall (1990), Lovell (1993), Ali and Seiford (1993), Lovell (1994), Charnes *et al.* (1995), and Seiford (1996). DEA was first advanced by Charnes, Cooper and Rhodes (1978), and led to a large number of papers extending its application.

The output-based Malmquist productivity change index was specified by Fare *et al.* (1989) as:

$$m_o(y_s, x_s, y_t, x_t) = \left[\frac{d_o^s(x_t, y_t)}{d_o^s(x_s, y_s)} \times \frac{d_o^t(x_t, y_t)}{d_o^t(x_s, y_s)}\right]^{1/2}. \tag{3}$$

The index computes the productivity index for one production point (say for x_t and y_t) relative to another period's production point (say x_s and y_s). For values of m_o greater than 1, this represents TFP growth from the base period. Similarly, with a decline in the value of m_o from the base period, a decrease in productivity growth is implied.

The Malmquist index is in fact a geometric mean of two output-based Malmquist TFP indices, where one index uses period (s) technology and the other, period (t) technology. The computation of the Malmquist index using the constant returns to scale (CRS) assumption is only appropriate when all Decision Making Units (DMU's) operate in the flat portion of the long-run average cost curve (Coelli, 1996). Given that a firm may be subjected to various factors that inhibit it from operating in this region, the CRS model should be extended to take into account circumstances involving variable returns to scale (VRS). These extensions are explained in Banker *et al.* (1984). The use of the CRS assumption in a production process that displays VRS will lead to technical efficiency estimates that are overstated (since they include scale efficiencies). Therefore, the ability to specify a VRS assumption will provide more accurate estimates of technical efficiency.

An equivalent way of writing the productivity index is:

$$m_o\left(y_s, x_s, y_t, x_t\right) = \frac{d^t(y_t, x_t)}{d^S(y_S, x_S)}\left[\frac{d_o^s\left(x_t, y_t\right)}{d_o^t\left(x_t, y_t\right)} \times \frac{d_o^s\left(x_s, y_s\right)}{d_o^t\left(x_s, y_s\right)}\right]^{1/2} \tag{4}$$

The ratio in the outside bracket measures the change in the output-oriented measure of Farrell technical efficiency between years (s) and (t); that is, the efficiency change is equivalent to the ratio of the Farrell technical efficiency in period (t) to the Farrell technical efficiency in period (s).

$$\text{Efficiency change} = \frac{d^t(y_t, x_t)}{d^S(y_S, x_S} \tag{5}$$

The geometric mean of the two ratios inside the bracket captures the shift in technology between the two periods evaluated at x_t and x_s

$$\text{Technical change} = \left[\frac{d_o^s\left(x_t, y_t\right)}{d_o^t\left(x_t, y_t\right)} \times \frac{d_o^s\left(x_s, y_s\right)}{d_o^t\left(x_s, y_s\right)}\right]^{1/2} \tag{6}$$

The decomposition of efficiency and technical change is illustrated in Figure 15.2 using a CRS technology and involving a single input and single output.

In Figure 15.2, the firm produces at points D and E in periods s and t, respectively. In both periods, the firm is operating below the technology for that period. Therefore, the efficiency and technical change can be described following equations (5) and (6) as:

$$\text{Efficiency change} = \frac{y_t / y_c}{y_s / y_a} \tag{7}$$

$$\text{Technical change} = \left[\frac{y_t / y_b}{y_t / y_c} \times \frac{y_s / y_a}{y_s / y_b} \right]^{1/2} \qquad (8)$$

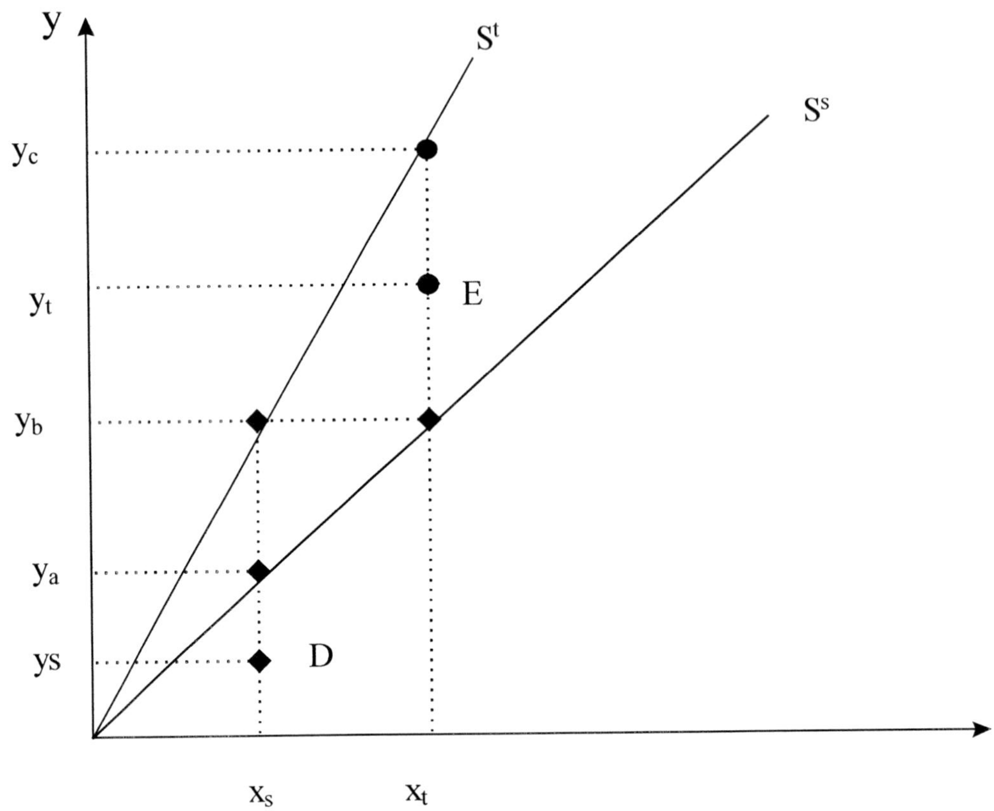

Figure 15.2. Illustration of Malmquist Index.

The Malmquist productivity index used in this study is computed by estimating the four component distance functions of equation (3) using the Data Envelopment Program (DEAP) (Coelli, 1996).

The production frontier was estimated for a single outputs, the Gross Domestic Product in millions of US dollars. The inputs are defined as follows:

X_1 population in millions as a proxy for labour;
X_2 gross fixed capital formation in millions of US dollars;
X_3 electricity consumption in millions of KWH;
X_4 government education expenditure in millions of US dollars as a proxy for education level.

The data for the study was obtained from ADB database. The period for which data were available was from1981 to 2004 (24 years). Due to missing data for PICs, only Fiji, PNG and Samoa are examined in this paper.

3. Results and Discussion

The DEA results are presented in Table 15.5 below. The results in the table shed some interesting light on PIC economies. First, efficiency change has not been gained in Fiji and Samoa. However, there has been a 2% gain for PNG. With respect to technological change, there is a decline for all three countries under study. For Fiji, technological change has declined by 51%. For Samoa, its has declined by 40% while for PNG, the decline was 48%. This decline in technological contribution has brought down TFP for all three countries. For Fiji, it has dropped from 1.52 to 1.01, a decline of 51%. For PNG, it has declined by 1.46 to 1.01, a decline of 45%. Similarly, for Samoa, the TFP has declined from 1.41 to 1.01, a fall of 40%.

Table 15.5. Efficiency, Technology and Total Factor Productivity Change, 1982-2004

Year	Efficiency Change			Technological Change			Total Factor Productivity Change		
	Fiji	PNG	Samoa	Fiji	PNG	Samoa	Fiji	PNG	Samoa
1982	1	1.006	1	2.009	1.949	1.946	2.009	1.962	1.946
1983	1	0.915	1	1.534	1.477	1.322	1.534	1.351	1.322
1984	1	1.027	1	1.326	1.257	1.185	1.326	1.29	1.185
1985	1	0.99	1	1.211	1.229	1.217	1.211	1.217	1.217
Mean1986/90	***1***	***0.9845***	***1***	***1.52***	***1.478***	***1.4175***	***1.52***	***1.455***	***1.4175***
1986	1	1.018	1	1.201	1.137	1.205	1.201	1.158	1.205
1987	1	0.948	1	1.14	1.164	1.062	1.14	1.104	1.062
1988	1	0.988	1	1.184	1.092	1.026	1.184	1.079	1.026
1989	1	1.108	1	1.067	1.037	1.12	1.067	1.149	1.12
1990	1	1.026	1	1.051	1.078	1.088	1.051	1.106	1.088
Mean 1991/5	***1***	***1.0176***	***1***	***1.1286***	***1.1016***	***1.1002***	***1.1286***	***1.1192***	***1.1002***
1991	1	0.938	1	1.036	1.083	1.079	1.036	1.016	1.079
1992	1	0.98	1	1.089	1.025	1.048	1.089	1.004	1.048
1993	1	0.973	1	0.973	1.033	1.058	0.973	1.004	1.058
1994	1	0.968	1	1.104	1.036	0.841	1.104	1.003	0.841
1995	1	0.961	1	1.039	1.044	1.07	1.039	1.004	1.07
Mean 1991/5		***0.964***	***1***	***1.0482***	***1.0442***	***1.0192***	***1.0482***	***1.0062***	***1.0192***
1996	1	0.98	1	1.107	1.031	1.007	1.107	1.01	1.007
1997	1	0.996	1	1.044	1.041	1.003	1.044	1.037	1.003
1998	1	1.012	1	0.92	1.001	1.03	0.92	1.013	1.03
1999	1	0.997	1	1.017	1.022	1.03	1.017	1.018	1.03
2000	1	0.83	1	1.134	1.126	1.003	1.134	0.935	1.003
Mean 1996/0		***0.963***	***1***	***1.0444***	***1.0442***	***1.0146***	***1.0444***	***1.0026***	***1.0146***
2001	1	1	1	0.967	0.989	1.003	0.967	0.989	1.003
2002	1	0.938	1	1.035	1.024	1.025	1.035	0.96	1.017
2003	1	1.062	1	1.009	0.976	1.011	1.009	1.037	1.011
2004	1	1.035	1	1.022	1.002	0.993	1.022	1.037	0.993
Mean 2001/4	***1***	***1.00875***	***1***	***1.00825***	***0.99775***	***1.008***	***1.00825***	***1.00575***	***1.006***

The results provide a new dimension to economic growth analysis of PICs. The PICs economies low growth rates can now be attributed to falling TFP. In particular, there is no efficiency improvement and there appears to be a technological regress. While the data used is only for three PICs, given the commonalities, it does suggest the same could be true for the other small economies.

4. Summary and Conclusion

There are a plethora of studies attempting to explain the sluggish growth performance of PICs economies. The arguments presented in all these papers indicate that bad governance, lack of appropriate economic policies and institutions and political instability are the key causes of low or negative growth in PICs. The exact impact of the fundamentals or the transmission mode has yet to be pointed out.

This paper brings forth a new dimension to these findings. That is, these factors affect efficiency and productivity of the factors of production, thus making economic growth slow. The results of this study reveal that three of PIC economies have not become efficient over the last 24 years. Furthermore, the economies have undergone technological regress over the same period.

Efficiency and technological change are two ways in which economies can grow without increasing their total outlay of inputs. In particular, when resources are scarce and limited, efficiency and productivity growth are the ways to increase output. In a competitive market, efficiency and technological gain can provide the required competitive edge to survive in the market.

References

Ali, A.I., and Seiford, L. M. 1993. The Mathematical Programming Approach to Efficiency Analysis, in H.O. Fried, C.A.K. Lovell and S.S. Schmidt (Eds), *The Measurement of Productive Efficiency*, Oxford University Press, pp. 27-44.

Arnade, C.A. 1994. Using Data Envelopment Analysis to Measure International Agricultural Efficiency and Productivity, *Technical Bulletin* No:1831, Economic Research Service, USDA, pp. 22.

Avkiran, N. K. 1999. The Evidence on Efficiency Gains: The Role of Mergers and the Benefits to the Public, *Journal of Banking and Finance*, 23(2):991-1013.

Banker, R.D., Charnes, A and Cooper, W. W. 1984. Some Models for Estimating Technical and Scale Inefficiencies in Data Envelopment Analysis, *Management Science*, 30(2):1078-1092.

Berg, S.A., Forsund, F and Jansen, E. 1992. Malmquist Indices of Productivity Growth During the Deregulation of Norwegian Banking, 1980-1989, *Scandinavian Journal of Economics*, 88(2):211-28.

Berg, S. A., Forsund, F and Jansen, E. 1991. Technical Efficiency of Norwegian Banks: a Nonparametric Approach to Efficiency Measurement, *Journal of Productivity Analysis*, 2(1):127-42.

Berg, S.A., Forsund, F., Hjalmarsson, L and Souminen, M. 1993. Banking Efficiency in Nordic Countries, *Journal of Banking and Finance*, 17(1):371-38.

Borger, B. D and Kerstens, K. 2000. The Malmquist Productivity Index and Plant Capacity Utilisation, *Scadinavian Journal of Economics*, 102(2):303-310.

Caves, D.W., L.R. Christensen, and Diewert, W. E. 1982. The Economic Theory of

Index Numbers and the Measurement of Input, Output, and Productivity, *Econometrica,* 50(1):1393-1414.

Charnes, A., Cooper, W. W and Rhodes, E. 1978. Measuring the Efficiency of Decision Making Units, *European Journal of Operations Research*, 2(2):429-444.

Charnes, A., Cooper, W. W., Lewin, A. Y., and Seiford, L. M. 1995. *Data Envelopment Analysis: Theory, Methodology and Applications*, Kluwer, pp. 243.

Coelli, T.J. 1996. A Guide to Data Envelopment Analysis (Computer) Program: Deap Version 2.1, mimeo, Department of Econometrics, University of New England, Armidale, Australia, pp.44.

Elyasiani, E., and Mehdian, S. M. 1995. The Comparative Efficiency Performance of Small and Large US Banks in the Pre-and Post Deregulation Eras, *Applied Economics*, 27(2):1069-79.

Fare, R., Grosskopf, S., Lindgren, B., and Roos, P. 1989. *Productivity Developments in Swedish Hospitals: A Malmquist Output Index Approach*, Department of Economics, Southern Illinois University, Carbondale, pp. 25.

Farrell, M.J. 1957. The Measurement of Productive Efficiency, *Journal of the Royal Statistical Society*, 120(3): 11-290.

Fulginiti, L.E and Perrin, R. K. 1993. Prices and Productivity in Agriculture, *Review f Economic and Statistics*, 75(1):471-482.

Fukuyama, H. 1995. Measuring Efficiency and Productivity Growth in Japanese Banking: a Nonparameteric Frontier Approach, *Applied Financial Economics*, 5(3):95-107.

International Monetary Fund (1997) “Globalisation and the Opportunities for Developing Countries” in *World Economic Outlook,* May, Chapter 4,”, pp. 1-275.

Lovell, C.A.K. 1993. Production Frontiers and Productive Efficiency, in Fried, H.O., C.A.K. Lovell and S.S. Schmidt (Eds*), The Measurement of Productive Efficiency*, Oxford University Press, New York, 3-67.

Lovell, C.A.K. 1994. Linear Programming Approaches to the Measurement and Analysis of Productive Efficiency, *Top*, 2(1):175-248.

Neal, P. 2004. X-Efficiency and Productivity Change in Australian Banking, *Australian Economic Papers*, 22(1):174-191.

Seiford, L.M. 1996. Data Envelopment Analysis: The Evolution of the State of the Art (1978-1995), *Journal of Productivity Analysis*, 7(2):99-138.

Reddy, M (1998) *Production Economics Analysis of Fiji Sugar's Industry,* Unpublished Ph.D Dissertation submitted to Department of Agricultural and Resource Economics, University of Hawaii, Honolulu Hawaii, pp. 210.

Seiford, L.M., and Thrall, R. M. 1990. Recent Developments in DEA: The Mathematical Approach to Frontier Analysis, *Journal of Econometrics*, 46(2):7-38.

Shephard, R.W. (1970). *Theory of Cost and Production Functions.* Princeton, New Jersey, Princeton University Press.

Solow, R.M. (1956). “A Contribution to the Theory of Economic Growth”, *Quarterly Journal of Economics*, 70:65-94.

Swan, T., 1956, "Economic growth and capital accumulation," *Economic Record,* 32: 334-61.

Umetsu, C. 1996. Population Pressure and Agricultural Intensification: Technology Adoption and Resource Management in the Agricultural Sector in the Philippines, A report submitted to the Foundation of Advanced Studies on International Development, Tokyo, Japan, pp 1-160.

Walker, G. 1998. Economics of Scale in Australia Banks 1978-1990, *Australian Economic Papers*, 37(1):71-87.

In: Development Problems and Prospects in Pacific Islands ISBN: 978-1-60021-793-7
Editors: B. C. Prasad, D. C. Roy, pp. 229-245

Chapter 16

THE THIRD SECTOR AND SOCIAL DEVELOPMENT IN SMALL PACIFIC ISLAND COUNTRIES: CONSTRAINTS AND OPPORTUNITIES IN FIJI ISLANDS

Manoranjan Mohanty

1. INTRODUCTION

Since the 1980s there has been a change in the development paradigm from a top-down to a bottom–up approach. In the quest for an alternative development model that is humanising, equitable and environmentally sustainable, a people-centered development with greater people's participation and more grass-roots involvement, has been accepted as a new developmental discourse. Enlargement of people's choices, empowerment, capacity building, equitable development and a more participatory approach are the focus areas in development. A democratisation of development processes and good governance are the prerequisites for achieving sustainable development. Good governance in turn demands for more decentralisation, participation, partnerships, and institutional strengthening.

With increasing globalisation, liberalisation and de-regulation, the international forces have influenced the economic and social problems at the national and local levels, thus resulting in an increasing disempowerment and powerlessness of the people, particularly the poor and marginalised sections of the society. There is a greater need for empowerment of these groups economically, socially and politically. Development of people's organizations, i.e. the organizations, that are controlled by the people, is an effective means of the process of empowerment.

Non-governmental organizations (NGOs) with their participatory and humane approach, people's mobilising capacity, closeness to grass-roots, innovative and experimental approaches and better insights into the needs of the citizen have emerged as alternative development agents. A global 'associational revolution' appears to be underway around the world today (Salamon, 2001:17). NGO activities now touch the lives of about 250 million people in developing countries (UNDP, 1993: 93). The NGO and civil society are grouped as a distinct sector and variously referred to as 'non-profit', 'non-partisan' or the 'third sector'.

They have emerged clearly as a 'third sector' in the process of development, which is placed between the state (first sector) and the private enterprises (second sector). Civil society is one of the three 'spheres' that interfaces with state and market in the making of democratic societies. No country today, probably, can achieve development in a sustained way without the active involvement of civil society in its process of development and governance.

Growing social problems, rapid urbanization, liberalization, globalization and a consequent shrinking of state functions and growing market forces, all demand for more institutional building and institutional strengthening. Now the emphasis is more towards non-state sectors such as the private/ business sector and civil society. Anheier, Carlson and Kendall, (2001:2) emphasized that the nonprofit sector has come to receive more attention by policy makers, and occupy a more central role in discussion about the future of economic and social policies in a wide variety of fields. The civil society as a 'third sector' has emerged as an institutional framework and a non-state sector to serve as catalyst for change and development. As Salamon and Anheier (1996) pointed out that the proliferation of civil society organizations represent the 'great social innovation of the twentieth century'.

The paper explores the emergence of 'third sector', the complexities in definitions of NGOs and civil society organizations (CSOs) and identifies NGO diversity in Pacific Island countries and their role particularly, in the context of social development in Fiji islands. It also identifies some constraints and opportunities that exist in the 'third sector' in Fiji.

2. Third Sector: Origin, Definitions, Diversity and Role

The term 'third sector' was used by the Filer Commission, the Commission on Private Philanthropy and Public Needs in USA, in 1973, on the initiative of John D. Rockefeller III (Douglas, 1983:11). The Commission in its Report entitled, *Giving in America* described voluntary and philanthropic organizations as the 'third sector'. According to Douglas (1983:28), the 'voluntary collective identification' characterizes the 'third sector' as 'exchange' characterizes the market sector and 'authority', a government sector. The theories of 'failure of market' and 'failure of government' are the explanations given for the rationale of a 'third sector' (Douglas, 1983; Dollery and Wallis, 2003). The genesis of voluntary sector (or third sector) according to Dollery and Wallis (2003:7) lies in either market failure, 'characterized as the inability of a market or a market system to provide goods and services in an economically optimal manner', or government failure, defined as 'the inability of public agencies to achieve their intended objectives'.

3. Definitions and Diversity

The terms such as 'voluntary sector', 'civil society', 'nonprofit sector' and 'third sector' are synonymously used and the definitions are widely contested. A definitional problem becomes apparent when one looks at the host of organizations that are active in diversified fields. NGOs and CSOs are found in different forms and sizes and called by different names such as for example, a voluntary association, voluntary agency (VA) or voluntary organisation (VO); non-governmental development organizations (NGDOs); social action group; social work agency; citizen's group; self-help organization; grass-root organizations (GOs); welfare organization; are community development organisation (CDOs). The concept of civil society is much broader and is defined as 'the associations of people, families and communities which are independent and autonomous of the government on the one hand and economic enterprise on the other' (UNDP, 1993). Voluntary organisations (VOs), community based organizations (CBOs) or people's organizations (POs), are the subset of NGOs and the NGOs are the subset of a civil society. NGOs are at the heart of civil society and they are considered as the 'voice' of civil society. The definitions of civil society move beyond a narrow focus on NGOs to include trade unions, business associations, employers' associations, advocacy groups, and recreational groups and so on. Civil society provides institutional space where people discuss civic matters and community life. It can be created by empowering and strengthening a network of NGOs and CBOs.

Voluntary organizations are 'formal, self-governing, independent of government, not profit distributing (and primarily non-business) and voluntary (Salamon and Anheier, 1993). In contrast, community-based organizations (CBOs) are 'peoples organizations' or grassroots organizations, which are distinct from other NGOs in their nature and purpose. People's organizations are 'democratic organizations that represent the interests of their members and are accountable to them' (UNDP, 1993: 84). They are distinct from other NGOs in the sense that they are normally 'membership' organizations made up of a group of individuals who have joined together to further their own interests (e.g. women's groups, youth clubs, and farmer associations).

The term NGO encompasses many different types of organization. NGOs include formal/informal, non-profit –making and profit-making bodies. They include wide range of organizations such as social welfare organisations, educational and health organisations, religious bodies, environmental organisations, human rights, women and youth organisation, orphanage, old age home, sports associations.

The definitions of NGOs include elements/characters of organization that are independent and autonomous, non-governmental and formed either voluntarily or involuntarily, they are either informal or formal with certain common interests and collective action. Although a vast majority of NGOs are formally independent and have non-profit ethos, the definition of civil society becomes complex/controversial as many government/political party/business oriented NGOs are included in the spectrum. We can not draw boundaries between the three sectors: public, private and civil society. Governments some time 'make use of Third Sector institutions as agents to carry out their tasks' (Douglas, 1983: 14). There are also many NGOs initiated by business houses (called BONGOs) for profit and they are commercially oriented. Similarly others are either government-sponsored NGOs (GONGOs), political party-sponsored NGOs (PONGOs) or donors/funding agency –sponsored NGO (FUNGOs). NGOs can be classified on the basis of their size, organisational form/legal status, source of inspiration: ideological/philosophical/religious affinity; type/area/level of operation; functional role; activities; target group and forms of control or governance (Mohanty and Singh, 2001: 25-28).

As Foster (2003:5) notes, `strong civil society' does not just refer to the number of NGOs, but rather to citizens' community-based and mass social movements. The citizens are at the heart of governance. NGOs are important only insofar as they contribute to `avenues and structures for citizen participation, building cohesion and solidarity, and facilitating partnerships (with the state) for progressive development outcomes (ibid).

4. Role of NGOs and Civil Society

The nature of NGOs and civil society has undergone considerable transformation over past decades with the changing nature of society and its problems. Accordingly the role of NGOs and civil society has undergone a revolutionary change. At least four dominant roles can be identified (Mohanty and Singh, 2001:21). Firstly, NGOs perform the traditional role of delivery of services to the deprived and underprivileged sections of the society. Secondly, they have a 'watchdog' role, which is more fundamental to social development and good governance. These include prevention and misuse of governmental authority; limitation of and economically powerful interests in perpetuating social injustices and arresting the trends of inefficiency and non-accountability of public administration. Thirdly, they have a supplementary role in cooperating with government agencies and supplementing their efforts in the implementation of their key programmes. Finally, NGOs and civil society perform a functional role becoming involved into social welfare and developmental activities; emergency relief and rehabilitation; disaster management; human rights; protecting the environment; and providing community services. They promote participatory development, empowerment and capacity building, and help in process of conflict resolution and peace building, and good governance. There are at least four areas where the civil society can make a contribution to good governance: public policy and decision making; enhancing state performance; improving transparency and flow of information; and social justice, human rights and the rule of law. The 'indirect impact of NGOs is often much wider than their direct contribution' (UNDP, 1993:92).

5. Third Sector and Social Development

The non-governmental development organizations (NGDOs) and civil society have taken prominent role in social development, particularly since the World Summit for Social Development in 1995. Today, they 'cover most facets of social development: reducing poverty and exclusion; improving access to basic services; conflict prevention; fostering democracy; influencing public policies, etc'(Fowler, 2000,iv). The most fundamental attribute of the NGDO as an effective agent of social change is 'its ability to interact with, and change, other actors and institutions' (ibid 20).

5.1. Pacific Islands Context

Small Islands Developing States (SIDS) particularly, the small Pacific Islands States, are structurally constrained. They are vulnerable economies, heavily depending on international trade and external assistance. The smallness, limited natural and human resources and other intrinsic limitations on the one hand and the growing problems- social, economic and environmental on the other make them more vulnerable. Their vulnerability increases due to their proneness to natural as well as environmental disasters and their limited capacity to respond to such disasters. Human resources and cultural heritages are their most significant assets for their survival. The need is great for the promotion of human resource development including education, training and skills development. There is also a need for enhancing national capacities and self reliance. Their institutional capacities must be strengthened at all levels: government, private and non-governmental. This can be achieved by their partnerships, cooperation and information sharing between them. All efforts should be to put people/ community at the centre of the development process.

NGOs and civil society with their people-centered approach have a critical role to play in achieving sustainable development and Millennium Development goals. Several international conventions, such the Earth Summit in Rio de Janeiro (1992), the Barbados Declaration on Sustainable Development of SIDS (1994), the World Summit on Social Development in Copenhagen (1995), World Summit for Sustainable Development in Johannesburg (2002), and the Mauritius Strategy Meeting for Sustainable Development of Small Islands Developing States (2005) all reaffirmed the special role of NGOs and CSOs. They also stressed the importance of a healthy partnership between government, intergovernmental organisations and NGOs and CSOs, and the private sector. 'Small islands, big issues' was the slogan used in the Barbados Conference in 1994. The Pacific Plan that has been adopted by the Pacific Islands Forum countries in 2005 is a milestone in Pacific regionalism. Sutherland Robertson et.al (2005) found that there is a great need to strengthen regional cooperation through enhanced engagement with civil society.

Table 16.1. Developmental and Social Indicators in Selected Pacific Countries

Countries	GDP per capita (US$) 2001	Human Development Index			Adult illiteracy rate(%) 15yr and above 2002/2003	Life Expectancy at birth (year) 2002	Human Poverty Index %
		Index value 2002	Global Ranking 1998	Global Ranking 2003			
Cook Is.	4, 388	0.789	62	-	1.0	71	-
Fiji Islands	2, 046	0.667	101	92	7.1*	67	21. 3
Kiribati	468	0.592	129	-	8.3	64	-
Marshall Is.	1, 938	0. 665	121	-	4.7	68	-
Nauru	2, 500	0.652	103	-	1.0	55	-
Niue	NA	0.741	70	-	2.7	70	-
PNG	545	0.414	164	137	42.7*	54	40. 5
Samoa	1, 402	0.731	117	74	1. 3*	73	-
Solomon Is.	760	0.410	147	128	33.9	61	-
Tonga	1, 284	0.718	107	-	1.1*	71	-
Tuvalu	1, 342	0.653	118	-	0.3	63	-
Vanuatu	1,085	0.586	140	118	26.0*	67	24. 7

Source: UNDP, Human Development Report, 2005, Pacific HDR, 1999, Draft Pacific HDR, 2006 World Statistics Pocket Book- Small Island Developing States, 2003. * The figure for 2003.

The growing incidence of income poverty and poverty of opportunities, lack of or low access to education, health services and increasing health issues such as HIV/ AIDS, growing domestic violence, violence against women and children and rapid urbanisation and its social, economic and environmental ramifications and a host of social development issues in the small Pacific Island countries are the main concerns today. The Pacific island countries have wide disparities in their social and human development. Table 16.1 shows wide variations in some developmental and social indicators in the Pacific Island countries. In 2001, the GDP per capita income ranged between US$4,388 in Cook Islands to US$468 in Kiribati. The Human Development Index (HDI) values varied between 0.789 in Cook Islands to 0.410 in Solomon Islands. Similarly, in terms of HDI ranking, the Cook Islands depicted a high rank in the Pacific region, while PNG ranked the lowest in the region in 1998 (Table 16.1). Fiji Islands, a middle income country in the Pacific, had a HDI value of 0.667 and a global rank of 92 in 2003. The adult illiteracy rates remain high in the Melanesian countries of Papua New Guinea, Solomon Islands and Vanuatu. Similarly, life expectancy at birth remains low in these countries (Table 16.1). The social problems of most vulnerable groups such as women, children, disabled, youth, and squatter dwellers are multidimensional and call for massive developmental and welfare services and a greater role for NGOs and civil society.

5.2 NGO Diversity

The whole of the Oceania region and particularly the South Pacific Island countries have diversified and growing NGO groupings. According to one estimate the 'third sector' in Oceania had just over 8,701 international NGOs in 2000 (World Resources Institute, 2003:1). This represents about 291 NGOs per million populations. On the basis of level of operations, the NGO sector in Pacific includes at least five broad types:

a. *Local/Grass-root/Community -based NGOs:* e.g., youth and women groups and other CBOs in Fiji, Kosre Community Action Program (KCAP), and Yap Community action Program in Federated States of Micronesia etc.
b. *National/ Umbrella Organisations:* National level NGOs or 'intermediary' umbrella NGOs are active in Social and community development. Examples include, in Fiji, the Fiji Council of Social Services (FCOSS), Fiji Women's Crisis Centre (FWCC), Fiji Disabled People's Association (FDPA), Solomon Islands Development Trust (SIDT) in Solomon Islands, Kiribati Association of NGOs, Tuvalu Association of NGOs and Vanuatu Association of NGOs.
c. *Regional NGOs:*The Pacific Islands Association of NGOs (PIANGO) is the apex regional body that facilitate networking among NGO's at all levels throughout the region. PIANGO has national Liaison Units and interim members. Some of the objectives of PIANGO are to enable NGOs to better understand, fulfill and develop their roles and functions, and strengthen their organisation and program capacities; to assist in identifying, monitoring and analysing the needs of people in the Pacific, and ways of increasing the role of the people of the Pacific in their own development, with greater emphasis on Pacific women and youth and to play an active role in promoting a regional Pacific identity and Pacific ways of thinking and responding. Capacity building; information and communication; and coalition and alliance building are some of the functional areas of PIANGO. The other NGOs of a regional nature include, Pacific Concerns Resource Centre (PCRC), Pacific Conference of

Churches (PCC), The Foundation for the Peoples of the South Pacific International (FSPI) and Ecumenical Centre for Research, Education and Advocacy (ECREA) etc.

d. *orthern NGOs:* e. g OXFAM-UK, Save the Children Fund and Australian Council of Social Services (ACOSS).
e. *International NGOs (INGOs):* e.g. Salvation Army, Red Cross, Green Peace, Lions Club, Helpage International etc.

6. NGO Activities in the Pacific

Apart from other donors, AusAID provides assistance to Pacific NGOs under its AusAID-NGO Cooperation Program (ANCP). On the basis of an analysis of AusAID funding pattern in 2003-2004, and Table 16.2 reflects the dimensions of NGO activities in the Pacific countries. Solomon Islands received the largest volume of AusAID during the period followed by Fiji, Vanuatu, Samoa, Tonga and Kiribati (Table 2). NGOs are more active in these countries. In other Pacific countries such as Marshall Islands, Cook Islands and Tuvalu, NGO activities though limited but are growing phenomenon.

Table 16.2. NGO Activities in Selected Pacific Countries

Country	Volume of Aus-Aid received by NGOs (in 000AU$) 2003-2004
Solomon Islands	3,797.1
Fiji	1,258.4
Vanuatu	1,248.0
Samoa	1,107.5
Tonga	839.9
Kiribati	611.0
FSM	169.1
Marshall Islands	150.3
Cook Islands	141.1
Tuvalu	20.3

Source: AusAID-NGO Cooperation - Statistical Report, 2003-2004, Australia.

7. NGOs and Social Development in Fiji Islands

7.1. NGO Growth

Fiji has a vibrant NGO sector, with the largest NGO groupings next to Papua New Guinea in the Pacific region. The civil society in Fiji covers a wide spectrum of organisations and located in the length and breadth of the country ranging from small, loose knit local organisations to well established national umbrella/'intermediary' organizations and the international NGOs. Although there is no comprehensive study, the size of NGO sector in Fiji has witnessed a dramatic growth in number of NGOs and CBOs over time. According to one estimate, there were 651 international NGOs in Fiji in 2000 (World Resources Institute, 2003:1). Besides the national umbrella organisations and international and 'northern' NGOs in Fiji, there are large number of women groups, environmental NGOs and residential social welfare NGOs such as Home of Compassion, Pearce Home, Veilomani Boys Home and Dilkusha Children's Home. Most of the NGOs in Fiji are registered under the legal framework of the Charitable Trusts Act, 1945.

7.2. NGO Activities in Fiji: role in Social Development

The civil societies in Fiji have wide ranging activities including charity and philanthropy; relief/rehabilitation; disaster management; human rights; social welfare activities for women, children, old people, the disabled; beggars; street children and youth; counseling; education and training and advocacy; health/medical services; religious/cultural activities; fund raising; environmental protection/conservation ; developmental activities including income generating and poverty alleviation; rural development, community services/development and natural resource management.

There are many environmental, human rights, developmental and welfare, advocacy NGOs and women groups in Fiji. There are more registered NGOs in southern divisions in Fiji, particularly in Suva City, whereas other divisions have more community based groups (CBOs) such as women's groups, youth groups, religious groups (Fiji Department of Social Welfare, 2003:16). Some of the leading women organisations in Fiji are for example, National Council of women, Fiji Women's Crisis Centre (FWCC), Fiji Women's Rights Movement (FWRM), Women Action for Change (WAC), Fiji Association of Women Graduates (FAWGMS), and Nai Soqosoqo Vakamarama. The FWCC is actively involved in advocacy and providing counseling services, and is more involved in support for women victims of domestic violence and sexual abuse.

There are many environmental NGOs working in Fiji, for example, the South Pacific Action Committee on Human Ecology and the Environment (SPACHEE), Foundation for the Peoples of the South Pacific International, Greenpeace, Pacific Concern Resource Centre, WWF South Pacific Programme and the Wildlife Conservation Society (WCS). The Citizen's Constitutional Forum (CCF) is an NGO coalition on human rights in Fiji. Over the years CCF has established strong relationships with other NGOs in Fiji and the Pacific. Many NGOs and CSOs in Fiji are actively involved in social and community development: educational development, health/medical services (e.g. HIV), housing development, poverty alleviation and income generation, and social enterprise activities. Some are actively involved in welfare of children, the elderly, orphans, the disabled, beggars, street children and women.

7.3. Educational Development in Fiji: Role of NGOs

NGOs play an important role in the education sector and promote human resource development and build the capacity in Fiji. The civil society in Fiji remains the key provider of formal education from preschool to higher secondary level. In 2002, there were 957 schools in Fiji. Of this about 96% schools are run by NGOs and 3% are directly controlled by the government primarily the Ministry of Education. Almost all primary schools (99%) in the country are in the NGO sector. Similarly the non-formal education is the sole domain of the CSOs (Fiji Council of Social Services, 2003). About 90% of secondary schools and technical vocational schools are in the non-government sector (Table 16.3). Of the total school in Fiji about 69% schools are Committee-run schools (Fiji Ministry of Education, 2006).

Table 16.3. Schools in Fiji by Controlling Agency, 2004

Agency	Primary Schools		Secondary Schools		Special Schools		Technical Vocational		Teacher Training		Total Schools	
	No	%	No	%	No	%	No	%	No	%	No.	%
Govt.	3	0. 4	16	10. 0	-	-	6	9.7	2	50. 0	27	2. 8
Private	5	0.7	2	1. 3	-	-	-	-	-	-	7	0. 7
NGOs	706	98. 9	142	88. 7	17	100.0	56	90.3	2	50. 0	923	96. 5
Total	**714**	**100.0**	**160**	**100.0**	**17**	**100.0**	**62**	**100.0**	**4**	**100.0**	**957**	**100.0**

Source: By the Author based on data from Ministry of Education, *Annual Report,* 2004. Parliamentary Paper No 95 of 2006.Table No. 8, p. 13.

Some of the leading NGOs involved in running schools in Fiji are for example, Arya Pratinidhi Sabha, Shri Sanatan Dharam Pritinidhi Sabha of Fiji, the Sangam Association, Gujarat education society, Catholic Archdiocese, Methodist Church of Fiji, Seventh Day Adventist and Anglican Churches.

The number of schools in the NGO sector in Fiji has increased over the years (Table 16.4).

Table 16.4. Growth of Schools in Fiji by Agency, 2002-2004

Controlling Authority	Total Schools		% Share to total 2004	% Change 2002- 2004
	2002	2004		
NGO Sector	905	923	96. 4	2. 0
Private/ International	7	7	0. 7	0. 0
Govt . Sector	25	27	2. 8	7. 4
Min. of Education	21	22	2.3	4. 8
Grand Total	**937**	**957**	**100. 0**	**2. 1**

Source: Ministry of Education, *Annual Report,* 2002 and 2004.

7.4. NGOs in Health and Medical Services

Many NGOs are actively involved in health and medical services in Fiji including disability, HIV/AIDS prevention and rehabilitation for example, Fiji Disabled People's Association (FDPA), Fiji Crippled Children Society, Fiji Rehabilitation Council, Fiji Society for the Blind (FSB), (JP) Bayly Trust in medical services, Partners in Community Development (PCDF), Home of Compassion- a national medical care centre run by Catholic Church, FCOSS , Fiji Red Cross Society, and the Pacific Islands AIDS Foundation (PIAF).

HIV/AIDS is a grave and growing health issue in the small Pacific Island countries particularly in Fiji. The number of HIV cases in the region is increasing rapidly. The estimated number of HIV cases (adults and children) in Fiji was 600 in 2004 (UNDP, 2006). People living with HIV/AIDS need treatment and follow up care and support. They are the most socially vulnerable group. The Fiji National HIV/AIDS Strategic Plan, 2004-2006 revealed that people who are HIV positive are experiencing discrimination at the workplace (UNDP, 2006). NGOs have a greater role in prevention of AIDS and the discrimination of HIV positive persons at work place, at community and societal level through awareness generation programmes, and the rehabilitation of infected persons. The Fiji AIDS Task-force is the lead agency for a regional NGO-CBO initiative aimed at strengthening the work of Pacific NGOs engaged in AIDS related work (ibid.). The Taskforce collaborates with the Pacific Islands AIDS Foundation (PIAF), a regional NGO working with support networks for Pacific Islanders living with HIV/AIDS, based on the Cook Islands.

7.5. NGOs in Housing Development

Housing development is another area where NGOs play a significant role in Fiji. Two prominent NGOs working in housing development are the Housing Assistance and Relief Trust (HART) and Habitat for Humanity, Fiji (HFH). HART has about 600 housing units located in villages in Fiji at Suva-Nausori, Labasa, Rakiraki, Ba and Lautoka. HART shelters more than 3,000 destitute families. Government provides grants to HART for housing development in Fiji. In addition, HART also undertakes social welfare oriented programmes including counseling and providing educational assistance to children.

7.6. NGOs and Poverty Alleviation

Many reports on poverty IN Fiji are now available. According to UNDP's- Fiji poverty report, nearly one-third of the households of Fiji were under relative poverty and 26 % basic costs poverty (UNDP, 1997: 38). Many NGOs in Fiji, for example, the Fiji Council of Social Services (FCOSS) are active in poverty alleviation. The 11th National Conference on Social Development with the theme Poverty Eradication: Civil Society Responsibility Plan of Action was adopted in Nadi-Fiji on 26- 28 August 1996 by the Fiji Council of Social Services. The civil society's commitment to poverty eradication includes a 'National Anti Poverty Campaign' and creation of a 'National Poverty Eradication Fund'.

A poverty alleviation program is one of the major program of the Ministry of Women, Social welfare and Poverty Alleviation. NGOs in Fiji supplement the activities of the Ministry through the social welfare services and community based programs aimed at alleviating poverty. A policy framework for partnership between government and NGOs in alleviating poverty is now in place.

To fight poverty and promote development is to build, not only strong processes and institutions of government, but also to encourage the participation of a strong civil society, which engages the power of the people (Barr, 2004).

7.7. NGOs and Community Empowerment

Community or social enterprise is a recent development in the NGO sector in Fiji. Micro finance and small business development and social entrepreneurial activities are the new areas in which some of the NGOs in Fiji are actively involved. A social enterprise is a business with a social purpose. Many of the NGOs in Fiji are engaged in income generation activities and small businesses such as handicrafts and mat making and honey collection etc. The Peace Corps beekeeper in Fiji is involved in honey bee projects, and FCOSS is actively involved in micro finance and has a Social Enterprise and Entrepreneurship Programme (SEEP). The Housing Assistance and Relief Trust (HART) also provides small loans to the poor house tenants to run small businesses. The concept of social enterprise is quite established in many developing countries. For example, in India, the Self-Employed Women's Association (SEWA) aims at enhancing women's income earnings and their working environment; in Bangladesh- the Grameen Bank provides micro-credit to the poor having no access to banking facilities and the Bangladesh Rural Advancement Committee (BRAC) provides non-formal primary education and healthcare services to the needy; and in Sri Lanka, the Sarvodaya Sharamadana Movement runs income-generating programmes for the poor (UNDP, 1993). The vast majority of social enterprises in these countries are grassroots-based organizations.

7.8. Funding to NGOs

NGOs in Fiji mobilise resources both from internal and external sources. They get funds from various donors including bilateral and multilateral agencies and from the Northern NGOs. The funding to NGOs by the overseas governments constitutes one of the main sources of funding. In many developing countries, India for example, the funding to NGOs by the overseas governments constituted over 7% of the total external aid to India in 1994 (Mohanty,1996 :15). The official flow of assistance from overseas governments to NGOs in Fiji accounted for about 3% of the total personal remittances to Fiji in 2004 (Table 16.5). The foreign assistance to NGOs in Fiji, primarily in the form of gifts and donations, has declined dramatically over the years. The flow has declined from F$ 37 million in 1999 to F$ 9 million in 2004 (Table 16.5). Barr (2004) pointed out that 'after the political upheaval of May 2000, various donor countries suspended all new aid programmes to Fiji'.

Many NGOs receive government funding for their endeavour for example, HART, Fiji National Council of Disabled Persons (FNCDP) and the Home of Compassion. The Ministry of Women, Social Welfare and Poverty Alleviation provides grants to voluntary organizations for social welfare activities. In 2001, for example, the total approved funding to NGOs was F$ 201,817 and NGOs providing services to disabled members of the community received about 43% of the Ministrys' grants. Another 24% each was received by community service-oriented NGOs and the NGOs working for children and elderly persons (Table 16.6).

Table 16.5. Flow of Foreign Assistance from Overseas Governments to NGOs in Fiji, 1999-2004

Year	Foreign government assistance to NGOs* (F$ million)	% change to previous year
1999	36.70	-
2000	28.84	-21.4
2001	36.60	+26.9
2002	19.89	- 45.7
2003	10.98	- 44. 8
2004	8.89	- 19. 0

Source: Reserve Bank of Fiji, 2005. * includes assistance in the form of gifts and donations.

Table 16.6. Categories of NGOs receiving the Social Welfare Ministry Grants in Fiji, 2001

NGO Activities	% Government Grant
Disabled	43. 0
Community	24. 0
Children	15. 0
Elderly	9. 0
Single mothers	3. 0
International	3.0
Residential	3.0

Source: Fiji Department of Social Welfare, *Annual Report,* Suva, Fiji.

7.9. Constraints

The NGOs face enormous structural, operational and financial constraints in their endeavours. Broadly the constraints can be grouped as: organizational and non-organiZational issues. The organisational constraints include: funding and other resource constraints ; human resource problemS including lack of trained and dedicated staff, professional workers and problem of staff turnover; leadership crises; an overdependence on external funding jeopardizing the NGO independence and autonomy ; infrastructure facilities and operational constraints; management issues and NGO transparency, accountability, code of conduct and best practices. The non-organiZational constraints include the relationships between: NGO and government, NGO- Donor, NGO-community, NGO-NGO, civil society and private sector. These are the critical issues and the major constraints in NGO operations. The NGO relationships with communities are conventionally understood in terms of ‘people’s participation’.

7.9.1. NGO-government Relationships

The NGOs-government relationships are controversial and complex. The relationships, however, are dynamic and ever-changing in nature. The state plays a role as regulator, funder, promoter and partner of civil society. The relationships depend much on the communication and dialogue between the two. The government-NGO collaborations normally can be seen at three levels: at the central ministries/national government level, local government level and at national/ public forum or national debates on development policies/strategies. In many countries collaboration between central and local governments and NGOs has been forged to strengthen initiatives on social development at the local level (UNESCAP, 1997). For example, in China, the National Association for Social Development (NASD) was founded to work closely with NGOs on social development.

Commonwealth guidelines on good NGO policy and practices (Commonwealth Foundation, 1995) suggest that the governments create the right environment by giving recognition to NGOs, outlining legislation and official procedures for NGOs and providing a platform for consultation and partnerships; providing framework and mechanisms to facilitate communication and consultation with them and to provide financial/ technical support to them. The government of Fiji has now an NGO policy framework for social welfare and development especially, for poverty alleviation.

7.9.2. NGO-Private Relationships

Today, it is acknowledged worldwide that the private sector can play a greater role in poverty reduction and in social development. The interface between government, private sector and civil society is crucial in achieving this goal. An effective interaction between the three sectors is vital. The interface between government and private sector is usually provided by various trade associations. Many governments have specific policies on the relationships between government and private sector, and between government and the civil society. In Pacific countries, an enabling environment for dialogue between private sector and civil society do not clearly exist and have yet to evolve.

7.9.3. Weaknesses in NGO Sector

Some of the major weaknesses in the NGO sector in Fiji can be identified as: the limited financial and management expertise; limited institutional capacity; poor human resource development; lack of professionalism; low capacity building; poor resource (financial and material) base; low levels of self-sustainability; isolation/lack of coordination; poor networking and information sharing between NGOs; poor internal governance system; and an inadequate understanding of the broader social or economic development issues.

7.9.4. Challenges to the NGO Sector

The civil society in Fiji is still evolving stage and they are struggling to occupy an effective institutional space within the society. This depends much on the government-NGO relationships. The relationships between these two developmental actors arise over various issues: resource mobilization; service delivery; implementation of programmes; and in a broader context, the social and economic changes. One of the basic challenges in the 'third sector' in Fiji is strengthening relationships among government, private sector, donors, the NGOs and the community. Overdependence on donors for financial assistance has much impact on the autonomy and independence of NGOs. They are generally donor-driven and over-dependent on donors for funding. The key challenges in the NGO sector are: to achieve long-term sustainability, institutional and financial; to establish effective collaborations and partnerships with the other two sectors; to improve sectoral professionalism; creating environment for internal NGO governance, code of conduct and best practices, changing the perceptions and building the confidence of donors, private sector, government and the community and people at large; to resolve leadership issues; to reduce over-dependence on institutional funding and maintaining independence and autonomy and to pursue an ethical voluntarism. The ultimate challenge to NGO/the third sector in a small island state such as Fiji is to strengthen and create an effective civil society.

7.9.5. Opportunities

Opportunities, however, exist in Fiji for an effective civil society. The organizations in Fiji share many unique cultural attributes that can help in strengthening NGOs and civil society. Being a small island country, Fiji should find it easy to develop an effective NGO networking. Governments can easily identify and control NGOs in a limited area of operation. The Island community's social networks, social capital and close knit community structure are some of the strengths that can help in easy and quick dissemination of information and adaptation of social development programmes. Besides, these positive attributes can help establishing healthy cooperation and partnerships between the three sectors.

The power of advocacy of NGOs in Fiji is their greatest strength. Another strength lies in their ability to respond quickly and effectively during emergencies. Besides, the strengths of NGOs that put them in positions for an effective implementation of social policies and programmes are: their strong grassroots links; field-based development expertise; people's mobilising capacity; the ability to innovate and adapt; process-oriented approach to development; use of participatory methodologies and tools; long-term commitment; and above all their cost-effectiveness.

7.9.6. Good NGO Policy and Practice

The Commonwealth Foundation (1995) guidelines on good NGO policy and practice advise that NGOs should follow the code of conduct and the following practices:

- The value based objectives of NGOs should be clearly defined and should be based on the desire to advance and improve the human condition. They should maintain high ethical standards both at organisational and personal level.
- to ensure that NGOs remain transparent in all their functions they should make clearly known who they are and what they do. They should publish and disseminate annual and financial reports/ reports on activities.
- NGOs should adopt appropriate legal structures.
- NGOs should have a constitution, by-laws, memorandum of association or similar document that establishes a framework for the governance of the organization. This should vest control of the organization in the hands of a board of management and the members of the board may be either be nominated or elected.
- The general and financial management practices of NGOs should be of high standard and aim to strengthen institutional capacity and sustainability.

- NGOs should commit themselves to being transparent in their fundraising practices to all stakeholders and they should establish an effective financial monitoring system through a proper accounting system.
- NGOs should build and strengthen their capacities in order to meet the increasing demand for services.
- NGOs should recognise the need to build and strengthen sustainable partnerships based on equality, trust and honesty.
- Networking, coordination, cooperation and communication among and between NGOs are required to be established based on shared values, visions and objectives.

8. Conclusions

The non-profit sector or the 'third sector' in the process of development is at the crossroads. The 'third sector' has emerged as a catalyst for change and development. This sector in order to be a viable and effective sector needs to follow good policies, code of conduct and ethical practices. Accountability, transparency, information sharing and networking are the critical issues before the sector can become an effective institutional framework and to help create a more sustainable society. There is a great need for strengthening NGO networks and developing and strengthening partnerships between civil society, governments and the private sector. The effective collaborative partnerships between these sectors should be based on open, transparent, accountable and mission-oriented approaches. The relationships can be sustainable if they are promoted and nurtured with trust, confidence and goodwill. Partnership, collaboration, sharing of information and resources between the three sectors is the best way forward for achieving the sustainable and Millennium development goals.

References

Anheier, H. K., L. Carlson and J. Kendall (2001) "Third sector policy at the cross roads", in H. K. Anheier, and J. Kendall (eds) *Third Sector Policy at the Crossroads: An International Nonprofit Analysis,* London and New York: Routledge. pp. 1-16.

Barr K. J. (2004) "Fiji and the Pacific: Competing paradigms of good governance, human rights and democracy", A Paper for the *Reality of Aid.* Quezen City, The Philippines http://www.realityofaid.org/roareport.php?table=roa2004&id=61

Commonwealth Foundation (1995) "Non-governmental Organisations: Guidelines for Good Policy and Practice", London: Commonwealth Foundation.

Dollery, B. E. and J. L. Wallis (2003) "Public policy approaches to the voluntary sector", in Dollery, B. E. and J. L. Wallis, *The political Economy of the Voluntary Sector: A Reappraisal of the comparative Institutional Advantage of Voluntary organisations,* Edward Elgar, Cheltenham, United Kingdom, pp. 102-128 and 129-64.

Douglas, J. (1983). *Why Charity? the case for a Third Sector,* London and New Delhi: Sage.

Fiji Council of Social Services (2003) *Annual Report 2003,* Suva, Fiji: Fiji Council of Social Services.

Fiji Department of Social Welfare (2003) *Annual Report, 2001,* Parliamentary Paper No. 44, Department of Social Welfare, Suva, Fiji.

Fiji Ministry of Education (2006) *Annual Report 2004,* Parliamentary Paper No. 95, Ministry of Education, Suva, Fiji.

Foster, J. W (2003) "Crisis Time: Repossessing Democratic Space — Governance and the Promotion of Rights in International Cooperation and Aid", A Discussion Paper for the *Reality of Aid.* The North-South Institute. Canada. http:www.nsi_ins.ca/english/pdf/foster_reality_of_aid-paper.pdf#

Fowler, A (2000) *Civil Society, NGDOs and Social Development: Changing the Rules of the Game.* Geneva. Switzerland: United Nations Research Institute for Social Development.

Kendall, J. and H. K. Anheier (2001) "The third sector and the European Union policy process", in H. K. Anheier, and J. Kendall (eds) *Third Sector Policy at the Crossroads: An International Nonprofit Analysis,* London and New York: Routledge. 126-52.

Mohanty, M. (1996) *Foreign Aid and NGOs.* New Delhi: VANI.

Mohanty, M. and A. Singh (2001) *Voluntarism and Government: Policies, Programme and Assistance.* New Delhi: VANI.

Salamon, L. M. (2001) "The nonprofit sector at a crossroads: The case of America", in H. K. Anheier, and J. Kendall (eds.), *Third Sector Policy at the Crossroads: An International Nonprofit Analysis,* London and New York: Routledge. 17-35.

Salamon L. M. and H. Anheier (1993) "A comparative study of the non-profit sector: purposes, methodology, definition and classification" in S Saxon-Harrold and J. Kendall (eds), *Researching the Voluntary Sector,* Volume 1, Tonbridge: Charities Aid Foundation.93-121.

Salamon L. M. and H. Anheier (1996) *The Emerging Nonprofit Sector,* New York: Manchester University Press.

Sutherland, W., R. Robertson etal.(2005). "Strengthening regional cooperation through enhanced engagement with civil society", Suva, Fiji; Development Studies, PIAS-DG, University of the South Pacific.

UNDP(1993) "People in community organizations" in chapter 5, *Human Development Report, 1993* , New York: UNDP.84-99.

UNDP (1997) Fiji *Poverty Report,* Suva, Fiji: UNDP

UNDP (2006) "HIV situation in Fiji", youandaids, Country report, HIV/AIDS Portal for Asia and Pacific. http://www.youandaids.org/Asia%20Pacific%20at%20a%20Glance/Fiji/index.asp

UN ESCAP (1997) "Review of national progress achieved in the implementation of the Agenda for Action on Social Development in the ESCAP region, in the context of the programme of Action of the World Summit for Social Development" , Social Policy Section, Social Development Division, United Nations ESCAP. http://www.un.org/Depts/escap/sps/paper2a.htm

World Resources Institute (2003) "Environmental Institutions and Governance-Fiji", Country Report, Earth Trends, Washington, D. C. http://earthtrends.wri.org/pdf_library/country_profiles/env_cou242.pdf

In: Development Problems and Prospects in Pacific Islands ISBN: 978-1-60021-793-7
Editors: B. C. Prasad, D. C. Roy, pp. 245-258

Chapter 17

TOWARDS BETTER GOVERNANCE: FIJI'S RECENT REFORM EXPERIENCES

Mohammad Habibur Rahman and Alka Ashwini

1. INTRODUCTION

Over the last few decades, the roles of governments around the world have gone through a number of changes. These changes instigated by the World Bank and the IMF were geared towards public sector reforms in the context of development. This paper seeks to describe the particular reform as it is applied in a developing country, Fiji Islands. It focuses on the introduction of this concept and the outcomes in Fiji.

This paper is divided into three parts. The first part expresses the ideology and conceptualization behind reforms in the contemporary world. The next part takes a look at the government of Fiji, gives a profile the country's developmental challenges and explores some of its recent reform experiences towards better governance to combat those challenges. The final part highlights reform applications in the world and outlines possible policy improvements for Fiji. This paper draws its findings and observations solely from government sources and available recent literature.

2. QUEST FOR REFORM

A number of governments in countries around the world have embarked upon reform programmes that are anticipated to make public sector organizations achieve better. This comes as no surprise as public management reforms or administrative reforms were initiated as early as the 1980s in the OECD world and such reform is considered to be a fashionable concept or perhaps the 'in' thing for today. At present reforms are believed to have reached pandemic proportions, that is, it is no longer a new terminology for it has been tested and tried one too many times since its inception(Boyne et al, 2003). However, the results of reforms around the world are rather mixed.

Our discussion on administrative reform (AR) will be comprehensive so it is essential that we develop a common understanding of the term. A number of definitions have been used and expressed by prominent authors and organizations over the years and no doubt all have had their fair share of criticism and limitations, which one will come to realize towards the end of this paper.

Caiden (1969, cited in Khan, 1998) was one of the first scholars who attempted to understand and define the concept of AR. He described AR as "the artificial inducement of administrative transformation against resistance". His definition and insight in to the concept gave way to many more interpretations that have assisted in the better understanding and operationalizing of the concept.

According to Saxena (1980, cited in Khan, 1998) "reform is generally identified with 'improvement' or the creation of good administration". Likewise Leemans (1976, cited in Khan, 1998) asserts that AR refers to "changes of broad scope and high intensity in the governmental organization". He further puts forward two important aspects of the term. The first that AR will in actual fact include the reorganization of the machinery of the government as a subsystem of the larger system containing the political and bureaucratic element, and the second, that the success of the reform in the reorganization process is entirely dependent on the people involved, their influence and their dedicated support for it.

The UN (1983, cited in Khan, 1998) definition for AR is quite simple and helps portray the general dynamics of AR. UN describes AR "as the deliberate use of authority and influence to apply new measures to an administrative system so as to change its goals, structures and procedures with a view to improving it for developmental purposes". This definition can be strengthened with that of Abueva (1970, cited in Khan, 1998) who views AR "essentially as a deliberate attempt to use power, authority and influence to change the goals, structure or procedures of the bureaucracy and therefore to alter the behavior of its personnel" (Khan 1998: 1-7).

These definitions are rather useful and when looked at together make a whole lot of sense. We describe AR as a process that is clearly intentional and may be imposed on public bureaucrats or civil servants and the machinery of government for the purpose of improved development of the organization. On the brighter side, AR helps to sow seeds in productivity, efficiency, accountability and so forth. On the contrary, given that AR is deliberate, it will result in a lot of resistance and this is the one dreaded factor that may hinder the overall progress. Nevertheless, AR must not be viewed as difficult, rather it must be perceived positively with an open mind for it to develop into a success.

Having come to a common understanding and a simplified definition of AR, we shift to the reasons for reform and the so-called 'waves' of reform. The first reforms began in the late 1970s as a result of the increasing magnitude of governments and the difficulty in sustaining and affording them. This fiscal pressure actually stimulated the two waves of reform. The first wave was an effort to curb the aggregate expenditure of government, making it more efficient. This effort was generously backed by the European Union and success came in most OECD countries. Reduction in expenditure took place by means of avoiding unnecessary commercial activities and downsizing.

The second wave of reforms was directed towards 'better government'. This particular reform was prompted by the public, who demanded for improved services and a more responsive administration acting to serve the citizens rather than just dictate to them. Consequently, transparency was improved in administration, participation was welcomed, accessibility was increased and accountability was put into practice. In addition to the above, a decentralized way of government was sought. Overall, this particular reform recognized the need for greater involvement and participation of the public or the citizens for a more united government.

While the above reforms are directed towards betterment it should be noted that the speed and the methods of AR are more or less country specific, therefore outcomes tend to vary. Currently, many OECD countries are now in what may be called the third stage or wave of reform. This stage is in fact more delicate and valuable for it involves mammoth efforts in preserving the "good innovations of the previous years while jettisoning the ones that have proven to be too costly or counterproductive" (Schiavo-Campo and Sundaram, n.d).

As can be gathered, the traditional model of administration has been totally replaced by public management as a result of the reform process as has been described above. The reform process may not have been welcomed with joy by the ones affected but it has indeed been initiated with the hope of improvement. Still, it is vital to note that "any process of change will involve winners and losers and among the losers may be some valued parts of the traditional model of administration" (Hughes, 2003).

The discussion that follows, portray these ideological and administrative changes for reform prospects in one country in the Pacific region namely Fiji Islands. Among the South Pacific Island countries, Fiji is the second largest in land area and population. Fiji has a growing economy based on agriculture, manufacturing and service sector. Like other post colonial societies, Fiji too depended on its public sector for nation-building and socio-economic development (Sarker and Pathak, 2003).

3. Fiji Government Setup

The Constitutional Amendment Act 1997 highlights a number of things that are unique to the constitutional history of Fiji. We will touch only a few main ones. To begin with, Fiji was ceded to Great Britain after the signing of the Deed of Cession in 1874. Second, Fiji became an independent sovereign state when Her Majesty Queen Elizabeth II promulgated the Fiji Independence Order under which the Fiji Constitution of 1970 came into being and finally the Republic of the Fiji Islands is a sovereign democratic state where the Constitution is the supreme law of the state (Constitution of the Republic of the Fiji Islands, 1998).

Under this Constitutional structure, the President serves as the head of state and is appointed for a 5-year term by the Great Council of Chiefs, which is a traditional ethnic Fijian leadership body. The President in turn appoints the Prime Minister (head of government) and Cabinet from among the elected members of parliament, who must be able to command the support of a majority of the House of Representatives. The function of Cabinet is to advise the President and to be collectively responsible to Parliament for all Government policies and the operation of Government services.

The Cabinet is also collectively responsible to the House of Representatives for the governance of the state. The Senate, which may not initiate legislation but may veto most bills, comprises 32 members chosen by the Great Council of Chiefs, the Prime Minister, the Leader of Opposition, and the Rotuma Island council. The more powerful House of Representatives consists of 71 members, of whom 25 are elected by universal suffrage and 46 from communal electoral rolls representing the Fijian (23), Indo-Fijian (19), Rotuman (1) and minority (3) communities.

Moreover, Fiji maintains an independent judiciary consisting of a Supreme Court, a Court of Appeals, a High Court and magistrates courts. The judiciary remained independent even though the coups of 1987, 2000 and 2006 has affected its functioning.

There are four administrative divisions (central, eastern, northern and western), each under the charge of a commissioner. Ethnic Fijians have their own administration in which councils preside over a hierarchy of provinces, districts, and villages. The councils deal with all matters affecting ethnic Fijians. The 55-member Great Council of Chiefs *(Bose Levu Vakaturaga* in Fijian) includes 3 representatives from each of Fiji's 14 provinces and 1 dependency, 3 ex-officio members (the President, Vice-President, and Prime Minister), and 6 government appointees; former Prime Minister Sitiveni Rabuka is a life-member. The Great Council of Chiefs advises the government, and also functions as an electoral college to appoint the President of the Republic, as well as 14 of the 32 Senators. It is considered just about compulsory for the government to consult and secure the approval of the Council before making major changes to the Constitution, although nothing in the Constitution requires it to do so.

The Great Council of Chiefs should not be confused with the House of Chiefs, which is a larger body including all hereditary chiefs, although membership of the two bodies overlaps to a considerable extent. One may also find this Great Council of Chiefs unique to Fiji only and that most members of the Great Council are selected by the larger Council of Chiefs (i.e. House of Chiefs) from among themselves.

Unlike the political appointees, who hold their seats for four-year terms, those appointed by the Council of Chiefs serve for life. Despite Fiji now being a republic, the Great Council still recognizes Queen Elizabeth II as its Paramount Chief. (Wikipedia Encyclopedia, 2005).

4. Developmental Challenges in Fiji

Like any other typical developing society, Fiji too has its share of developmental problems and challenges.

Firstly there is a need for the preservation of law and order for sustained socio economic development. Law and order in Fiji has been severely challnged with political instability and insecurity not to mention the two coups in 1987 and one in May 2000 and the most recent in December 2006 that severely eroded public confidence and caused disruptions to the economy. In addition, activities such as drugs, money laundering, prostitution, sexual offences against the weak that is women and children along with petty criminal offences have placed even more pressure for government to quicken their pace of reform.

Secondly, is the issue of good governance. Coupled with the problems mentioned above Fiji faces isolation from the international community. This could indeed cripple Fiji's current economic state. Good governance requires that the basic institutions of the State perform their functions in line with their constitutional provisions and be seen to be doing so. The Fiji Government values what good governance preaches and recognizes the Public Service Commission's independence and responsibility in executing its functions impartially and transparently, along with strengthening of the Office of the Auditor General and tabling a Freedom of Information Bill in Parliament.

Third is the issue of quality of life, as measured by the UNDP Human Development Index. Here, however Fiji was ranked 81st in the world in 2003 - far above than many of the current booming economies such as China and India (UNDP, 2004). The fourth concern is that of poverty levels, which have gradually increased from the years 1983 to 1996 and this figure, was further accentuated with the May 2000 coup. Nonetheless, Fiji's poverty has also grown by two thirds (Naidu and Barr, 2002). Government with the help of NGOs is responsible to undertake poverty alleviation programs. Next is the health situation. Fiji has recorded 104 cases of HIV/AIDS in the year 2002 as confirmed by the Ministry of Health statistics. This along with the poor nurse patient ratio calls for immediate action. Also is the issue of education primarily literacy rates in urban and rural areas. No doubt the problem dominating here is the lack of services and facilities in rural areas in comparison to urban areas. Consequently, rural children tend to have poor results. This problem has been further aggravated with the emigration of teachers. The next issue is that of low rural incomes and living standards which are inflamed with poor accessibility, roads, electricity as well as the issue of land resettlement. This area needs quick looking into as a large portion of Fiji's revenue is dependent on exports of local produce.

In addition, the failure to include disadvantaged groups such as parts of indigenous Fijian community, women and disabled persons into the development process. These groups have potential to contribute to the economy only with the support and encouragement from the government. The next problem is that of urban population growth that has resulted from lack of jobs and financial distress. Urban population growth creates a number of social problems like poor sanitation, overcrowding, poor diet, crime and so forth. The last challenge under social development is that of environmental vulnerability to natural disasters and man made problems like waste management, land degradation, air and water pollution etc that again undermines people's quality of life.

5. Three Major Streams in Reform in Fiji: The Agendas

The Asian Development Bank (ADB), the International Monetary Fund (IMF) and the World Bank (WB) have actively promoted structural reforms in the South Pacific region. This is regarded as necessary because of the poor economic performance accompanied with unemployment, corruption and rent seeking, increased levels of borrowing and debt and the lack of savings and investment. This depressing performance of the Pacific Island states over the last two decades has placed even more pressure to carry out structural and economic reforms (Prasad and Reddy, 2002).

Public Sector Reform in Fiji was first introduced in 1992 during the government's 1993 Budget address to Parliament (Appana, 2003). It was believed to be a strategy for economic growth. Public Sector Reform in Fiji is divided into three major areas with our focus being on the latter two.

The first one is Financial Management Reform that focuses on improving the financial systems and instruments of Government. The broad objective of this reform is to strengthen and mordernise the current financial management framework. This would promote better alignment of policy priorities with budget resources, effective expenditure control and improved accountability and transparency (Ministry of Finance and National Planning, 2003).

According to Waqabaca (2002) these are "policy measures designed to deregulate and transform the financial system and its structure with a view to achieving a liberalized market oriented system within an appropriate regulatory framework". Hence policies and regulations have been removed over the years 1980-2000 to permit better market orientation. Furthermore, various institutions have been restructured and created with grants of bank leases to promote competition. Consequently capital markets in Fiji have become more sophisticated.

The second major reform is the civil service reforms (CSR). The Fiji CSR programme was the key feature to the change cycle that was set in place to align Fiji with other countries in regard to making Fiji more united, prosperous and better able to meet the challenges of globalization. Pressure for CSR in Fiji came from the excessive overhead costs especially wages incurred in the operations of Government due to its size and the inefficiencies existing in the delivery of public services. The aim of this reform in Fiji was to develop a productive and efficient public service that would not only satisfy taxpayer expectations, but at the same time ensure transparency and accountability in their operations.

Key components of the CSR in Fiji are reforms in productivity management, service delivery management (e.g. e-governance), change management (e.g. CEO leadership), organizational management, and human resource management. These reform areas are to practise increased leadership, fairness and ethics, accountability and innovation (see figure 1). In order to demonstrate utmost fairness and equity and workplace diversity, Government passed the Bill of Rights and an Equal Employment Policy. This sets an ethical standard for the above reforms.

The PSC exists to promote excellence in public service delivery. In order to perform this role PSC has not only statutory power to review the machinery of government but also constitutional and statutory powers to be the central personal authority to CEO in 2002. PSC currently focuses on the strengthening of leadership capacity in Ministries and Departments and at the same time developing a human resources management framework for the public service workforce. This particular framework design must guarantee continued innovation and improvement, accountability and transparency in public services delivery. Other contributions of PSC include better corporate planning and the setting of a clear framework through collaborative efforts by Ministries and departments and their respective CEO's, proposed establishment of an e-government and the reorganization of state properties including office accommodation and quarters.

6. The PMS-COLA Dilemma: A Policy Failure?

Since the beginning of the new millennium, the PSC has been showing much initiative towards civil service reforms including the much talked-about performance management system (PMS), which was introduced in January 2004 to motivate and develop a professional productive workforce along with extensive training programs[1]. However, towards the end of 2005, the government was not sure what to do with PMS as it had proved to be too costly.

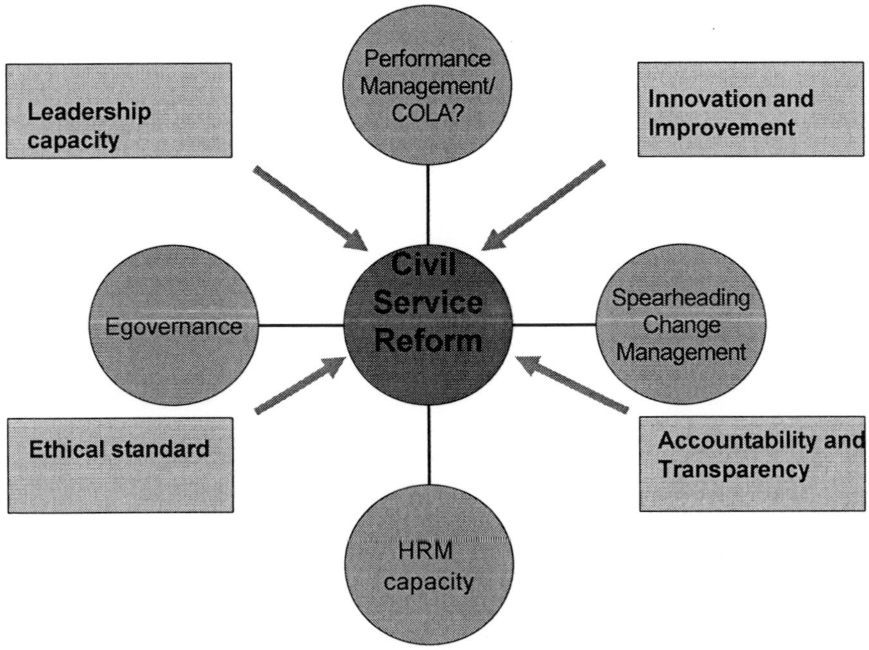

Figure 17.1. Key Civil Service Reform Components.

The government finally returned to the Cost of Living Adjustment (COLA) approach and provided a 3 percent COLA payment for the year 2004 on 22 December 2005 (Fiji Government Press Release for December 22, 2005). This payment is designed to maintain the purchasing power of the existing wages of all civil servants in the case of inflation. In fact, it is paid to all public servants and acts like a safety valve rather than a reward. But the PMS was a system to act both as a reward and a compensation for inflation. Although the PMS system was implemented for a good reason, it had a fair share of criticism. There were several disputes on PMS and hearings took place. The hearings commenced on 16 May 2005 and lasted a total of 14 days ending on 15 July 2005. At the end of all the hearings, parties submitted reports to the Tribunal for an official decision. The Tribunal pointed out a number of shortfalls of the PMS system and these are described below:

PMS is thought to help maintain the purchasing power of the existing wages of all public servants but apparently this is has not been the case.

There are number of shortfalls such as a lack of objectivity, difficulty in measuring performance and excessive and confusing paperwork.

The efficiency of the present PMS has been questioned.

---

[2] As part of an agreement between PSC and the University of the South Pacific, the mid-level Fiji civil servants are undergoing a Graduate Certificate in Public Sector Management. Started in January 2004, the Program has so far trained 50 civil servants and currently another 30 are enrolled in the Programme. The goal of the Programme is to develop and deliver an accredited training programme for Fiji senior managers and administrators to enhance their academic knowledge and governance skills to become able managers and successful implementers of reform in all arenas of the service.

The tribunal believes that the present PMS does not promote equity in pay determination. They have justified this by saying that 10-30 percent of civil servants will not qualify for a performance increase in any given year.

The present PMS is not sustainable in terms of its cost.

It does not ensure that the Commission will necessarily achieve their objective of reduced operation costs.

The above are reasons for the failure of PMS. The Government probably embarked on PMS a bit too soon to follow the footsteps of Australia and New Zealand. They were ill prepared for the disruptive symptoms of PMS and they did not realize that assessing the thousands of civil servants in the state workforce would be a nightmare. On the other hand, COLA, which seems to be a feasible option, has its problems too. In order to accommodate COLA increases as a permanent part of the budget cycle, government may have to cut the size of its civil service itself (Pacific Islands Report, 2005). However, this kind of dilemma (the pendulum effect of COLA-PMS-COLA) create uncertainties in service and therefore affects productivity.

Public enterprise reform assesses the viability of some agencies to operate on a commercial basis and restructuring the institutions to run on either a commercial, corporate or a private basis, thus reducing the size of the service in the process. With the passing of the Public Enterprises Act in 1996, the Fiji government has already restructured and reorganized a number of its public enterprises under this legal framework. The Government of Fiji has in fact adopted a three-stage approach towards reform.

The first stage, which is commonly referred to as reorganization or commercialization, is the process of commercializing the activities of a public enterprise so as to make it an effective and profitable commercial entity. In this reform the legal status of an enterprise does not undergo any change; rather it aims to put into action business-oriented managerial practices (Sarker and Pathak, 2003).

According to Tadulala (1998), commercialization is quite similar to corporatization and he defines it as "the reorientation of an organization away from being a social service providing government body to a commercial enterprise".

The second stage is known as corporatisation. Here, commercial activities that are viewed separately from the social responsibilities are identified and then the enterprise is corporatized. The enterprise does not operate as a direct arm of the government, meaning it is now set up with a board of directors that is in charge of policy directions and reports to the Minister, who has considerable powers over the enterprise (Samy, n.d). In this scenario the government pretty much remains the sole shareholder.

Tadulala (1998) stresses that corporatization is very much the reorganization and the restructuring of a public enterprise, statutory body or Government department into a commercial company or entity, thus making the new entity more accountable to its owners for its operations. Furthermore, corporatisation is a pre–requisite for privatization, which is the final stage of reform.

The last stage is privatization. This involves "the transfer, in whole or part, to the private sector the government's shareholding in public enterprises" (Sarker and Pathak, 2003). Doing this reduces the role of government and increases the role of the private sector in any activity or in the ownership of assets. As a privatized entity he reorganized body has its shareholding completely diversified among its several shareholders. Moreover, the sole objective of privatization is to enhance the performance of public enterprises and at the same time reduce the burden it places on government budget.

Since the deregulation and restructuring programme started in 1989, the following enterprises have been corporatized in Fiji: Post and Telecommunication department, firstly becoming Fiji Post and Telecommunications Ltd (FPTL) and later splitting into Telecom Fiji Ltd and Post Fiji Ltd, Ika Corporation becoming Ika Corporation Ltd in January 1990; Fiji Pine Commission becoming Fiji Pine Ltd in January 1990 and finally National Marketing Authority becoming National Trading Corporation Ltd in 1992. For our discussion we shall look at the reform process and contents of two of Fiji's major earners. Illustrated in table 17.1 are the various organizations in Fiji that have undergone or are undergoing reforms.

Table 17.1. Public Enterprises Reform in Fiji

Government Commercial Company	Commercial Statutory Authority
Port Terminal Limited	Civil Aviation Authority of the Fiji Islands
Fiji Broadcasting Corporation	Maritime Ports Authority of Fiji
Fiji Hardwood Corporation Limited	Housing Authority
Airports Fiji Limited	Public Rental Board
Fiji Ships and Heavy Industries Limited	Fiji Electricity Authority
Rewa Rice Limited	Others
NATCO	PAFCO (Pacific Fishing Co. Ltd.)
Viti Corps Limited	Fiji Daily Post Co. Ltd.
Yaqara Pastoral Company Limited	
Post Fiji Limited	
Unit Trust of Fiji (Mgmt) Limited	

The Posts and Telecommunications Department became Fiji Post And Telecommunication Ltd in January 1990. In 1996 a split occurred and Telecom Fiji Ltd and Post Fiji Ltd came into being. It was assumed that the corporatization process would trim down the financial burden of government making it more commercialized. This would allow the organization to become more customer driven, more efficient in the provision of goods and services and more profitable. It was hoped that this new organization would now be in a better position to take advantage of the emerging telecommunications market such as email, internet, cellular phones and a host of new information and communication needs of the business world along with an ever increasing demand for personal telephone services. Obviously the public expected more efficient services than were provided under the government/civil service structure. Early 1997 the Minister for Telecommunications advised Telecom Fiji that its exclusive domestic operating licecse or its 25-year monopoly would be opened up for competition.

Fiji Pine Limited: This was the second government owned institution to be corporatized. Fiji Pine Limited was incorporated in September 1990 but then took over the assets, liabilities and obligations of the Fiji Pine Commission on 1 January 1991. There are two shareholders in this company. The first one is the Government of Fiji, that holds 99.8% of the shares and second is the Fiji Pine Trust that holds the minute number of remaining shares.

The indigenous landowners on whose land pine trees are grown solely own the Trust. The main activity of the company is the growing and selling of the pine timber, which it does with the help of its subsidiary company Tropik Wood Industries Limited. This subsidiary company is responsible for the processing and the marketing of sawn timber and woodchips as the main products. Fiji Pine Limited and Tropik Wood Industries are economically interdependent.

Fiji Pine Limited plays an important role in implementing government's socio-economic policies and is also expected to contribute to the development of the country by means of expanding the economic base of the country through the creation of an industry based on plantation forest, implementing governments corporatisation and privatization programme, providing a vehicle for direct participation of landowners, generating foreign exchange earnings and contributing to the protection and conservation of the environment (Reddy, 1997).

7. Reform Results

The Public Service Commission has exerted a lot of effort and resources in its initiatives towards good governance or in Fiji's civil reform process. These efforts reveal interesting results. The thought of a productive workforce is certainly desirable but PSC is faced with the enormous challenge of changing the culture and mindset with its innovative programs. However, productivity is an ongoing effort as in most departments the old culture which worship processes rather than outputs still dominates.

PSC has also made serious efforts in setting Individual Work Plans and Position Descriptions for Civil servants to ensure that they are accountable for their actions. Yet again there is much resistance from individuals in accepting responsibility for their actions. Corporate planning still needs to be thoroughly practiced by those involved. PSC's research and observations over the period show that there is an absence of active participation and consultation with relevant stakeholders and clients. If there is any sort of coordination taking place, it is more or less one way. The typical scenario involves just senior managers in the corporate planning exercise with no substantial input from key operational managers. Only the senior and key personnel are involved in decision making and designing the appropriate frameworks. The other important point to note is that foreign consultants are usually involved in the planning stage hence making implementation challenging, the plan is not locally owned or aligned. Efforts to set up an e-government is still underway and PSC's idea of reorganization of state properties, as worthy as it sounds, is subject to much disagreement.

Until recently, the progress of Government corporatization/privatization has achieved mixed results" (Tadulala, 1998). The restructuring of public enterprises was expected to improve performance but over the years only a few have shown signs of economic recovery and profits. In actual fact most still remain loss making entities. The reality is that the overall performance of the public enterprise sector has remained weak with the return on assets to the government averaging barely 2.7% since 1992 (Sarker and Pathak, 2003).

Even though post and telecommunications activities have been separated into two separate companies their reform process still remains incomplete. The reform process came as no easy task. Once corporatized, FPTL faced a number of challenges. First was that it had to change from a civil service – based service provider to a more customer focused and driven organization. The usual laidback civil service ethic and attitude had to be abandoned to bring about speed and efficiency. This required the adoption of a new corporate culture that is evidently not easy to achieve in any organization in the world. For this new culture to be functional employees had to change their attitude and this required endurance and training and awareness workshops.

The next challenge was to maintain the staff morale during the transition phase. There are obviously diehards in any organization who find it very difficult to leave the old ways. Thus there were continuous disagreements and conflicts between the higher levels in the organization. There was no consensus and this created distrust and divisiveness within the FPTL. Other challenges included improving performance and better return to the shareholders, upgrading of technology and providing improved telephone services to the larger community.

FPTL is currently performing reasonably well but there are the usual tensions and arguments and this requires consensus and collective agreement between employees and management and relevant stakeholders in order for FPTL to progress.

Fiji Pine too has had its fair share of problems, the major one being that the employees of the company were members of two different trade unions. The salaried staff were members of the Fiji Public Service Association (FPSA) and the remaining permanent staff were members of the Public Employees Union. Obviously the two separate unions held different views and perspectives and there was conflict and disagreement. To solve this problem a new company-based union Fiji Pine Employees Union was registered in 1992 and had more than fifty percent membership. This disturbed the FPSA, who argued that they were the legal representatives of the workers and obviously did not like the reduced membership and size. This led on and an industrial dispute took place but Fiji Pine vigorously challenged the FPSA. FPL went through the higher courts via a Judicial Review and won the case.

Currently the Fiji Pine Limited Employees Union continues to be the sole representative of the workers in the company. As the union is new, it lacks independent unionism and union expertise. This drawback has led to problems within the membership where union officials are viewed as puppets and representatives of the Management rather than the employees. This is the challenge that needs to be overcome and can only be successful once the union reaches the desired membership so that it is able to direct more resources to engage a full time and professional trade unionist.

The corporatiZation process has provided both these organizations the necessary legal framework to separate from a government department to a registered company with its own board of directors, corporate and management structure. Hence we can confirm that the corporatiZation process has been a success and reached completion. On the other hand, both these organizations have failed to operate on a commercial basis as was assumed. This is attributed to the fact that these new companies were basically under government directive to provide employment to basically all employees under controlled conditions of employment. As a result now, some six to seven years later, the work culture has still not changed and the employees today are the same ones who were there before corporatization began.

8. Global Reform Experience and Some Policy Thoughts for Fiji

The twenty-first century brings with it opportunities and challenges for countries around the world. This concluding section includes discussion on how other countries have reformed their public services to face the challenges of the twenty-first century and recommendations or prescriptions as to how the public service in Fiji can be enhanced and reformed in order to be in pace with the rest of the world.

Over the last decade New Zealand has made considerable changes to its public management. These changes have taken countries by surprise, as they demand radical changes to the structure, governance and basis for management in government agencies. The New Zealand reforms value and reveal elements of "new public management" such as budgeting for results and the devolution of management control over inputs. Similar changes are also evident in other developed countries like the United Kingdom and Australia but one fact that remains is that New Zealand is indeed the leader in implementing change. Comparable transformations can be seen in other countries, particularly the United Kingdom and Australia but nothing like the New Zealand reforms which are not only sophisticated in the truest sense but also complex and unique to the country (Laking, n.d).

Nevertheless hope must not be lost as all public service reform programmes in any country in the world require a common set of variables. These are perhaps the basic components of the reform framework. These so called variables are political commitment, credibility, a reliable body to monitor progress, shared ownership, institutionalizing systems of feedback, working with the civil society organizations and interest groups and acceptance and continuous pursuit of change (Khan, 1998).

The public service reforms in Fiji have had an early start and have in fact secured many of the variables in the above mentioned framework. This means that resistance to change by public servants is perhaps lessening, sending out a positive signal to the initiators of change that this may indeed be the perfect time to quicken the pace of reform in Fiji with slight modifications. The prescriptions that follow focus on what should be done to further enhance the reform of the public services in line with global trends.

The PSC as part of its functions spearheaded the civil service reform, which concentrates on upgrading the overall Public Service culture to a new level of efficiency, effectiveness and productivity. As commendable as PSC's actions may be there are still many improvements to be made. For starters, PSC must get regular feedback from ministries and departments so that reform programmes are consistent and in line, ensuring that deadlines are met on time. Moreover to make PSC's role in this effort easier, government must ensure its utmost support as well as demonstrate political commitment at all times. Generally speaking, public sector reform is likely to be affected by changes in governments and their approaches and attitudes on reforms.

However, government can work on passing proper corruption legislation to avoid abuse and corruption and setting clear measurements for ethics regulated in the Public Service Regulations 1999. There is a desperate need for clearer goals and strategies so that public servants are given no excuse to escape punishment for wrongful behaviour and laxity. So the government must enhance its leadership and guidance roles.

The establishment and management of an information system is perhaps called for. This will help keep track of the implementation of reforms and it will also keep the relevant parties connected and informed at all times. Thus healthy networking takes place.

New work and organizational culture is still vague to many civil servants, resulting in lack of commitment and ownership from the wider public service. To overcome this there is a need for greater networking between change agents in ministries and more awareness programmes. Continuous training and awareness of civil servants at all levels on issues such as good governance and client orientation should be considered. Reform champions should be encouraged to lead changes and help progress reform. These all will indeed aid in the facilitation of cohesive coordination towards collective reform goals. Furthermore the partnership and harmonious working relationship with stakeholders especially the public sector unions is important for the advancement of reform initiatives. It should always be remembered that human resources are the key assets and factors that will make changes a success, therefore investment in their well being and development must be prioritized.

Government needs to pass a policy whereby all ministries and departments take full ownership of the devolution /delegation and decentralization of powers by the PSC, that is, PSC's role in the reform programme must be regarded and respected as a facilitator and not as a doer. As can be judged from the discussion above, reforms are very time consuming and are difficult to bring about, therefore it is advisable that changing governments guaranteed support for ongoing reforms, rather than causing serious disruptions by imposing new rules and concepts.

With regard to performance management, the overall initiative would be to get the relevant parties involved and to work towards performance management (and an old COLA process) that is outcome based rather than input or output, but one that is affordable. What can be envisioned is a change to involve communities at large to oversee and monitor the performance of civil servants in which the communities should get involved not only as reflexive stakeholders but as active participants.

Reflections on theory and practice of reforms have generated a lot of hope and ways to best carry out reform in its easiest form. There are positive trends and opportunities and there is every reason to believe that reforms can be carried out in Fiji as successfully as in the case of New Zealand reforms. At the same time it must be kept in mind that all good reforms begin by the filling up of gaps in the reform framework through the above prescriptions and other promising united approaches.

REFERENCE

Appana, S. (2003). "New Public Management and Public Enterprise Restructuring in Fiji". *Fijian Studies* ,v.1(1):51-73.

Boyne et al. (2003). *Evaluating Public Management Reforms,*Buckingham: Open University Press.

Constitution of the Republic of the Fiji Islands, (1998). Suva: Government Printers.

Fiji Government Press Release (2005). Arbitration Tribunal-Awards 52-57-2004 COLA. [Online]. (Accessed from: http://www.fiji.gov.fj) [March10, 2006].

Fiji Government Press Release (2005). Cola Payout Tomorrow. [Online]. (Accessed from: http://www.fiji.gov.fj) [March10, 2006].

Government of Fiji (1991). *Opportunities for Growth*, Suva.

Government of Fiji (2002). "Rebuilding Confidence for Stability and Growth for a Peaceful, Prosperous Fiji". Parliamentary Paper No.72 of 2002, Fiji: Government Printers.

Great Council of Chiefs (2005). Wikipedia Encyclopedia [Online] http://en.wikipedia.org/wiki/Great_Council_of_Chiefs_(Fiji) [2005,January 20] http://www.flp.org.fj/04_ADC/final_poverty.htm

Hughes, O.E (2003). *Public Management and Administration*, 3rd ed, New York: Palgrave Macmillan.

Khan, M. M. (1998). *Administrative Reforms in Bangladesh*, Dhaka, Bangladesh: The University Press.

Laking, R. (mimeo).A New Zealand Approach to Public Management Reform in Mongolia.

Ministry of Finance and National Planning (2003). Presentation to Ministries and Departments on Financial Management Reforms.

Naidu, V. and Barr, K. (2002). *Comment on Poverty for Fiji Update 2002.* Paper presented by the National Centre for Development Studies, Asia pacific School of Economics and Management, The Australian National University and University of the South Pacific.

Pacific Islands Report (2005). Pay Raises Worsen Fiji Civil Service Woes. [Online]. (Accessed from: http://www.fijitimes.com) [March10, 2006].

Prasad, B and Reddy, M (2002). Structural Reforms, political instability and economic growth in Fiji: Sustainability in the long run. [Online] Available: Http://www.fdc.org.au/files/prasad.pdf [2004, August 25].

Reddy, N. (1997). "The Implications of Public Sector Reforms on Human Resource Management in the South Pacific: The Case of Fiji." A paper presented at the conference on Human Resources and Future Generations in Islands and Small States', 6-8 November, University of Malta, Valletta, Malta.

Samy, S.N (mimeo) "The Process of Commercialization, Corporatisation and Privatization in Fiji". Working Paper, USP, Fiji.

Sarker, A.E. & Pathak, R.D. (2003) "Public Enterprise Reform in Fiji Islands". *Public Organisation Review, - A Global Journal*, Vol.3, 2003, pp.55-75.

Schiavo-Campo, S and Sundaram, P (mimeo). To Serve and to Preserve: Improving Public Administration in a Competitive World. (66-69).

Tadulala, M (1998). Background Paper: Government Corporatisation, Privatisation Policy/Strategy.

UNDP (2004) Human Development Report 2003, UNDP website

Waqabaca, C (2002). Financial sector development and Reform in Fiji. Working paper 2000/2005, Reserve Bank of Fiji, Fiji.

In: Development Problems and Prospects in Pacific Islands ISBN: 978-1-60021-793-7
Editors: B. C. Prasad, D. C. Roy, pp. 259-279

Chapter 18

A MACROECONOMETRIC MODEL FOR FIJI

Rup Singh

1. INTRODUCTION

There are three stages in economic research, viz, purpose, summary of facts and interpretation. From this perspective, econometric techniques have a limited role and only help to prepare summaries of facts. If alternative techniques yield similar summaries, our confidence in those summaries will increase. In this paper we have used a simpler time series technique known as the general to specific approach (GETS). It was developed by the econometricians at the London School of Economics such as Saragan, Mizon and Hendry. Hendry is currently its strongest proponent. We have used this technique because in a limited number of empirical studies we have found that it gives similar summaries of facts compared to some alternative techniques like the Phillip-Hansen FMOLS and the Johansen VECM.

However, GETS is relatively more flexible than these two techniques and especially useful for estimating small to medium sized models with a limited number of observations. In this respect, this paper is exploratory as it applies a single equation method to estimate the key structural equations for Fiji and develop a model for the entire economy with a view to examine how well it explains the macroeconomic variables.[1]

Where possible, we have also used VECM and FMOLS to check our estimates of GETS. However, we have not had substantial differences in the results obtained with these alternative techniques. At Uinversity of the South Pacific, we are extending our model to incorporate policy variables so that it can be used for policy analysis.

To date, only one conventional econometric model and a Computable General Equilibrium (CGE) model has been developed for Fiji. Murphy (1992) estimated a macroeconometric model using annual data from 1974 to 1986. While his work provides

[1] Our approach is similar to the past practice of estimating models with the single equation methods. Some examples are: the Nevile model of Australia, the St.Louis model for the USA, the RBA model of Beechey et.al., the Shand and Tredgold model for PNG and the Murphy model for Fiji. In all these models partial adjustment specifications have been used to capture the dynamics. In contrast GETS uses more general dynamic specifications.

some useful insights in structural modeling, no further attempts have been made to refine or update this model. The Murphy model is aimed at analyzing shocks affecting the Fiji economy and a significant proportion (40 out of 58 equations) of the model are identities. The model is not suitable for forecasting. Details of the Murphy model and some important estimated equations can be found in Singh (2005a). However, Murphy failed to provide sound theoretical justifications for his equations and has used either OLS or partial adjustment models (PAM) to estimate the relevant parameters. It is well known that estimation using these standard methods with unit root variables give spurious summaries. Nonetheless, Murphys attempt is pioneering and important.

Levantis (1999) developed a CGE model for Fiji which he has revised in 2003. Nonetheless, both his works are important for policy institutions like the National Planning Office (NPO) and the Reserve Bank of Fiji (RBF). At its inception, the Levantis model was extensively used by the RBF to compare the validity of its own forecasts.[2] While there are limitations in static CGE models, these models give a detailed breakdown of the effects of changes in exogenous variables. However, it would be even more valuable if a traditional time series dynamic econometric model and a CGE model are used together, often to check and re-affirm each other's predictions. The advantage of the conventional models is that they can generate the actual dynamic adjustment paths of variables, which provides insightful information and room for assessment.

Currently there does not seem to be a reliable and usable structural macroeconometric model for Fiji. Even at the RBF, only single equation framework is being used to generate inflation forecasts.[3] Moreover, forecasts of national accounts and other key statistics represent a judgmental consensus between the major policy institutions on which, in many occasions, both academic and professional economists have had disagreements. Therefore, attempts to construct macroeconometric models for forecasting and policy are enormously supported and encouraged in empirical research in Fiji and perhaps in other PICs. Thus, in this respect, our work is a starting point for further works aimed at developing structural models for policy.

This paper is organized as follows: The next section presents the basic structure of our model followed by the full exposition and a brief discussion of the dynamic model that is used for simulations. Section 4 details the simulation results and evaluation tests and conclusions with limitations are stated in the final section.

2. The Basic Structure of Our Model

The hypothesized basic structure of our macroeconometric model, abstracted from its dynamics, is as follows. There are 11 endogenous variables (C, I, X, RM, M1, P, CPI, W, Y^d, Y^S and Y) and therefore 11 equations. Given the estimated parameter values of these equations, if the actual values of the 13 exogenous variables ($\bar{G}$, YD, R, RL, E, PM, PF, YT, K, L, POIL, PM and Y^*) and for the 9 dummy variables, (COUP, COUP1 SS, DEV, DEV2,

[2] While at the RBF, I had the first-hand experience in generating macroeconomic forecasts and analyzing the effects of various shocks using the CGE. However, due to software licensing problems, the Bank restricted further use of this model. There are indications that it is hardly being used by the NPO as well.

[3] While there are indications that RBF is developing a macroeconometric model for policy, we are not privy to details.

VAT1, VAT2, DUM8991 and DUM8996) are provided, the model gives time paths for the endogenous variables.

2.1. The Equilibrium Specifications

$$ln\, C_t = \alpha_0 + \alpha_1 lnYD_t + \alpha_2 R_t + \epsilon_{1t} \quad (1)$$

$$ln\left(\frac{I_t}{Y_t}\right) = \beta_0 + \beta_1 ln\, Y_t + \beta_2 RL_t + \epsilon_{2t} \quad (2)$$

$$ln\left(\frac{M1_t}{P_t}\right) = \lambda_0 + \lambda_1 ln\, Y_t + \lambda_2 RS_t + \epsilon_{3t} \quad (3)$$

$$ln\, P_t = \pi_0 + \pi_1 ln\, PM_t + \pi_2 T + \epsilon_{4t} \quad (4)$$

$$ln\, X_t = \gamma_0 + \gamma_1 ln\, YT_t + \gamma_2\, ln\left[\frac{P_t}{E_t \times P_{Ft}}\right] + \epsilon_{5t} \quad (5)$$

$$ln\, RM_t = \tau_0 + \tau_1 ln\, Y_t + \tau_2\, ln\left[\frac{P_t}{E_t \times P_{Ft}}\right] + \epsilon_{6t} \quad (6)$$

$$ln\, W_t = \omega_0 + \omega_1 ln\, CPI_t + \epsilon_{7t} \quad (7)$$

$$ln\, CPI_t = \phi_0 + \phi_1 ln\, P_t + \epsilon_{8t} \quad (8)$$

$$Y_t^d = C_t + I_t + \overline{G}_t + X_t - RM_t \quad (9)$$

$$ln\, Y_t^s = \theta_0 T + \theta_1 ln\, K_t + (1-\theta_1) ln\, LL_t + \epsilon_{10t} \quad (10)$$

$$Y_t = \eta_1 Y_t^d + \eta_2 Y_t^s \quad (11)$$

The specification of the behavioural equations is based on economic theory and various empirical works on Fiji and other developing countries. However, controversy still persists over the structural specifications of macroeconometric models and macroeconomic relationships in general. In this respect, our work addresses some of these issues, but all the relevant issues can not be adequately addressed within the scope of this paper. Each equation is estimated with the two aforesaid time series methods, viz, GETS and JML. While it is hard to comment which method gave better results, we included the most preferred equations from both the estimators and selected the ones that produced better simulation results. In doing so, we noted that most of the equations included in the model are based on GETS; see the dynamic model below. The estimation details are not presented here to conserve space but a brief explanation is given after each dynamic equation.[4] Data is derived from the RBF Quarterly Reviews and the Current Economic Statistics (various years) and the IMF-CD ROM (2003). Specific data construction and definition of variables are in appendix A and the standard unit root test results are given in Appendix B.

The aggregate demand Y^d obtained by adding the levels of expenditures in (9) can be said to be only a proxy to Y^d. Therefore, we assume that actual output adjusts to this proxy aggregate demand and aggregate supply (in 10), which is estimated with a production function. Unlike in many models where aggregate supply is ignored, we have used a Cobb-Douglas production function (unadjusted for capacity utilization) for Fiji estimated by Rao and Rao (2005) using GETS.[5] The intersection of the two determine the equilibrium level of output Y_t given in (11). This approach is based on Rao (2003) and Nevile and Rao (1996) who argue that such an exposition of the ADAS where AD is derived from the ISLM framework is inconsistent because the price flexibility implied in the ADAS model is inappropriate since the labour and goods markets are fixed price markets in the ISLM. This calls for an ADAS model based on the assumption that these are disequilibrium markets. A simpler alternative is to close the ISLM by augmenting with the Phillips curve type price adjustment equation or both price and quantity adjustment equations. Therefore, some Keynesian economists augment the ISLM model with the Phillips curve, but use the inverted Phillips curve as aggregate supply. Goods prices are determined as a mark-up on the wage costs augmented with a demand pressure variable. This is a pragmatic compromise and we follow this approach by developing wage and price equations in our model. Other equations in our model either explain the dis-aggregated components of Y^d and prices. The government expenditure which includes both current and capital spending of government is treated as exogenous. The estimated dynamic model is given below:

2.2. The Dynamic Model For Simulation

Consumption Function

$$
\begin{aligned}
\Delta lnC_t = & -0.105\left[lnC_{t-1} - (0.811 lnYD_{t-1} + 0.408R_{t-1})\right] \\
& \quad (-1.43) \qquad\qquad (8.16)^{*} \qquad\qquad (1.44) \\
& - 0.699\Delta lnC_{t-1} - 0.451\Delta lnC_{t-2} - 0.258\Delta lnC_{t-3} \\
& \quad (-4.30)^{*} \qquad\qquad (-4.10)^{*} \qquad\qquad (-2.54)^{*} \\
& - 0.285\Delta lnYD_{t-1} - 0.019\Delta R_{t-1} \\
& \quad (-1.84)^{**} \qquad\qquad (-3.38)^{*} \qquad\qquad\qquad (1')
\end{aligned}
$$

$$\bar{R}^2 = 0.675, SER = 0.035 \quad Period: 1975 - 2002$$

$$\chi^2_{sc1} = 0.047, \chi^2_{ff} = 2.855, \chi^2_{n} = 0.732, \chi^2_{hs} = 0.371$$

[4] Detailed discussions can be found in Singh (2005). Also see, Rao and Singh (2004), (2005a), 2005b), and Singh (2005) for details of consumption, demand for money, exports & imports and investment equations, respectively.

[5] Rao used the GETS approach to tackle the unit roots in the variables of the production function.

Briefly, consumer expenditure depends on current and past values of disposable income (YD) and availability of consumer credit (R). Past values of consumption are also significant. The financial variables such as the real rate of interest have no implications for consumption in Fiji since low and volatile consumer incomes together with less developed bonds market offer limited opportunities for inter-temporal substitution. Rao (2005) and Rao and Singh (2004) have also made these observations. Thus, targeting consumption with the rate of interest such as what the RBF is doing is inappropriate. None of the χ^2 summary statistics for the first order serial correlation ${\chi_{(sci)}}^2$ functional form mis-specification ${\chi_{(ff)}}^2$ normality in residuals ${\chi_{(n)}}^2$ and heteroscedasticity ${\chi_{(hs)}}^2$ are significant at the 5% level.

The Investment Equation

$$\begin{aligned}
\Delta ln\left(\frac{I_t}{Y_t}\right) = & -6.693 - 0.119(\Delta RL_t + COUP) - 13.374\Delta^2 lnP_{t-1} \\
& (-7.81)^* \quad (-7.75)^* \qquad\qquad (-6.40)^* \\
& - 0.261[\Delta ln(I/Y)_{t-2} + \Delta ln(I/Y)_{t-4}] + 0.038\,T \\
& (-2.88)^* \qquad\qquad\qquad\qquad (7.00)^* \\
& - 7.898[\Delta^2 lnP_t + \Delta^2 lnP_{t-2}] - 2.589\Delta lnY_t \\
& (-5.00)^* \qquad\qquad\qquad (-4.81)^* \\
& + 0.050\Delta RL_{t-4} - 0.688ECM_{t-1} \\
& (2.93)^* \qquad\qquad (-4.12)^*
\end{aligned} \qquad (2')$$

$$\bar{R}^2 = 0.761, SER = 0.127 \quad Period: 1976-2002$$

$$\chi^2_{sc1} = 2.590, \chi^2_{ff} = 0.202, \chi^2_{n} = 1.154, \chi^2_{hs} = 0.161$$

The private investment ratio depends on two important variables, viz, real output and the real long-term interest rate taken as a proxy for the user cost of capital. Political coup seems to have a permanent negative impact on investment while accelerating inflation and inflation expectations seem to reduce investment. The implied long-run output elasticity is unity and the elasticity of the real rate on interest at its mean of 2.80 is around -0.40. This implies that an increase in real interest rate by 1 percentage point (pp) will reduce the investment ratio by around 0.20pp and therefore the recent RBF stance on interest rate is harmful to private investment. None of the χ^2 summary statistics are significant and around 70% adjustments to long-run equilibrium are completed in one year.

Demand for Money

$$\Delta ln\left(\frac{M_t}{P_t}\right) = -3.047 - 1.114ECM_{t-1} - 0.039(\Delta RS_t - \Delta RS_{t-1})$$
$$(-10.94)^{*} \quad (-11.05)^{*} \quad (11.05)^{*}$$
$$- 0.820(\Delta lnY_{t-2} - \Delta lnY_{t-4}) + 1.114\Delta^2 lnY_t$$
$$(-3.59)^{*} \quad (6.43)^{*}$$
$$+ 0.279COUP - 0.114DEV2 - 0.002T$$
$$(5.93)^{*} \quad (1.93)^{**} \quad (-0.71) \qquad (3')$$

$$\bar{R}^2 = 0.857, SEE = 0.055 \quad Period: 1976 - 2002$$
$$\chi^2_{sc1} = 0.169, \chi^2_{ff} = 3.94, \chi^2_n = 1.053, \chi^2_{hs} = 0.642$$

Real income and the nominal rate of interest determines the demand for narrow money. The income elasticity is unity and interest rate elasticity at its mean rate of 6.76 is around -0.35. The demand for money is stable (stability test results may be obtained upon request) and none of the χ^2 statistics are significant. This implies the RBF to target the level of money supply rather than the rate of interest.

GDP Deflator Equation

$$\Delta lnP_t = 0.777 - 0.287[lnP_{t-1} - (0.244\ lnPM_{t-1} + 0.028T)]$$
$$(6.70)^{*} \ (-4.27)^{*} \quad (-2.08)^{*} \quad (5.06)^{*}$$
$$+ 0.362\Delta^2 lnP_t + 0.188\Delta^2 lnP_{t-1} + 0.025\Delta lnPOIL_{t-1}$$
$$(4.45)^{*} \quad (2.55)^{*} \quad (1.88)^{**}$$
$$+ 0.054COUP1$$
$$(3.60)^{*} \qquad (4')$$

$$\bar{R}^2 = 0.901, DW = 1.56, SEE = 0.020, Period: 1974 - 2002$$
$$\chi^2_{sc1} = 2.253(0.13), \chi^2_{ff} = 0.911, \chi^2_n = 1.126, \chi^2_{hs} = 0.139$$

The import price and time trend are significant determinants of output price in Fiji. The dynamics are captured by current and lagged inflation and oil price growth. COUP1 indicates sudden upswings in prices due to precautionary demand during the political crisis and none of the χ^2 summary statistics are significant at 5% level.

The Exports Equation

$$\Delta lnX_t = 0.311 - 0.157(\Delta lnX_{t-2} + ECM_{t-1}) + 0.0004SS_{t-2}$$
$$(6.50)^* \quad (-5.33)^* \quad (3.78)^*$$
$$- 0.752\Delta ln\left[\frac{P_{Dt}}{E_t \times P_{Ft}}\right] - 0.310(\Delta lnYT_{t-2} + COUP)$$
$$(11.76)^* \quad (-13.79)^* \qquad (5')$$

$$Period: 1974 - 2002$$
$$\bar{R}^2 = 0.817, SER = 0.061, Period: 1973 - 2002$$
$$\chi^2_{sc}(1) = 1.819, \chi^2_{ff}(1) = 0.641, \chi^2_{nn}(2) = 0.813, \chi^2_{hs}(1) = 3.454$$

The estimated coefficients are significant and have the expected signs. The implied long-run trading partner output elasticity is around unity and relative price elasticity is around -1.108. These results indicate that exports is an engine of growth for Fiji. The political coup seems to have a negative impact and the average sugar productivity (SS) seems to increase exports. The speed of adjustment is reasonable and none of the χ^2 summary statistics are significant at 5% level.

Import Equation

$$\Delta lnRM_t = -1.425 + 0.416\Delta ln\left[\frac{P_{Dt}}{E_t \times P_{Ft}}\right] + 0.416\Delta ln Y_{t-4}$$
$$(-4.49)^* \ (4.26)^* \quad (3.17)^*$$
$$+ 0.785\Delta lnYT_t - 0.716ECM_{t-1} + 0.021T$$
$$(2.52)^* \quad (-5.55)^* \quad (2.21)^*$$
$$- 0.288COUP - 0.005SS_{t-2}$$
$$(-4.16)^* \quad (3.92)^* \qquad (6')$$

$$\bar{R}^2 = 0.80, DW = 2.00, SER = 0.05, Period: 1975 - 2002$$
$$\chi^2_{sc}(1) = 0.072, \chi^2_{ff}(1) = 1.668, \chi^2_{nn}(2) = 2.476, \chi^2_{hs}(1) = 0.179$$

The long-run output elasticity is 0.81 and relative price elasticity is 0.60. The impact of coup and supply shock seem to be negative. To improve the current account balance, Fiji needs to improve international competitiveness since the absolute value of the sum of the two relative price elasticities exceeds unity. Note, the speed of adjustment is reasonable and none of the χ^2 summary statistics are significant at 5% level.

Wage Rate Equation

$$\Delta lnW_t = -0.175[lnW_{t-1} - 0.147\ lnCPI_{t-1}] + 0.283\Delta^2 lnW_{t-1}$$
$$(9.46)^* \qquad (9.54)^* \qquad (4.65)^*$$
$$+ 0.424\Delta^2 lnW_t + 0.130[\Delta ln(Y/LL)_{t-1} + \Delta ln(Y/LL)_{t-2}]$$
$$(6.36)^* \qquad (1.78)^{**}$$
$$+ 0.047VAT2 - 0.043DUM8991$$
$$(3.07)^* \qquad (-1.96)^* \qquad (7')$$

$$\overline{R}^2 = 0.875, DW = 1.59, SEE = 0.026, Period: 1974 - 2002$$
$$\chi^2_{sc1} = 1.154, \chi^2_{ff} = 0.008, \chi^2_n = 0.386, \chi^2_{hs} = 2.003$$

The implied long run elasticity of wages with respect to CPI is significant at around 0.15. The dynamic factors are the lagged changes in GAP, wage rates, average productivity of labour and a temporary VAT dummy lead to higher wage rate in Fiji. The dummy variable (DUM8991) which marks government's massive tax free programs for producers seems to have led to higher demand for labour. Note, none of the χ^2 summary statistics are significant at 5% level.

The CPI Equation

$$\Delta lnCPI_t = -0.264[lnCPI_{t-1} - (1.015\ lnP_{t-1})] + 0.036DEV$$
$$(-3.49)^* \qquad (145.70)^* \qquad (3.04)^*$$
$$+ 0.100[\Delta lnPM_{t-1} + \Delta lnPM_{t-2} + \Delta(lnY - lnY^*)_{t-2}]$$
$$(4.08)^*$$
$$+ 0.220\Delta lnCPI_{t-2} + 0.317\Delta lnP_t$$
$$(2.66)^* \qquad (3.98)^* \qquad (8')$$

$$\overline{R}^2 = 0.828, DW = 1.61, SEE = 0.015, Period: 1974 - 2002$$
$$\chi^2_{sc1} = 1.255, \chi^2_{ff} = 0.007, \chi^2_n = 1.135, \chi^2_{hs} = 0.074$$

The GDP deflator has a strong positive effect on CPI and has an implied long-run unit elasticity. All other variables are correctly signed and the change in GAP seems to have a positive impact on CPI. The lagged growth of import prices is significant and the devaluation seems to have increased consumer prices. The VAT dummies, both temporary and permanent, were insignificant at conventional levels.

$$\Delta lnY_t^s = -3.900 - 1.195\, lnY_{t-1}^s + 0.264\, lnK_{t-1} + 0.736\, lnLL_{t-1}$$
$$(-7.05)^* \quad (-6.94)^* \quad (8.53)^* \quad (8.53)^*$$
$$+ 0.737\Delta lnLL_t + 1.005\Delta lnK_t + 0.028DUM8995 + 0.013T$$
$$(5.93)^* \quad (3.50)^* \quad (1.94)^{**} \quad (10')^*$$

$$R^2 = 0.987, DW = 2.29, SER = 0.028, Period: 1971 - 2002$$
$$\chi_{sc}^2(1) = 1.41, \chi_{ff}^2(1) = 2.00, \chi_{nn}^2(2) = 0.37, \chi_{hs}^2(1) = 0.00$$

The Production Function

The production function has two inputs, labour and capital and a time trend has been added to capture the impact of the Hicks neutral technical progress. In spite of the preliminary nature of his estimates, his production function gave good results. These have been improved further in the growth accounting equations; see Rao and Rao (2005). Note the $\bar{R}^2$ which is impressive, and that none of the χ^2 summary statistics are significant at 5% level.

.Aggregate Output

$$Y_t = 3.261 + 0.298Y_t^s + 0.280Y_t^d$$
$$(9.17)^* \quad (2.74)^* \quad (1.99)^* \qquad (11')$$

$$\bar{R}^2 = 0.911, DW = 1.598, SER = 0.040, Period: 1977 - 2002$$
$$\chi_{sc}^2(1) = 0.87, \chi_{ff}^2(1) = 1.46, \chi_{nn}^2(2) = 0.47, \chi_{hs}^2(1) = 0.79$$

The aggregate output adjusts to both demand and supply conditions with similar impacts. Note that none of the χ^2 summary statistics are significant at 5% level.

3. A Note on Simulations

Model simulations are performed for a variety of reasons. However, given our objectives, we perform only historical simulation and evaluate the results based on standard model evaluation criteria, viz, the root mean squared errors (RMSE), root-mean-squared percentage errors (RMSPE), Theils inequality measure (U) and its decompositions. Generally, the RMSE should be compared with the actual size of the variables, say proxied by its sample mean. In practice, the RMSEs are often high, since they penalize large individual errors more heavily. Low RMSPE is only one of the desirable measure of simulation fit. A statistic related to RMSE is the Theils inequality coefficient (U). The values of U close to zero means a perfect fit. This inequality can then be defined in proportions of Um, Us and Uc, which are called the bias, variance and covariance proportions, respectively, which are useful breakdowns of simulation errors into its characteristics sources. Large values of Um signal systematic bias and imply the need for revision of the model. The variance proportion, Us, indicates the model's ability to replicate the degree of variability in the variables, i.e, either the actual or the simulated series have more fluctuations than the other. This would also signal model revision. Finally, the Uc measures unsystematic errors which is less worrisome.

Sometimes, a model may perform well in some of these criteria, but may fail in others. Thus one has to apply judgment and understand the trade-off between alternative criteria. Unfortunately as yet, econometrics does not offer a unified statistic, which gives model's performance consistent with all these desirable attributes. Further, one should check if the model tracks turning points well in data. This indicates if there is specification bias. Moreover, evaluation should depend on the purpose for which the model is built. Since our main objective is to develop a macroeconometric model using recent developments in time series methods, it is important to check if the equations are well specified, with the correctness of the signs and the magnitudes of estimates, which are shown to be appropriate and consistent with economic theory and our expectations. Note each equation fits historical data reasonably well with low SERs, high $\bar{R}^2$ and satisfy other important summary statistics. However, when combined as a system, we hope that the complete model will accurately replicate the actual data series. The simulation results and evaluation tests of the complete model are given below.

4. Simulation Results

We now turn to simulation results and conduct standard simulation evaluation tests. We compute various summary statistics to examine how well the model captures the dynamics of output, its disaggregated components, inflation and wages during the sample period. However, before we analyze the simulation results, it is important to highlight some of the major problems that we faced in simulating the model. First, all equations were specified in logarithms and their re-conversion to levels, at best, is an approximation. We found it difficult to balance the national accounting identity. This was further aggravated by the lack of consistent data for the full sample on capital consumption and other important components of the national accounts. Therefore, instead of linking the national income and disposable income with identities, we have assumed that the disposable income is a proportion of GDP, determined by the tax rate. This approach was also taken by Murphy (1992). Further the aggregate demand Y^d obtained by adding the levels of expenditures, is only a proxy of Y^d. Therefore, we assumed that actual output adjusts to this proxy aggregate demand and aggregate supply.

In our simulations, output in the short-run is assumed to adjust to both demand and supply conditions. In a way, this adjustment process captures the missing quantity adjustment equation in the dis-equilibrium models. While some model builders make slope and intercept adjustments in their simulations, we found that small adjustments to the intercepts of our consumption function, which did not fit the data well, adversely affected the simulation results for other variables. Therefore, we had to experiment with alternative estimates of the consumption equation, which is given in (1'). Nonetheless, in spite of some weaknesses, our simulation results satisfy various criteria used to judge the quality of simulation results.

The in-sample simulations plots of actual and simulated values of the endogenous variables are given are in Figures 18.1-18.8, see Appendix-18.3. These are based on dynamic simulation and all quantity variables are in real terms and given in their logarithms. The predicted series are indexed with z. Figure 1 shows the dynamic time path of consumption. Although the simulation results were not impressive of our estimates of consumption equation given in (1'), it is noted that the model replicates turning points reasonably well. Therefore, we had to fit an OLS equation between the actual and predicted values of consumption and the results are given in Figure 18.2. It may be noted that there is a remarkable improvement in predictions and a near to perfect fit between the two is noteworthy.

In Figure 18.3, we have plotted private investment against its simulated values. Except for the mid-1980s, the model gives a good prediction for changes in investment given the volatility of investment in general. However, based on the evaluation criteria of Theil's's, see next section, our predictions are quite reasonable. None of the decomposed Theil's indices are high and the RMSE is low at 0.016. The money demand is shown in Figure 18.4. Apart from the slight unexplained deviations in 1986, which may be due to political problems, the predictions are impressive. All simulation test statistics are well determined.

Real exports and imports are given in Figures 18.5 and 18.6, respectively. The predictions are not perfect only in 1986-87 and in late 2000. These may be due to the two political coups during these periods. However, the overall simulation results for both, exports and imports together with the RMSPE are noteworthy. The Theil's statistic and its decompositions are low. The graph shows good fit of data.

Figures 18.7-18.9 show simulation results of price equations. All the variables, viz, the GDP deflator, CPI and the nominal wage rate have perfect fit implying that their dynamics are well captured by the model.

Figure 18.10 shows predictions of real GDP, which is derived using the output equation. Note there is a close association between the actual and predicted values, although the fit is not perfect. However, the results are reasonable given the size and limitations of our model and data. However, there are no serious problems according to the simulation evaluation tests as given in Table 181.

All the summary statistics are impressive except for the original consumption equation which has been improved upon in C_t' see the third row. Both RMSPE and Theil's U are low for all variables. The highest RMSPE is 0.118 for the wage variable and is lowest for the alternative consumption and GDP deflator equations at 0.003. The U is 0.010 for the wages but this is still low. The Um and Us decompositions are small, which indicates that there are no serious errors in specification and that the variations in dependent variables are adequately captured in all equations. While Um is around 0.15 for investment and exports equations, they are respectful, given our sample size, data limitations and single equation approach to estimation. Further, Pindyck and Rubinfeld (1991) suggest that Um above 0.2 may be troublesome, which is not the case in ours. The last three columns in Table 81.1 give the basic statistics based on OLS fit of the actual and the simulated values of respective variables. It may be said that there exists close to perfect fit between the actual and simulated values for all the endogenous variables. The $\bar{R}^2$ s are high, slope coefficients are close to unity and the intercepts are around zero. Thus, our dynamic simulation results indicate that our methodology is useful for developing other models for policy and forecasting. However, there are no alternative models for comparing our results and building another model for this single purpose is beyond the scope of this paper.

Table 18.1 EX-post Simulations: Summary Statistics

	RMSE	RMSPE	U	Um	Us	Uc	α	β	$\bar{R}^2$
lnC_t	0.085	0.012	0.006	0.921	0.026	0.053	0.990	0.583	0.930
lnC_t^a	0.019	0.003	0.001	0.001	0.000	0.999	0.033	0.996	0.990
lnI_t	0.092	0.016	0.008	0.135	0.002	0.863	0.121	0.918	0.974
$lnM1_t$	0.042	0.008	0.004	0.061	0.052	0.888	0.238	0.961	0.983
lnX_t	0.059	0.008	0.004	0.161	0.008	0.831	-0.008	1.004	0.984
$lnRM_t$	0.058	0.008	0.004	0.107	0.000	0.893	0.099	0.989	0.970
lnP_t	0.014	0.004	0.002	0.009	0.025	0.966	-0.021	1.005	0.999
$lnCPI_t$	0.015	0.003	0.002	0.025	0.000	0.975	0.003	0.999	0.975
lnW_t	0.042	0.118	0.010	0.043	0.067	0.890	-0.008	1.010	0.998
lnY_t	0.037	0.005	0.002	0.000	0.021	0.979	0.000	1.000	0.918

lnC_t^a represents the alternative consumption function used in simulations. The α and β are, respectively, the intercept and slope of the fit between the actual and simuated values. The $\bar{R}^2$ measures the goodness of fit.

5. Conclusions and Limitations

In this paper, we have used alternative time series techniques to estimate a small macroeconometric model for Fiji. A brief survey of literature suggests that an up-to-date macroeconometric model useful for forecasting or policy does not exist in Fiji. Our single equation approach for estimation is not new because systems methods are not pragmatic given the quality and frequency of data in developing countries compared to the number of coefficients of the model. Further, it is not yet known how these time series methods can be modified to estimate models consisting of more than two or three equations. The complete model is then simulated over the historical period and standard model evaluation tests are performed. The simulation predictions are noteworthy with small RMSPE and impressive Theils inequality coefficients. The decomposed Theils indices indicate that there are no serious systematic or specification errors. Based on these results, we claim that our methodology, which is a mixture of the Cowles Foundation tradition to specification and time series approach to estimation, seems to have produced good results and therefore is useful for developing large scale forecasting or policy models.

However, a few limitations should be noted. First, we are unable to extend our work in lines of forecasting and policy analysis. However, these require further revision of our model, which we are currently persuing at USP. Second, we have ignored structural breaks and their implications on unit root tests as implied by Perron (1989) whose work stimulated several interesting developments because a major limitation in it is that the date of the break should be known *a priori*; for a comprehensive survey see Maddala and Kim (1998). However, we argue that there are practical problems in utilizing these tests when there are only a limited number of annual observations, i.e, suppose the tests show that there is a single or double break in the series, it would be necessary then to partition the data into sub-samples and estimate the cointegrating vectors for each. Such a partition is not practical for a small sample such as ours. Nonetheless, we do not argue that structural change methodology is not useful, but in our view, it has only limited use for developing countries. However, we have conducted the usual TIMVAR stability test, which suggest that all the estimated equations are stable. The stability test results are not reported in this paper but are available upon request.

Given these limitations and the exploratory nature of our work, we do not claim to have estimated a model satisfactory for policy or forecasting at this stage but suggest that our approach based on simple techniques like GETS gives promising and more reliable estimates for building better models. With these controversial methodological debates, our findings should be treated as preliminary until they are refuted by other work. Nonetheless, we are hopeful that it will be a useful starting point for future work and may encourage other researchers to develop large-scale models. We envisage that our model can form the basis for manageable and easy-to-use models for forecasting or policy for Fiji and for some of the PICs where data are available at least at the national accounts level.

APPENDIX 18.1. DATA AND DEFINITIONS

C_t = Nominal private consumption expenditure including durables and non-durables deflated by GDP deflator. Source: Current Economic Statistics, Bureau of Statistics (various years).

P_t = Real GDP deflator. Source: International Financial Statistics CD-ROM, (December 2003).

YD_t = Real private sector disposable income computed as YD = Y_t*(1-Tx)+RGNT_t , where Tx is the average (direct) tax rate and RGNT_t is the sum of grants and current transfers received by the private sector, deflated by GDP deflator. The tax rate is computed as a ratio of direct tax levied on wages and profits as a proportion of gross disposable income accrued to labor and capital. Source: Current Economic Statistics, Bureau of Statistics (various years).

Y_t = Nominal GDP at factor cost deflated by GDP deflator. Sources: Reserve Bank of Fiji, Quarterly Reviews (various years) and International Financial Statistics CD-ROM, (December 2003).

R_t = Credit availability proxy computed as the spread between the nominal short term (RBF 91-day bond or treasury bill rate, which ever is available) and the long term interest rates (5yr government bond yields). Sources: International Financial Statistics CD-ROM, (December 2003) and Reserve Bank of Fiji, Quarterly Reviews (various years).

I_t = Nominal private sector investment deflated by GDP deflator. It also includes investment expenditure of statutory bodies. Source: Reserve Bank of Fiji, Quarterly Review, (December 2003).

Y^*_t = Real potential GDP, de-trended values of real GDP using HPF method in Microfit 4.1.

RL_t = Real long term interest rate, computed as the difference between nominal long term interest rate and GDP deflator inflation rate.

SS_t = Average Sugar production per hector used as a proxy for the supply side dummy. Source: Current Economic Statistics, Bureau of Statistics, (December 2003).

CPI_t = Annual average index of the consumer prices. Sources: Current Economic Statistics (December 2003) and Reserve Bank of Fiji, Quarterly Reviews (various years).

GAP_t = Is computed as the difference between ln Y_t and ln Y^*_t in Microfit 4.1.

W_t = Is the nominal annual average daily wage rate in all productive sectors classified by the FSIC categories. Source: Current Economic Statistics and Fiji Employment Survey, both of Bureau of Statistics, (various years).

LL_t = Labor force in paid employment. Sources: Reserve Bank of Fiji and Fiji Employment Survey, (various years).

K_t = Real capital stock data is derived by adjusting the capital stock series used by Gounder and Morling (2000). Sources: Reserve Bank of Fiji's Quarterly Review, (December 2003) and Gounder and Morling (2000).

RS_t = Nominal simple average of 1-3 years savings deposit rates. Sources: Reserve Bank of Fiji Quarterly Review (various years) and International Financial Statistics CD-ROM, (December 2003).

$M1\_t$ = Narrow money balance consisting of currency in circulation, demand deposits and bills payable. Source: Reserve Bank of Fiji Quarterly Review (various years) and the International Financial Statistics, (December 2003).

X_t = Quantity of exports determined by nominal (FOB) export value deflated with domestic export unit value index. Sources: Current Economic Statistics, Bureau of Statistics (various years) and International Financial Statistics CD-ROM, (December 2003).

E_t = Nominal exchange rate - the price of a unit of foreign currency in terms of domestic currency. Sources: International Financial Statistics CD-ROM, (December 2003) and Reserve Bank of Fiji, Quarterly Reviews (various years).

P_Ft = Foreign prices computed as trade-weighted average of GDP deflator (1995 = 100) of Fiji's major trading partner countries. The trading partner countries are Australia, New Zealand, USA, EU/England and Japan. Trade weights are computed as respective trade shares of these economies on Fiji's total trade with them. Sources:

International Financial Statistics CD-ROM, (December 2003) and Reserve Bank of Fiji, Quarterly Reviews (various years).

PM_t = Import prices computed as import-weighted average export unit value indices (1995 = 100) of Fiji's major trading partner countries. Import weights are computed as respective shares of import from these economies on Fiji's total imports. Sources: International Financial Statistics CD-ROM, (December 2003) and Reserve Bank of Fiji Quarterly Reviews (various years).

Y_F = Trade weighted real GDP Index of trading partner countries expressed in 1995 prices.

RM_t = Quantity of imports of goods and services, determined by nominal imports deflated with PM_t. Sources: Current Economic Statistics and Reserve Bank of Fiji Quarterly Reviews, (various years).

POIL_t = Brent crude oil prices Index (1995 = 100). Source: International Financial Statistics CD-ROM, (December 2003).

COUP = Dummy variable for the two political coups in Fiji. Data constructed as 1 since the first coup in 1987 to 2002 and 0 in all other periods.

COUP1 = Dummy variable to capture the temporary impact of the two coups. Data constructed as 1 in 1986 to 1988 & 2000 and zero in all other periods.

NBF = Dummy variable for the collapse of the National Bank of Fiji. Data constructed as 1 for 1996 to 1998 and 0 for all other periods.

DEV = Dummy variable for the two devaluations of the Fiji dollar. Data constructed as 1 for 1987-88 & 1997-98 and 0 for all other periods.

DEV2 = Dummy variable for the second devaluation. Data constructed as 1 for 1997 to 98 and 0 for all other periods.

VAT = A permanent dummy for the introduction of VAT in 1992. Data constructed as 1 from 1992 onwards and zero for other periods.

VAT2 = Temporary VAT dummy for the introduction of Value Added Tax in Fiji. Data constructed as 1 for 1992-1994 and zero in all other periods.

DUM8991 and DUM8995 are dummy variables to proxy, separately, the post 1989 to 1991/95 period of high private sector confidence following the major tax incentives in tax free zones and export promotion policies.

APPENDIX 18.2: UNIT ROOT TESTS

Variable	ADF	PP	Variable	ADF	PP	m
RI_t	2.55	1.71	ΔRI_t	4.43	4.28	
	0.11	0.42		0.00	0.00	[1,1,3,3]
$\ln\left(\frac{I_t}{Y_t}\right)$	0.90	1.55	$\Delta \ln\left(\frac{I_t}{Y_t}\right)$	6.40	8.27	
	0.31	0.53		0.00	0.00	[1,3,1,1]
$\ln(Y_t - Y_t^*)$	5.40	8.14	$\Delta \ln(Y_t - Y_t^*)$	5.90	15.85	
	0.00	0.00		0.00	0.00	[4,4,4,4]
$\ln C_t$	2.44	2.58	$\Delta \ln C_t$	4.14	6.58	
	0.23	0.11		0.01	0.00	[1,1,1,1]

APPENDIX 18.2. CONTINUED

$\ln YD_t$	2.33	2.88	$\Delta \ln YD_t$	5.27	6.24	
	0.33	0.33		0.00	0.00	[1,1,1,1]
R_t	2.05	1.15	ΔR_t	6.28	10.08	
	0.27	0.22		0.00	0.00	[2,1,1,1]
$\ln P_t$	3.39	3.34	$\Delta \ln P_t$	4.08	4.08	
	0.07	0.08		0.02	0.02	[0,1,0,0]
$\ln Y_t$	1.23	1.48	$\Delta \ln Y_t$	4.46	7.89	
	0.15	0.53		0.00	0.00	[1,2,1,1]
$\ln P_t^F$	1.88	0.72	$\Delta \ln P_t^F$	4.81	3.08	
	0.97	0.98		0.01	0.00	[1,1,2,2]
$\ln M1_t$	2.73	0.02	$\Delta \ln M1_t$	6.46	7.94	
	0.44	0.43		0.00	0.00	[1,1,1,1]
RS_t	1.79	2.26	ΔRS_t	4.49	32.15	
	0.61	0.96		0.00	0.00	[2,5,1,1]
$\ln X_t$	2.74	2.42	$\Delta \ln X_t$	6.57	5.91	
	0.23	0.24		0.00	0.00	[0,0,1,1]
$\ln YT_t$	2.93	2.00	$\Delta \ln YT_t$	3.51	4.59	
	0.33	0.58		0.01	0.00	[1,1,1,1]
$\ln\left(\frac{P_t}{E_t * PF_t}\right)$	2.71	2.86	$\Delta \ln\left(\frac{P_t}{E_t * PF_t}\right)$	6.38	6.08	
	0.06	0.08		0.00	0.00	[1,1,1,1]
$\ln RM_t$	2.26	3.64	$\Delta \ln RM_t$	6.09	13.21	
	0.43	0.71		0.00	0.00	[2,2,1,1]
$\ln PM_t$	2.27	1.37	$\Delta \ln PM_t$	2.97	3.02	
	0.44	0.85		0.04	0.04	[1,1,1,1]
$\ln POIL_t$	2.34	2.47	$\Delta \ln POIL_t$	3.89	6.10	
	0.17	0.13		0.01	0.00	[1,1,1,1]
$\ln CPI_t$	2.79	1.86	$\Delta \ln CPI_t$	4.00	5.15	
	0.28	0.75		0.03	0.03	[1,1,1,1]
$\ln XP_t$	2.94	1.96	$\Delta \ln XP_t$	4.67	5.31	
	0.13	0.60		0.00	0.00	[4,4,1,1]
$\ln W_t$	1.97	1.98	$\Delta \ln W_t$	3.61	4.86	
	0.59	0.59		0.04	0.00	[0,2,3,3]
$\ln APL_t$	2.46	3.10	$\Delta \ln APL_t$	4.64	8.25	
	0.13	0.12		0.00	0.00	[1,0,1,1]
$\ln Lb_t$	2.70	1.79	$\Delta \ln Lb_t$	4.85	6.98	
	0.24	0.37		0.00	0.00	[1,0,1,0]
$\ln K_t$	2.84	1.79	$\Delta \ln K_t$	3.19	3.02	
	0.27	0.27		0.10	0.14	[1,1,0,1]
SS	1.46	1.33	ΔSS	3.48	14.08	
	0.54	0.20		0.02	0.00	[6,6,6,6]

1. ADF is the standard augmented Dicky-Fuller F-test and the PP is the Phillips-Perron test. For both the tests the p-values are given in parenthesis.
2. m is the lag length of the first differences of variables included, for example, [1,1,2,2] means that one lagged first difference is found to be adequate in each test in levels and two lags are optimal for their first differences.
3. The sample chosen for the tests are 1972-2002 for levels and 1973-2002 for first the differences of variables.
4. A time trend (T) is included for levels but only for the first difference if it is significant. Microfit 4.1 and E-Views 5.0 are used to compute the test statistics.
5. The unit root test results indicate that all variables except the output gap ln Y_t - ln Y*_t) are I(1) in levels but are stationary in first difference at 5% level. The KPSS test for ln P_t and ln [(P_D/E_t)* P_F] are, respectively: 10.529 and 0.954 against the critical value of 0.146. It rejects the null of stationarity at 5%. The KPSS for Δ ln K_t was 0.441 against 0.463 at 5\% level. Thus we accepted that the two prices are I(1) and Δ ln K_t is I(0).

APPENDIX 18.3 SIMULATION RESULTS (GRAPHS)

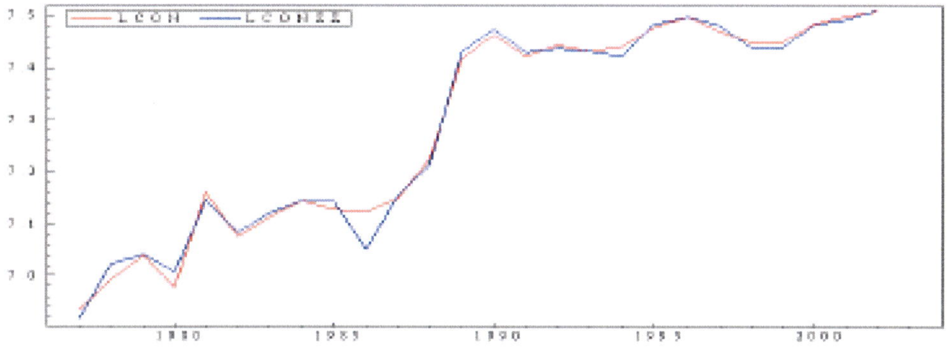

Figure 18.1.

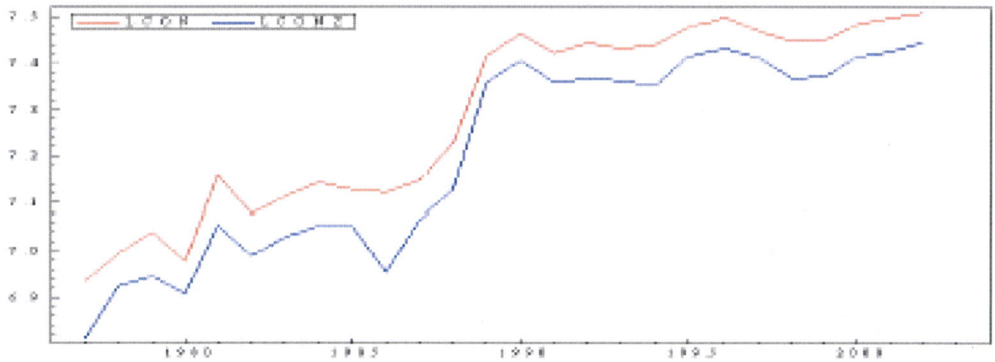

Figure 18.2.

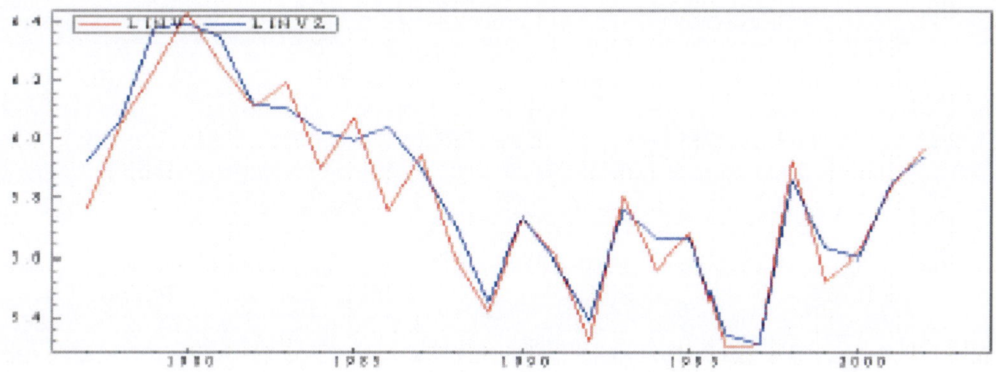

Figure 18.3.

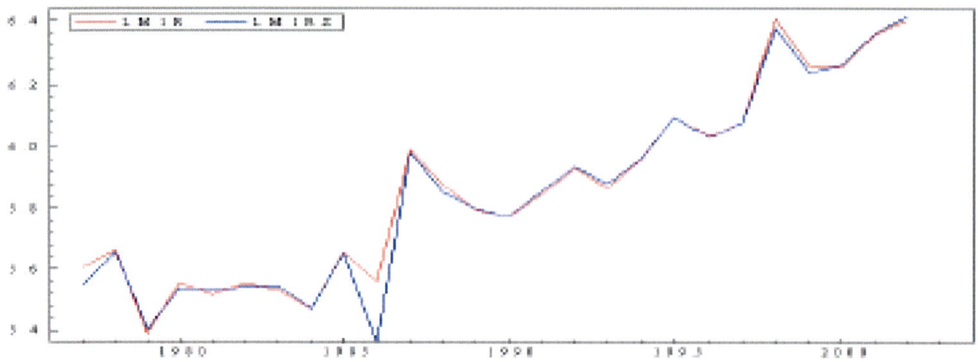

Figure 18.4.

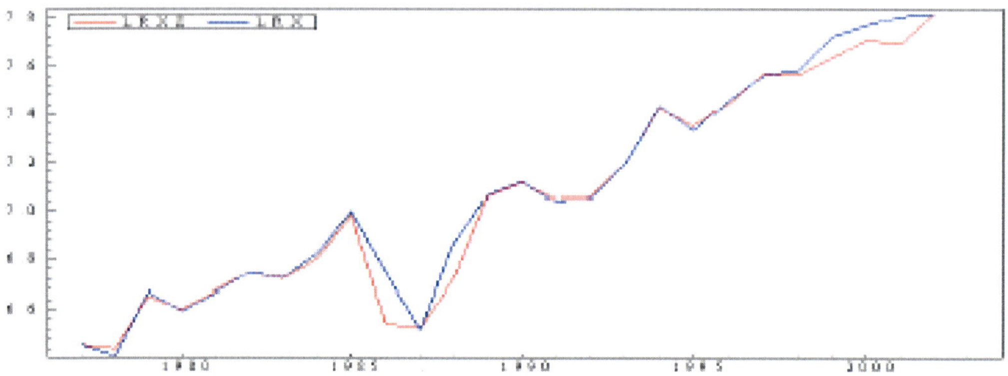

Figure 18.5.

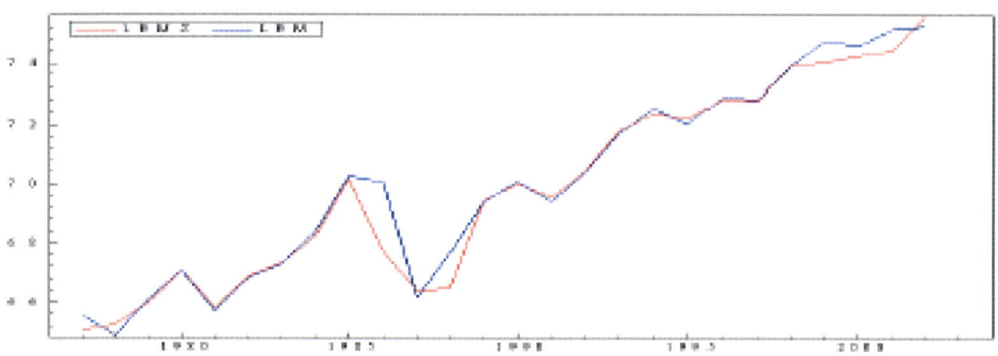

Figure 18.6.

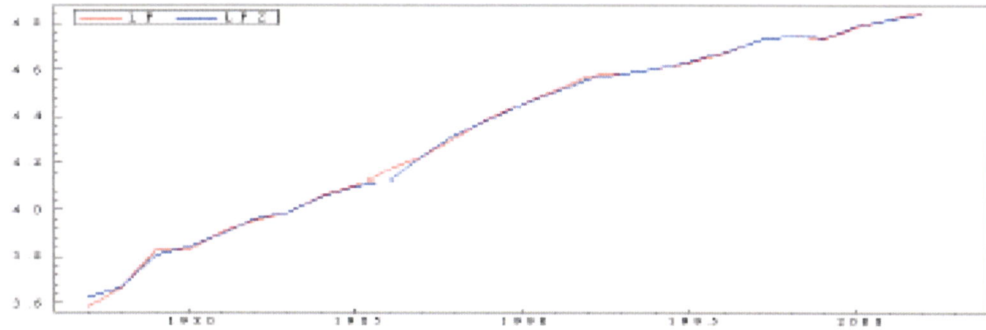

Figure 18.7.

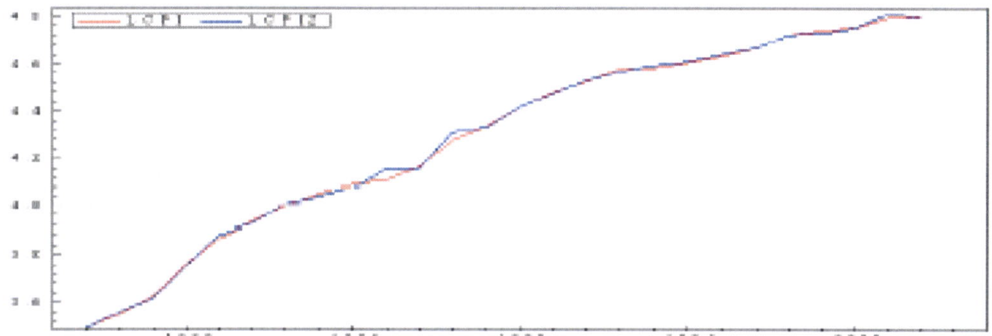

Figure 18.8.

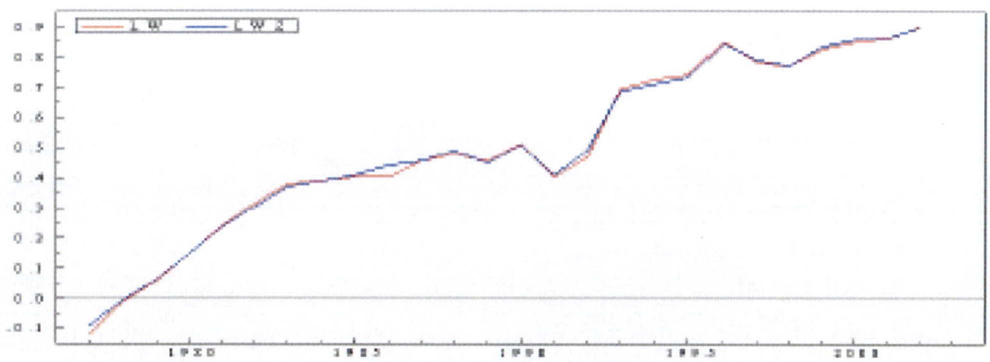

Figure 18.9.

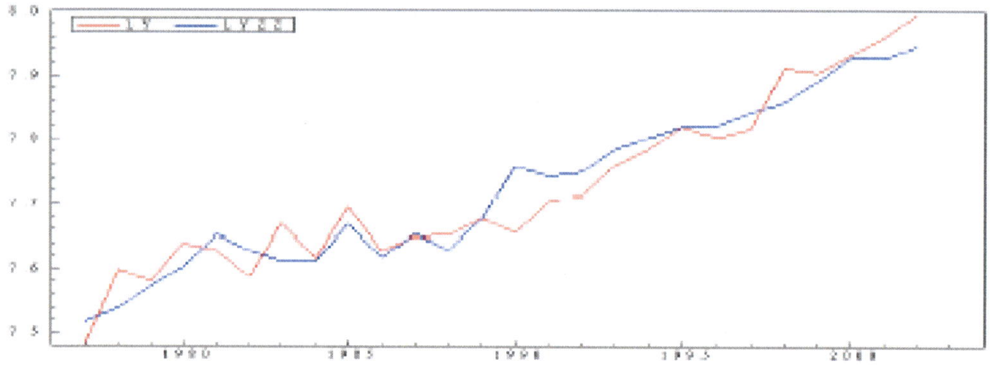

Figure 18.10.

References

Bureau of Statistics, (various years) *Current (Key) Economic Statistics.* Suva: The Fiji Island Bureau of Statistics.

——— (2003) *Fiji Employment Survey.* Suva: The Fiji Island Bureau of Statistics.

E-views 5.0. (2004) *A Quantitative Micro-Software.* Irvine, CA: U.S.A.

International Monetary Fund. (2003) *International Financial Statistics, IMF CD-ROM (December).* Washington DC: The International Monetary Fund.

Levantis, T. (1999) A *Computable General Equilibrium Model for the Fiji Economy.* Canberra: The Australian National University.

Maddala, G., and Kim, I. (1998) *Unit-Roots, cointegration and Structural Change.* Cambridge: Cambridge University Press.

Murphy, C. (1992) ``Macroeconometric Model for Fiji," *Staff Working Paper (04/1992).* Canberra: The Australian National University.

Nevile, J., and Rao, B. (1996) *``The Use and Misuse of Aggregate Demand and Supply Functions,"* Manchester School, 64(2): 189-207.

Perron, P. (1989) ``The Great Crash, the Oil Price Shock and the Unit Root Hypothesis," *Econometrica,* 57(6): 1361-1401.

Pindyck, R., and Rubinfeld, D. (1991) *Econometric Models and Economic Forecasts,* 3rd edition. New York: McGraw-Hill.

Rao, B. (2005) ``Testing Hall's Permanent Income Hypothesis for a Developing Country: The Case of Fiji," *Applied Economics Letters,* 12(4): 245-248.

——— and Singh, R. (2004) ``A Consumption Function for Fiji," *The ICFAI Journal of Applied Economics,* 4(3): 7-14.

——— (2005a) ``Cointegration and Error Correction Approach to the Demand for Money in Fiji," *Pacific Economic Bulletin,* (June): 72-86.

——— (2006) ``Estimating Export Equations," *Staff Working Paper (02/2006).* Suva: The University of the South Pacific.

Rao, B. and Rao, M. (2005) `` *Determinants of Growth Rate: Some Methodological Issues With Time Series Data From Fiji,"* Staff Working Paper. Suva: The University of the South Pacific.

Rao, B. (2003) ``The Nature of ADAS Model based on the ISLM Model," *Staff Working Paper (09/2003)*. Suva: The University of the South Pacific.

Singh, R. (2005) ``A Macroeconometric Model for Fiji," *Masters Thesis* Suva: The University of the South Pacific.

Singh, R. (2005) ``An Investment Equation for Fiji," *Staff Working Paper (01/2006)* Suva: The University of the South Pacific.

In: Development Problems and Prospects in Pacific Islands ISBN: 978-1-60021-793-7
Editors: B. C. Prasad, D. C. Roy, pp. 281-286

Chapter 19

DEVELOPMENT EXPERIENCES AND CHALLENGES FACING THE PACIFIC ISLANDS

Biman Prasad and Kartick Roy

1. INTRODUCTION

Pacific Island countries (PICs) are undergoing fundamental economic changes with the objective of reaping benefits of global economic integration. Many of the PICs since independence pursued import-substitution policies to promote economic growth. Many of the smaller ones also continued to rely on foreign aid for the development of their infrastructure. Countries such as Samoa, Tonga, Tuvalu and Niue also depended heavily on remittances from their emigrated citizens. Since the late 1980s, led by Fiji and Papua New Guinea, PICs began to move away from the protectionist and interventionist import substitution policies to a more outward looking export-oriented policies. The merits and demerits of the open economic policy approach are still being debated and many scholars and commentators on the Pacific Islands and small economies in general are still apprehensive about the supposed benefits from globalisation and international trade.[1] On the other hand, trade optimists believe that PICs with limited resources and vulnerable to natural disasters and political instability would be better off by pursuing export oriented policies. The international organisations such as the International Monetary Fund (IMF), World Bank, and World Trade Organisation (WTO) have also lent their support to the PICs to undertake trade policy reform to ensure that these small economies benefit from global trade. Regional organisations such as the Asian Development Bank (ADB) and Pacific Islands Forum Secretariat (PIFS) have also provided technical support and policy advice for PICs to change their economic policy direction.

From a theoretical perspective, openness of trade regimes provides welfare gains to countries based on benefits derived as a result of comparative advantage. There is evidence that trade liberalisation has generally led to better export performance and hence economic growth in countries that have actively pursued export-oriented strategy for growth.

---

[1] See for example Boris and Hughes (1982) Brigulio (1995,1998), Ismail, (2006), McKee and Tisdell, C. (1990), Streeton (1993), Srinivasan (1986), Grynberg (1999,2000), Prasad and Tisdell (2006).

2. Development Policies in the PICs

In this book the authors provide different perspectives on the development progress and challenges of PICs. Clem Tisdell in Chapter 2 argues that "it is by no means clear that growing economic globalisation involving freer international markets will stimulate economic development in all Pacific countries". He shows that in the case of Fiji trade openness did not lead to an increase in private investment. In fact, in Fiji's case private investment has remained just about 5% of GDP and its economic performance in the last two decades has been sluggish. Tisdell, further points out that it is possible that some of the PICs could suffer further economic and demographic decline as more and more capital and labour flows out of these countries.

In chapter 2, Robbie Robertson provides a useful discussion of the Pacific Plan and how this may provide opportunities for labour mobility which would help PICs to over come the problem of unemployment and low-income poverty. The Pacific Plan is a regional strategy to enhance the participation of PICs in the global economy and to use more and better regional cooperation to benefit from each other's economic progress and through trade. Robertson, while optimistic that PICs could benefit from further regional integration, lends strong support to the call for labour mobility within the region. He also, however, cautions that if PICs do not put in place policies to enhance education, health and skills development of people, the benefits of regionalism and regional trade integration may not be realised. Regional trade integration and benefits of regional free trade agreements such as Pacific Islands Countries Trade Agreement (PICTA) and Pacific Agreement on Closer Economic Relations (PACER) would be hard to realise if PICs do not build capacity to increase their exports. In fact one of the major issues for PICs is to raise exports. The majority of them are face increasing trade deficits. This gives more reason to sceptics of trade to believe that PICs will lose from free trade. Trade deficit occurs because of constraints on the supply side. Yenteshwar Ram, Biman Prasad and Ron Duncan in chapter 4 discuss some of the supply side constraints facing Pacific Islands. Using case studies of Fiji, Papua New Guinea, Solomon Islands and Vanuatu they point out that limited and poorly-maintained physical infrastructure, lack of well-defined property rights to land, the absence of a skilled and experienced workforce, natural disasters, man-made disasters (coups, ethnic conflicts, violent crimes, etc), the challenges of conducting trade including geographical isolation, poor trade facilitation, and limited access to trade finance are some of the major constraints to increasing exports in these countries. Putting in policies to attract foreign direct investments (FDIs) could help in resolving the difficulties of physical infrastructure in these facilities. However, these FDIs can be attracted only if these PICs create a stable macroeconomic and legal environment and have transparent and efficient institutions.

M.D. Sharma and Uriam Timiti in chapter 5 discuss the role of development banks and stress the point that development banks need to concentrate more on social development. A key challenge to ensure institutional relevance/responsiveness and viability is for development banks to continue to reinvent themselves; which is tantamount to ensuring that their roles are modelled on and consistent with the demands of changing political and socio-economic environments in which they operate. The seeming dependence on legal instruments and charters as guiding documents to define the role of development banks has long been viewed as inadequate as such documents are usually too general and vague. They identify critical development issues and priorities, the use of a macro level SWOT analysis, which in their view provides a systematic and dynamic framework to identify an appropriate role model for development banks to ensure that they continue to be responsive to the needs and aspirations of people. Development Banks were traditionally designed to support rural and agricultural development and small business. However, these roles have changed more towards providing funding for developments in the urban manufacturing sector. As a result the agriculture sector in the PICs has remained relatively underdeveloped with declining productivity (Reddy and Duncan, 2006).

PICs have historically depended on foreign aid. Smaller island countries still depend on foreign aid for all development projects and also to fund their recurrent expenditure. Larger PICs have also depended on aid and more recently on remittances to address the problem of increasing poverty. Cathrin Thodock in chapter 6 combines the discussion of foreign aid, remittances and the role of the informal sector to discuss the development process in island nations and its impact on poverty. The effectiveness of aid to the Pacific is still being debated amongst policy makers and commentators. Some like Helen Hughes (2003) have pointed out that aid has been less than effective whereas others believe that aid if properly directed and not tied to donor policies and priorities could provide meaningful resources for development and capacity building in the region. Cathrin Thodock goes further to point out that the informal sector ought to be supported as a policy measure to support many of the poor who derive their income from this sector. There is no doubt that the agricultural sector in the PICs has been shrinking while the manufacturing sector has not been developing well to absorb those released from the agricultural sector. The natural absorber of many of those in unemployment is the urban informal sector. Government policies, therefore, cannot ignore the role of the informal sector and hence policies will have to developed to support those dependent on the informal sector.

3. Governance and ICT Development in PICs

Bad governance corruption and mismanagement have affected economic growth in many PICs. This has affected their ability to raise the level of economic growth and hence many have failed to reduce poverty in their countries. Recent aid effort from Australia, New Zealand and the European Union have been directed towards improving governance in the PICs. Indra Jeet Mistry and Charmaine Rodrigues in Chapter 7 and Pramila Devi in Chapter 8 have identified the importance of the development of Information and Communications Technology (ICT) for social and economic progress in the PICs. Pramila Devi points out that the development of ICT could be an important step in reducing the gender inequity. Using the example of distance learning at the University of the South Pacific, she points out that the use of ICT and distance education has helped many women to upgrade their qualifications and also attain university education. This has positive effects on reducing gender inequality in the PICs. Related to ICT development in the PICs, Graham Hassall in Chapter 9 provides an analysis of Pacific parliaments and how they make use of ICT to disseminate information. While some have well developed websites, others still lag behind and do not make use of websites and ICT in general to make the operation of their legislature more efficient. Good governance in many of the PICs will depend to a large extent on their ability to use ICT in various government activities.

4. Public Finance and Productivity Issues

In Chapters 10, 11 and 12, Mahenrda Reddy and Monovi Amani; Ajay Chandra and T.K. Jayaraman; and Rukmani Gounder respectively, provide a useful discussion of Fiji public finance policies. Fiji is one of the leading economies and the hub of the Pacific. The majority of the PICs suffer from poor public finance management. Public debt in many of them has been rising in the last two decades. In the case of Fiji the authors point out that domestic debt, largely as a result of government borrowing from the superannuation funds in Fiji, is a major problem. Reddy and Monovi and Chandra and Jayaraman point out that the rising level of debt for Fiji, which currently stands at about 52 percent of GDP, may already be unsustainable. Reddy, Kumar and Karan in chapter 15 also provide an analysis of total factor productivity in PICs with reference to Fiji, Papua New Guinea and Samoa. They find that bad governance, political instability and institutional factors affect productivity of factors of production. In addition, their study reveals that little technological advance has been made in these countries, which further explains the lack of growth of productivity in these economies. Narayan and Singh in Chapter 13 provide an analysis of energy consumption in Fiji and find that energy consumption is vital for economic growth. Many of the PICs are energy dependent countries. All of them rely on imported fuel and any constraint on the supply could have serious negative consequences on GDP growth.

5. Role of Agriculture, Foreign Aid and Remittances in Development.

Agriculture, foreign aid and remittances still account for a significant part of the PIC economies. While the contribution of the agriculture sector has been declining in some of the countries it remains a significant contributor to GDP in others. In the case of Fiji, the contribution of agriculture has declined from about 22 % in the late 1980s to about 16 percent of GDP. This has happened precisely because of deliberate government policies, which lay more emphasis on the development of the urban manufacturing sector. In other larger PICs (Papua New Guinea, Solomon Islands and Vanuatu) agriculture remains a major contributor to GDP. Phillip Hone, Henry Haszler and Apenisa Tuicakau in Chapter 14 show that despite official figures showing a decline in the contribution of the agricultural sector to GDP, the actual contribution may have been underestimated. They find that in the case of Fiji, the contribution of subsistence agriculture has not been taken into account in the calculation of the contribution of agriculture to GDP. In Chapter 16 Manoranjan Mohanty discusses the role of the non-government organizations (NGOs) in the social development of Pacific Islands. He emphasises the need to strengthen the role of NGOs to promote meaningful development in PICs. Partnership between NGOs, government and the private sector can help in adopting appropriate policies for social and economic progress. Rahman and Ashwini in Chapter 17, using the example of Fiji, provide a description of the difficulties of undertaking public sector reforms in the Pacific Islands. Often, the intentions and policy prescriptions do not match the actions undertaken on the ground. public sector in many of the PICs is a large drain on public funds and in many instances bad governance leads to poor delivery of public services to the people. Reform of the public sector, therefore is vital, to improve the delivery of services, especially to the poor. Rup Singh in Chapter 18 reports on development of macroeconometric model for Fiji to assess its overall performance. This model could also be used for other PICs to make appropriate macroeconomic assessments. Many of the PICs lack data collection ability and the relative unavailability of official statistics is always a problem.

6. Concluding Remarks

Pacific Islands countries face an increasing number of challenges to achieve economic and social progress. Some of these challenges come from their own inability to promote good governance, their inability to reform their institutions and continuing political instability in some of them. Other challenges come from the forces of globalisation and the move towards freer world trade under the direction of the World Trade Organisation (WTO). Many of the smaller PICs are still dependent on foreign aid for their development. The larger PICs have all made attempts to develop their export sectors and in particular their services sectors. Fiji, Papua New Guinea, Solomon Islands and Tonga are already members of the WTO and have to meet the commitments they have made within the WTO rules. This is likely to put pressure on these countries to raise their export capacity as a main strategy for growth. With progressive reduction of tariff rates and other protectionist measures, these PICs have to ensure that they are able to raise their exports of goods and services and raise revenue from alternative means. Evidence so far shows that many of them are struggling to raise their level of exports of goods. The tourism industry is one which promises to be the leading sector in many of these PICs. However, in the long term these countries would need support and investment to increase their capacity through expansion of tourism related infrastructure. Tourism is also one area that is very vulnerable to natural disasters and political instability. These two threats are clearly evident in many of them and this may not help the tourism industry in the long term.

Despite these challenges, the long-term prosperity of these countries will depend on their ability to develop sustainable economic policies to promote the services sector. The bigger PICs should also concentrate on raising productivity in the agricultural sector as this sector could provide a complementary role to the tourism sector. Developed country partners such as the EU, Australia and New Zealand would have to understand the special challenges facing these countries and would therefore have to make some concessions where trade agreements are concerned. Mutually beneficial trade agreements can only come about if the developed partners provide some special and differential treatment to the PICs. PICs on their part will have to adhere to the principles of democracy and good governance, and promote regionalism as a tool to achieve benefits from regional cooperation.

References

Boris, B. and Hughes, H. (1982) "Growth Experience of Small Countries" In B. Jalan, ed. *Problems and Policies in Small Economies.* New York, St. Martin's Press: 85-102.

Brigulio. L. (1995) "Small Developing States and Their Economic Vulnerabilities", *World Development,* Vol.23 (9), pp.1615-1632.

Brigulio, L. (1998) "Small Country Size and Returns to Scale in Manufacturing", *World Development,* Vol.26 (3), pp.507-15.

Grynberg, R. (2000) *The Pacific Island States and the WTO: Towards a Post-Seattle Agenda for the Small Vulnerable States.*Paper presented at the Global Conference on the Development Agenda for Small States, London, 17-18 February 2000.

Grynberg, R. (1999) Trade Implications for Vulnerable States of the Global Trade Regime.Paper presented at the World Bank–Commonwealth Secretariat Conference on Small States, St. Lucia, February 17-19, 1999.

Hughes, H. (2003) *Aid has failed the Pacific,* Issues Analysis No.33. Centre for Independent Studies: Sydney.

Ismail, F. (2006) "How Can Least Developed Countries and Other Small, Weak and Vulnerable Economies Also Gain from the Doha Development Agenda on the Road to Hong Kong?", *Journal of World Trade,* 40 (1), 37-68.

McKee, D. and Tisdell, C. (1990) *Development Issues in Small Island Economies,* New York: Praeger.

Prasad, B. and Tisdell, C. (1996) *Institutions, Economic Performance and Sustainable Development: A Case Study of the Fiji Islands,* Nova Science Publishers, New York.

Reddy, M and R. Duncan (2006) "Productivity of Pacific Islands Agriculture: Issues and Challenges", *ICFAI Journal of Agricultural Economics,* 3 (2):16-31.

Streeton, Paul (1993) "The Special Problems of Small Countries". *World Development,* Vol.21, No.2, pp.197-202.

Srinivasan, T.N. (1986) "The Cost and Benefits of Being A Small, Remote Island, Landlocked or Ministate Economy", *World Bank Research Observer,* Vol.1, No.2, pp.205-218.

INDEX

A

B

C

D

E

F

G

H

I

J

K

L

M

N

O

P

Q

R

S

T

U

V

W

Y